S0-AUX-645

EDUCATION AND THE BRAIN

EDUCATION AND THE BRAIN

The Seventy-seventh Yearbook of the National Society for the Study of Education

PART II

By

THE YEARBOOK COMMITTEE

and

ASSOCIATED CONTRIBUTORS

Edited by

JEANNE S. CHALL AND ALLAN F. MIRSKY

Editor for the Society

KENNETH J. REHAGE

19  78

Distributed by THE UNIVERSITY OF CHICAGO PRESS • CHICAGO, ILLINOIS

The National Society for the Study of Education

The purposes of the Society are to carry on investigations of educational problems and to publish the results of these investigations as a means of promoting informed discussion of important educational issues.

The two volumes of the seventy-seventh yearbook (Part I: *The Courts and Education* and Part II: *Education and the Brain*) continue the well-established tradition, now in its seventy-eighth year, of serious effort to provide scholarly and readable materials for those interested in the thoughtful study of educational matters. The yearbook series is planned to include at least one volume each year of general interest to all educators, while the second volume tends to be somewhat more specialized.

A complete list of the Society's past publications, including the yearbooks and the recently inaugurated series of paperbacks on Contemporary Educational Issues, will be found in the back pages of this volume.

It is the responsibility of the Board of Directors of the Society to select the subjects to be treated in the yearbooks, to appoint committees whose personnel are expected to insure consideration of all significant points of view, to provide for necessary expenses in connection with the preparation of the yearbooks, to publish and distribute the committees' reports, and to arrange for their discussion at the annual meeting. The editor for the Society is responsible for preparing the submitted manuscripts for publication in accordance with the principles and regulations approved by the Board of Directors.

Neither the Board of Directors, nor the Society's editor, nor the Society is responsible for the conclusions reached or the opinions expressed by the Society's yearbook committees.

All persons sharing an interest in the Society's purposes are invited to join. Regular members receive both volumes of the current yearbook. Those taking out the "comprehensive" membership receive the yearbook volumes and the volumes in the current series of paperbacks. Inquiries regarding membership may be addressed to the Secretary, NSSE, 5835 Kimbark Avenue, Chicago, Illinois 60637.

Library of Congress Catalog Number: 77-15768

Published 1978 by

THE NATIONAL SOCIETY FOR THE STUDY OF EDUCATION

5835 Kimbark Avenue, Chicago, Illinois 60637

First Printing, 9,000 Copies

Printed in the United States of America

Officers of the Society
1977-78

(Term of office expires March 1 of the year indicated.)

N. L. GAGE

(1979)
Stanford University
Stanford, California

JACOB W. GETZELS

(1978)
University of Chicago, Chicago, Illinois

JOHN I. GOODLAD

(1980)
University of California, Los Angeles, California

A. HARRY PASSOW

(1978)
Teachers College, Columbia University, New York, New York

KENNETH J. REHAGE

(Ex-officio)
University of Chicago, Chicago, Illinois

HAROLD G. SHANE

(1979)
Indiana University
Bloomington, Indiana

RALPH W. TYLER

(1980)
Director Emeritus, Center for Advanced Study in the Behavioral Sciences
Stanford, California

Secretary-Treasurer

KENNETH J. REHAGE
5835 Kimbark Avenue, Chicago, Illinois 60637

The Society's Committee on Education and the Brain

JEANNE S. CHALL

(Cochairman)
Professor of Education and Director, Reading Laboratory
Graduate School of Education
Harvard University
Cambridge, Massachusetts

ALLAN F. MIRSKY

(Cochairman)
Professor of Psychiatry (Neuropsychology) and Neurology
School of Medicine
Boston University
Boston, Massachusetts

RICHARD HELD

Professor of Experimental Psychology and Chairman,
Department of Psychology
Massachusetts Institute of Technology
Cambridge, Massachusetts

JEROME KAGAN

Professor of Developmental Psychology
Harvard University
Cambridge, Massachusetts

HORACE W. MAGOUN

Professor Emeritus, University of California at Los Angeles
Los Angeles, California

RICHARD L. THOMPSON

Professor of Psychobiology
University of California at Irvine
Irvine, California

SHELDON H. WHITE

Professor of Psychology
Harvard University
Cambridge, Massachusetts

MERLIN C. WITTROCK

Professor of Educational Psychology
Graduate School of Education
University of California at Los Angeles
Los Angeles, California

Associated Contributors

MARTHA BRIDGE DENCKLA, M.D.

Assistant Professor of Neurology, Harvard Medical School
Director, Learning Disabilities Clinic, Children's Hospital Medical Center
Boston, Massachusetts

HERMAN T. EPSTEIN

Professor of Biology
Brandeis University
Waltham, Massachusetts

SEBASTIAN P. GROSSMAN

Professor of Behavioral Sciences (Biopsychology)
University of Chicago
Chicago, Illinois

KENNETH M. HEILMAN, M.D.

Professor of Neurology
J. Hillis Miller Health Center
College of Medicine, University of Florida
Gainesville, Florida

MERRILL HISCOCK, M.D.

Assistant Professor of Psychology and Clinical Instructor in Psychiatry
University of Saskatchewan
Saskatoon, Saskatchewan, Canada

MARCEL KINSBOURNE, M.D.

Professor of Pediatrics and Psychology, University of Toronto
Toronto, Ontario, Canada
Professor of Pychology, University of Waterloo
Waterloo, Ontario, Canada

PAUL D. MAC LEAN, M.D.

Chief, Laboratory of Brain Evolution and Behavior
National Institute of Mental Health
Bethesda, Maryland

RITA G. RUDEL

Associate Clinical Professor of Psychology
Columbia-Presbyterian Medical Center
Presbyterian Hospital
New York, New York

TIMOTHY J. TEYLER

Associate Professor of Neurobiology
College of Medicine, Northeastern Ohio University
Rootstown, Ohio

Editors' Preface

Education and the Brain is the first volume in the yearbook series of the National Society for the Study of Education to be devoted to the brain sciences and education. In a sense, its publication is similar to the publication in 1942 of *The Psychology of Learning,* which appeared as Part II of the Society's Forty-first Yearbook and was devoted entirely to psychology and education.

Educators have been interested in the neurosciences for some time. As early as the 1950s, for example, researchers and clinicians were looking to the neurosciences for explanations of the causes of severe reading and language disabilities and for better methods of treating those disabilities. Educational and developmental psychologists, as well as workers in the field of special education, were also turning to the neurosciences for explanations of strengths and weaknesses in cognition and learning that were not based primarily on motivation, parent-child relations, emotional or other psychological factors.

By the early 1960s, the neurosciences had begun to have a considerable impact on the diagnosis and treatment of children who have severe difficulty in learning academic skills. Increasingly, the neurologist tended to be the director of the interdisciplinary team evaluating academic difficulties in place of the psychiatrist or clinical psychologist who had directed the team in previous years. The recommended treatments also seemed to change. In the 1940s and 1950s, psychotherapy or counseling were often recommended for children who were failing in school. In the 1960s, it was more common to recommend training in visual perception, auditory perception, and visual-motor coordination for the treatment of underlying psychoneurological deficits. It is well to note that this form of treatment has also come into question recently.

During the 1960s the concepts of minimal brain dysfunction (MBD), learning disabilities, and hyperactivity gained recognition and wide use in schools and clinics. Physicians often prescribed medication, particularly for hyperactivity, to be given during school hours, often under the supervision of the school staff. This practice opened up a host of concerns, such as whether the drugs were in fact beneficial for learning and behavior and whether they might be contributing to later drug addiction. And, of course, there was great concern regarding the responsibility that schools should take in administering the prescribed medication to pupils.

By the early 1970s, educators and schools had become very much involved with the neurosciences in seeking new ways of working with children with severe learning disabilities, in the assessment of those disabilities, and in special instruction. Many popularized articles have appeared since the early 1970s. While these articles are extremely interesting, serious researchers claim that many of them are misleading. This is not surprising, since the complex knowledge of the neurosciences comes from many disciplines, among them neurology, psychiatry, neuropsychology, cultural anthropology, chemistry, biology, nutrition, educational psychology, and from the fields of reading, language, and learning disability. In their attempts to communicate in a popular fashion ideas that are essentially quite complex, many authors have resorted to oversimplification.

In 1973, Jeanne S. Chall submitted to the Board of Directors of the National Society for the Study of Education a proposal for a yearbook on the neurosciences for educators—for researchers, administrators, and teachers. The proposal was in due course accepted by the Board. Many eminent scholars in the neurosciences and in related fields were consulted for their comments and suggestions. Among those consulted and from whom invaluable assistance was obtained were Richard Held and the late Hans Lukas Teuber, both of the Massachusetts Institute of Technology; Jerome Kagan, of Harvard University; George Miller, of Rockefeller University; Horace W. Magoun and Louise H. Marshall, of the University of California, Los Angeles; and Allan F. Mirsky, of the Boston University Medical Center. All these gave generously of their time and counsel and with their help the yearbook committee was formed. Others who helped either in the initial or later planning included David Rose, of Tufts University, and Helen Popp and Jeffrey Schnitzer, both of Harvard University. In January,

1976, the final plan for the volume was drawn up at a meeting of the coeditors, members of the yearbook committee, and Kenneth J. Rehage, Executive Secretary of the National Society for the Study of Education and editor of its publications.

Our purpose was to present an overview of current scholarship in the neurosciences that has implications for educational theory, research, and practice. The authors of the chapters in this volume include noted scholars in the neurosciences who were asked to bring their knowledge to interested workers in other fields. In view of the many popular and often oversimplified articles appearing in the general and educational press we believed that what educators needed was not a journalistic treatment but rather the kind of serious analysis characteristic of the Society's yearbooks. Since the disciplines represented are many and complex, the reader will find much that will need careful study. We have included many illustrations, which we hope will assist the reader in acquiring an understanding of the basic concepts and processes relating to the brain.

The yearbook is divided into five parts. Part One consists of Timothy Teyler's chapter, "The Brain Sciences: An Introduction," a veritable primer on the neuroanatomy, neurochemistry, and neurophysiology of the brain. Teyler's opening sentence sets the tone for the chapter and for the volume: ""The human brain is probably the most complex organized matter in the universe." The complexity theme is continued: "To understand a bit of how the brain works, quite literally, is to gain insight into how man works." Teyler also anticipates a point frequently made in later chapters when he stresses the influence of environmental factors on the brain: "Rats reared in an enriched environment (with litter mates in a cage full of 'interesting' objects) show marked changes in brain development as compared to rats reared in impoverished environments. Furthermore, it has been shown that brain processes present at birth will degenerate if the environmental stimulation necessary to activate them is withheld."

Part Two contains chapters on some of the basic processes of the brain: attention, cognition, motivation, language, and cerebral lateralization. In chapter 2, "Attention: A Neuropsychological Perspective," Allan F. Mirsky dramatizes the central importance of attention: "There is scarcely any human performance which is not dependent on some attentive capacity on the part of the subject." Attention is defined as "a focussing of consciousness or awareness on some part of the multitude of stimuli from the environment, usually on the basis of learning or training." An individual's attentive capacity at any given moment is modified by past experience, training, motivation, and level of interest in a particular task. Interaction of attention with motivation is particularly complex. Thus, "motivation that is too high can be as deleterious for performance requiring attention as motivation that is too low."

Merlin C. Wittrock's chapter, "Education and the Cognitive Processes," is directly concerned with education, drawing implications for teaching, learning, and curriculum development. Much of this chapter is concerned with hemispheric specialization. "The left cortical hemisphere," Wittrock notes, ". . . specializes somewhat in a propositional, analytic-sequential, time-oriented serial organization well adapted to learning and remembering verbal information. . . . The right hemisphere specializes somewhat in an appositional synthetic-gestalt organization well adapted to processing information in which the parts acquire meaning through their relations with the other parts." Of particular interest and use to educators will be the research reported by Wittrock on novel ways of teaching (left hemisphere) verbal skills through stimulation of the right hemisphere. Also of interest is the section on cognitive styles and the recent research relating these styles to models of cognitive processing in the brain.

In chapter 4, "The Biology of Motivation," Sebastian P. Grossman focusses on the theories and research relating to motivation. Most psychological theories of motivation, he notes, "are strongly influenced by the motivational consequences of starvation or water deprivation as studied mainly in the ubiquitous albino rat." Grossman takes great pains to delineate the tentativeness of the evidence, which should give pause to the educator who might think of making direct applications from neuropsychological research to teaching and learning. Also of special interest to educators is Grossman's discussion of arousal theory, where he points out that animals as well as man will work to obtain access to novel or interesting environments. Animals do not tolerate "prolonged exposure to conditions that sharply limit sensory input; and [they do] voluntarily engage in activities that involve certain dangers." Grossman's chapter ends as it began by emphasizing the complexity of motivation and the wide differences of opinion that exist in this particular area of inquiry.

Kenneth M. Heilman's chapter on "Language and the Brain" concentrates on a fundamental understanding of the neuropsychological processes underlying language. Although the educator may not need such knowledge in a clinical setting, Heilman believes an understanding of the neuropsychological processes underlying behavior is essential, not only for understanding how the brain works but also for understanding the common problem of learning disorders. One of the practical outcomes of understanding brain mechanisms has been the development of predictive tests that allow early educational intervention. Furthermore, "an understanding of the brain mechanisms underlying language may also enable educators to develop educational methods that best use the innate capability of language-processing systems of both normal and abnormal children and adults." The chapter also treats handedness and language, the aphasias, reading and writing disorders, and recovery of language functions.

In their chapter on "Cerebral Lateralization and Cognitive Development" Marcel Kinsbourne and Merrill Hiscock open with a provocative statement: "Few topics in the neurosciences can match the study of cerebral lateralization in its power to stimulate the imagination of people." And they satisfy our curiosity with a fascinating, almost detective-story account of how the different theories, research interpretations, and means of measuring laterality have developed. The chapter begins with an examination of the notion that "faulty" cerebral dominance is related to learning disabilities. The empirical evidence regarding this notion is outlined and some of the ambiguities and deficiencies are pointed out. Kinsbourne and Hiscock then devote the remaining and major portion of their chapter to the assumptions underlying the various theories of lateralization and to the basic research relevant to those assumptions.

Part Three, which deals with brain dysfunctions and recoveries, begins with Martha B. Denckla's chapter on "Minimal Brain Dysfunction." Denckla treats many problems of great interest for all types of education, particularly in light of the current concern with mainstreaming. She gives special attention to some issues that have universal importance for the development and learning of all children and young people: maturational lag and whether it is possible to catch up; whether children with one type of brain organization do better than children with a different type of brain organization; whether sex differences are related to brain differences; whether medication is helpful for children with specific kinds of minimal brain dysfunction. In her concluding statement, Denckla calls for greater collaboration between medicine and education to "broaden and elevate the callings of both parent and teacher while restoring to the physician the educational role implicit in the title of 'Doctor'."

In her chapter on "Neuroplasticity," Rita G. Rudel is concerned with the capacity of the brain to recover from the effects of damage and with what this means for human development and for education. The time at which the brain damage occurs is important, with the long-term effects of early damage to the brain usually less destructive than similar later damage. Research on both animals and humans indicates that the stimulation and experiences of those with early brain damage have a considerable effect on their recovery. Thus, even test experiences given to monkeys as part of experiments have led to improvement in their functioning. Control monkeys with the same injury were not given test experiences and did not make as much progress. For children, recovery of function after brain damage is also enhanced by experience, even though the experience may not appear to be immediately effective. One comes away from reading this chapter with a great sense of hope and of optimism because of the capacity of the brain to heal itself when proper stimulation (that is, education) is provided.

Part Four comprises two chapters, in the first of which Paul D. MacLean reaches into our evolutionary past to present a remarkable and fascinating picture of what the brain "knows of itself." Like other authors in this volume, MacLean regards the brain as the "most complicated and remarkable instrument in the known universe." The human forebrain retains the basic features of three formations that reflect our ancestral relationship to reptiles, early mammals, and recent mammals. "Radically different in structure and chemistry, and in an evolutionary sense countless generations apart, the three formations constitute a hierarchy of three brains in one, or what may be called for short a *tri*une brain"—a primal mind, an emotional mind, and a rational mind. Throughout the chapter we are intrigued with statements such as "the human predisposition to routine has its roots in the older parts of the forebrain." MacLean points out that "observations of reptiles reveal that they are slaves to routine, precedent, and ritual." Like authors of preceding chapters, MacLean stresses the importance of experience at critical times for brain development. "There is now abundant anatomical and behavioral evidence that if neural circuits of the brain are not brought into play at certain critical times of development, they may never be capable of functioning. Chimpanzees reared in darkness may be forever blind. Is it possible that if empathy is not learned at a critical age, it may never become fully developed? Kubie, who dealt extensively with the education of the young scientist, emphasized that adolescents not only need to be exposed to human suffering, but also to be given the responsibility for ministering to it."

In chapter 10, Herman T. Epstein proposes a theory of stages of brain development which may well be correlated, if not causally related, to stages of mental development. The brain growth spurts, or stages, proposed by Epstein fall within the following intervals: three to ten months, two to four, six to eight, eight to twelve or thirteen, and fourteen to sixteen or seventeen years. These stages correlate well, says Epstein, with the traditionally described stages in mental growth, in particular with the stages of intellectual development as described by Piaget. The implications for learning and particularly for school learning are many, among them the hypothesis that "intensive and novel intellectual inputs to children may be most effective during the brain growth stages." Epstein also proposes that insight into cultural differences in school achievement and more effective ways of evaluating experimental programs may be gained from an application of the theory of stages in brain growth.

Part Five contains the concluding chapter in which we point

to the major implications of preceding chapters for education and call attention to the one central theme running throughout the volume—the potential for the constructive influence of education on the growth and optimal development of the brain.

We hope that readers of this volume will be as enriched by its contents as we have been.

JEANNE S. CHALL
ALLAN F. MIRSKY
Cambridge and Boston, Massachusetts
January, 1978

Acknowledgements

Education and the Brain has been brought to completion only because many very busy and very competent authors have been willing to devote a great amount of time to the enterprise. We are especially grateful to the coeditors, Jeanne S. Chall and Allan F. Mirsky, whose involvement in the project has been intensive from the beginning. Professor Herman G. Richey again graciously agreed to prepare the index, as he has done for all the yearbooks published since his retirement as Secretary-Treasurer of the Society and as editor of its publications. The Society wishes in this way to acknowledge its indebtedness to all these individuals, as well as to those who assisted with the planning of the volume in the early stages of its development.

Kenneth J. Rehage
Secretary-Treasurer

Table of Contents

Part One

CHAPTER I

The Brain Sciences: An Introduction

TIMOTHY J. TEYLER

Introduction

The human brain is probably the most complexly organized matter in the universe. Unravelling its mysteries has occupied the minds of scientists from a variety of disciplines. The three most basic disciplines upon which the brain sciences rest are anatomy, physiology, and chemistry. Each of the individuals in these disciplines is seeking to answer the question, what is the brain and how does it function? The anatomist answers: "A collection of specialized cells, complexly arranged, yet with commonalities." The physiologist answers: "An electrochemical machine that interacts with its environment and itself in particular ways." The chemist replies: "An incredible biochemical system, specialized for the processing of information."

The brain is rarely given much thought by the nonprofessional, although it is the source of all thought. Virtually everyone would agree, however, that all behavior, as well as all human thought, emotion, memory, and knowledge, is generated by the brain, to be expressed by muscles and glands. The hypothetical answers above, from an anatomist, a physiologist, and a chemist, represent the three basic sciences upon which the brain sciences, or neurosciences, rest. The goals of individual scientists differ—all desire to know more of the workings of the brain—but it is useful to remember that most scientists are interested in: (a) What are the components of the brain, and how are they connected one to another? (b) What are the functions of those components, and how do they work together? (c) What are the chemical and electrical phenomena underlying the functioning of the components? The answers to these questions are being sought today. When the answers have been obtained, we will have progressed significantly in our quest to understand the workings of the human brain and thus the human mind.

To certain nonprofessionals, these are interesting questions today—and as knowledge of the brain is gained, allowing man to manipulate its fabric, they will later become important questions to all. Knowledge of the workings of the brain is a potentially powerful tool to benefit mankind. The problems are waiting to be solved: mental retardation and mental illness, for example. But like most powerful tools, there also exists the potential for misuse. The ability to alter the fabric of the brain represents the application of a power more awesome than that contained in the nucleus of the atom. Only through education and awareness can we insure that this powerful tool will be employed for the benefit of mankind.

On a more pedestrian level, knowledge of the stuff of the brain could prove to be a fascinating topic to many readers—the brain is, after all, responsible for all that we are and can become. To understand a bit of how the brain works, quite literally, is to gain insight into how man works.

The Neuron

THE NEURONAL CELL

The unit of the brain is the *neuron.* The brain of man at birth has been estimated to contain between 20 and 200 billion neurons. Surprisingly, we never have more neurons than when we are born. After birth we lose thousands daily, never to be replaced, and apparently not missed until the cumulative loss builds up in very old age (and even then, not all individuals are affected similarly). Each of these neurons communicates with as many as a thousand other neurons, making the total number of connections and the "wiring diagram" very complex indeed. Neurons are very similar across species, although the neurons of lower organisms communicate with one another primarily by "electrical" contacts between neurons, and those of higher organisms (particularly the vertebrates) communicate primarily by "chemical" contacts (to be discussed below). As can be seen in figure 1, neurons come in a variety of shapes and sizes: some with one or two processes ex-

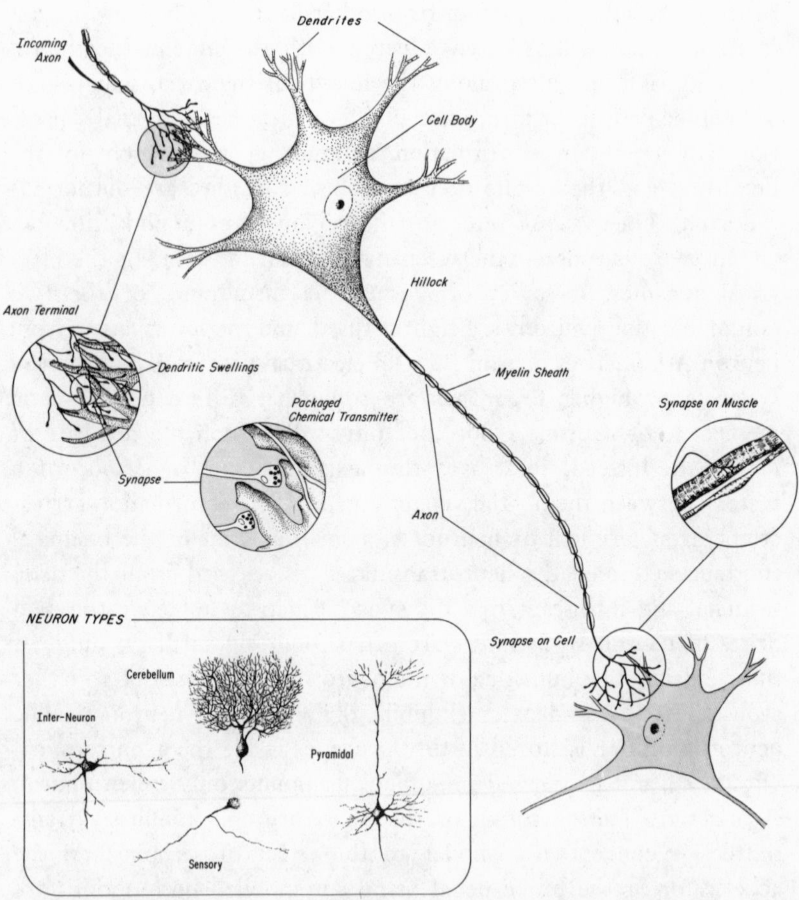

FIG. 1. The neuron. A prototype neuron showing its processes and communication (synapse) with other neurons and with muscle. Inset: several of the types of neurons encountered in various parts of the brain.

tending from the cell body of the neuron; others with richly branching processes resembling a tree in winter.

A neuron is like other cells in the body in that it possesses a continuous cell membrane enclosing the cytoplasm. Neurons have a cell nucleus and the metabolic machinery necessary to maintain life. In addition, they are specialized for the integration and transmission of information. A prototype neuron is shown in figure 1. The short, branching processes extending from the cell body are *dendrites* (known collectively as the dendritic tree). These processes receive information from other neurons. The long process is the *axon*, which is often covered with the myelin sheath. Information is transmitted along the length of the axon, which ends at another neuron or at a muscle. The neuron has a normal "direction" of operation: information is input at the region of the dendrites, and the results of a neuron's processing are output via the axon. The *synapse* refers to the region of communication between two neurons (or between neuron and muscle). In the electrical synapses of lower organisms, the membranes of the two communicating neurons are tightly fused, and the information from neuron A influences neuron B by an electrical process. The chemical synapses of higher organisms are somewhat different. The axon membrane of neuron A does not physically touch the dendrite of neuron B. Instead, there is a tiny gap (about 1/50,000,000 of a meter) between them—the synaptic gap. When information arrives at the axon terminal of neuron A, a small amount of the chemical substance (termed the neurotransmitter) is released from the axon terminal and diffuses across the synaptic gap to influence the dendrites of neuron B. Synapses are often found on small swellings of the dendrite. The influence of the neurotransmitter can be to either arouse (excite) or depress (inhibit) the activity of neuron B. The neurotransmitter is stored in tiny packages inside the axon terminal (figure 2) and is released in sufficient amounts only when neuron A is active. The operation of the excitatory and inhibitory transmitters is conceptually similar to the effect of stepping on the accelerator or the brake pedal of an automobile—both actions are similar, yet they influence the behavior of the automobile in a diametrically opposed fashion. After use the neurotransmitter is removed from the synapse and "recycled" for use again.

BASIC NEUROPHYSIOLOGY

What causes the release of the packaged transmitter? To answer this question, we must examine how a neuron becomes "active." The membrane of a neuron is like a sieve, allowing the passage of small molecules and charged atoms (ions) from one side of the membrane to the other, but preventing the movement of larger molecules and ions. In addition, the membrane contains a "pump" that expels the positively charged sodium ion (Na^+) and takes in

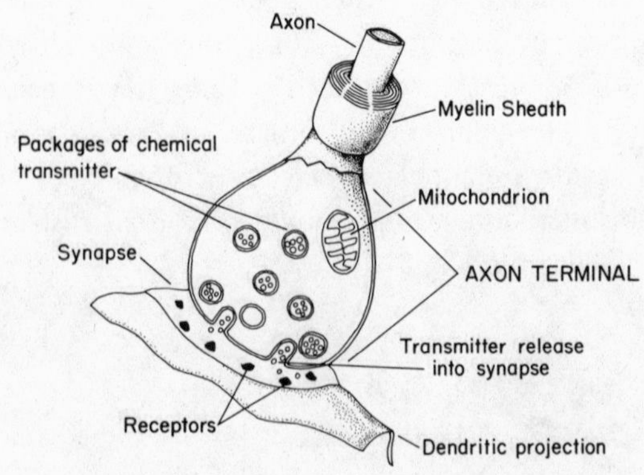

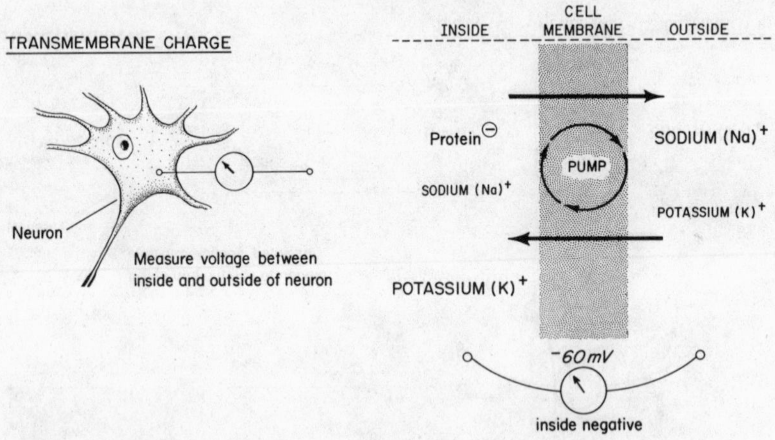

FIG. 2. The synapse. Top: cut-away view of an axon terminal showing the packaged transmitter chemical and the synaptic region. Bottom: features of the resting neuron showing the transmembrane charge (left) and the unequal distribution of charged molecules and ions due to the Na+/K+ pump (right).

the similarly charged potassium ion (K+). The net result of the leaky membrane, the Na+/K+ pump, and the presence of negatively charged protein molecules inside the cell is an electrical potential between the interior and exterior of the neuron (see figure 2). The potential is such that the interior is negative with respect to the exterior. The nonactive, or resting, neuron displays a potential (termed the transmembrane potential) of about –60 millivolts. If the transmembrane potential is lowered (made less negative) to about –50 millivolts, the neuron will initiate an "action potential" in its axon. The action potential is a transient opening of minute "gates" in the axon membrane, first allowing Na+ to rush into the

THE ACTION POTENTIAL

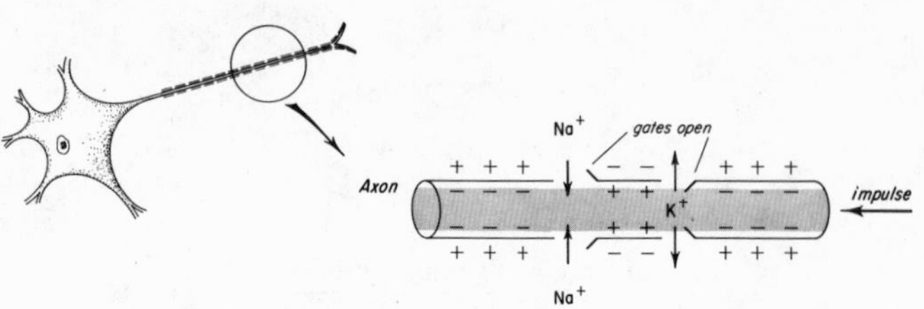

THE SYNAPTIC POTENTIAL

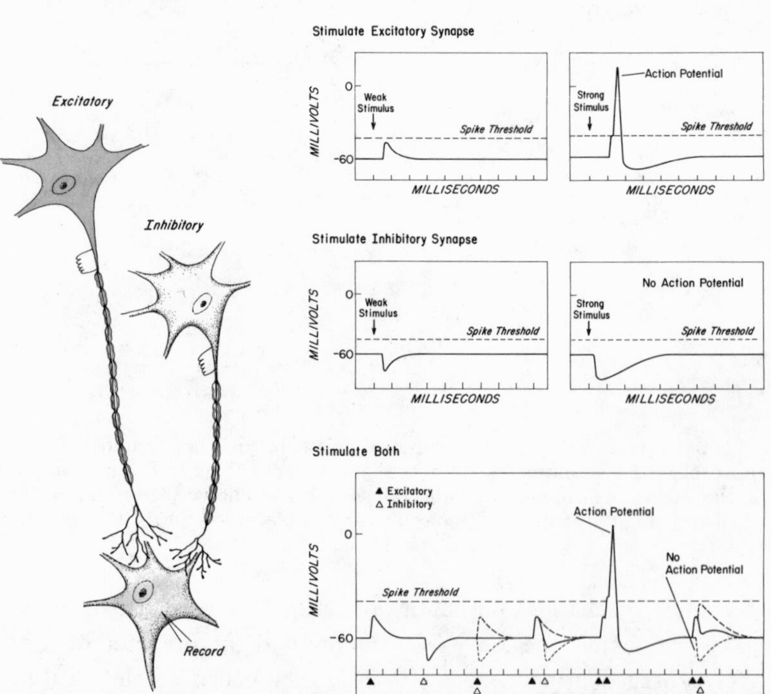

FIG. 3. The action potential. Top: expanded view of a section of axon showing a "snapshot" of an action potential traveling down the axon. Opening

axon, and then allowing K+ to rush out. An electrode measuring the transmembrane charge during an action potential would see an abrupt swing from the resting level of –60 millivolts to approximately + 10 or + 20 millivolts due to the inflow of the positively charged Na ion. The subsequent elimination of the positively charged K ion results in a return (and brief negative overshoot) to the resting level (see figure 3). One of the functions of the Na+/K+ pump is to redress the ionic imbalance brought about by the ion flow during an action potential.

The action potential begins at the hillock of the axon and travels down the axon at speeds up to 300 feet per second. This is slow compared to the velocity of a purely electrical potential (186,000 miles per second), and is due to the fact that while electrical potentials are associated with an action potential, the phenomenon itself is a time-consuming process involving the opening and closing of ion gates in the membrane and the flowing of ions through the membrane gates. When the action potential arrives at the axon terminals, it causes the release of some of the packaged neurotransmitter. The transmitter diffuses across the synaptic gap to attach to receptor sites on the membrane of the dendrites. There it has an excitatory or inhibitory effect on the recipient cell.

An action potential is initiated by lowering the transmembrane charge through the action of excitatory neurotransmitters at the synapse. Excitatory neurotransmitters lower the transmembrane

---

of sub-microscopic gates in the axon allows the passage of ions in the direction indicated by the arrows. The ion movement and altered transmembrane charge they produce constitute the action potential. Bottom: upon arriving at an axon terminal, the action potential causes the release of a neurotransmitter into the synapse. Synapses are either excitatory or inhibitory, depending upon the neurotransmitter chemical released and the properties of the receptor. Shown in the graphs are the effects of weak and strong activation of an excitatory synapse (top) and an inhibitory synapse (middle). Prior to stimulation, the recipient neuron is at resting level (minus 60mV). After the neurotransmitter reaches the receptors on the recipient neuron (allowing time for the action potential to traverse the axon), it causes the transmembrane charge to go toward spike threshold for excitatory synapses and to go away from spike threshold for inhibitory synapses. Strong stimulation of the excitatory synapse will result in an action potential in the recipient cell. When both excitatory and inhibitory synapses are activated (as is normally the case), their effects algebraically sum. This is shown in the bottom graph where the dashed lines indicate the contribution of the excitatory and inhibitory synapses, and the solid line represents their sum and thus their influence on the recipient cell.

charge toward the action potential threshold, while inhibitory neurotransmitters raise (make more negative) the transmembrane charge. The dendritic synapses are some distance away from the hillock of the axon, the site of action potential initiation, and their contribution is diminished as a function of distance. Rarely is the activity of a single synaptic contact sufficient to trigger an action potential, which is called a "spike." Thus, several excitatory synaptic inputs must be active more or less simultaneously (within milliseconds) to raise the transmembrane charge to threshold and fire a spike. In contrast, an active inhibitory synapse on one portion of a dendrite can counteract the effect of an active excitatory synapse on an adjacent portion of the dendritic tree. These properties are depicted graphically in figure 3. A neuron has hundreds or thousands of synapses, many of which are active at any given time. The transmembrane charge, and thus the initiation of a spike, is dependent on the net synaptic influence on the neuron. More excitatory input relative to inhibitory input will trigger a spike; more inhibition than excitation will not.

Synapses in the brain are the primary site for intercellular communication—yet any individual synapse is not a "secure" communication channel. The ability of a single synapse on the typical neuron to produce an action potential depends upon many factors, such as: the type of neurotransmitter (excitatory or inhibitory); the transmembrane charge, as influenced by prior activity on other synapses; the amount of neurotransmitter released; the distance of the synapse from the action potential trigger zone on the axon hillock; the simultaneous activity of other synapses on the recipient cell; and the past history of the synapse (many synapses are altered by their prior "experience" and are said to be "plastic"—a characteristic presumably present in synapses that play a role in behavioral learning). An analogy can be drawn to a political demonstration. When many individuals are shouting different slogans at the same time, it is difficult to understand the message. In this setting, information would be best communicated either by shouting in unison or by silence on the part of the crowd while listening to a spokesperson.

In summary, the neuron will release neurotransmitter from its axon terminals provided that its synaptic excitation exceeds its synaptic inhibitions sufficient to reach spike threshold. In one sense, the neuron behaves like a hybrid computer: operating as an analog computer in the dendritic tree, and operating as a digital computer in the axon. The reader should be warned that the whole story can not be presented here. Unfortunately for neuroscientists interested in unravelling the complexities of the brain, all neurons are not as simple as has been outlined above. To provide only two examples: some neurons are capable of generating spikes in their dendritic trees, and some synapses are reciprocal (information can pass in both directions).

The Brain

THE CORTEX

An examination of the surface of the human brain will show it to be a large (3+ pound) bilaterally symmetrical, wrinkled organ. The outer surface, or *cortex*, contains billions of neurons and the processes that connect neurons. As we shall see, the cortex contains subdivisions of highly specialized functions. Toward the rear of the brain the cerebellum can be seen protruding from under the cortex. It, too, is a highly wrinkled, or convoluted, tissue, concerned primarily with the coordination of commands to muscles. The convoluted cortex of the brain represents a phylogenetically recent adaptation, rendering more surface area available and thus more neurons. The effect is similar to crumpling a piece of paper into a ball whose outer surface area is much less than the area of the paper itself. Since the major difference between the human brain and the brains of other mammals is in the number of neurons they possess, the brains of related species, for example, primates and cetaceans (whales and porpoises), are similarly convoluted but to a lesser degree.

Underlying the convoluted layer of cortical neurons are axon tracts that extend from and carry messages from cortical neurons to other neurons and vice versa. Examination of these fiber tracts with the unaided eye would show them to be relatively more white than the pinkish-gray of the cortex. This is due to the fact that the lengthy axonal processes are often covered with the specialized myelin sheath of fatty tissue which appears white. The myelin sheath serves both to insulate the axon from its immediate surroundings and to speed its message-transmitting capacity by a factor of 10 or so. The process of myelinization is far from complete at birth, in some brain regions it is not completed until puberty.

The cortical surface is not without regional distinctions. It is common to divide each hemisphere of the cortex into four *lobes* (figure 4). These are, from front to back: Frontal, Parietal, Tem-

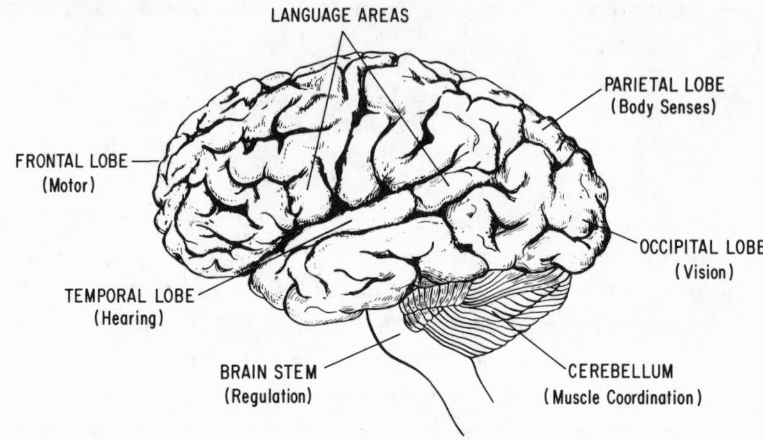

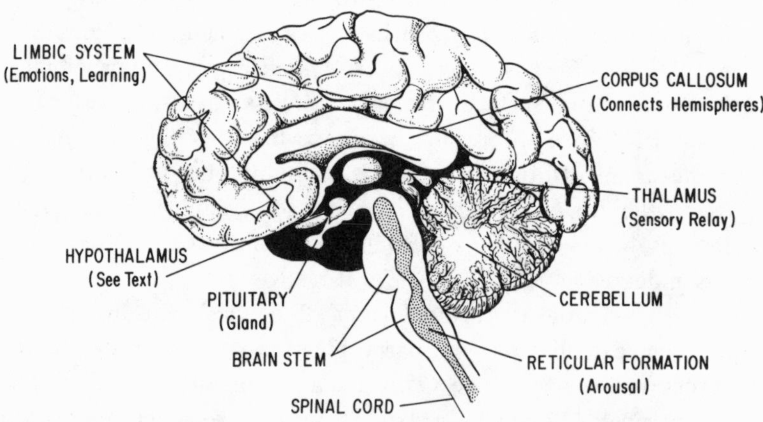

FIG. 4. The human brain. Top: the surface of the left hemisphere of the human brain, with major areas and their functions labelled. Bottom: a midline view of the right hemisphere with the major areas/structures and their functions labelled.

poral, and Occipital. Each lobe has somewhat different functions. All lobes in man can be divided into zones that are sensory or motor, and into zones that are termed "associational." A word of explanation is in order. The sensory and motor zones are just that: areas for bodily sensation, such as touch and temperature, and regions concerned with the control of muscular contractions. Sensory zones contain neurons that receive information from sensory organs and further process this information. Motor areas have neurons whose axons ultimately influence the musculature to produce movement. The cortex is only several millimeters thick but contains a number of distinct layers in which are found (a) the terminations of information bearing axons, (b) output neurons, (c) local processing neurons, and (d) other nonneuronal cells (the glia). The appearance of the layers under the microscope differs from one cortical zone to the next, with sensory zones having an expanded layer containing the terminations of information bearing axons. Usually there are several separate zones for each sense; for example, the visual area of cat and monkey contains three zones, and the motor area contains two zones. In some cases we understand the functional differences of the various zones; for example, the three visual zones (termed V1, V2, and V3) contain neurons that respond to different aspects (edges versus moving angles) of the visual scene.

The *association* zones function neither as sensory analyzers nor motor programmers. In many cases we are almost totally ignorant of the precise function(s) of the association zones. In other cases we know them to be involved, for example, with the understanding of language or the perception of complex sensory information. A clue to their function comes from observations of the amount of association cortex in other species. Rats have a tiny amount; dogs and cats have much more; primate and cetacean brains come as close to the brain of man as do any. Since the amount of association cortex parallels the phylogenetic progression, and since the function of the association cortex for which we have clear information suggests a role in the more cognitive aspects of behavior, it is assumed that these functions are associated with association cortex. The increase in cognitive abilities across species nicely parallels the expansion of the association cortex. In short, it is probably association cortex that separates us from our fellow creatures.

Cortical specializations are found in each of the four lobes. (In addition, each lobe of the human brain contains association cortex.) In the *frontal lobe* are the motor areas for all the skeletal muscles in the body. Cells in these zones send axons to neurons in other parts of the brain as well as long axons (three feet in man, thirty feet in the blue whale) to neurons in the spinal cord which, in turn, send axons directly to muscle. The *parietal lobe* contains bodily sense areas receiving axon projections from other brain areas (subcortical areas) whose function is to process and pass on body sense information gained from receptors located in the skin, joints, and other tissues. In the *temporal lobe* are the auditory sense areas receiving information indirectly from the cochlea of the ear. There are multiple auditory analyzers in the temporal lobe, each probably dealing with a different aspect of the auditory world. Finally, in the *occipital lobe* are the cortical sensory analyzers for information from the retina of the eye. A large bundle of fibers, the corpus callosum, serves to connect the two cortical hemispheres. The corpus callosum will be the topic of several of the chapters that follow.

The registration of sensory information on cortical neurons is not a simple one-to-one affair. There are numerous subcortical "relay" areas that do not simply relay the information, but process it at each stage in its journey from receptor to cortical receiving area. In addition, there is a considerable degree of convergence, the coming together of various signals to a single point, and divergence, the radiating of a signal to many points. These seemingly contradictory processes work together in the processing of information by the brain. As information about the sensory world ascends through the processing stations of the brain on its way to the cortical receiving areas, the signal, while changed, does not lose its form or pattern. Take, for instance, the registration of a spot of light on the retina, analogous to viewing an illuminated ping-pong ball in a darkened room. A certain portion of the retina is activated and neural impulses stream toward the brain. As the optic fibers terminate on their subcortical relay station in the thalamus, they form a "pattern" of the retina in the thalamus. Similarly, the fibers going from the thalamus to terminate in the visual cortex of the occipital lobe retain the pattern of the retina. Thus, the spot of retina activated by light from the ping-pong ball is represented on the visual cortex by a spot of activated cortical tissue. This general rule holds for all sensory projections—they project to the cortex (and intermediate relay stations) such that the surface of the receptor (retina, skin, cochlea) is mapped out on the surface of the cortex. The mapping is, however, quite distorted, although all parts are present. In the bodily senses of touch and temperature, the distortion is such that in man, the fingers, lips, and tongue are grossly out of proportion, being much larger than would be the case with a one-to-one mapping. The reason for this apparent distortion is that the brain allocates cortical space not by surface area but by receptor density. Humans have the highest density of skin receptors in the fingers, lips, and tongue. The bodily sense cortical projections of a house cat would have a grossly large area devoted to the sensory receptors supplying the whiskers of the face and a relatively small paw representation.

THE SUBCORTEX

Underlying the cortex is a virtual panoply of subcortical brain structures, most of which we will conveniently ignore. For our purposes, we have adopted the convention of dividing the brain into four parts: the *forebrain*, of which the cortex is a part; the *midbrain*; the *brain stem*; and the *spinal cord*. The changes across phylogeny that were mentioned earlier are, by and large, limited to the forebrain. The midbrain, brain stem, and spinal cord are little changed across a wide range of species. As we have seen, the *thalamus*, a forebrain tissue, acts to process and relay visual information to the cortex. To accomplish these tasks it has a specialized collection of neurons, known as the nucleus. The thalamus, as the major sensory relay in the brain, contains relay nuclei for each of the senses. In addition, it possesses other nuclei specialized for other jobs—such as widespread activation of the cortical association areas, a function presumably linked to arousal processes. Mammals deprived of sensory cortex due to a genetic accident or surgical removal experience only the crudest aspects of sensory experience such as intensity and frequency; the fine patterning of the sensory world is unavailable to them.

The other forebrain structure of interest to us is not a single nucleus, nor even a collected group of nuclei, but rather a physically widespread yet closely interconnected group of structures known collectively as the *limbic system.* The names of some of the structures are intriguing: amygdala, hippocampus, septum. Equally as intriguing and mystifying to neuroscientists is the function of the limbic system. Humans deprived of the hippocampus through surgery to control epilepsy suffer an inability to store events into permanent memory. Animals apparently do not share this deficit, but display a diverse symptomology which has spawned many theories as to hippocampal function, ranging from a role in inhibiting no longer relevant behaviors to keeping track of objects in space. We simply do not know the function of this brain area.

The *midbrain*, located not surprisingly in the middle of the brain, is made up of the reticular formation and the hypothalamus/pituitary. Running up through the base of the brain and ending in the midbrain is a diffuse structure known as the *reticular formation* (figure 5). This core of neural tissue receives sensory information on route to the thalamus and cortex. Unlike the thalamus, its fibers do not project to circumscribed areas of the cortex; rather, they are widespread and have diffuse connections with many brain regions. Electrical stimulation of the reticular formation in a sleeping animal will awaken the animal—suggesting a role in arousal. This is confirmed by experiments in which the reticular formation was inactivated, producing a continual somnolent state, and by noting that sedative drugs act at this location. Some of the neurons in this area have incredibly long projections, with thousands of connections established throughout the brain—further attesting to the widespread nature of reticular formation effects.

If a case could be made for one "brain center," the only viable candidate would have to be the *hypothalamus*, a nuclear structure, located above the roof of the mouth in man. The reasons for choosing the hypothalamus as the brain area of major importance are as follows: (a) it has widespread connections with many other brain areas; (b) it is intimately connected with the master endocrine gland—the pituitary; (c) and it has been found to be involved in a wide variety of behaviors and processes. Since entire books the size of this one could be, and have been, written on the hypothalamus, we shall again summarize. The hypothalamus has one over-

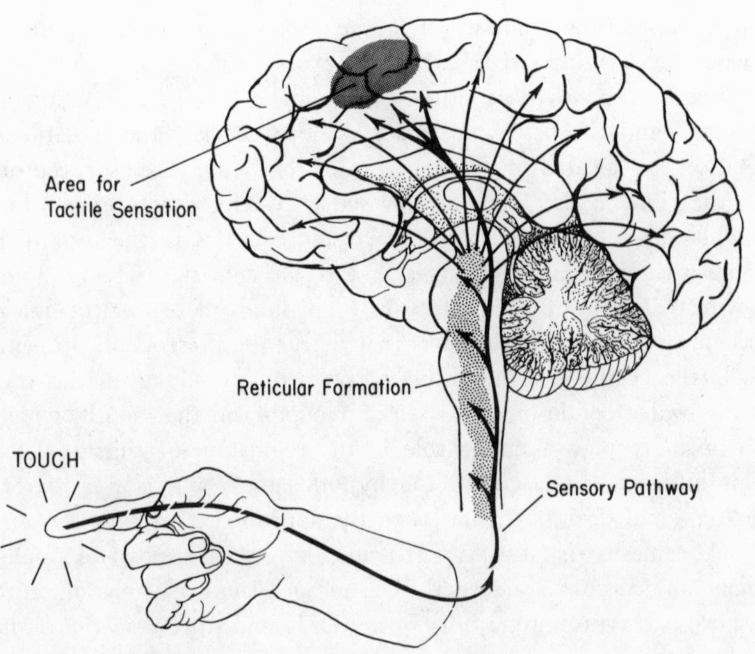

FIG. 5. The reticular activating system. Incoming sensory information from touch receptors on the finger is fed into the reticular formation (stippled area). The reticular formation activates the entire cortex by means of a widespread fiber system. The touch information is relayed by the thalamus to the cortical area for tactile information (shaded area located on the lateral surface of the hemisphere).

riding duty—the maintenance of relatively constant internal conditions, termed *homeostasis*.

The body is not unlike an incredibly complex factory, wherein separate assembly lines must be coordinated such that the output meets the demand of the marketplace—if demand increases, this information must be "fed back" to the assembly lines to enable them to produce more. So, too, the hypothalamus regulates many activities by the judicious application of "feedback." Such behaviors as eating and drinking, and such physiological functions as temperature regulation and reproduction, are largely governed by the hypothalamus. We will briefly examine one system governed by the hypothalamus in order to appreciate its function and its execution of that function.

Drinking water is vitally important, as most organisms cannot store appreciable amounts of water. There is a limited range of water levels within the body; any excess water is excreted, any deficit brings into play water-seeking behaviors (the sensation of "thirst" and the behaviors undertaken to alleviate the sensation). Sensors are located in various parts of the body: stretch receptors in the vessel walls of the cardiovascular system, which signal a loss in blood and thus water volume; osmoreceptors in the hypothalamus that respond to changes in the salt content of body fluids (with dehydration, the salinity of body fluids increases); chemical receptors in the hypothalamus that detect the presence of a chemical (the hormone angiotensin) secreted by the kidney under low body water conditions; and sensor receptors in the mouth, which surprisingly play a minor role in the regulation of thirst. All of this information is sent to the hypothalamus, where it is "interpreted" and decisions made as to the appropriate response.

The means that the hypothalamus has at its disposal to implement its decisions are several. The hypothalamus can manufacture a hormone (antidiuretic hormone, ADH) and store it in the pituitary to be released upon a neural command from the hypothalamus. ADH acts upon the kidney to cause it to conserve body water by concentrating the urine output. In addition, the hypothalamus is presumably involved in the sensation of thirst (and the converse, satiation) and the water-seeking behaviors that accompany it, although the means by which the rest of the brain is interfaced to the hypothalamus in this behavior is by no means understood.

The hypothalamus is intimately connected to the *pituitary* by a slender stalk. The two tissues work in concert; in fact, the division between brain and gland is somewhat arbitrary. To give an idea of the "holistic" nature of the brain/gland system, consider that in many situations the pituitary gland is driven into activity (and secretes a hormone into the blood) by a "local hormone" released by the hypothalamus. The hormone secreted by the pituitary causes activity elsewhere (for example, the gonads) and, in turn, activates the secretion of gonadal hormone into the blood where it is sensed by the hypothalamus. Thus, the hypothalamus is involved with information regarding the "effectiveness" of its action and is in a position to increase or decrease the output of its "local hormone." This principle of control is seen in many everyday situations, for example, adjusting the flow of water out of a lawn sprinkler. Your hand (hypothalamus) turns on a faucet (hormone), and you adjust the flow depending upon the area covered by the sprinkler (circulating levels of target gland hormone).

Proceeding further down into the brain, we are confronted with a portion of the brain that has least changed across species—the *brain stem.* Many brain nuclei and nerve tracts exiting from higher brain centers and incoming sensory fibers are found here. In addition, this area contains nuclei of the autonomic nervous system—a relatively involuntary division of the nervous system that innervates the visceral organs, vessels, and ducted glands. The autonomic nervous system has two divisions: the sympathetic, which increases its activity in times of stress or arousal, and the parasympathetic, which exhibits more activity during quiescence. Most organs are supplied with nerves from both divisions of the autonomic nervous system. Nuclei concerned with motor control are located in the brain stem as well. Although technically not considered a brain stem structure, the *cerebellum* communicates with the rest of the brain via the brain stem and, of course, is involved in the control and cooperation of muscles and muscle ensemblages.

The last structure on our quick anatomical tour is the *spinal cord*—in man the diameter of your little finger—it contains ascending and descending nerve tracts, large neurons (motor neurons) whose job it is to induce muscular contraction, and smaller neurons whose job in part is to contribute to motor control and facilitate reflexive behavior.

Much can be gained by examining the brains of different species and the developing brain of a single species. Figure 6 graphically depicts a phylogenetic comparison across several species, and the ontogenetic development of the human brain. Phylogenetically, the brain stem is very similar across species, with marked differences in the forebrain—to the point of some species having no forebrain. The growth of the forebrain, particularly the cortex, is evident. Since the basic unit of the brain, the neuron, is similar across a wide phylogenetic span, man's ascendancy in large part must rest upon his tremendous cortical endowment—rivalled only by the whales

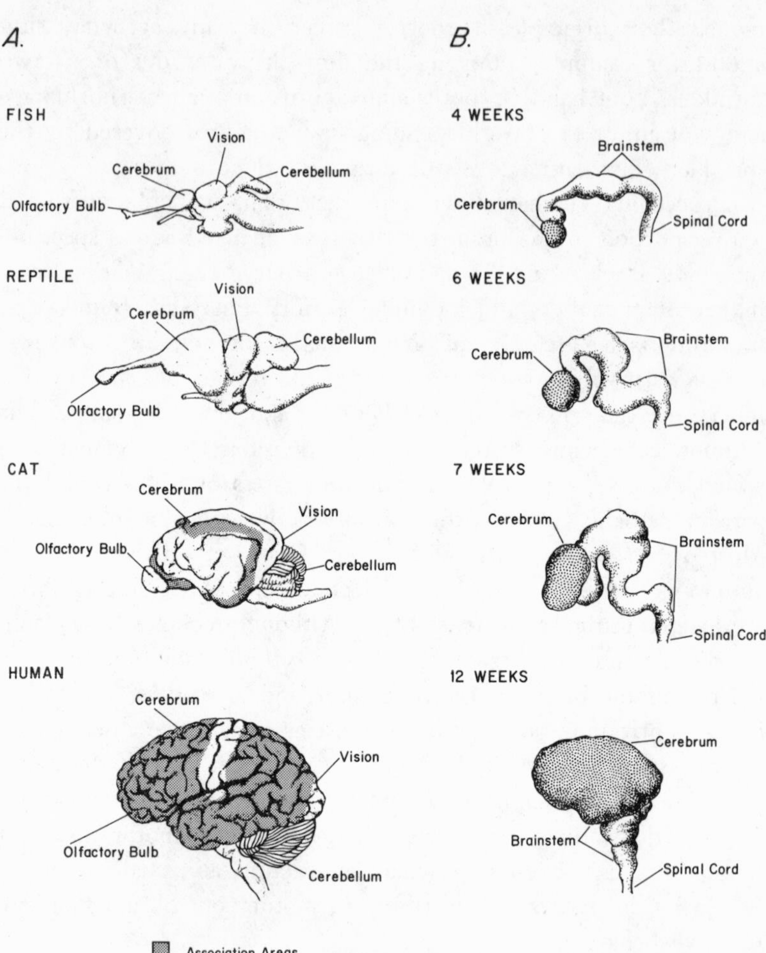

Fig. 6. A. A comparative view of brain anatomy. The drawings of the brains of fish through man are not to scale. Note the diminished predominance of the olfactory bulb and the tremendous increase in the size of the cerebrum. Association cortex is absent in fish and reptile, and is fully elaborated in the human brain. B. The development of the human brain in the first 4-12 weeks of life. The basic structure is established at 12 weeks, with cell division and brain growth proceeding rapidly up to the time of birth.

and dolphins. Note the shaded cortical areas; they represent association cortex in which the phylogenetic disparity is even more pronounced.

Across ontogeny, the brain differentiates out of a mass of neuron precursors—the neuroblasts. Cell division in the embryo proceeds at a rapid rate such that the basic architecture of the brain is complete at birth, to be modified and expanded by its subsequent environment. Out of a primitive neural tube the forebrain, midbrain, and brain stem rapidly emerge to form identifiable structures even at the earliest ages. Cell division before birth is occurring at a furious pace (doubling every few days in some instances) in contrast to the absence of cell division after birth. All the while, neurons are migrating about in the embryonic brain to eventually assume their final and correct locations—an awesome phenomenon that has remained a mystery for years.

BASIC NEUROCHEMISTRY

We have seen that neurons communicate with each other via neurotransmitters. Research has shown that there are several varieties of neurotransmitters, some of which are located only in particular areas of the brain. Knowledge of neurotransmitters is important in relation to their role in neurological disease, psychopathology, and learning disorders. In addition, drugs of abuse, particularly addicting drugs, appear to operate by mimicking naturally occurring neurotransmitters. Therefore an understanding of these agents may have profound implications for the alleviation of many individual and societal problems.

The scientific criteria for establishing the identity of a synaptic neurotransmitter are exceedingly stringent. To date, only one neurotransmitter has been completely identified in the central nervous system—acetylcholine, an excitatory transmitter at the skeletal nerve-muscle junction and the autonomic nervous system. Acetylcholine has also been identified in the cortex and thalamus of the brain by assaying for the presence of the agent (an enzyme) that inactivates the neurotransmitter. Other neurotransmitters in the brain and their areas of localization have not been definitively identified, although substantial evidence exists concerning their roles as suspected neurotransmitters.

Dopamine. Dopamine is an inhibitory neurotransmitter found in subcortical motor nuclei and in limbic system connections to the cortex. This candidate neurotransmitter, a catecholamine, has been linked to Parkinson's disease, a condition characterized by a pronounced muscular tremor. This disease is associated with a degeneration in the major dopamine nucleus—the substantia nigra. Dopamine itself, if injected or ingested, would not gain entry into the brain, being blocked by a system of protective barriers known as the "blood-brain-barrier." Dopamine has also been linked to mental illness by the observation that the most effective antipsychotic pharmaceutical agents act by blocking dopamine synaptic transmission (sometimes giving rise to "Parkinson-like" side effects).

Norepinephrine. One synthetic step beyond dopamine is the inhibitory neurotransmitter norepinephrine. Like dopamine, norepinephrine is obtained from dietary phenylalanine. A region of the brain stem, the locus coeruleus, is a major source of the widely projecting norepinephrine nerve fibers. These fibers project to the cortex, limbic system, hypothalamus, spinal cord, and elsewhere.

Serotonin. Serotonin is an inhibitory neurotransmitter that has been implicated in cognitive functions, mental illness, and sleep cycles. The cell bodies of serotonin releasing fibers are found in the raphé nuclei of the brain stem. One of the drugs of abuse of the early 1970s, LSD, bears striking chemical similarities to this neurotransmitter. Several other suspected neurotransmitters have been discovered, and more are sure to come. It is possible that each of the various specialized brain "circuits" possesses a unique neurotransmitter. The study of the "chemical anatomy" of the brain is expected to answer this and many other questions.

The brain, as we have seen, is an electro-chemical machine. Not surprisingly, it can be altered in its function by the addition of "foreign" chemicals. Many drugs have little or no central nervous system action, primarily because they are prevented access to the brain by the blood-brain-barrier. Those that do gain access interact with various processes in the brain. Alcohol, for example, is a central nervous system depressant and is similar in action to the barbiturates. While the precise mechanism of action of this drug is being actively investigated, it is not improbable that it acts by interfering with brain metabolism, or acts at the ion gates referred to above. The effect of alcohol and the barbiturates, which were or are used as general anesthetics, is also observed with over exposure to certain paint thinners, glue, and industrial solvents which contain benzene, toluene, and xylene. These agents are powerful brain depressants and, when abused, can lead to serious complications or death.

Other drugs are central nervous system excitants. Examples include the amphetamines. These drugs, too, have been subject to much abuse. Their mechanism of action in the brain appears to involve the facilitated release of packaged neurotransmitters from axon terminals, such that neural excitability is increased due to the elevated synaptic concentrations of the neurotransmitters. When abused, these agents are particularly dangerous, as addiction develops and heavy use can lead to the development of both a drug-induced psychosis and deterioration of brain tissue.

The narcotics, derivatives of opium such as heroin, are technically analgesics in that they alter the perception of pain. The property leading to their abuse is the euphoria associated with the drug. These agents are addicting. Their mechanism of operation is being pursued. It appears that they activate certain naturally occurring receptors on neurons to produce their effect. Once their mechanism of action is known, we may be able to prevent or treat drug addiction more effectively than at present.

Several drugs are rather similar in chemical structure to naturally occurring neurotransmitters, and have a powerful effect on awareness and perception. Among these psychotomimetic drugs are: mescaline (derived from the Peyote cactus), with a structure similar to one of the catecholamines; LSD, with a structure similar to serotonin; and marijuana—a mild psychotomimetic that does not have structural similarities to any known neurotransmitter. An understanding of the mechanism of action of these agents may shed light on normal brain processes and may provide insight into the reasons for their abuse.

Brain Processes

Our knowledge of brain processes is most complete with regard to sensory functions or motor control. We know relatively little of brain processes associated with thinking, reasoning, motivation, and other more "cognitive" processes. An examination of known brain processes may provide us with an understanding of general principles of brain functioning. These general principles may also prove to hold for cognitive processes of which we have only fragmentary knowledge today.

The analysis of sensory events by the brain operates by a principle of feature extraction. As sensory information is relayed through the brain, neurons respond to particular aspects of the stimulus; some neurons code aspects of patterning, some code movement, and some code other aspects such as color or pitch. An example of feature extraction in the visual cortex of a cat is seen in figure 7. It is as if the sensory signal were being passed through

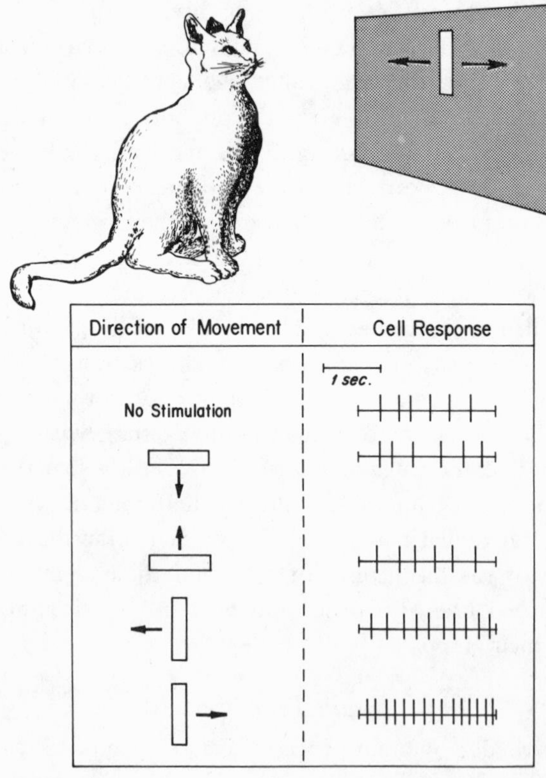

FIG. 7. Feature extraction. An electrode capable of detecting the activity of a single neuron in the visual cortex has been painlessly implanted in the cat's brain. The cat watches a bar of light move across a screen. Simultaneously, the activity of the neuron is recorded—each vertical line represents an action potential. This cell is most responsive to a movement to the right, as shown by its discharge rate.

an array of tuned filters, with each sensory event activating a different set of filters. It is easy to conceive of how such an analyzer would work, but very difficult to understand how the result of this analysis is entered into our conscious awareness of the world. We perceive the results of activation of the retina as vision, not because of some unique property of the information being sent from the retina to the brain, but rather because of the particular connections of the fibers from the retina to the rest of the brain. If it were possible to rewire the brain such that the optic nerve fibers could be connected to the auditory areas of the brain, we would undoubtedly "hear" light. Surprisingly, there are documented cases of individuals who apparently register any sensory event in all of their sensory analyzers. One individual, a Soviet citizen, when exposed to an auditory stimulus, not only hears sound but also experiences a visual pattern and color as well as a particular taste and smell. It is not known how this individual's brain differs from a normal brain.

We have seen that feedback is an important aspect of brain functioning. Without feedback control, however, we would experience difficulty performing even the simplest act. We are able to stand upright without falling over by integrating the various relevant signals and adjusting the musculature appropriately. In this example, information from pressure receptors on the feet, the semicircular canals of the vestibular system, and visual information are analyzed. Given perturbation of the system (for example, a gust of wind), similar information would be registered in several sensors and the appropriate correction made. The system can be confused by providing discrepant information to the sensors. An example of the latter is the "tilting room" of a fun house, in which the room visually appears to be tilted. In this case, the visual input is at odds with the other sources of information. The brain integrates this discrepant visual information with the other sources—the result is that people adjust their bodies to compromise the discrepant information from the various sensors. A person with his eyes closed in the tilting room would, of course, stand upright. Upon opening his eyes, he will tilt his body to adjust for the discrepant information, but not as much as would be determined by the visual input alone. So, too, do we compromise our cognitive responses to sources of disparate information. Children confronted with diverse reactions to their inappropriate behavior will not be able to determine what behavior patterns are desired, and as a consequence may select a behavioral solution that represents a compromise to the conflicting demands. If the reactions are too diverse, causing the feedback loop to fail, the reactions will be ineffective in modifying the child's behavior—with unfortunate results. So, too, in the tilting room example; if the information is too discrepant, an individual will simply fall down—a failure of feedback control due to conflicting information input of an excessive nature.

LEARNING AND MEMORY

Learning implies a relatively permanent alteration in behavior as a result of experience. It also implies the relatively permanent storage of the results of learning. The search for brain correlates of learning and memory is confounded by the existence of an apparent paradox. The electrical stimulation of discrete areas of the brain in unanesthetized neurosurgical patients often results in vivid memories of past events, some of which were apparently "forgotten" by the patient. This suggests two things. First, the brain has an infinite capacity for memory, although it may not always be possible to retrieve certain memories. Indeed, no one has ever "filled up" the brain with memories such that further remembering is impossible. Second, it would appear that there exist discrete locations where memory is stored. Herein lies the apparent paradox. Early experiments with animals wherein portions of the brain were surgically removed indicated that specific memories were *not* deleted. Rather, the degree of behavioral deficit was related to the amount of tissue removed *rather* than to its specific location. Thus, on the one hand, it appears that memories are localized, while on the other hand they appear to be diffuse. Subsequent experiments have not all supported these early lesion studies. Indeed, substantial evidence exists that certain brain areas are specialized for learning certain behaviors or certain types of tasks. In many animals, including man, lesions of parts of the frontal lobes produce defects in learning tasks that require the subject to delay or withhold its response. Similarly specific deficits are produced in animals surgically deprived of portions of their temporal lobes

—in this case the defect is seen in tasks requiring a visual discrimination between objects.

The hypothetical memory trace is often referred to as the *engram.* The search for the engram has been approached in a variety of ways. One of the most promising involves recording the activity of neurons throughout the brain in an animal with permanently implanted electrodes while the animal is learning a task. These experiments have shown that while there are some areas that seem particularly involved with the learning process (for example, the hippocampus), and some areas that are apparently not involved at all, many areas of the brain do show neural changes associated with behavioral learning. It is, therefore, possible that the engram has no discrete location but is represented by a diffuse and perhaps redundant network of altered neurons.

The nature of the alteration in the brain as a result of information storage is unknown. This is not to say that potential mechanisms have not been proposed and examined—they have. Among them are: changes in neuronal RNA and protein (which could permanently alter the neuron's response to the transmitter); changes in the amount of transmitter released; growth of new synaptic contacts; and changes in the physical/chemical properties of the synapse. In some simple systems (invertebrates) the synaptic mechanism responsible for decrementing synaptic transmission (habituation) has been delineated; it involves a decrease in transmitter release from axon terminals. It is by no means certain that all neurons will be found to employ the same mechanism of change. Ultimately, we may understand these mechanisms and be in a position to modify their processes—thus modifying the ability of an organism to learn and to remember.

The process of converting a learned behavior into a relatively permanent engram has been found to be a time-dependent process. When a behavior has been learned, it is susceptible to interruption for a brief period of time, thus preventing its "consolidation" into an enduring engram. This is the period of "short-term" memory. Amnesia following a trauma to the brain is a common occurrence in accident victims, and is also seen following psychiatric electro-shock therapy. These persons cannot remember events immediately preceding the trauma. Once consolidated in "long-term" storage, memories are no longer affected by these treatments which primarily modify the ionic properties of the neuron membrane. Long-term memory can be disrupted by treatments that inhibit the synthesis of proteins (structural proteins are presumably involved in any enduring engram). Thus it is thought that memory consolidation involves two phases: the first, a transient change in the neural membrane, and the second, a relatively enduring structural change of the neuron. There are documented cases of individuals incapable of forming long-term memory engrams. These persons, who suffer from damage to the hippocampus, can learn normally and have intact short-term memory, but are incapable of long-term storage (or retrieval).

INFORMATION PROCESSING

A defining characteristic of the human species is the presence of a formal language. Research has delineated two regions on the dominant hemisphere (usually the left hemisphere for right-handed individuals—subsequent chapters will deal with hemispheric specialization in some detail) specialized for language. They are Broca's area in the frontal lobe and Wernicke's area in the temporal lobe. Damage due to injury or stroke to Broca's area results in a person incapable of producing smooth, well-articulated speech, although the content and meaning are normal. Damage to Wernicke's area results in well-articulated speech almost totally devoid of content. These observations, and others, have led to the notion that Broca's area is primarily concerned with language production, and that Wernicke's area is primarily concerned with semantic aspects of language. Both of these areas are considered association cortex. It should be noted that careful study usually reveals some general language problems associated with damage to any language area of the brain.

Much of what we learn are motor skills. Riding bicycles, typing, operating machinery, and playing the piano are all highly skilled motor behaviors. The acquisition and retention of motor skills are somewhat different than for more cognitive skills. Once acquired, they appear to endure for long periods of time, even in the absence of practice. Skilled motor behaviors often are produced with such rapidity as to question if each movement is consciously directed, as in the playing of an experienced pianist. The hippocampal damaged patient referred to earlier, suffering from a lack of long-term memory, has no trouble remembering newly learned motor skills for long periods of time. Yet he is unable to *verbally* report having any recollection of the skill or of how to perform it.

The fabric of the brain is set down as a result of the interaction of genetic blueprints and environmental influences. While the basic features of brain organization are present at birth (cell division is essentially complete), the brain experiences tremendous growth in neural processes, synapse formation, and myelin sheath formation, declining around puberty. These processes can be profoundly altered by the organism's environment, as will be detailed in a subsequent chapter. Rats reared in an enriched environment (with litter mates in a cage full of "interesting" objects) show marked changes in brain development as compared to rats reared in impoverished environments. Furthermore, it has been shown that brain processes present at birth will degenerate if the environmental stimulation necessary to activate them is withheld. It appears that the genetic contribution provides a framework which, if not used, will disappear, but which is capable of further development given the optimal environmental stimulation. The social and political implications of this fact of brain functioning are obvious and far-reaching.

To the beginning student of the neurosciences, it is often informative to outline the pattern of information flow in the brain. While this cannot be done with complete confidence, it is illustrative of the regions activated by a simple sensory and motor event. In figure 8, the information flow resulting from touch receptors on the finger is diagrammed. On the top is the sensory registration of the event relayed from the thalamus to the parietal lobe, accompanied by widespread reticular formation activation of the cortex. In this depiction, the event is being evaluated cognitively by the frontal association cortex to result in the issuance of a motor command (figure 8, bottom) to move the hand and finger. The motor output originates in the frontal motor area, is further modulated by subcortical motor areas and the cerebellum, and projects into the spinal cord to terminate on motor neurons projecting to the appropriate muscles (not shown). It must be noted that many

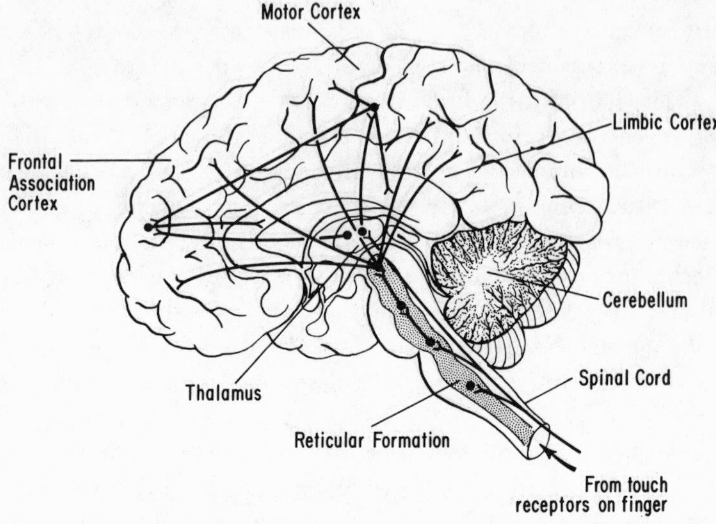

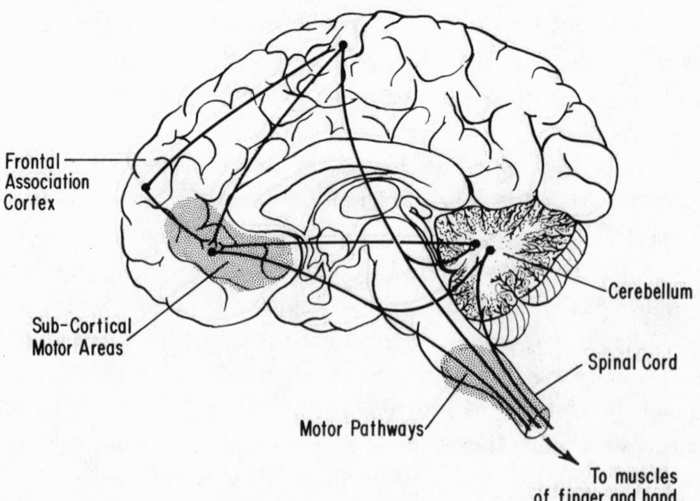

Fig. 8. Information flow in the brain. Top: brain areas activated by sensory information from touch receptors on the finger. Bottom: brain areas involved in the issuance of motor commands to muscles of the finger and hand. In the interest of legibility, many brain areas involved in this simple situation are not shown.

relevant brain areas involved in this simple stimulus-response have been omitted for the sake of clarity. Even for this elementary behavior, widespread areas of the brain are engaged.

MEASUREMENT OF BRAIN ACTIVITY

The measurement of brain activity is a limiting factor in our understanding of its function. Restrictions are imposed because of the technical limitations of the procedure and the intrusive effects of the recording device on the normal operation of the brain. In human beings, the only widely used means of directly measuring brain activity is through the use of scalp electrodes. These electrodes measure the summed activity of millions of neurons lying under the skull. When the neurons are synchronously active, the resultant record (the electroencephalogram, EEG) shows rhythmic waves of various frequencies. When the neurons are asynchronously active, the EEG becomes less rhythmic. An analogy can be drawn to a crowd of people on a basketball court. When they all jump up and down in concert, the floor rebounds up and down in large swings. When the individuals in the crowd each jump independently, the undulations of the floor are smaller and of higher frequency. By measuring the floor vibrations, we can get some idea of the activity of the population of individuals. Since the EEG records the activity of a large population of neurons, it is not particularly valuable for examining the fine tuning of the brain. It has proved of use in measuring the general state of arousal of an individual as is shown in figure 9. Recent claims have appeared regarding the correspondence between EEG patterns and measured intelligence. These claims have not been widely accepted by the scientific community.

The most precise information regarding neural activity comes from recording the activity of single neurons, particularly with electrodes that are capable of penetrating the cell membrane to detect the transmembrane charge. While this provides a great deal of information about neural processing, it is technically difficult and faces the rather nasty problem of sampling the activity of a very few cells out of the billions in the brain. These recording techniques are intrusive and are not normally used in examining human brain functioning.

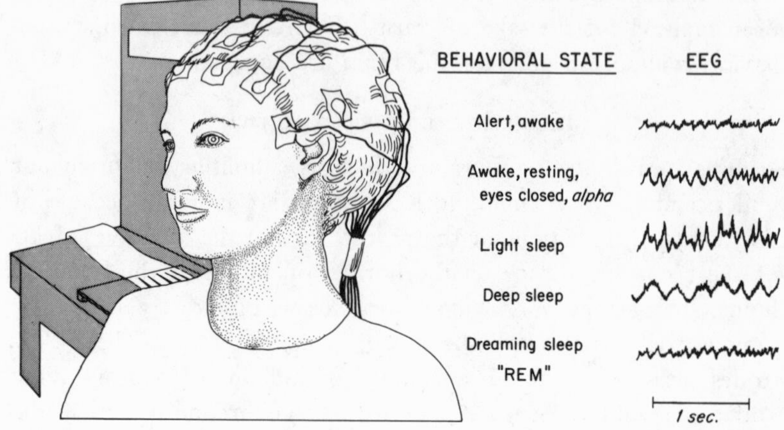

FIG. 9. The electroencephalogram (EEG). Scalp electrodes can measure the activity of large populations of neurons. When the neurons act in synchrony, waves can be recorded, i.e., alpha waves—associated with relaxed wakefulness. Particular EEG patterns are associated with behavioral states as is depicted here.

In summary, the brain is an incredibly complex electro-chemical machine. The neurosciences are still in their infancy, but are progressing rapidly in uncovering the mysteries of the brain. We do know that it is an exquisitely built tissue capable of being modified, for good or bad, by its environment. It is not altogether ridiculous to draw an analogy between the brain and the United States, in which the citizens represent neurons and the cities represent nuclei. Cities are connected by lines of communication and often perform specific duties, for example, commerce, tourism, manufacturing. Individuals in the cities work at these duties and influence other individuals, but few are really indispensable. The sum of society's knowledge (memory) is distributed throughout the citizenry. And, finally, the country is influenced, for good and bad, by its environment—both natural and man-made.

FOR FURTHER READING

In this final section of the chapter some additional readings are suggested for those readers desiring information beyond what it has been possible to provide in this brief introduction.

For general purposes, the reader will find Timothy J. Teyler,

A Primer of Psychobiology (San Francisco: Freeman, 1975), an elementary introduction to the brain that assumes no relevant background. Richard F. Thompson, *Introduction to Physiological Psychology* (New York: Harper and Row, 1975), is a college-level textbook that provides broad coverage of the brain and behavior. A higher-level book emphasizing mechanisms of neural operations is Steven W. Kuffler and John G. Nichols, *From Neuron to Brain* (Sunderland, Mass.: Sinauer, 1976). In Michael S. Gazzaniga and Colin Blakemore, *Handbook of Psychobiology* (New York: Academic Press, 1975), a book that assumes an introductory knowledge of the brain, readers will find chapters devoted to current research areas. In Mark R. Rosenzweig and Edward L. Bennett, *Neural Mechanisms of Learning and Memory* (Cambridge, Mass.: MIT Press, 1976) there are chapters devoted to current research on brain processes of learning and memory in man and animals. Horace W. Magoun's *The Waking Brain* (Springfield, Ill.: Charles C Thomas, 1963) is an engaging book dealing with brain mechanisms of arousal and sleep.

Those particularly interested in neuroanatomy will find the following volumes useful: Charles R. Novack and Robert J. Demarest, *The Nervous System: Introduction and Review* (New York: McGraw-Hill, 1972), an easy to read, well-illustrated beginning book on brain anatomy; Ernest Gardner, *Fundamentals of Neurology*, 6th ed. (Philadelphia: Saunders, 1975), an integrated presentation of brain anatomy and physiology, moderately advanced; and Alf Brodal, *Neurological Anatomy*, 2d ed. (New York: Oxford University Press, 1969), a more difficult anatomy text that does an admirable job of integrating structure and function.

On the subject of neurophysiology, Robert F. Schmidt's *Fundamentals of Neurophysiology* (New York: Springer-Verlag, 1975) is an intermediate-level textbook with emphasis on motor, sensory, and homeostatic systems. John C. Eccles, *The Understanding of the Brain* (New York: McGraw-Hill, 1973) is an intermediate-level text with sections on brain development and cognitive functions. For a more difficult book dealing with the biophysics of neural function, see Bernard Katz, *Nerve, Muscle, and Synapse* (New York: McGraw-Hill, 1966).

Those interested in neurochemistry will find Robert M. Julien,

A Primer of Drug Action (San Francisco: Freeman, 1975) an introductory book on the chemistry of the brain and the effect of drugs on the brain. Jack R. Cooper, Floyd E. Bloom, and Robert H. Roth, *The Biochemical Basis of Neuropharmacology*, 2d ed. (New York: Oxford University Press) is a difficult but comprehensive book on the biochemistry of the brain and synaptic transmission.

Part Two

CHAPTER II

Attention: A Neuropsychological Perspective

ALLAN F. MIRSKY

Definition and Comparison with Other Related Fields of Inquiry

We may define attention, for the purposes of this chapter, as a focussing of consciousness or awareness on some part of the multitude of stimuli from the environment, usually on the basis of learning or training. The study of attention or of the attentive process in neuropsychology includes all of the events from the impinging of stimuli on the receptor organs of the body (including but not limited to the eyes, ears, nose, tongue, and skin) through the central processing of the information in the brain, to the final expression of the process, usually in some motor or muscular act. The body of material included under the study of consciousness, which includes attention, overlaps to a considerable extent with research on the process or orientation and habituation and with the study of the phenomena of sleep and wakefulness. By orientation we mean the mechanisms, learned and unlearned, which cause an organism to direct some part of its sensory receiving apparatus toward noval environmental stimuli (the way a dog pricks up his ears and turns in the direction of a sound in the night). Habituation refers to the gradual disappearance of the orienting response, as a once novel stimulus becomes repetitive and familiar (as the dog will sleep undisturbed through a sound to which he has become accustomed). Research on sleep and wakefulness, on the other hand, is concerned with the mechanisms and principles that underlie the

Support for some of the research described in this chapter and for the preparation of the chapter came from research grants NS-12201, MH-12568, and K5-14,915 (Research Scientist Award) from the U.S. Public Health Service.

regular, daily cycling of the level of alertness which characterizes most animals that have been studied.[1]

We do not imply that consciousness, orientation-habituation, and sleep-wakefulness are all distinct and separate phenomena or that they are necessarily served by different brain mechanisms. To some extent the distinctions are artificial and refer to the ways in which various investigators have structured their experiments. On the other hand, disorders or illnesses that involve disturbance in one or another of these functions are clearly not equivalent in the way these terms are commonly used. Disturbed "attention" is not equivalent to disturbed "consciousness"; the latter can be considerably more grave, especially when it follows brain damage or disease. Some clarity, perhaps, is added by reference to figure 1, which

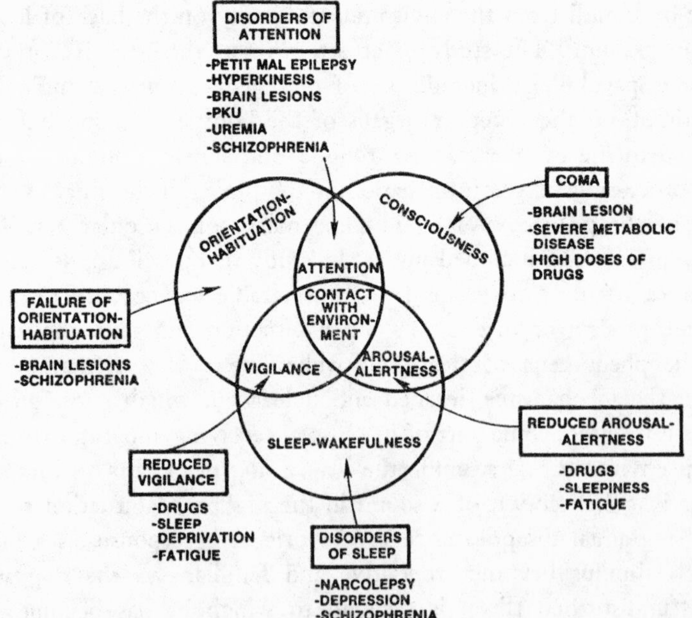

FIG. 1. Heuristic-conceptual diagram of the relationship among areas of research concerned with organism-environment interaction

Source: Allan F. Mirsky and Merle M. Orren, "Attention," in *Neuropeptide Influences on the Brain and Behavior*, ed. L. H. Miller, C. A. Sandman, and A. J. Kastin (New York: Raven Press, 1977), pp. 233-67. Reprinted with permission.

1. Truett Allison and Domenic V. Cicchetti, "Sleep in Mammals: Ecological and Constitutional Correlates," *Science* 194 (1976): 732-34.

presents a heuristic-conceptual model of the relationships among the three bodies of work. What is common to all is an interest in understanding the principles and mechanisms governing contact between the organism and its environment.

Examples of various patient groups or diagnostic entities in which disturbances of some of these functions occur are also provided in figure 1. Some of these will be discussed in later sections of this chapter. The reader is also referred to two recent collections of papers in this area of work, and in particular to the clear and cogent discussions of the problem by Berlyne.[2]

Neurological Bases of Attention

The information we have concerning the neurological bases of attention is derived for the most part from studies of the structures in the brain that are necessary for maintenance of consciousness. The data stem largely from two sources: postmortem study of patients who either through disease or accident sustained injury to the brain, which injury was accompanied by profound and permanent disturbance or loss of consciousness ("coma"), and research studies of animal subjects in which various portions of the brain were destroyed for experimental purposes. The information from these two approaches to the problem is in substantial agreement in that both suggest that a critical area for the maintenance of consciousness lies deep within the brain, in a structure known as the brain stem.[3] The borders and exact boundaries of the brain stem are not precisely defined from an anatomical point of view, but most anatomists would agree that it consists of the most anterior ("rostral") portion of the spinal cord (some refer to this as the "lower" brain stem) as well as more anterior portions called the midbrain (mesencephalon) and portions of the forebrain (that is,

2. Daniel E. Berlyne, "The Development of the Concept of Attention in Psychology," in *Attention in Neurophysiology*, ed. Christopher R. Evans and Thomas B. Mulholland (London: Butterworths, 1969), pp. 1-26; idem, "Attention as a Problem in Behavior Theory," in *Attention: Contemporary Theory and Analysis*, ed. David I. Mostofsky (New York: Appleton-Century-Crofts, 1970), pp. 25-49.

3. Elliot M. Marcus, "The Electroencephalogram: Seizures, Sleep, Coma, and Consciousness," in *An Introduction to the Neurosciences*, ed. Brian A. Curtis, Stanley Jacobson, and Elliot M. Marcus (Philadelphia: Saunders, 1972), pp. 710-52.

midline structures of the thalamus and the hypothalamus). The relation among these structures is presented in figures 4 and 5 of chapter 1.

The whole brain stem is not thought to be involved in a critical way in the maintenance of consciousness; more specifically this responsibility appears to reside in a medially located structure or system lying within the brain stem, which is referred to as the reticular formation or reticular system. This system, which itself contains a number of separable, identifiable nuclei or structures, comprises many millions of nerve cells and fibers (axons, dendrites) that interconnect and also connect to or are part of all the major ascending and descending pathways of the brain. In ways which are not yet understood fully, all neural messages that course between the sensory receptors and the brain, and between the brain and the effectors (muscles, glands), are registered in the reticular system. In addition to being registered there, neural messages can be regulated and modified. The regulation of neural messages takes place in two ways: the potency and (perhaps the salience) of a particular sensory signal can be modified by action of the reticular formation; further, the general tone or level of activity (or degree of "activation") of the entire brain can be modified by action of the reticular formation. There is evidence to suggest that the activation process itself is rather complex and can be subdivided into two types: a short-lived or "phasic" activation that may be due to action of the more anterior (thalamic) portions of the reticular system and a more long-lasting or "tonic" activation due to the more posterior ("lower" brain stem) portions of the reticular formation.[4]

One further important bit of complexity needs to be emphasized in this picture, although it has already been noted, at least by implication. The reticular formation is not in sole command of the activation and sensory modification functions of the brain. There are manifold reciprocal two-way neural connections and pathways between the cerebral cortical masses and the reticular formation so that the regulation of consciousness, on which all of this discussion bears, is obviously under the joint control of both cerebral

4. Henri H. Jasper, "Recent Advances in an Understanding of Ascending Activities of the Reticular System," in *Reticular Formation of the Brain*, ed. Henri H. Jasper et al. (Boston: Little, Brown and Co., 1958), pp. 319-31.

cortex structures in the reticular formation.[5] This is a rather oversimplified version of what is known about the regulation of consciousness; many details have been omitted. Hopefully, it is clear that for the normal regulation of conscious processes there must be a harmonious relation between the cerebral cortex and the brain stem reticular formation. Lesions in the medial portions of the brain stem can disrupt this harmony and are particularly likely to cause impaired consciousness; however, there can be functional "lesions" (that is, those in which structural damage may be difficult to demonstrate or verify) in cortex or reticular formation which may presumably be equally disturbing to consciousness.

This account thus far has concerned primarily the neural bases of consciousness. May we assume that all of this information applies equally well, or at least in some aspects, to attention and its disturbances? If attention is assumed to be some subregion of consciousness (related also to orientation-habituation as suggested by figure 1) this must be the case. Information from human subjects is difficult to obtain directly; usually disorders of attention or of attentiveness are not associated with some fatal illness which would allow pathologists to examine the brains of such persons and thereby to draw some inference about the central nervous system pathology (if any) that has produced this particular symptom. We are thus forced to rely on inferences or hunches. One inference would be that defects in attention, which are not severe enough to be called impaired consciousness, may represent small amounts of pathology in the same region of the brain known to be necessary for consciousness. If the pathology were larger in amounts, more disturbance of environmental contact or "loss of consciousness" would ensue. Another inference would be that defective attention is due to some temporary, functional disturbance of this area of the brain which is not detectable in any structural way (that is, as loss or damage to nerve cells). This does not exhaust the possible inferences, but these are two that are commonly made. Another way of gaining information on this point is to study experimental animals, whose brains can be manipulated in various ways so as to allow us to test our inferences or hypotheses about what may be wrong

5. Jasper et al., *Reticular Formation of the Brain.*

with the brain in persons with a particular kind of attentional defect. This technique of animal "modeling" is very frequently used in biological science and especially neuroscience. The assumption being made here is that the brains of higher animals (especially monkeys) are similar enough to human brains so that the information gained from the animal research is applicable in large measure to the understanding of human problems. Animal research concerned with central nervous system factors in attention has usually involved the following kind of experimental sequence. First, the animal subject is trained on some procedure that requires attention to some environmental stimuli and some kind of overt (usually motor or muscular) response. Second, some manipulation of the brain of the animal is made to see whether it will impair or improve the attentive capabilities of the animal. Such manipulations can be direct and permanent, for example, creating small experimental lesions in various brain areas (most often by the passage of electrical current in amount sufficient to destroy cells). Or the manipulation can be direct and temporary, for example, by injecting small amounts of drugs, or by passing electrical current in amounts insufficient to destroy tissue but sufficient to cause short-lasting disruption of the normal electrical activity of cells. This latter technique in particular has been used to model forms of epileptic disorder, which presumably represents naturally occurring disturbed electrical activity of brain cells.[6] Indirect manipulations of the brain have also been used in attention research. These involve such methods as injecting drugs into the bloodstream or depriving animals of oxygen or sleep.[7]

The general thrust of the findings in this area is that much of the same regions are involved in attention as are involved in consciousness, although regulation of attention may be far more complex. There is reason to believe that certain areas of the cerebral cortex and of the limbic system may play a role that they do not play in consciousness. Thus, in recent years, a considerable litera-

6. Eva B. Pragay et al., "Effect of Electrical Stimulation of the Brain on Visually Controlled (Attentive) Behavior in Macaca Mulatta," *Experimental Neurology* 49 (1975): 203-20.

7. Allan F. Mirsky and Susana Bloch-Rojas, "Effects of Chlorpromazine, Secobarbital, and Sleep Deprivation on Attention in Monkeys," *Psychopharmacologia* 10 (1967): 388-99.

ture has accumulated which suggests that the parietal lobe in man, and possibly the right inferior portion of this cortical structure, may be critical for certain kinds of attention behavior. Patients with right parietal lobe lesions may neglect the left side of their body and visual field almost entirely. Such behavior is referred to as the "hemi-inattention" or "unilateral neglect" syndrome.[8] Other research involving brain-damaged patients, primarily by Russian investigators, has implicated certain areas of the frontal lobes in the maintenance of sustained attention.[9] However, not all studies of the effects of frontal lobe damage have confirmed such findings.[10]

The apparent greater complexity of the maintenance, control, and regulation of attention as compared with consciousness seems to accord with our general understanding of factors influencing attention as we know it in man (or animals). Thus, the subject's past experiences, training, motivation, or level of interest in a particular task at a particular time can modify his apparent attentive capacity at a given moment. We know that cortical structures are necessary, in part, to register and benefit from experience. Motivation is also related to the functioning of some limbic and cortical structures. The interaction between motivation and attention can be complex. Motivation that is too high can be as deleterious for performance requiring attention as motivation that is too low. The precise nature of the contribution of various brain areas and the relationship among them in attention is being studied actively at this time.

Neurophysiological Correlates of Attention and Alertness

THE ELECTROENCEPHALOGRAM (EEG)

Many of the investigations alluded to in the previous sections made use of one or another kind of measurement of brain electrical

8. Edwin A. Weinstein and Robert P. Friedland, eds., *Advances in Neurology*, vol. 18: *Hemi-Inattention Syndromes and Hemisphere Specialization* (New York: Raven Press, 1977).

9. Alexander R. Luria, "The Frontal Lobes and the Regulation of Behavior," in *Psychophysiology of the Frontal Lobes*, ed. Karl H. Pribram and Alexander R. Luria (New York: Academic Press, 1973), pp. 3-26.

10. Allan F. Mirsky and Merle M. Orren, "Attention," in *Neuropeptide Influence on the Brain and Behavior*, ed. Lyle H. Miller, Curt A. Sandman, and Abba J. Kastin (New York: Raven Press, 1977), pp. 233-67.

activity. In most instances, the electroencephalogram (EEG) is in itself a reasonably accurate and sensitive measure of variations of the level of arousal or alertness (fig. 9, chap. 1), particularly as it is a reflection of stages of sleep or wakefulness. We repeat here for emphasis (fig. 2) some examples of the kind of EEG that are seen

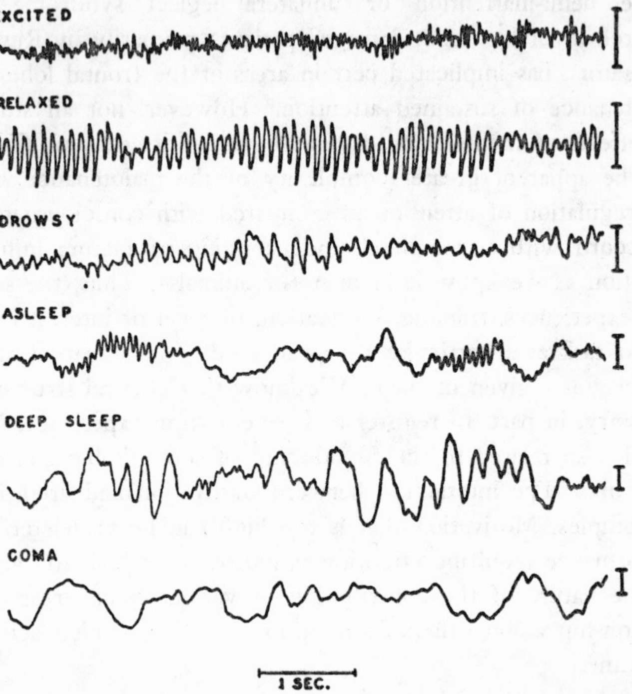

FIG. 2. EEG patterns associated with differing levels of consciousness
Source: Wilder Penfield and Henri H. Jasper, *Epilepsy and the Functional Anatomy of the Human Brain* (Boston: Little, Brown and Co., 1954). Reprinted with permission.

in varying states of alertness. The EEG is also a sensitive index of the effects of many agents or conditions (drugs, lack of oxygen, brain lesions, or brain disease) that can alter attention or alertness. Figure 3 provides examples of EEG tracings seen following administration of two drugs that impair attention—secobarbital, a barbiturate which is used to induce sleep, and chlorpromazine, a tranquilizing drug of the type which can induce sleepiness in many persons. The samples shown in figure 3 are particularly instructive since they were obtained in a study of the effects of these drugs on visual attention in the monkey.[11]

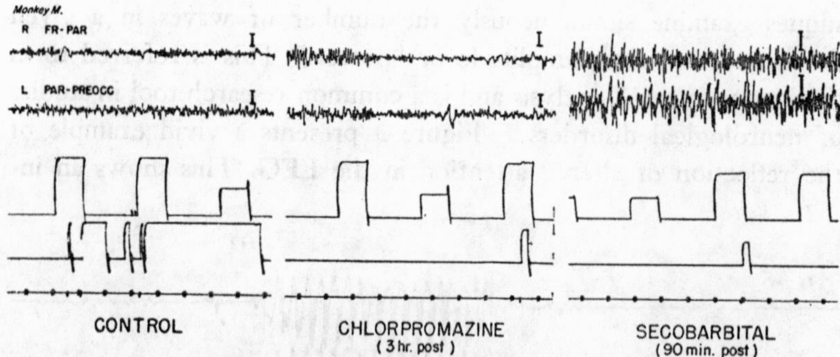

FIG. 3. Sample EEG and behavior tracings obtained under control, chlorpromazine, and secobarbital conditions from Monkey M. The top two channels (calibration = 100 μV) are EEG from fronto-parietal and parietal-preoccipital placements respectively. The third channel represents the stimuli: the smaller deflections from the baseline are negative (blue or green) stimuli, the larger deflections are positive (red). On the fourth channel appear the bar-press responses. Below this are indicated one-second time marks and (smaller deflections) reinforcements. In the control sample from this water-trained animal, the animal responded correctly to two positive stimuli and was reinforced each time. In the chlorpromazine sample, an omission error occurred to the first red stimulus, accompanied by high voltage EEG activity. The animal responded correctly to the second red stimulus (note lower voltage EEG) and was reinforced. Under secobarbital, the omission error cannot be distinguished electrographically from the correct response.

Source: Allan F. Mirsky and Eva B. Pragay, "EEG Characteristics of Impaired Attention Accompanying Secobarbital and Chlorpromazine Administration in Monkeys," in *Attention: Contemporary Theory and Analysis*, ed. David I. Mostofsky (Engelwood Cliffs, N.J., Prentice-Hall, 1970), pp. 25-49. Reprinted with permission.

Many experiments have used quantitative measurements of EEG as a neurophysiological index. These methods usually entail some computer-assisted techniques such as a count of the number of EEG waves in a particular frequency band or of a particular amplitude. In general, low amplitude fast waves (so-called beta activity, which can range from 14 to 40 Hz or cycles per second) tend to be positively correlated with attentiveness; high amplitude slow waves (such as theta activity or waves of 4 to 7 Hz or cycles per second) are negatively correlated with attentiveness.[12] Some tech-

11. Allan F. Mirsky and Eva B. Pragay, "EEG Characteristics of Impaired Attention Accompanying Secobarbital and Chlorpromazine Administration in Monkeys," in *Attention: Contemporary Theory and Analysis*, ed. Mostofsky, pp. 403-17.

12. Allan F. Mirsky et al., "EEG Correlates of Impaired Attention Performance under Secobarbital and Chlorpromazine in the Monkey," *Psychopharmacologia* 41 (1975): 35-41.

niques examine simultaneously the number of waves in a given frequency and their amplitude or "power." This is referred to as "power spectrum" analysis and is a common research tool in studies of neurological disorders.[13] Figure 4 presents a vivid example of the reflection of altered attention in the EEG. This shows an in-

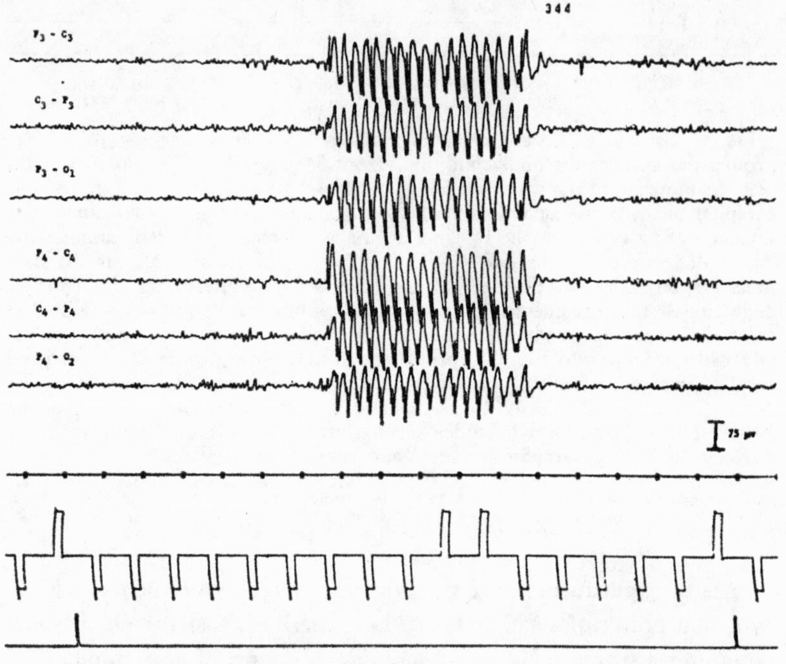

FIG. 4. Relation between a burst of spike and wave activity and CPT performance in a patient suffering from petit mal epilepsy. The top six channels in the tracing represent a standard anteroposterior EEG run, with electrode placements determined by the "10-20" system. (See Penfield and Jasper, *Epilepsy and the Functional Anatomy of the Human Brain.*) The seventh channel below this is a one-second time mark. Below this in channel 8 are represented the stimuli (duration = 0.2 sec.) shown to the patient; those requiring a response (the letter "X") are seen as deflections above the baseline; other letter stimuli appear as deflections below the baseline. The patient's response appears on channel 9 as an upward deflection. In this sample, the patient responded correctly to "X's" presented before and after the spike and wave burst but failed to respond to the two occurring within the burst.

Source: Allan F. Mirsky and Joseph J. Tecce, "The Analysis of Visual Evoked Potentials during Spike and Wave EEG Activity," *Epilepsia* 9 (1968): 211-20. Reprinted with permission.

13. Peter Kellaway and Ingemar Petersen, eds., *Quantitative Analytic Studies in Epilepsy* (New York: Raven Press, 1976).

stance of what is referred to as a paroxysmal or seizure discharge in the EEG, or the type that is found in persons suffering from petit mal epilepsy. In this instance the presence of the "burst" of abnormal EEG activity was perfectly correlated with complete inattention to sensory stimuli (visually presented letters of the alphabet in the example shown). The sensory inattention in cases of this kind can be the only obvious sign of abnormal functioning.[14] The French term for this phenomenon is quite descriptive; it is called the "absence."

EVOKED POTENTIALS

Aside from the EEG itself, there are other possibly more subtle measures derived from the EEG that have been shown to be sensitive measures of the attentive state of an individual. We will mention two examples. Both of these electrical measures are considered to be "evoked" from the brain by some environmental event or circumstance, as opposed to so-called "spontaneous" brain activity. One of these, the sensory evoked potential,[15] is a measure of the summated or averaged electrical brain response to a specific sensory input such as a flash of light (visual evoked potentials), a tone or sound (auditory evoked potentials), or an electrical impulse applied to the skin (somatosensory evoked potentials). Laboratory computers are used to "extract" the "signal" reflected in the EEG from the background EEG, which is considered to be random "noise" for the purposes of this procedure. The procedure assumes that there is a repetitive signal that is time-locked to the sensory event but can only be appreciated when many such signals are added together or averaged. The number of trials that has to be averaged to yield a satisfactory evoked potential depends, in part, on the size of the signal being studied. The number ranges from fifty or less to several thousand in some experiments. The random background fluctuations will themselves average to zero if they are truly random with respect to the occurrence of the sensory evoked potential. This type of signal or signal analysis has long been used

14. Wilder Penfield and Henri H. Jasper, *Epilepsy and the Functional Anatomy of Human Brain* (Boston: Little, Brown and Co., 1954).

15. David Regan, *Evoked Potentials in Psychology, Sensory Physiology, and Clinical Medicine* (London: Chapman and Hall, 1972).

by brain scientists in studying sensory areas of the central nervous system. Usually, the signal is derived from electrodes or probes placed directly on or in brain tissue. The advent and access to laboratory computers has permitted a new use of the method: the extraction of very small signals from the scalp of human subjects. This method requires no more inconveniencing of the subject than does the usual EEG examination, that is, a temporary pasting of recording electrodes onto the scalp. Some examples of the characteristic wave forms elicited by sensory stimuli are shown in figure 5.

Of particular interest for this discussion is the fact that alterations in the size of evoked potentials have been reported by some workers to be correlated with "attention" to a particular stimulus. A frequent, although not invariant, finding has been that stimuli that are attended have larger amplitudes than those that are not. Moreover, it is possible to reverse the size differences to stimuli on the basis of the instructions given to the subject. An example of this phenomenon is presented in figure 6. A finding that may be related to this is that altered evoked potentials may be found in persons who have difficulties with attention (as well as other cognitive difficulties). Some examples include persons with schizophrenic illness, children characterized as hyperactive or diagnosed as minimal brain-damaged, and some who are mentally retarded.[16] The brain mechanisms responsible for the evoked potentials (or for alterations in them) are not fully understood. The data suggest, however, that the series of waves which comprise the evoked potential (see fig. 5) represent the contribution of a number of regions of the brain to the elaboration of a sensory signal. In the case of the auditory evoked potential, for example, it has been shown that some early components (appearing within ten milliseconds after stimulus onset) actually reflect the transmission of a signal from the auditory nerve through various way stations within the brain stem.[17] These waves (so-called "brain-stem potentials") are quite small in size and require specialized recording techniques. Analysis and measurement of these waveforms are being used clin-

16. Enoch Callaway, ed., *Conference on Event Related Potentials in Man* (New York: Academic Press, forthcoming).

17. Don L. Jewett, M. N. Romano, and John S. Williston, "Human Auditory Evoked Potentials: Possible Brainstem Components Detected on the Scalp," *Science* 167 (1970): 1517-18.

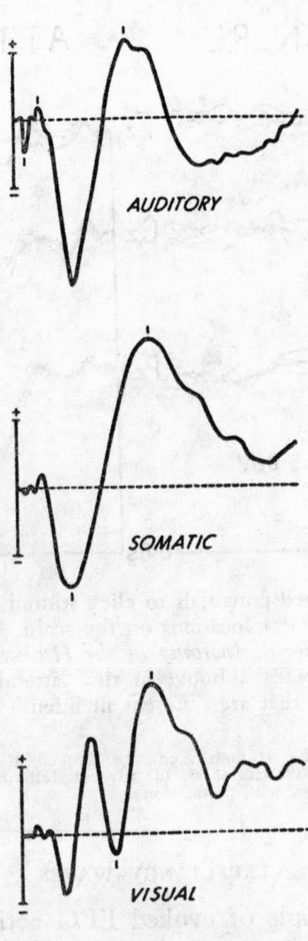

Fig. 5. Averaged evoked responses obtained from eight adult subjects. Each tracing is the average of 4800 individual responses. Calibration = 10 μV, 100 msec/division (negative down).

Source: H. G. Vaughan, Jr., "The Relationship of Brain Activity to Scalp Recordings of Event-related Potentials," in *Average Evoked Potentials: Methods, Results, and Evaluations*, ed. E. Donchin and D. B. Lindsley (Washington, D.C.: U.S. Government Printing Office, 1969), pp. 45-94. Reprinted with permission.

ically for the examination of patients suspected of brain-stem damage.[18] Consequently there is the eventual hope that sophisticated analysis of evoked potentials, say, associated with an attention defect, may be able to pinpoint the area of the brain that is functioning improperly and gives rise to the defect.

18. Callaway, *Conference on Event Related Potentials in Man.*

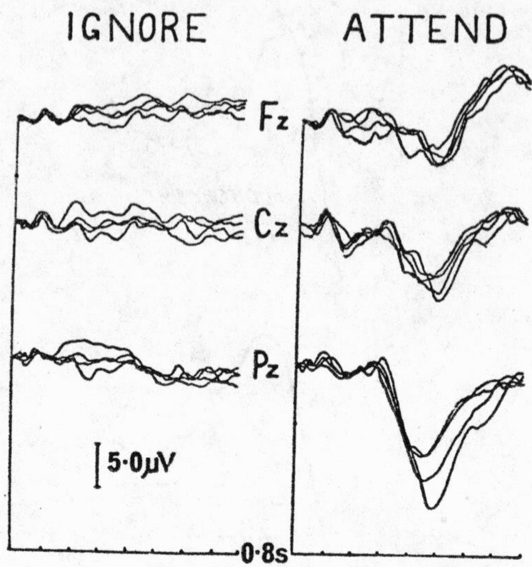

FIG. 6. Auditory evoked potentials to click stimuli from Frontal (Fz), Central (Cz), and Parietal (Pz) locations on the scalp. (See Penfield and Jasper, *Epilepsy and the Functional Anatomy of the Human Brain.*) In the "ignore" condition the subject reads a book; in the "attend" condition the subject counts occasional clicks that are different in intensity or frequency from the majority.

Source: R. Galambos, "The Human Auditory Evoked Response," in *Sensation and Measurement*, ed. H. R. Moskowitz et al. (Dordrecht-Holland: D. Reidel Publishing Co., 1974), pp. 217-21. Reprinted with permission.

EXPECTANCY WAVES

The second example of evoked EEG activity, the expectancy wave, is in principle similar to the evoked potential, although the technical details for recording differ somewhat from those used for evoked potentials. The basic paradigm for eliciting these waves is one in which the subject is told that two stimuli are going to be presented to him sequentially (say, a light flash followed within two seconds by a tone). The first (S_1) then is a preparatory or warning signal; the second or "imperative" signal (S_2) will require some response, such as pressing a key or lever. Within the interval between the preparatory and imperative signals a steady rise in the background or baseline (D.C. or direct current) level of the EEG can be seen, which is not the same as the frequency and amplitude variables that are usually examined. This rise in baseline level falls more or less precipitously to the pre-warning-signal level when the response has been executed. As in the case of evoked potentials, these waves can best be seen when there is averaging of a number of trials, although satisfactory wave forms can be seen with an average of twelve to twenty-five trials. In the conventional parlance used in EEG recordings, an upward rise is considered to be an increase in the negative charge in the baseline. Since the increased negativity is contingent on the experimental situation described above, the term "contingent negative variation" or CNV is often used in place of the term "expectancy wave." An example of the CNV is seen in figure 7. A number of explanations have been of-

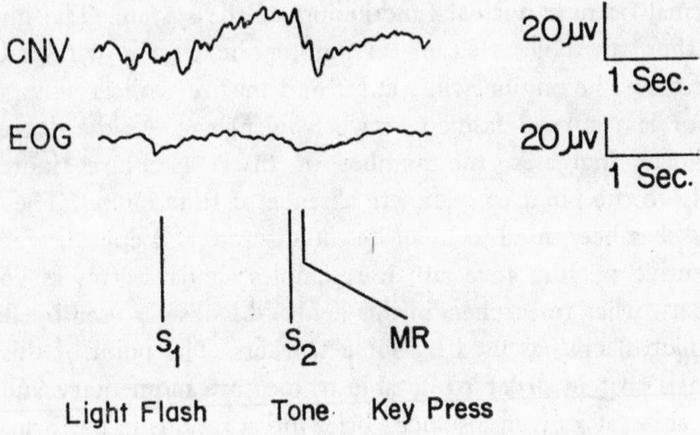

FIG. 7. CNV or "expectancy wave" (top tracing; EOG, that is, electro-oculogram record of eye movements (second tracing). See text for further description.

Source: Joseph J. Tecce, "Contingent Negative Variation (CNV) and Psychological Processes in Man," *Psychological Review* 77 (1972): 73-108. © 1972, American Physiological Association. Reprinted with permission.

fered for the CNV phenomenon.[19] It is clear, however, that the "expectancy" reflects at least partly the degree of arousal or activation of the subject, and this measure has been used in attention research. Thus, under some conditions in which reduced attention is seen (for example, administration of depressant drugs) reduced amplitudes of CNV waves have also been seen.

19. Joseph J. Tecce, "Contingent Negative Variation (CNV) and Psychological Processes in Man," *Psychological Bulletin* 77 (1972): 73-108.

Behavioral Measurement of Attention

MODELS OF ATTENTION DEFICIT

An important consideration in the design of tasks measuring attention has to do with the theoretical view as to how impairment of this function may occur. In a study of sleep deprivation effects on behavior, Williams and his colleagues contrast two models of attention failure.[20] They make the important point that attention impairment (as studied by them) does not occur so much as a gradual diminution of a function (the way a generator slows down when its fuel supply is cut off). Rather it is characterized by a series of sporadic or episodic brief failures interspersed with periods of normal or near-normal functioning of the system. The impairment thus resembles that of an automobile engine with a dirty carburetor. The engine will sputter and misfire while running in a more or less normal fashion between misfirings. As the degree of impairment increases, the number of discrete failures increases, possibly to the point of complete absence of functioning. The term "lapses" has been used to describe the discrete and episodic failures in attentive performance and it resembles similar terms as coined by other earlier researchers in this field: "blocks" as used by Bills[21] and "microsleeps" as used by some workers. The point of this discussion is that in order to be able to measure momentary and unpredictable (at a given instance) brief interruptions in performance, it is necessary to have a reasonably sustained sample of behavior, rather than a series of discrete trials.

An alternative way of describing or conceptualizing this distinction is to speak of the difference between experimenter-paced and subject-paced tasks. In the former, the spacing and sequencing of the trials is controlled by the experimenter and the subject performs as best he can; in the subject-paced task the subject controls the occurrence and sequence of individual trials. Lapses may be difficult to measure in such a situation, since the failure to initiate

20. Harold L. Williams, Ardie Lubin, and Jacqueline J. Goodnow, "Impaired Performance with Acute Sleep Loss," *Psychological Monographs* 73, no. 14 (1959): 1-26.

21. Arthur G. Bills, "Blocking: A New Principle of Mental Fatigue," *American Journal of Psychology* 43 (1931): 230-45.

a trial because of a lapse may not be distinguishable from failure due to other causes. This distinction is reflected (see below) in the way in which the tasks to study attention may be designed. It is also important to note that it is by no means certain that all behaviors considered under the rubric of impaired attention necessarily conform to the lapse model. Studies of drug effects on attentive behavior, for example, have indicated that the effects of barbiturates do in fact resemble the gradual slowing down of a system (as reflected in reaction time measures) whereas the effects of phenothiazine drugs (such as chlorpromazine) resemble more the episodic-failure model. Some research has been directed at comparison and contrast of these two types or models of attention impairment, as reflecting (possibly) different kinds of nervous system malfunctions.[22] The two types of impairment may, in fact, never exist in pure form but may always be present at least to some extent in combination. In any event, the design of the behavioral methods has reflected this theoretical view.

STATE VERSUS TRAIT

A consideration which sometimes enters into the construction of attention tasks, but more often into the classification of subjects or experimental designs, has to do with whether impaired attention results from a particular experimental condition (for example, a "state" which is produced by such treatments as administration of drugs, prolonged work on a task, or deprivation of sleep) or is an enduring characteristic or "trait" of a given population of subjects (for example, persons with mental retardation or with certain psychiatric or neurological disorders). The distinction has to do with the relative degree of permanence of the impairment: a state of impaired attention can be produced in any person, for example, by the appropriate dosage of certain drugs, and it will dissipate when the drugs have worn off. On the other hand, some schizophrenic persons may have chronically impaired attention, which persists as long as the illness. Also, as noted earlier, patients with lesions of the parietal lobe may have chronic (if partial) attention deficits.

22. Mirsky et al., "EEG Correlates of Impaired Attention Performance under Secobarbital and Chlorpromazine in the Monkey."

BROADENED VERSUS NARROWED ATTENTION

A distinction that has proved useful in some studies and does not necessarily imply impairment concerns whether the attentive focus of the subject is relatively broad or narrow.[23] Broadened attention implies that the subject can scan or perceive a relatively large number of stimuli (or stimulus aspects) simultaneously; narrowed attention requires a more restrictive focus on a limited number of stimuli or stimulus attributes. Normal persons can shift flexibly from the one attitude to the other depending on the task requirements. Moreover there is evidence that some centrally acting drugs can facilitate either broadened or narrowed attention.

ATTRIBUTES OF ATTENTION TASKS

There is scarcely any human performance that is not dependent on some attentive capacity on the part of the subject. This has posed something of a problem for those who wish to study attention or attentiveness per se. One solution to this problem has been to design tasks in which the problem-solving, memory, or learning requirements are simple or are kept to a minimum and in which the motor requirements are not complex, but in which sustained concentration or continuous attentive effort is necessary. Tasks conforming to these requirements have frequently been used in studies of "vigilance" such as is required by watchkeeping in military contexts, in repetitive or boring industrial occupations, or in long-distance truck driving or aircraft operation. An example of such a task is the Mackworth clock,[24] in which the subject observes a clock-like object watching for unusual (double step) movements of a clock hand. One characteristic of such tasks is that most of the time the subject is performing no responses except for observing some display. Responses are required infrequently, but in the applied context to which they pertain, the occurrence of the response may be of crucial importance (for example, noting an unidentified

23. Enoch Callaway and George Stone, "Reevaluating Focus of Attention," in the tracing represent a standard anteroposterior EEG run, with electrode John Wiley, 1960), pp. 393-98.

24. Broadened versus narrowed attention as well as the problem of vigilance and the Mackworth "clock" are discussed in Harry J. Jerison, "Vigilance, Discrimination, and Attention," in *Attention: Contemporary Theory and Analysis,* ed. Mostofsky, pp. 127-47.

object on a radar screen, or avoiding an obstruction on a road at night). Although developed in some cases for vigilance studies, which by our definition (fig. 1) reflect some alteration in the state of wakefulness, such tasks have also been used and are useful in studies of attention. In these contexts the alteration in the subjects' level of contact with the environment may bear little or no obvious relation to the sleep-wakefulness continuum.

Most of the tasks that have been used in neuropsychological or psychopharmacological research share certain common features:

1. The subject attends to some stimulus source, usually visual or auditory, but somatosensory stimuli (that is, electrical, vibratory, or other mechanical impulses to the skin) are occasionally used. The subject may be required to monitor two or more stimulus sources or two or more aspects of the stimulus (for example, color and form or pitch and intensity) depending on the experimental purpose.
2. The subject usually has to discriminate among stimulus conditions, so as to decide (a) whether or not a stimulus has appeared (as in the Mackworth clock) or (b) whether a stimulus is "critical" or "imperative" or "positive" (the terms are more or less interchangeable). In terms of the instructions given to the subject, the critical stimulus is the one requiring a response.
3. The subject makes some response to critical stimuli, usually some overt muscular response, such as pressing a button or displacing a lever. The response may be internal, such as counting the number of flashes of light, or the number of tones. The subject's verbal report of the number observed may be deferred until the end of a series of trials. In such cases the accuracy of the count may be irrelevant, since the experimental interest may lie in the effect of the attention condition per se on the electrophysiological (or other) variable (see fig. 6).
4. The duration of an experimental session is sufficiently long so as to allow some assessment of sustained attentive capacity. Durations used in some experiments have ranged from five to thirty minutes, although longer experimental sessions are not unusual. This is probably a key attribute of adequately designed experimental studies of sustained attention (at least, in accordance with the lapse model of attention failure).

EXAMPLES OF ATTENTION TASKS

Although many techniques have been devised to measure attentive behavior, we will present here some examples of methods that have been used primarily in the assessment of weakened or impaired attention in the clinical situation.

Reaction time. In "simple" reaction time the subject monitors a visual or auditory stimulus source and responds as rapidly as possible (usually by lifting a finger off a telegraph key) when the stimulus appears. There may be a ready or warning signal in one stimulus modality followed by an imperative signal in a different modality. Or, both may be in the same modality. The fore period (interval between warning and imperative signal) may be regular (for example, always four seconds) or irregular and unpredictable (for example, two, four, one, ten, six seconds). Most subjects are able to benefit from a regular foreperiod and achieve faster reaction times in this predictable situation than when the foreperiod is variable. As a group, schizophrenic persons are unable to derive this benefit; this is part of the information which has been used to categorize them as deficient in some aspects of attention behavior.[25] A common variation on the reaction time paradigm is the so-called "choice" reaction time, in which the subject is instructed to respond to a critical or positive stimulus only. Choice reaction times are invariably longer than simple reaction times; some theorists have suggested that the differential represents the time necessary for decision making to occur within the brain. The primary dependent variable is response latency.

The Continuous Performance Test (CPT). This experimenter-paced procedure, developed originally by Rosvold and associates,[26] has been used extensively in studies of attention in patients with neurological, psychiatric, and metabolic disorders, as well as in studies of drug effects on normal persons. The usual form of the task presents visual stimuli (letters of the alphabet, numbers, colors, pictures) for a brief exposure (0.1–0.4 second) at regular intervals of about one per second. Auditory versions of the task have also

25. Eliot H. Rodnick and David Shakow, "Set in Schizophrenia as Measured by a Composite Reaction Time Index," *American Journal of Psychiatry* 97 (1940): 214-25.

26. H. Enger Rosvold et al., "A Continuous Performance Test of Brain Damage," *Journal of Consulting Psychology* 20 (1956): 343-50.

been used. The subject is instructed to respond to a given critical stimulus only, for example, the letter "X," or the letter "X" if it follows the letter "A." The subject is allowed about 0.7 seconds to respond in order for a response to be scored as correct, and he performs on the task for five to fifteen minutes, depending on his age and other experimental variables. Dependent variables, or measures of performance yielded by this task, include errors of omission (failure to respond to critical stimuli) and errors of commission (responses to noncritical stimuli). A form of the task has been used by some investigators in which the task becomes more difficult as a function of the subject's performance; thus, correct responses result in shorter stimulus durations, allowable response times, and interstimulus intervals. The subject thus yields, by his own performance, the optimum level of which he is capable.

The Stroop Test. This method has had some applicability in the study of broadened versus weakened attention, although it was developed originally as a technique for studying perceptual interference.[27] A number of components are or have been included in the task, but the basic procedure requires the subject to read a page of color names, which are printed in inks of contrasting colors. The length of time taken and/or the number of errors made in reading this page is contrasted with the same measures when the subject is required instead to call off the colors of the inks, ignoring the lexical content. As Callaway has used the technique, narrowed attention is reflected in relative success in naming the colors as contrasted with reading the color words.[28] Broadened attention is the reverse, that is, relatively better performance in reading the words than in naming the colors. Other investigators have used the Stroop test simply as a measure of attention.

The Bourdon Test. This ancient and honorable procedure presents the subject with sheets of paper on which are printed various symbols or dot patterns.[29] The instructions require the subject to cross out as many of a critical stimulus or pattern as possible within a given time interval.

27. J. Ridley Stroop, "Studies of Interference in Serial Verbal Reactions," *Journal of Experimental Psychology* 18 (1934): 643-62.

28. Callaway and Stone, "Reevaluating Focus of Attention."

29. Benjamin Bourdon, "La perception et désignation des nombres," in *Entre Camarades* (Paris: Felix Alcan, 1901).

Other measures of attention. Some procedures that have been used less frequently as measures of attention (and which also may be more difficult to interpret in terms of some of the other factors involved in the performance) include digit span recall; performance on Progressive Matrices (paper and pencil mazes of gradually increasing difficulty); identification of embedded figures (simple geometric forms contained in a background of similar lines and shapes); and tachistoscopic recognition (accuracy of visual stimulus identification under conditions of brief exposure).[30]

Clinical States in which Impaired Attention is a Symptom

Although a number of methods have been used to study impaired attentiveness in clinical populations, possibly more groups have been studied with the continuous performance test (CPT) than with any other technique. Table 1 summarizes a number of these investigations and includes some comments on the nature of the impairment seen and on any relevant empirical or theoretical consideration that applies to that particular study.

A full discussion of all the studies included in table 1 would go beyond the scope of a single chapter, but some overriding theoretical considerations are presented in the next section of this chapter. A more complete treatment may be found elsewhere.[31] It may be emphasized, however, that references numbered 4, 11, and 13 through 17 in table 1 include children suffering from disorders likely to be encounted in educational settings (for example, petit mal epilepsy, hyperkinetic behavior, mental retardation, learning disability). It is of some interest that difficulty in sustained attention tasks may be a significant contributing factor to the educational problems that members of these groups may have in school.

Theories of Impaired Attention

As we have indicated in a preceding section of this chapter, the brain structures and neurophysiological mechanisms involved

30. Allan F. Mirsky and Conan Kornetsky, "The Effects of Centrally Acting Drugs on Attention: A Review 1956-1966," in *Psychopharmacology: A Review of Progress, 1957-1967*, ed. Daniel E. Efron (Washington, D.C.: U.S. Government Printing Office, 1968), pp. 91-104.

31. Mirsky and Orren, "Attention."

in the regulation of attention are complex. Nevertheless, the central role of the brain stem reticular formation has been emphasized in a number of theoretical approaches to attention impairment, particularly as seen in some of the clinical populations described in the previous section. Some of these approaches have leaned heavily on information provided from experiments with animal subjects.

It seems fair to say that there is no overriding theory or explanation of all or even a major portion of the human states in which attention impairment is seen. There are, however, a number of explanations that have been adduced to account for a specific clinical condition or drug-induced state. Some of these are noted here.

THE HYPERAROUSAL EXPLANATION

This account is derived from a more general explanation of the relationship between performance level and degree of arousal or activation. It states that the relationship between these two variables is in the nature of an inverted U. Thus, as activation or arousal increases, there is an improvement in performance to some optimum level; as activation is increased further, performance falls. This phenomenon is illustrated in figure 8. The impaired attention behavior of some schizophrenic persons has been interpreted in terms of this relationship: these persons perform more poorly on attention tests because they are overaroused and this relates to an increased level of activity in the brain stem reticular formation. There is substantial behavioral, physiological, and pharmacological evidence of the "overaroused" state of many schizophrenic persons.[32] There is no clear cut or consistent evidence of brain stem pathology in the brains of schizophrenic persons; however, the putative disturbance may be biochemical, that is, functional in nature and possibly related to abnormal levels or metabolism of brain transmitter substances (see chap. 1). A key part of this theoretical account relates to the effect of distraction; thus, several studies with schizophrenic persons (both in the acute stage of illness and in re-

32. Allan F. Mirsky, "Neuropsychological Bases of Schizophrenia," *Annual Review of Psychology* 20 (1969): 321-48; Conan Kornetsky and Allan F. Mirsky, "On Certain Psychopharmacological and Physiological Differences between Schizophrenic and Normal Persons," *Psychopharmacologia* 8 (1966): 321-48.

TABLE 1
SUMMARY OF STUDIES INVESTIGATING SUSTAINED ATTENTION DEFECT AS A SYMPTOM OF SOME CLINICAL DISORDER/ENTITY

CLINICAL DISORDER OR ENTITY	REFERENCE NUMBER	CPT IMPAIRMENT DESCRIBED	COMMENT
Petit mal epilepsy	1	Yes	Contrasted with other groups of epileptic patients
Petit mal epilepsy	2	Yes	Contrasted with other groups of epileptic patients
Petit mal epilepsy	3	Yes	Behavioral-physiological study
Petit mal epilepsy	4	Yes	Epileptic children studied
Schizophrenia	5, 6 7, 8	Yes, in 40 percent of cases	Theoretical implication of reticular formation involvement "hyperarousal"
Schizophrenia	7, 8, 9	Yes, but with distraction only	Theoretical implication of reticular formation involvement "hyperarousal"
Remitted schizophrenia	7, 8, 10	Yes, but with distraction only	Theoretical implication of reticular formation involvement "hyperarousal"
Mother with schizophrenia "high risk"	11, 12	Yes, but only in five-year-olds, not six-year-olds	Genetic disorder?
Hyperkinetic children	13	Yes	Brain damage suspected in some children; heterogeneous disorder
Hyperkinetic behavior	14	Yes, but reversible with stimulants	Brain damage suspected in some children; heterogeneous disorder
Mental retardation (MR) and brain damage (BD)	15, 16	Yes, MR + BD worse than MR alone	Diffuse and/or heterogeneous brain damage
Learning disability	17	Yes, in 2d grade children	Development delay suspected; brain damage uncertain
Chronic alcoholism	5	No	Damage to brain is cortical and/or subcortical but may spare reticular systems
Korsakoff's syndrome	18	No	Damage to brain is cortical and/or subcortical but may spare reticular systems
Uremia	19, 20, 21	Yes, reversible with dialysis in some cases	Clear evidence of reticular formation damage in severe cases
Phenyketonuria	22, 23	Yes	"Petit mal-like" EEG
Psychosurgery patients	24	No	Normal performance for omission errors; some cases made excessive commission errors

Reference Numbers, Table 1

1. Allan F. Mirsky et al., "A Comparison of the Psychological Test Performance of Patients with Focal and Nonfocal Epilepsy," *Experimental Neurology* 2 (1960): 75-89.

2. Herbert Lansdell and Allan F. Mirsky, "Attention in Focal and Centrencephalic Epilepsy," *Experimental Neurology* 9 (1964): 463-69.

3. Allan F. Mirsky and J. M. Van Buren, "On the Nature of the 'Absence' in Centrencephalic Epilepsy: A Study of Some Behavioral, Electroencephalographic and Autonomic Factors," *Electroencephalography and Clinical Neurophysiology* 18 (1965): 334-48.

4. P. Fedio and Allan F. Mirsky, "Selective Intellectual Deficits in Children with Temporal Lobe or Centrencephalic Epilepsy," *Neuropsychologia* 7 (1969): 287-300.

5. Maressa H. Orzack and Conan Kornetsky, "Attention Dysfunction in Chronic Schizophrenia," *Archives of General Psychiatry* 14 (1966): 323-26.

6. Maressa H. Orzack and Conan Kornetsky, "Environmental and Familial Predictors of Attention Behavior in Chronic Schizophrenics," *Journal of Psychiatric Research* 9 (1971): 21-29.

7. Allan F. Mirsky, "Neuropsychological Bases of Schizophrenia," *Annual Review of Psychology* 20 (1969): 321-48.

8. Conan Kornetsky and Allan F. Mirsky, "On Certain Psychopharmacological and Physiological Differences between Schizophrenic and Normal Persons," *Psychopharmacologia* 8 (1966): 309-18.

9. Eugene C. Stammeyer, *The Effects of Distraction on Performance in Schizophrenic, Psychoneurotic, and Normal Individuals* (Washington, D.C.: Catholic University of America Press, 1961).

10. Gerald W. Wohlberg and Conan Kornetsky, "Sustained Attention in Remitted Schizophrenics," *Archives of General Psychiatry* 28 (1973): 533-37.

11. Henry Grunebaum et al., "Attention in Young Children of Psychotic Mothers," *American Journal of Psychiatry* 131 (1974): 887-91.

12. David Rosenthal and Seymour S. Kety, eds., *The Transmission of Schizophrenia* (New York: Pergamon Press, 1968).

13. Donald H. Sykes, "Virginia Douglas, and Gert Morgenstern, "Sustained Attention in Hyperactive Children," *Journal of Child Psychology and Psychiatry* 14 (1973): 213-20.

14. Donald H. Sykes et al., "Attention in Hyperactive Children and the Effect of Methylpheidate (Ritalin)," *Journal of Child Psychology and Psychiatry* 21 (1971): 129-39.

15. H. Enger Rosvold et al., "A Continuous Performance Test of Brain Damage," *Journal of Consulting Psychology* 20 (1956): 343-50.

16. Kenneth G. Crosby, "Attention and Distractibility in Mentally Retarded and Average Children," (Ed. D. diss., Boston University, 1968).

17. Nancy L. Ricks and Allan F. Mirsky, "Sustained Attention and the Effects of Distraction in Underachieving Second Grade Children," *Journal of Education*, Boston University 156 (1974): 4-17.

18. Unpublished data (1974) in personal communication from G. Glosser, N. Butters, and Maressa H. Orzack.

19. Benjamin J. Murawski, "The Continuous Performance Test: A Measure of Sustained Attention in Human Uremics," in *Proceedings of the Workshop on Bioassays in Uremia*, ed. R. B. Coletti and K. K. Krueger (Washington, D.C.: U.S. Government Printing Office, 1970), pp. 72-73.

20. S. Olsen, "The Brain in Uremia," *Acta Psychiologica Scandinavia* 36, Supplement 156 (1961): 129.

21. J. C. Jacob et al., "Electroencephalographic Changes in Renal Failure," *Neurology* 15 (1965): 419-20.

22. V. Elving Anderson et al., "Responses of Phenylketonuric Children on a Continuous Performance Test," *Journal of Abnormal Psychology* 74 (1969): 358-62.

23. Henri Gastaut et al., "Introduction to the Study of Functional Generalized Epilepsies," in *The Physiopathogenesis of the Epilepsies*, ed. Henri Gastaut, Henri Jasper, J. Bancaud, and A. Waltregny (Springfield, Ill.: Charles C Thomas, 1969), pp. 5-25.

24. Allan F. Mirsky and Maressa H. Orzack, "Final Report on Psychosurgery Pilot Study," in National Commission for the Protection of Human Subjects of Biomedical and Behavioral Research, *Psychosurgery* (Washington, D.C.: U.S. Government Printing Office, 1976), Appendix II, pp. 1-168.

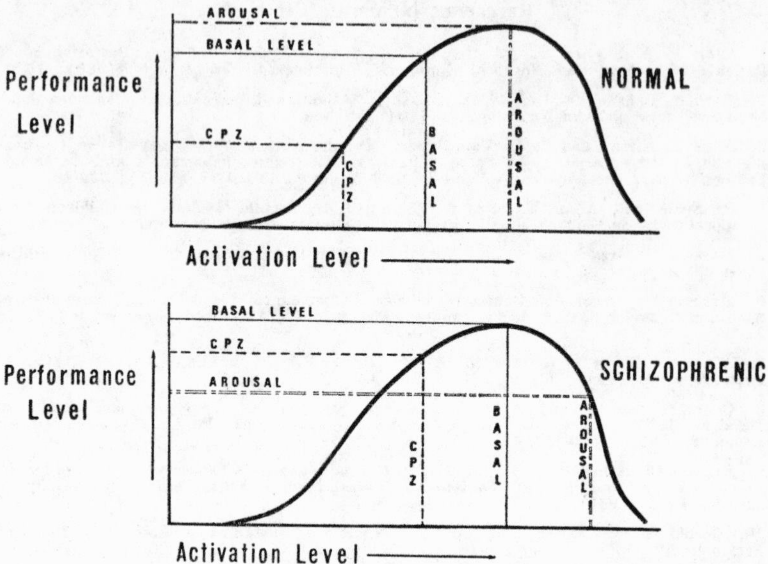

FIG. 8. A hypothetical inverted U model relating activation level with performance level. In this curve the assumption is made that the effects of chlorpromazine cause similar changes in activation level from basal level in both the normal and the schizophrenic, but that the basal arousal level of the schizophrenic is greater than that of the normal.

SOURCE: Conan Kornetsky and Allan F. Mirsky, "On Certain Psychopharmalogical and Physiological Differences between Schizophrenic and Normal Persons," *Psychopharmacologia* 8 (1966): 309-18.

mission) have shown a particularly deleterious effect of distraction during performance.[33] The effect of this condition is interpreted as increasing arousal level and thereby producing a further depression in performance. Some experiments with rats have provided indirect support of this general explanation; electrical stimulation in the reticular formation through implanted probes depresses performance of animals on attention tasks. Furthermore, tranquilizing drugs such as chlorpromazine, which are useful in the treatment of schizophrenia, can "protect" the rat from the deleterious effects of brain stimulation and restore attention performance to normal

33. Eugene C. Stammeyer, *The Effects of Distraction on Performance in Schizophrenic, Psychoneurotic, and Normal Individuals* (Washington, D.C.: Catholic University of America Press, 1961); Gerald W. Wohlberg and Conan Kornetsky, "Sustained Attention in Remitted Schizophrenics," *Archives of General Psychiatry* 28 (1973): 533-37.

levels.[34] In the normal rat (as in the nonschizophrenic human) this drug produces impairing effects on attention. It is conceivable that this explanation (that is, hyperfunction in the reticular formation) might account for the poor attention performance of some children with the diagnosis of hyperkinesis or of learning disability.

THE HYPOAROUSAL EXPLANATION

This might almost be viewed as a cognate or complementary explanation to the previous one. Some persons with the diagnosis of schizophrenia are viewed as massively underaroused and might in fact be unable to execute any tasks requiring attention, orientation, and the like. Hypoarousal has also been used to account for the effect of drugs such as secobarbital (see fig. 3). The effect that this compound produces is gradually to slow down responsivity, presumably due to an effect on transmission of impulses at the various and multiple synapses (junctures between nerve cells) required in the execution of attentive behavior.[35] Thus included are a number of synapses in the reticular formation of the brain, one of the loci of action of barbiturate-type drugs.

THE SENSORY INTERRUPTION EXPLANATION

This account has been used as a partial explanation of the interruptions in consciousness seen in patients with petit mal "absence" attacks. These episodes might serve as a prototypical example of the lapse type of attention impairment (see fig. 4). According to this view, the patient fails to respond to stimuli for the period corresponding to his "burst" of abnormal EEG waves (and possibly for a half second or more before this) because he cannot perceive them. Support for this view has been provided by some physiological evidence from human and animal studies obtained primarily with

34. Conan Kornetsky and Mona Eliasson, "Reticular Stimulation and Chlorpromazine: An Animal Model for Schizophrenic Overarousal," *Science* 165 (1969): 1273-74.

35. Mirsky et al., "EEG Correlates of Impaired Attention Performance under Secobarbital and Chlorpromazine in the Monkey"; Eva B. Pragay and Allan F. Mirsky, "The Nature of Performance Deficit under Secobarbital and Chlorpromazine in the Monkey: A Behavioral and EEG Study," *Psychopharmacologia* 28 (1973): 73-85; Jesus B. Otero and Allan F. Mirsky, "Influence of Secobarbital and Chlorpromazine on Precentral Neuron Activity during Attentive Behavior in Monkeys," *Psychopharmacologia* 46 (1976): 1-9.

visual stimuli.[36] This theoretical view postulates that some temporary disturbance, probably at the level of the reticular formation of the brain stem, produces a disruption of the transmission of sensory impulses, which for most modalities involves some processing and/or some way stations in the brain stem. If this explanation is correct, such a patient is in the most literal sense "bereft of his senses" (that is, sensory information) more or less for the duration of his abnormal EEG discharge. This view emphasizes the initial part of the sequence of any attention task—the reception and processing of sensory information. It is not entirely clear, however, whether this accounts entirely for the defective attention seen in absence attacks, or whether some disturbance in higher-order processing or decision making is also involved in these seizure discharges. There is some evidence that a lapse-type explanation, involving sensory processing, may in part account for the effects that the drug chlorpromazine has on attentive behavior.[37] This explanation has also been used to account for the effects of prolonged sleep deprivation on attentive behavior.[38]

Concluding Comments

This account has emphasized a particular view, approach, and body of research related to attention. As Grossman notes in his introduction to chapter 4, "The Biology of Motivation," there is no guarantee that other authors writing on the same topic would select the same material, or share this approach. Nevertheless, much of the thinking and work presented here is tied strongly to the clinical (or classroom) setting, and to human and animal research aimed at answering clinical questions about the maintenance and impairment of attention.

36. Allan F. Mirsky, Eva B. Pragay, and Sandra Harris, "Evoked Potential Correlates of Stimulation-induced Impairment of Attention in Macaca Mulatta," *Experimental Neurology* 57 (1977): 242-56; Merle M. Orren, "Visuomotor Behavior and Visual Evoked Potentials during Petit Mal Seizures" (Ph.D. diss., Boston University, 1974).

37. Mirsky et al., "EEG Correlates of Impaired Attention Performance under Secobarbital and Chlorpromazine in the Monkey"; Pragay and Mirsky, "The Nature of Performance Deficit under Secobarbital and Chlorpromazine in the Monkey"; Otero and Mirsky, "Influence of Secobarbital and Chlorpromazine on Precentral Neuron Activity during Attentive Behavior in Monkeys."

38. Williams, Lubin, and Goodnow, "Impaired Performance with Acute Sleep Loss."

CHAPTER III

Education and the Cognitive Processes of the Brain

M. C. WITTROCK

Introduction

Since the days of ancient Greece and Rome, the art of teaching has been influenced by knowledge and beliefs about learning, memory, and related functions of the human brain. Aristotle believed that we remember information only by forming images of it; and that we recall these images by ordering them in sequence, associating them with one another according to the principles of similarity, contrast, and contiguity.[1]

In ancient Greece and later in Rome, Aristotle's conception of memory and recall affected teaching. Students, teachers, lawyers, statesmen, and politicians were taught to generate images of the ideas they wished to remember, to associate the images with common objects in their homes, and to order these images and objects in unambiguous, easily remembered sequences.[2] The classical art of memory, based upon Aristotle's model of memory and Simonides' mnemonic system for ordering images in a sequence, persevered for over 1,000 years. It is today still the basis of some systems taught to facilitate memory.

In medieval times, Thomas Aquinas revived the classical art of memory, which lay dormant during the dark ages. He taught it widely to clergymen and to teachers. Saint Thomas used Aristotle's beliefs about memory to help many people to understand and to remember abstract religious ideas presented verbally.[3] Indeed, the

1. Aristotle, *On the Soul (De Anima); Parva Naturalia; and On Breath*, trans. W. S. Hett (Cambridge, Mass.: Harvard University Press, 1964).

2. Quintilian, *The Institutio Oratoria of Quintilian*, trans. H. E. Butler (New York: G. P. Putnam's Sons, 1921).

3. Frances Yates, *The Art of Memory* (London: Routledge and Kegan Paul, 1966).

statues, paintings, gargoyles, friezes, stained glass artwork, and mosaics adorning medieval cathedrals and public buildings were possibly designed, among other reasons, to facilitate teaching according to Aristotle's model of memory. In those days also, the art of teaching was built upon knowledge and beliefs about learning and memory.

In more recent times, when books, pens, paper, and pencils became widely available and often used, we changed our beliefs about learning, memory, and their relations to our brains. With these changes came further changes in the art of teaching. In the last seventy-five years in America, educational methods were influenced by behavioristic conceptions and studies of learning. The behavior and performance of the learners, rather than the constructive qualities of their mental processes, were emphasized in teaching and in instruction.

In research on learning, Aristotle's principles of order and association were interpreted to refer to the acquisition of behavior, peripheral observable events, not to memory and imagery, central unobservable events. In the beginning of modern scientific study of psychology and education in America, for reasons of theory and method it made sense to many researchers to emphasize the study of behavior and to minimize the study of mental and neural events.

Today, many researchers in cognition attempt to understand the finite human mental systems, processes, and organizations of information people use to generate infinitely variable actions. In recent studies of cognitive learning and memory, it has been shown that these cognitive processes include selective attention, imagery, verbal encoding, memory, and retrieval.[4] Even recent research in artificial intelligence and computer technology evidences a cognitive flavor, positing executives, buffers, and memory stores as internal structures and functions that mediate delayed performance.

Within the newly established interest in cognitive conceptions as old as Aristotle's model of memory, the recent findings about the human brain acquire further significance. They provide information about the nature and measurement of cognitive processes

4. Allan Paivio, *Imagery and Verbal Processes* (New York: Holt, Rinehart, and Winston, 1971).

and structures. In the following paragraphs we will describe and analyze the findings of some of the recent studies of several cognitive processes of the human brain. In concluding paragraphs of this chapter these findings about the brain will be synthesized and related to paradigms for educational research, to models of human learning, and to teaching.

Before beginning the description and analysis of recent research studies, it will be helpful to the readers to introduce three interesting relations between education and the cognitive processes of the brain that emerge from this review. First, for educational research, the recent findings about the brain suggest to me that process-oriented paradigms are useful in the study of the ways human learners construct meaning from instruction.

Second, the recent research on the brain is consistent with some findings in cognitive psychology regarding cognitive models of learning and memory. But when reading this review it should be remembered that cognitive functions cannot be reduced to neural structures, and psychological processes and educational methods should not be grafted onto the neurosciences. But the models and hypotheses developed to explain phenomena in learning, memory, attention, cognitive style, instruction, and teaching can be improved by relating them to other contexts, such as neurological models of the cognitive processes of the brain. For example, psychological research on imagery and verbal processes, the orienting reflex, and cognitive styles; anthropological research on cultural differences in language; and sociological research on social class differences in the use of analytic-verbal strategies for processing information can be juxtaposed with recent research on the hemispheric processes of the brain. Some interesting new directions for educational research, which are described in the concluding section of this chapter, emerge from these juxtapositions, with no need to overlay social science upon neuroscience.

Third, research on the human brain is consistent with some ancient ideas about the art of teaching. These ancient yet current ideas emphasize the importance of the mental elaborations of the learner. In a review of discovery learning written several years ago, in keeping with these ancient ideas about teaching, I suggested that the difference between rote and meaningful instruction is not to be found within the instruction, but within the learner's constructive mental processes.[5] That is, I maintained that instruction cannot be thoroughly understood by attending to the apparent qualities of treatments, such as their spatial and verbal or rote and meaningful qualities. The mental transformations performed by different people determine whether instruction is rote or meaningful, whether it stimulates verbal or spatial processes, and whether it facilitates learning and memory.

With these three relations in mind, we will now selectively review several interesting lines of research on the cognitive processes of the human brain. After the review of selected research studies, we will comment on their relations to educational research, learning, and teaching.

Recent Research on Cognitive Processes

THE BRAIN AS A MODEL BUILDER

One of the most interesting summary findings about the brain is that it actively constructs models of the world.[6] Luria and Trevarthen also find that the human brain actively selects, transforms, organizes, and remembers information.[7] The neural structures of the brain stem, midbrain, and cortical hemisphere not only receive and respond to sensory and somatic information, but these brain structures actively influence the selection and interpretation of information as well. The plans and intentions of the frontal lobes influence encoding, selective attention, and arousal. The descending reticular system exerts a decided effect upon arousal. The orienting response selectively directs attention to environmental information. Learners are not passive recipients of this information presented to them. They actively construct their own meanings from the information they are taught.

Learning and memory are influenced by the sets, intentions,

5. Merlin C. Wittrock, "The Learning by Discovery Hypothesis," in *Learning by Discovery: A Critical Appraisal*, ed. Lee S. Shulman and Evan R. Keislar (Chicago: Rand McNally and Co., 1966), pp. 33-75.

6. Harry J. Jerison, "Evolution of the Brain," in Merlin C. Wittrock et al., *The Human Brain* (Englewood Cliffs, N.J.: Prentice-Hall, 1977), pp. 39-62.

7. Alexander Luria, *The Working Brain: An Introduction to Neuropsychology*, trans. Basil Haigh (New York: Basic Books, 1973); Colwyn Trevarthen, "Analysis of Cerebral Activities that Generate and Regulate Con-

and plans generated in the neocortex of the brain, as well as by the information received from the immediate environment and from internal states, drives, and muscular responses. The reality we perceive, feel, see, and hear is influenced by the constructive processes of the brain, as well as by the cues that impinge upon it. The generative functions of the brain provide a theme that recurs throughout this chapter.

LEARNING AND ENCODING

One of the most dramatic findings of the recent research on the human brain is that, although there is a great deal of overlap and commonality in their functions, its cortical hemispheres characteristically organize and encode information in two different ways.[8] The left cortical hemisphere in about 98 percent of the right-handers and in about two-thirds of the left-handers specializes somewhat in a propositional, analytic-sequential, time-oriented serial organization well adapted to learning and remembering verbal information. For illustrative purposes, the sequential ordering of the words printed on pages exemplifies an organization characteristic of the left hemisphere. In these same groups of people, the right hemisphere specializes somewhat in an appositional, synthetic-gestalt organization well adapted to processing information in which the parts acquire meaning through their relations with the other parts. An example is the perception and interpretation of a painting or a photograph.

These recent findings about the hemispheric processes of the brain present a new perspective on some earlier puzzling results in the psychological research on verbal processes and imagery in learning, encoding, and memory. The recent brain research suggests that it is not only the verbal or spatial mode of the information but, more importantly, the type of organization or transformation performed upon it that characterizes its constructed and

---

sciousness in Commissurotomy Patients," in *Hemisphere Function in the Human Brain*, ed. Stuart J. Dimond and J. Graham Beaumont (New York: Halsted Press, John Wiley and Sons, 1974), pp. 235-63.

8. Joseph E. Bogen, "'Some Educational Aspects of Hemisphere Specialization," in Merlin C. Wittrock et al., *The Human Brain*, pp. 135-52; Roger W. Sperry, "Hemisphere Deconnection and Unity in Conscious Awareness," *American Psychologist* 23 (1968): 723-33.

remembered meaning. For example, an embedded figures test, which involves complicated spatial stimuli, presents problems that are analytically processed. By contrast, a parable is a verbal problem whose constructed meaning involves a synthesis or a juxtaposition of parts into wholes, perhaps by creating images of the events in the story, and by constructing relations between the story and one's own experience.

Before beginning the review of empirical studies of hemispheric brain processes, I wish to emphasize that the cortical hemispheres overlap greatly in ability and function and are richly connected with each other through the cerebral commissures and other tissues. For example, the right hemisphere comprehends, but cannot produce, speech.[9] The so-called dichotomy between the hemispheric functions probably results from a slight advantage one strategy has over the other strategy, which is sufficient to produce specializations of some functions. As Luria indicates in an excellent summary of the functional organization of the brain, it is hierarchically organized to integrate messages coming from lower sources.[10] The brain also specializes within each hemisphere as well as across hemispheres. No dichotomy of function does justice to the sophistication and complexity of the human brain.

Empirical support for the encoding strategies of the cortical hemispheres comes from research with commissurotomized patients, patients with unilateral brain damage, and normal people given dichotic listening tasks, dichoptic visual tasks, questions, sets, and instructions designed selectively to stimulate attention in one or the other cortical hemisphere. This extensive literature can only be sampled here to provide a context for discussion of some of its relations to education. Although Touwen indicates that laterality and dominance are inadequately differentiated in the literature,[11] I will use these terms as they are used in most research studies.

We will begin the review of the empirical studies of hemispheric processes with a now classic study by Sperry, who flashed words,

9. Alan Searleman, "A Review of Right Hemisphere Linguistic Capabilities," *Psychological Bulletin* 84 (1977): 503-22.

10. Luria, *The Working Brain*, chap. 1.

11. Bert C. L. Touwen, "Laterality and Dominance," *Developmental Medicine and Child Neurology* 14 (1972): 747-55.

such as KEYCASE, onto a rear projection screen for one-tenth of a second or less.[12] The letters KEY appeared only in the split-brain patient's left visual field, which is the area to the left of the point at which the subject is looking; and the letters CASE appeared only in the right visual field, which is the other half of the bisected visual field. Through the retinas of the eyes and neural pathways the left visual field connects directly to the right hemisphere, and the right visual field connects directly to the left hemisphere. By flashing words to commissurotomized people for intervals too brief for them to move their eyes, Sperry ingeniously insured that the word KEY was presented only to their right hemispheres and the word CASE only to their left hemispheres. When the patients were asked what they had seen, they said they saw the word CASE, such as in "case of fire" or "a case of beer." Sperry then placed several objects in a bag. He had the patients insert their left hands into the opaque bag and by touch alone retrieve the object they had just seen flashed on the screen. Each patient removed the key, even though he had earlier said he had seen the word CASE.

Kimura studied hemispheric cognitive processes in normal people by using dichotic listening tasks and visual-perceptual tasks to present different information to each hemisphere simultaneously.[13] For example, through headphones she presented two different melodies, one to each ear. By assuming that each ear is more directly connected to the contralateral (opposite) hemisphere than to the ipsilateral (same side) hemisphere, one can study the relative ability of the hemispheres to solve different kinds of problems. In normal right-handers, she found the left hemisphere better than the right hemisphere at tasks involving auditorily presented words, nonsense syllables and backward speech, visually presented letters and words, and skilled movements and gesticulations. The right hemisphere was better than the left hemisphere at auditory tasks involving melodies and nonspeech human sounds; at visual tasks involving locating points in two dimensions, dot and form enumeration, matching slanting lines, and steroscopic depth perception; and at

12. Sperry, "Hemisphere Deconnection and Unity in Conscious Awareness."

13. Doreen Kimura, "The Asymmetry of the Human Brain," *Scientific American* 228 (March 1973): 70-78.

manual tasks involving the determination of locations, such as locating a point in space under a table.

Kimura's results support those of Sperry and of Bogen and agree with a wide variety of different findings about hemisphericity, such as the finding that blind people tactilely perceive Braille dot patterns more quickly with their left hands than with their right hands. It seems that the hemispheres differ in their strategies, and perhaps somewhat in the type of information they process. In nearly all right-handers and in most left-handers, language and speech are analyzed predominantly in the left hemisphere, and spatial patterns and some auditory patterns, such as melodies, are synthesized predominantly in the right hemisphere. By implication, older notions about universal cerebral dominance do not explain the lateralized cognitive processes of the brain. With the exception of the production of speech, depending upon the type of problem or the appropriate strategy, either hemisphere may dominate the processing, or both of them may be involved in it. It is more precise to imply hemispheric dominance of a given function, or in a different sense, hemispheric lateralization of a given function, than it is accurate to imply that the same hemisphere is dominant for all functions.

Other research studies also support the specialization of brain functions indicated above. Geschwind presented a model of how the primary language areas are organized in the left hemisphere.[14] McAdam and Whitaker reported increased electrical activity over Broca's area, the speech production center in the left hemisphere, when normal subjects spoke polysyllabic words, but bilaterally increased electrical activity with analogous, nonspeech control gestures.[15] Morrell and Salamy measured cortical evoked electrical responses to speech stimuli presented to normal subjects.[16] The left hemispheres consistently produced the greatest amplitudes, with the greatest hemispheric differences occurring in the temporo-parietal region. Both in the production and reception of speech, we now

14. Norman Geschwind, "The Organization of Language and the Brain," *Science* 170 (1970): 940-44; idem, "Language and the Brain," *Scientific American* 226 (April 1972): 76-83.

15. Dale W. McAdam and Harry A. Whitaker, "Language Production: Electroencephalographic Localization in the Normal Human Brain," *Science* 172 (1971): 499-502.

16. Lenore K. Morrell and Joseph G. Salamy, "Hemispheric Asymmetry of Electrocortical Responses to Speech Stimuli," *Science* 174 (1971): 164-66.

have electrophysiological data to indicate support for ideas developed long ago by Paul Broca and Carl Wernicke about the neural organization of language in the brain.

Recently, it has been shown that a word, such as "fire," evokes a greater change in waveform in the left hemisphere than in the right hemisphere when the word is placed into a verbal context, such as "sit by the fire." With ambiguous contexts, these differences in waveforms disappeared.[17] With normal people, familiar abstract nouns showed a greater right visual field, that is, left hemispheric, superiority than did familiar concrete nouns,[18] which implies that an analytic strategy is involved in the recognition of familiar abstract words.

Seamon and Gazzaniga also report support for two separate encoding systems.[19] Verbal rehearsal strategies produced faster responses from the left than right hemisphere, while imagery strategies produced faster responses from the right than from the left hemispheres.

Another interesting area of research on hemispheric processes has focused upon the right cortical hemisphere. We will briefly review several studies on the cognitive processes of the right hemisphere.[20]

From research with patients with unilateral brain damage,[21] commissurotomized patients,[22] and normal people,[23] Nebes concludes that the right hemisphere processes spatial relationships and complex

17. Warren S. Brown, James T. Marsh, and James C. Smith, "Contextual Meaning Effects on Speech-evoked Potentials," *Behavioral Biology* 9 (1973): 755-61.

18. David Hines, "Recognition of Verbs, Abstract Nouns, and Concrete Nouns from the Left and Right Visual Half-fields," *Neuropsychologia* 14 (1976): 211-16.

19. John G. Seamon and Michael S. Gazzaniga, "Coding Strategies and Cerebral Laterality Effects," *Cognitive Psychology* 5 (1973): 249-56.

20. For a fine review of right hemispheric linguistic processes, see Searleman, "A Review of Right Hemisphere Linguistic Capabilities."

21. Arthur L. Benton, "Disorders of Spatial Orientation," in *Handbook of Clinical Neurology*, ed. P. J. Vinken and G. W. Bruyn, vol. 3 (Amsterdam: North Holland Publishing Co., 1969), pp. 212-28.

22. Robert D. Nebes, "Hemispheric Specialization in Commissurotomized Man," *Psychological Bulletin* 81 (1974): 1-14.

23. Murray J. White, "Laterality Differences in Perception: A Review," *Psychological Bulletin* 72 (1969): 387-405.

and difficult to name visual, tactile, and auditory stimuli.[24] The orientation of lines, spatial direction, spatial patterns, drawings of objects or complex shapes for which there are no names, music, and the recognition of faces exemplify so-called right hemispheric tasks.

Levy, Trevarthen, and Sperry presented visual chimeras to commissurotomized patients.[25] A chimera consisted of a right half of one stimulus joined to the left half of another stimulus, such as the halves of two different faces, or one half of an eye and one half of a rose. The chimeras were tachistoscopically flashed so that the midline of the chimeras coincided with the midline of the patients' right and left visual half fields, the point at which the eyes are focused. They found that each hemisphere, which had seen only half of the stimulus, constructed a bilaterally symmetrical whole stimulus, such as a whole rose, a whole eye, or a whole face. When the subjects verbally described the stimulus, they reported the face, object, or feature presented only to the left hemisphere. But when they used their right or left hand to point to the stimulus they had seen, they consistently pointed to the stimulus presented to their right hemisphere.

As long as no verbal transformation was required, the right hemisphere processed the visual stimuli and controlled the contralateral (left) or even the ipsilateral (right) hand in reporting what had been seen. When verbal processes were involved, such as in writing, the right hemisphere showed no comparable control over the motor system. It may be that the hemisphere with the most facility or most appropriate strategy controls the voluntary motor system, including on occasion at least, the ipsilateral muscles. Nebes also reports that the hemispheres differ in their bases for determining similarity among chimera.[26] The left hemisphere matches stimuli by verbal concepts and functions, while the right hemisphere matches stimuli by visual and structural similarity.

Several studies elaborate the cognitive processes of the right

24. Robert D. Nebes, "Man's So-called Minor Hemisphere," in Wittrock et al., *The Human Brain*, pp. 97-106.

25. Jerre Levy, Colwyn Trevarthen, and Roger W. Sperry, "Perception of Bilateral Chimeric Figures following Hemispheric Deconnection," *Brain* 95 (1972): 61-78.

26. Nebes, "Hemispheric Specialization in Commissurotomized Man."

hemisphere. Nebes tachistoscopically presented arrays of dots to the right or left visual fields of commissurotomized adults.[27] All patients correctly identified more patterns presented to the left than right visual field, implying a right hemispheric superiority for synthetic, spatial organization. Kumar used the Form Perception test, which is related to the Space Relations subtest of the Differential Aptitudes Test Battery, to measure the ability of five commissurotomized patients to recognize figural transformations, such as diagrams that when cut and folded exactly produce the unseen blocks felt only in one hand.[28] All patients performed better with their left than right hands, indicating a superiority of the right cerebral hemisphere for these figural transformations.

Umiltà et al. found that normal right-handers quickly discriminated easily named lines, such as vertical or horizontal lines, presented in the right visual field.[29] Other lines, for example, those inclined 150° or 30° from the vertical and not easily named, were more quickly discriminated when presented in the left visual field. The results were attributed to differences in the use of verbal mediators.

There are several interesting parallels between the research studies on the encoding processes of the brain and the recent psychological research on verbal processes and imagery in encoding. In recent research in psychology, dual process models of encoding that emphasize imagery and holistic processes, on the one hand, and verbal and analytic processes, on the other hand, are frequently studied.[30] In addition, for many years some commonly used dual factor tests of intelligence have emphasized verbal-linguistic and spatial-perceptual factors. The recently reported models of hemispheric brain processes suggest new support for these models of encoding and tests of intelligence, which will be explored next.

27. Robert D. Nebes, "Perception of Spatial Relationships by the Right and Left Hemispheres in Commissurotomized Man," *Neuropsychologia* 11 (1973): 285-89.

28. Santosh Kumar, "Cognition of Figural Transformation after Commissurotomy," *Perceptual and Motor Skills* 43 (1976): 350.

29. C. Umiltà et al., "Hemispheric Differences in the Discrimination of Line Orientation," *Neuropsychologia* 12 (1974): 165-74.

30. Paivio, *Imagery and Verbal Processes.*

MODELS OF HEMISPHERIC PROCESSES

Several researchers have questioned the accuracy of the verbal versus spatial dichotomization of the encoding processes of the brain. For example, trained musicians recognized simple melodies better in the right ear than in the left ear, while the reverse was true for nonmusicians.[31] The musicians analyzed the simple melodies into notes that they correctly named. Although the mode of presenting the information remained the same, its processing differed in trained and untrained musicians.

Bogen discusses problems with describing hemispheric cognitive processes in terms of verbal and nonverbal coding of stimuli.[32] The right hemisphere can read many words, understand some spoken sentences. The left hemisphere can analyze complex spatial diagrams. After Hughlings Jackson's suggestion, Bogen uses the term "propositional" to characterize the functions of the left hemisphere, and the term "appositional" to characterize the functions of the right hemisphere. In a recent publication Bogen has focussed upon the educational implications of his useful model of some of the cognitive processes of the brain.[33]

Luria and Simernitskaya also questioned the accuracy of characterizing hemispheric encoding functions as either linguistic or perceptual processes.[34] They suggest that language is one example of a conscious, logical coding process that is designed to enhance volitional control of behavior, the cognitive function of the left hemisphere. The cognitive activities of the right hemisphere they characterized as subconscious, automatic processes not under volitional control. They found that adult patients with lesions in their right hemispheres were more impaired on passive, unintentional memorization of lists of words than were normal people or patients with left hemispheric lesions. The patients with left lesions were

31. Thomas Bever and Robert J. Chiarello, "Cerebral Dominance in Musicians and Nonmusicians," *Science* 185 (1974): 537-39.

32. Joseph Bogen, "The Other Side of the Brain: II. An Appositional Mind," *Bulletin of the Los Angeles Neurological Society* 34 (1969): 135-62.

33. Bogen, "Some Educational Aspects of Hemispheric Specialization."

34. Alexander R. Luria and E. G. Simernitskaya, "Interhemispheric Relations and the Functions of the Minor Hemisphere," *Neuropsychologia* 15 (1977): 175-78.

more impaired than were the other two groups on the intentional memorization of word lists. It seems that each hemisphere contributes a different strategy, more than a different code, to the encoding task. Luria also distinguishes between simultaneous processing and successive processing, although he does not isolate each process within a hemisphere of the brain.[35]

In keeping with Luria's model, and consistent with Bogen's model, several studies compared dual information-processing strategies with verbal and spatial process models of encoding. In several factor analytic studies with children, Das, Kirby, and Jarman found their data better explained by Luria's model of simultaneous and successive information processing strategies than by an encoding model that distinguished between verbal and nonverbal codes. They write, "The brain stores neither words nor pictures, rather representations of both, as well as much more. The nature of these representations and how they are processed is of interest, but the verbal-nonverbal dichotomy tells us little."[36]

In another study, Das compared the use of simultaneous and successive information processing strategies by retarded and nonretarded six-year-old and thirteen- to fifteen-year-old children matched for mental age.[37] In tasks involving choosing the one of several visual arrays of dot patterns that best approximated the auditorily presented sequence of taps, the nonretarded children used simultaneous processing. The retarded children used a mixture of simultaneous and successive processing that resulted in poor performance. Research that focuses on the different processes used by learners can lead to an understanding of why some of them are having difficulty learning and can lead to some implications about what instruction might try to teach them.

There are interesting commonalities between some recent studies of the cognitive processes of the brain, the psychological research on dual process models of encoding, and the research on images and

35. Luria, *The Working Brain.*

36. J. P. Das, J. Kirby, and R. F. Jarman, "Simultaneous and Successive Syntheses: An Alternative Model for Cognitive Abilities," *Psychological Bulletin* 82 (1975): 99.

37. J. P. Das, "Patterns of Cognitive Ability in Nonretarded and Retarded Children," *American Journal of Mental Deficiency* 77 (1972): 6-12.

pictures in the facilitation of learning, memory, and instruction. We will now develop some of the educational implications of these converging lines of research by describing several training studies that report related findings.

Glass, Gazzaniga, and Premack studied seven global aphasic patients with massive left hemispheric damage that left intact little or no syntactic or grammatical ability, but that left intact some semantic ability and some ability to spell.[38] The patients were taught an artificial language system, using cut-out paper symbols for words, such as those used by Premack earlier to teach symbolic behavior to chimpanzees. After training, the patients all constructed syntactically correct sentences, each involving a subject, verb, and direct object, indicating that the right hemisphere has sophisticated cognitive ability which can be developed, or at least expressed, when proper teaching procedures are devised.

Jones found that patients with left temporal lobe lesions could compensate somewhat for defects in verbal memory by using an imagery strategy to learn paired-associates.[39] Patients with right temporal lobe lesions, but with normal, intact left hemispheres, learned the short paired-associate lists as well as did the normal subjects. In another study, visual imagery techniques produced promising improvements among some types of amnesic patients in encoding information into long-term memory.[40]

The effects of pictures, generated images, and instructions to image words upon encoding and retrieval is one of the most frequently studied problems in psychological research on learning and memory. The results with adults are sometimes impressive, resulting in threefold gains in retention in one study.[41] With children

38. Andrea V. Glass, Michael S. Gazzaniga and David Premack, "Artificial Language Training in Global Aphasics," *Neuropsychologia* 11 (1973): 95-103.

39. Marilyn K. Jones, "Imagery as a Mnemonic Aid after Left Temporal Lobectomy: Contrast between Material-specific and Generalized Memory Disorders," *Neuropsychologia* 12 (1974): 21-30.

40. Laird S. Cermak, "The Encoding of a Patient with Amnesia Due to Encephalitis," *Neuropsychologia* 14 (1976): 311-26.

41. Michael R. Raugh and Richard C. Atkinson, "A Mnemonic Method for Learning a Second-language Vocabulary," *Journal of Educational Psychology* 67 (1975): 1-16.

the gains are also impressive.[42] In one study when compared with remembering verbal definitions, pictures generated by elementary school children modestly enhanced the learning of definitions of words.[43] A dual process model of encoding, emphasizing imagery and verbal processes, was supported in two experiments with children and adults, indicating that the imagery value or the verbal meaningfulness value of the words to be learned influenced recall.[44]

In sum, some of the recent research on the brain indicates that teaching strategies that elaborate verbal information in a synthetic spatial or imagery strategy can facilitate memory with normal learners and with patients with left lesions. Some of the research on the brain also indicates that dual process models of encoding that emphasize verbal-analytic processes and holistic imagery make an important point about the encoding operations of the brain. In agreement with models of encoding, the hemispheric functions of the brain are distinguished more by the way they organize or represent information than by the type of information they organize. To explore the educational utility of that notion, studies are needed to examine the facilitation of learning that occurs when analytic or holistic strategies are intentionally stimulated among students learning subjects taught in schools.

DEVELOPMENT OF THE COGNITIVE PROCESSES OF THE BRAIN

The development of the attentional and encoding processes of the brain from birth to maturity is a complex, educationally relevant field of study. Several models of the development of the processes of the brain reflect some of the important, educationally relevant problems currently under study.

42. Joel R. Levin, "What Have We Learned about Maximizing What Children Learn?" in *Cognitive Learning in Children: Theories and Strategies*, ed. Joel R. Levin and Vernon L. Allen (New York: Academic Press, 1976), pp. 105-34; William D. Rohwer, Jr., "Images and Pictures in Children's Learning: Research Results and Instructional Implications," *Psychological Bulletin* 73 (1970): 393-403.

43. Britta L. Bull and Merlin C. Wittrock, "Imagery in the Learning of Verbal Definitions," *British Journal of Educational Psychology* 43 (1973): 289-93.

44. Merlin C. Wittrock and Sheila M. Goldberg, "Imagery and Meaningfulness in Free Recall: Word Attributes and Instructional Sets," *Journal of General Psychology* 92 (1975): 137-51.

Lenneberg argues that the cortical hemispheres are initially undifferentiated in function.[45] Lateralization of function occurs with the learning or acquisition of each function, such as language.

With regard to language, some researchers find lateralization is complete at early ages, while others find lateralization incomplete until adolescence or later. Krashen finds that lateralization of language is often complete by age five.[46] Fromkin et al. report that Genie, a girl isolated from language by her parents until she was thirteen years, nine months old, subsequently acquired some language facility.[47] In dichotic listening tasks, however, Genie showed a decided left-ear, right-hemisphere advantage for language and nonlanguage auditory stimuli. She was strongly right lateralized for language and nonlanguage functions. One person is far from an adequate number of subjects to support any hypothesis about the development of lateralization of hemispheric function. Genie's behavior, however, suggests the hypothesis that in early life linguistic stimulation is important in the development of left hemispheric specialization for language and linguistic competence.

With an ingeniously constructed optical device that allows prolonged unified presentation of visual stimuli to commissurotomized patients, Zaidel found that the right hemisphere cannot decode nonredundant sequential verbal phrases,[48] for example, a big red square, whose meaning is simply the concatenation of the individual sequential terms, each of which can be decoded by the right hemisphere. He found a variety of different age levels of ability for different linguistic processes in the right hemisphere of adults, some levels as high as age twelve. These results cast doubt upon the notion that lateralization of language to the left hemisphere is complete by age four.

45. Eric H. Lenneberg, *Biological Foundations of Language* (New York: John Wiley and Sons, 1967).

46. Stephen D. Krashen, "The Left Hemisphere," in Wittrock et al., *The Human Brain*, pp. 107-30.

47. Victoria A. Fromkin et al., "The Development of Language in Genie: A Case of Language Acquisition beyond the 'Critical Period'," *Brain and Language* 1 (1974): 81-107.

48. Eran Zaidel, "Unilateral Auditory Language Comprehension on the Token Test following Cerebral Commissurotomy and Hemispherectomy," *Neuropsychologia* 15 (1977): 1-18.

In research on so-called right hemispheric processes, proficiency sometimes develops into the school years at least. With the recognition of faces flashed to the left or right visual fields, normal right-handed children ages five, seven, and eleven showed a left-field, right-hemisphere advantage.[49] Carey and Diamond found that children under age ten remembered upside-down faces as well as right-side up faces.[50] After age ten, the right-side up faces were better remembered than the upside-down faces, which they interpret to indicate that configurational spatial ability continues to develop at least until age ten. Another interpretation is that linear analytic processes used to encode named directions, such as right-side up, continue to develop at least until age ten. It has also been found that if massive injury occurs to one hemisphere in infancy the other hemisphere can acquire the functions of the injured one, although with some deficit remaining.[51] Again proficiency and perhaps degree of hemispheric specialization seem to develop at different rates for different functions.

From research in educational psychology it has been found that until age six or seven children cannot effectively generate their own images to facilitate paired-associate learning.[52] Prior to those ages, however, pictures given to them facilitate paired-associate learning, as do self-generated sentences.[53] These latter two studies imply a development of function, but not necessarily a development of lateralization of function.

Another approach to the development of the cognitive functions

49. Andrew E. Young and Hadyn D. Ellis, "An Experimental Investigation of Developmental Differences in Ability to Recognize Faces Presented to the Left and Right Cerebral Hemispheres," *Neuropsychologia* 14 (1976): 495-98.

50. Susan Carey and Rhea Diamond, "From Piecemeal to Configurational Representation of Faces," *Science* 195 (1977): 312-14.

51. Maureen Dennis and B. Kohn, "Comprehension of Syntax in Infantile Hemiplegics after Cerebral Hemidecortication: Left Hemisphere Superiority," *Brain and Language* 2 (1975): 472.

52. Levin, "What Have We Learned about Maximizing What Children Learn?"

53. Ann E. McCabe, Joel R. Levin, and Peter Wolff, "The Role of Overt Activity in Children's Sentence Production," *Journal of Experimental Child Psychology* 17 (1974): 107-14.

of the brain assumes that lateralization exists at birth.[54] Some data indicate anatomical asymmetries in the brain,[55] and functional asymmetries at birth in handedness,[56] and in language.[57] In the left temporal and parietal lobes some of the regions associated with verbal processes, such as speech, are larger or at least differently shaped than their right hemispheric counterparts.[58]

Kinsbourne suggests that the development of hemispheric functions involves increases in proficiency and in learning to allocate attention to the hemispheric processes, rather than increases in degree of lateralization.[59] In Kinsbourne's model lateralization is an attentional phenomenon.[60] Each hemisphere activates its respective brain stem attentional mechanism to favor anticipated input from the contralateral side. In anticipation of a verbal stimulus, the left hemisphere voluntarily shifts attention to the right ear, right visual field, or both. These strategies of shifting attention can be learned, differently with different stimuli, different ages, and different groups, not because of any difference in lateralization of function.

The Kinsbourne model leads to predictions, discussed later, about how instructions, sets, and intentions prime or induce right or left hemispheric processing, and how different strategies learned in different social classes by boys and girls might explain observed differences in laterality of function. In the new field of neuro-

54. Marcel Kinsbourne, "Cerebral Dominance, Learning, and Cognition," in *Progress in Learning Disabilities*, vol. 3, ed. Helmer R. Myklebust (New York: Grune and Stratton, 1975), pp. 201-18.

55. Norman Geschwind, "The Anatomical Basis of Hemispheric Differentiation," in *Hemisphere Function in the Human Brain*, ed. Dimond and Beaumont, pp. 7-24.

56. Minna Giesecke, "The Genesis of Hand Preference," *Monographs of the Society for Research in Child Development* 1, no. 5 (1936): 1-102.

57. Dennis L. Molfese, "Cerebral Asymmetry in Infants, Children, and Adults: Auditory Evoked Responses to Speech and Musical Stimuli," *Journal of the Acoustical Society of America* 53 (1973): 363.

58. Alan B. Rubens, Mark W. Mahowald, and J. Thomas Hutton, "Asymmetry of the Lateral (Sylvian) Fissures in Man," *Neurology* 26 (1976): 620-24.

59. Kinsbourne, "Cerebral Dominance, Learning, and Cognition."

60. Marcel Kinsbourne, "The Control of Attention by Interaction between the Cerebral Hemispheres," in *Attention and Performance*, vol. 4, ed. Sylvan Kornblum (New York: Academic Press, 1973), pp. 239-56.

sociology, TenHouten hypothesizes that proficiency in verbal analytic processes correlates highly and positively with socioeconomic status in industrialized societies.[61]

ATTENTION

Since the days of William James, attention has been a centrally important topic in the study of learning, perception, encoding, learning disabilities, and even mental retardation. Zeaman and House suggest attention deficits as an explanation for mental retardation.[62] Dykman, Ackerman, Clements, and Peters hypothesize that learning disabilities, such as hyperactivity, are caused by attentional deficits.[63] Dykman et al. emphasize the important role of the cortex in determining attention via the descending reticular system:

> But the most important initiator of reticular activity is not, we believe, the classical sensory system but rather the descending (reticular) system mentioned above. Through these fibers, past associations or memories may enter to initiate and sustain reticular excitation and make it more specific.[64]

In a classic study, Moruzzi and Magoun described the ascending reticular activating system.[65] It is a diffuse system of polysynaptic fibers that extends from the spinal cord through the brain stem, thalamus or projecting nuclei of the thalamus to the cortex, including the limbic structures. Through these ascending and descending systems the neocortex influences selective attention via the orienting reflex or inhibitory mechanisms, and is, in turn, influenced by somatic and environmental stimulation.

61. Warren TenHouten, "More on Split-Brain Research, Culture, and Cognition," *Current Anthropology* 17 (1976): 503-11.

62. David Zeaman and Betty House, "The Role of Attention in Retardate Discrimination Learning," in *Handbook of Mental Deficiency*, ed. Norman Ellis (New York: McGraw-Hill Book Co., 1963), p. 159-223.

63. Roscoe A. Dykman et al., "Specific Learning Disabilities: An Attentional Deficit Syndrome," in *Progress in Learning Disabilities*, vol. 2, ed. Myklebust, pp. 56-93.

64. Roscoe A. Dykman et al., "Children with Learning Disabilities: V. Conditioning, Differentiation, and the Effects of Distraction," *American Journal of Orthopsychiatry* 40 (1970): 777.

65. Giuseppe Moruzzi and Horace W. Magoun, "Brain Stem Reticular Formation and Activation of the EEG," *Electroencephalography and Clinical Neurophysiology* 1 (1949): 455-73.

With this introduction to attentional mechanisms, we now return to Kinsbourne's attentional model of cognitive processes of the brain. Kinsbourne hypothesizes that each cerebral hemisphere directs attention to contralateral stimuli.[66] When both hemispheres are activated, they mutually inhibit the control of attention. When the left hemisphere of right-handers is activated, perhaps by linguistic stimuli or subvocal speech, attention orients to the right. When the right hemisphere of right-handers is activated, attention shifts to the left. Either the nature of the task itself, previously given instructions, or sets that activate one hemisphere more than the other should produce an attentional bias. When the instructions excite the hemisphere appropriate for the task, such as the left hemisphere for a verbal task, perception of verbal stimuli should be enhanced in the right visual field. But having a subject read words should produce a right visual field advantage for processing simple visual tasks. Kinsbourne's data reported in 1973 support the model,[67] and data from a later series of eight experiments give further support.[68] In the model attention is the vector sum of the activations of the cerebral hemispheres. Asymmetrical sums lead to lateralized hemispheric processes and to contralateral shifts of attention.

Gardner and Branski tested Kinsbourne's model in four experiments.[69] They used verbal stimuli or music to induce left or right hemispheric processing prior to presenting figures in the right or left visual fields. Perception of the figures was not enhanced. In two experiments the verbal stimuli or music retarded perceptual discriminability, perhaps by introducing competing stimuli, for example, music and forms, to be processed in the same hemisphere. However, in agreement with Kinsbourne's model, Klein, Moscovitch, and Vigna found that priming the left hemisphere with a

66. Kinsbourne, "The Control of Attention by Interaction between the Cerebral Hemispheres."

67. Ibid.

68. Marcel Kinsbourne, "The Mechanism of Hemispheric Control of the Lateral Gradient of Attention," in *Attention and Performance,* vol. 5, ed. Patrick M. A. Rabbitt and Stanislav Dornic (New York: Academic Press, 1975), pp. 81-97.

69. Elizabeth B. Gardner and Diane M. Branski, "Unilateral Cerebral Activation and Perception of Gaps: A Signal Detection Analysis," *Neuropsychologia* 14 (1976): 43-53.

verbal task reduced the left field superiority for recognizing faces, and priming the right hemisphere with a face recognition problem reduced a right visual field superiority for words.[70]

The interaction of priming stimuli and the task stimuli parallels the work in psychology by Paivio on the elusive interaction between verbal processes and imagery induced by instructional sets or by the verbal and imaginal qualities of words to be remembered. As Wittrock and Goldberg showed, the attributes of the words that have developed over years dominate the more transitory effects of the experimenters' instructions, at least when the two sources are in conflict with each other, such as when the learner is asked to process a high imagery word without using imagery.[71] In the tests of Kinsbourne's model, we would predict the task variables, rather than the instructions, often to exert a primary influence on attention.

Bowers and Heilman also supported, in part, Kinsbourne's attentional model of cognitive processes.[72] In agreement with the model, Cohen found that advance information facilitates cognitive processing, especially by the left hemisphere.[73]

Kinsbourne's model relates attention to encoding, and offers a new interpretation of much of the data on the encoding processes of the brain. In dichotic listening tasks, the results are usually explained by the lengths and directness of the paths between the ears and the cortical hemispheres. Kinsbourne's model suggests that the direction of the auditory stimuli, which is confounded with the ears in which they enter, as well as the nature of the preparatory stimuli, sets, and instructions produce the lateralization of hemispheric processes.

For education, research on the human brain indicates that attention is a highly fruitful area to explore. In particular, Kinsbourne's

70. Danny Klein, Morris Moscovitch, and Carlo Vigna, "Attention Mechanisms and Perceptual Asymmetries in Tachistoscopic Recognition of Words and Faces," *Neuropsychologia* 14 (1976): 55-66.

71. Wittrock and Goldberg, "Imagery and Meaningfulness in Free Recall."

72. Dawn Bowers and Kenneth M. Heilman, "Material Specific Hemispherical Arousal," *Neuropsychologia* 14 (1976): 123-27.

73. G. Cohen, "Hemispheric Differences in the Utilization of Advance Information," in *Attention and Performance*, vol. 5, ed. Rabbitt and Dornic, pp. 20-32.

attentional model of cognitive processes indicates ways to influence encoding. A second important implication is that attention is influenced by the past experiences and plans of the learners. The stimulation of attention might involve modifying a learner's goals and intentions, as well as it might involve novel instructional stimuli, subject matter, and textbooks.

In either case, the recent research on attentional mechanisms of the brain suggests a new interpretation of one commonly used attentional and motivational procedure, repetition and reinforcement. Regular, repeated reinforcements for responses seem more likely sometimes to produce habituation and a lack of interest, perseverance, attention, and motivation. The attentional mechanisms of the brain often respond to novelty, to the unexpected, in keeping with cognitive dissonance theory, or with some expectancy theories, or stimulus pattern theories. The interpretations made of the stimuli seem to depend upon the encoding processes engaged by the attentional mechanisms.[74]

INDICES OF COGNITIVE PROCESSES

In a number of electrophysiological studies of brain processes, electroencephalogram (EEG) data indicate asymmetries in brain wave patterns, especially in the temporal and parietal regions when verbal or spatial tasks are presented. These data imply two cognitive modes.

Galin and Ornstein indexed "idling" or inactivity in a hemisphere.[75] They constructed a ratio, called alpha power, to index the alpha waves produced by the cortical hemispheres. The higher the power ratio, indicating relatively greater alpha production in the right hemisphere, the greater is the involvement of the left hemisphere in the task, and vice versa. With verbal tasks and arithmetic, they found greater alpha production in the right than in the left hemisphere, indicating left hemispheric processing for the specific

74. For a comprehensive model, too detailed to be summarized adequately here, that relates arousal, activation, and motivation to the control of attention, see Karl H. Pribram and Diane McGuinness, "Arousal, Activation, and Effort in the Control of Attention," *Psychological Review* 82 (1975): 116-49.

75. David Galin and Robert Ornstein, "Lateral Specialization of Cognitive Mode: An EEG Study," *Psychophysiology* 9 (1972): 412.

tasks studied. With spatial tasks, they found relatively greater alpha production in the left hemisphere, indicating right hemispheric lateralization of function for those tasks.[76] The 8-13 Hertz alpha band produced the best discrimination between the hemispheres.

Occupational groups, ceramicists and lawyers, differed in degree but not in pattern of temporal-parietal EEG waves for verbal and spatial tasks.[77] Compared with the ceramicists, the lawyers showed greater left hemispheric processing of verbal tasks and spatial tasks. Dumas and Morgan found no difference in occipital alpha EEG asymmetries between male artists and male engineers given linguistic tasks, mathematical tasks, and spatial configurational tasks, such as a facial memory test.[78] The EEGs indicated that both groups tended to use their left hemispheres for the verbal tasks and their right hemispheres for the spatial tasks. Groups such as artists and engineers, or lawyers and ceramicists, do not seem to differ in the pattern of hemispheric processes they use for problems as much as they differ in the degree of use, or perhaps in the ability to use those respective processes.

Because EEG measures are today expensive and difficult to obtain, they are not ideal for use by educators who might wish to index cognitive processes used by different people to process instruction. In several studies the direction in which the eyes are moved, sometimes the head as well, indicates contralateral hemispheric activation.[79] When verbal problems are presented, typical right-handed people often look to the right, but with spatial prob-

76. Joseph C. Doyle, Robert Ornstein, and David Galin, "Lateral Specialization of Cognitive Mode: II. EEG Frequency Analysis," *Psychophysiology* 11 (1974): 567-78.

77. Robert Ornstein and David Galin, "Physiological Studies of Consciousness," unpublished paper.

78. Roland Dumas and Arlene Morgan, "EEG Asymmetry as a Function of Occupation, Task, and Task Difficulty," *Neuropsychologia* 13 (1975): 219-28.

79. Merle E. Day, "An Eye-movement Phenomenon Relating to Attention, Thought, and Anxiety," *Perceptual and Motor Skills* 19 (1964): 443-46; Paul Bakan, "Hypnotizability, Laterality of Eye-movements and Functional Brain Asymmetry," *Perceptual and Motor Skills* 28 (1969): 927-32; Marcel Kinsbourne, "Eye and Head Turning Indicates Cerebral Lateralization," *Science* 176 (1972): 539-41.

lems they often look to the left. These lateral eye movements (LEMS) are one index of contralateral hemispheric stimulation.

Kocel et al. found that verbal and arithmetical questions produced more right LEMS than did spatial and musical questions.[80] Kinsbourne found that right-handers moved their eyes to the right for verbal problems, indicating left lateralization for language, but showed less distinctive left movements for spatial problems.[81] Numerical problems produced no lateralization. Among left handers there was a different pattern of results, indicating that the same hemisphere, either right or left, was usually dominant for spatial and verbal problems, in about equal amounts.

Kinsbourne suggests testing Raquel Gur's explanation of conflicting data about eye movements.[82] Her hypothesis is that when facing the questioner, subjects move their eyes predominantly in one direction regardless of the type of question. When the questioner is situated behind the subject, right-handers move their eyes right for verbal problems and left for spatial problems. In a study with thirty-two right-handed and seventeen left-handed male college students, Gur, Gur, and Harris supported her hypothesis, and suggested that in a face-to-face situation perhaps greater anxiety and consequently greater reliance on a preferred hemisphere occurs.[83] On the other hand, Ehrlichman, Weiner, and Baker find no support for using horizontal eye movements to index hemispheric processes.[84]

With attention to Gur's hypothesis, eye movement measures should be used by educational researchers only when gathering data from a large number of people. For clinical use or for classroom

80. Katherine Kocel et al., "Lateral Eye Movement and Cognitive Mode," *Psychonomic Science* 27 (1972): 223-24.

81. Kinsbourne, "Eye and Head Turning Indicates Cerebral Lateralization."

82. Marcel Kinsbourne, "Direction of Gaze and Distribution of Cerebral Thought Processes," *Neuropsychologia* 12 (1974): 279-81.

83. Raquel E. Gur, Ruben C. Gur, and Lauren J. Harris, "Cerebral Activation, as Measured by Subjects' Lateral Eye Movements, is Influenced by Experimenter Location," *Neuropsychologia* 13 (1975): 35-44.

84. Howard Ehrlichman, Susan L. Weiner, and A. Harvey Baker, "Effects of Verbal and Spatial Questions on Initial Gaze Shifts," *Neuropsychologia* 12 (1974): 265-77.

use with individual students, the eye movement index of cognitive processes presents serious problems of reliability and validity. The potential utility of this unobtrusive, easily obtainable index warrants careful research and development.

HANDEDNESS AND COGNITIVE PROCESSES

Popular stereotypes about cognitive deficits of left-handers find no substantial support in the research literature. It is true that left-handedness occurs more frequently among twins than nontwins, among epileptics then nonepileptics, and among mentally retarded people than among nonmentally retarded people.[85] But it is also true that for statistical reasons alone, if brain damage early in life results in changes in handedness, these characteristics will be found slightly more frequently among left-handers than among right-handers. The reason is that there are many more right-handers than left-handers, who comprise from 5 to 11 percent of the population, to shift handedness early in life when brain damage occurs. But the frequency of shifts in handedness because of brain damage is not known.

The organization but usually not the proficiency of cognitive processes sometimes differs between right-handers and left-handers. Nearly all right-handers and about 60 to 70 percent of the left-handers have their speech centers in their left cortical hemispheres. Left-handers, especially those with a family history of sinistrality, are sometimes less well lateralized for speech and spatial processes than are right-handers.[86] Left-handers without a family history of left-handedness tend to be strongly left-handed with well lateralized cerebral functions typical, in degree and in location, of right-handed people.[87]

Kimura finds that during speaking right-handers gesture espe-

85. Jerre Levy, "Psychobiological Implications of Bilateral Asymmetry," in *Hemisphere Function in the Human Brain*, pp. 121-83.

86. Curtis Hardyck and Lewis F. Petrinovich, "Left-handedness," *Psychological Bulletin* 84 (1977): 385-404; Edgar B. Zurif and M. P. Bryden, "Familial Handedness and Left-Right Differences in Auditory and Visual Perception," *Neuropsychologia* 7 (1969): 179-87; David Hines and Paul Satz, "Cross-Modal Asymmetries in Perception Related to Asymmetry in Cerebral Function," *Neuropsychologia* 12 (1974): 239-47.

87. Hardyck and Petrinovich, "Left-handedness."

cially with the right hand, while left-handers during speaking make more gestures than right-handers, and use the hand ipsilateral to the cerebral hemisphere dominant for speech relatively more frequently than do right-handers.[88] Both groups used the contralateral hand more frequently than the ipsilateral hand. Left-handers show smaller visual field differences and smaller ear differences in dichotic listening tasks than right-handers,[89] and recover completely from aphasia more frequently than right-handers, again possibly indicating somewhat more symmetrical representation of cognitive functions than right-handers normally show. Briggs and Nebes suggest that mixed-handers should not be grouped with right-handers, nor with left-handers, nor with non-right-handers.[90] Mixed-handers showed the same patterns, but to a lesser degree, of ear advantages as did right-handers, while left-handers showed little or no pattern of ear advantages.

Left-handers seem to be more heterogeneous and more diffuse in hemispheric lateralization for speech and spatial processes than are right-handers. Although left-handers sometimes differ from right-handers in organization of cognitive processes, left-handers usually perform as well as right-handers on measures of cognitive ability. Newcombe and Ratcliff found that left-handers performed as well as right-handers on standard cognitive tasks, and that non-right-handed people with unilateral cerebral lesions compare favorably with right-handers with unilateral cerebral lesions.[91] Nebes finds that right-handers and left-handers do not differ in ability to use imagery.[92] McGlone and Davidson, however, found less spatial ability among one subgroup of left-handers, those with definite left-

88. Doreen Kimura, "Manual Activity during Speaking: I. Right-Handers," *Neuropsychologia* 11 (1973): 45-50; idem, "Manual Activity during Speaking: II. Left-Handers," *Neuropsychologia* 11 (1973): 51-55.

89. Levy, "Psychobiological Implications of Bilateral Asymmetry."

90. Gary G. Briggs and Robert D. Nebes, "The Effects of Handedness, Family History, and Sex on the Performance of a Dichotic Listening Task," *Neuropsychologia* 14 (1976): 129-33.

91. Freda Newcombe and Graham Ratcliff, "Handedness, Speech Lateralization, and Ability," *Neuropsychologia* 11 (1973): 399-407.

92. Robert D. Nebes, "The Use of Imagery in Memory by Right and Left Handers," *Neuropsychologia* 14 (1976): 505-8.

ear advantages in dichotic listening tests, indicating that they had right hemispheric speech.[93]

The implications of these studies of handedness are that the level of cognitive abilities does not differ according to handedness. But the organizations of the cognitive process, and perhaps the strategies of learning, may be somewhat different from those of right-handers, at least for some subgroups of left-handers, such as the left-handers with a family history of left-handedness. In sum, there is no solid basis for prejudice about the cognitive abilities of left-handers.

The measurement of handedness is complicated. The hand used in writing is one important element of handedness, but other uses of the hands are also relevant to determining handedness. To index multiple uses of the hands, paper and pencil questionnaires, such as the Edinburgh Handedness Inventory,[94] are often used in studies of brain processes. Several of the handedness inventories are listed in Touwen.[95] The reliability and internal consistency of these inventories is not well known. White and Ashton found two factors, handedness and mental imagery, involved in scores obtained from 406 college undergraduates given the Edinburgh Handedness Inventory.[96]

Levy and Reid derived a simple, unobtrusive index of cerebral lateralization of language based upon handedness during writing and posture of the writing hand.[97] Dextrals and sinistrals characteristically hold their writing hand either in a noninverted position, in which the hand lies below and roughly at a right angle to the line of writing, or in an inverted or hooked position, in which the hand is above and roughly parallel to the line of writing. Levy and Reid found that left-handers and right-handers who write with the

93. Jeannette McGlone and Wilda Davidson, "The Relation between Cerebral Speech Laterality and Spatial Ability with Special Reference to Sex and Hand Preference," *Neuropsychologia* 11 (1973): 105-13.

94. R. C. Oldfield, "The Assessment and Analysis of Handedness: The Edinburgh Inventory," *Neuropsychologia* 9 (1971): 97-113.

95. Touwen, "Laterality and Dominance."

96. K. White and R. Ashton, "Handedness Assessment Inventory," *Neuropsychologia* 14 (1975): 261-64.

97. Jerre Levy and Marylou Reid, "Variations in Writing Posture and Cerebral Organization," *Science* 194 (1976): 337-39.

noninverted or normal hand position have their language processes primarily in the contralateral hemisphere, while right-handers and left-handers who write with a hooked or inverted hand position have their language processes primarily in the ipsilateral cortical hemisphere.

In sum, left-handers are a heterogeneous group whose subgroups should be better identified. Some left-handers differ somewhat from most right-handers in their organization of cognitive processes. For statistical reasons, left-handers may include a slightly greater incidence of pathologically determined lateralizations. Nonetheless, the research data report no educationally important deficits in the cognitive abilities of left-handers. The age-old prejudices and stereotypes about the cognitive deficits of left-handers are ill-founded and without meaningful educational implications.

There is also a positive side to the diversity in handedness and in brain lateralization processes. Left-handedness contributes to a diversity among individuals and to a cultural richness. In education, some changes should be made to facilitate the learning of the 11 percent of the population who are left-handers. We could make a humble beginning by designing school furniture appropriate for them. We could make a fundamental beginning by providing understanding and equality to people who are left-handed.

SEX DIFFERENCES IN COGNITIVE PROCESSES

In a thorough review of the psychological literature on sex differences, Maccoby and Jacklin (1974) reported that the verbal abilities of boys and girls are quite similar until early adolescence.[98] At about age eleven and beyond the verbal abilities of females are superior, by about .25 of a standard deviation, to the verbal abilities of males. In adolescence and adulthood, males are superior by about .4 of a standard deviation to females on visual-spatial tasks, and after about age twelve or thirteen on mathematical tasks also. No sex difference was found in analytic ability, except for a male superiority when spatial ability was involved in disembedding complex figures.

The recent research on the cognitive processes of the brain

98. Eleanor E. Maccoby and Carol N. Jacklin, *The Psychology of Sex Differences* (Stanford, Calif.: Stanford University Press, 1974).

complements the above findings in several interesting ways. For over a decade a mild controversy has existed over the difference between the sexes in hemispheric distribution of language and spatial processes. Levy and Sperry argue that, compared with women, men have a greater degree of lateralization, with verbal processes in the left hemisphere and spatial functions in the right hemisphere, while women tend to have both verbal and spatial processes represented to a slightly greater degree in each hemisphere. Buffery and Gray argue nearly the opposite, believing that speech perception and consequently other verbal processes of girls develop earlier and become more strongly lateralized than those of boys, who have spatial processes more equally represented in both hemispheres.[99] Why a strong lateralization increases language ability in females, while its opposite, bilateral cerebral representation of nonlanguage skills, facilitates spatial ability in males is not made clear.

In the recent literature, Ray et al. report that males were lateralized for so-called right hemispheric or left hemispheric tasks, while no statistically significant differences between the same tasks were found for females.[100] Hannay and Malone found that males, but not females, showed a right visual field superiority for recognizing nonsense words, indicating less lateralization of linguistic functions in females than in males.[101] Witelson found spatial functions well lateralized in boys at about age six, but not in girls until about age thirteen.[102] On the other hand, Wolff and Hurwitz found earlier and greater left hemispheric specialization in girls for serial regulation of motor behavior, that is, keeping in time with a metronome and tapping a steady rhythm.[103] With biofeedback

99. A. W. H. Buffery and J. A. Gray, "Sex Differences in the Development of Spatial and Linguistic Skills," in *Gender Differences: Their Ontogeny and Significance*, ed. Christopher Ounsted and David C. Taylor (Baltimore, Md.: Williams and Wilkins, 1972), pp. 123-57.

100. William J. Ray et al., "Sex Differences and Lateral Specialization of Hemispheric Functioning," *Neuropsychologia* 14 (1976): 391-94.

101. H. Julia Hannay and Daniel R. Malone, "Visual Field Effects and Short-term Memory for Verbal Material," *Neuropsychologia* 14 (1976): 203-9.

102. Sandra F. Witelson, "Sex and the Single Hemisphere: Specialization of the Right Hemisphere for Spatial Processing," *Science* 193 (1976): 425-27.

103. Peter H. Wolff and Irving Hurwitz, "Sex Differences in Finger Tapping: A Developmental Study," *Neuropsychologia* 14 (1976): 35-41.

information about heart rate, females shifted to a greater right hemisphere activation than did males in an attempt to influence their heart rates.[104] Both sexes were equally effective at self-regulation of heart rate, although they used somewhat different strategies in attaining the equivalent outcomes.

Tucker studied analytic-spatial and synthetic-spatial tasks and found that males used their left hemispheres predominantly in the analytic task and their right hemispheres predominantly in the synthetic task.[105] Females used their right and left hemispheres in the analytic task, but showed a greater EEG difference between rostral and caudal (front and back) regions within the same cortical hemisphere. Bogen et al. found that black or white urban women do as well as men on the Street Gestalt Completion Test.[106]

In sum, sex differences in mean cognitive proficiency in different intellectual tasks are either nonexistent in most areas, or remarkably small in the remaining areas. They do not emerge until adolescence, suggesting an influence of culturally determined roles.

There is no educationally relevant empirical support in the studies reviewed here for the belief that one sex is more or less intellectually qualified than the other to pursue academic learning. The observed differences in hemispheric lateralization, which are still controversial, reflect a richness and diversity in the use of cognitive processes to attain equivalent outcomes and equal proficiency.

COGNITIVE STYLES

Cognitive styles are relatively stable ways individuals perceive, conceptualize, and organize information. Although perennially bothered with methodological problems, research on cognitive styles has potentially significant contributions to make to the individualization of instruction and to the development of process models of learning. In the following paragraphs, we will relate research on

104. R. J. Davidson and G. E. Schwartz, "Patterns of Cerebral Lateralization during Cardiac Biofeedback versus the Self-regulation of Emotion: Sex Differences," *Psychophysiology* 13 (1976): 62-68.

105. Don M. Tucker, "Sex Differences in Hemispheric Specialization for Synthetic Visuospatial Functions," *Neuropsychologia* 14 (1976): 447-64.

106. Joseph E. Bogen et al., "The Other Side of the Brain: IV. The A/P Ratio," *Bulletin of the Los Angeles Neurological Society* 37 (1972): 49-61.

cognitive styles to models of the processes of the brain and attempt to develop some educationally relevant implications from the emerging relationships.

Kagan, Moss, and Sigel introduced a model of conceptual styles in which the child's initial global percepts and concepts become more articulated and differentiated with development.[107] After they outlined two conceptual orientations (egocentric and stimulus centered) and three conceptual classes (analytic-descriptive, inferential-categorical, and relational) they reported seven studies that centered on analytic conceptual processes and their correlates. A person shows an analytic conceptual style by grouping stimuli by their similar elements, such as grouping a table and a chair together because they each have four legs. Nonanalytic groupings are based on commonalities of the whole or unanalyzed stimuli that are parts of one category (for example, people who are all soldiers) or stimuli that are functionally related to one another (for example, a table and chairs are used for dining). They found an analytic cognitive style to be related to a reflective differentiated style, which enables a child to ignore irrelevant, distracting stimuli. Nonanalytic children tended to be impulsive.

Zelniker and Jeffrey cogently related cognitive style to a model of cognitive processes of the brain.[108] They hypothesized that reflective children (that is, children who are above the mean on accuracy and above the mean for latency of response) differ from impulsive children (that is, children who are below the mean on accuracy and below the mean on latency of response) in their information-processing strategies. They found that the reflective children used a left hemispheric, analytic cognitive style and the impulsive children used a right hemispheric, global cognitive style. On problems involving matching figures by their details, because of their analytic style the reflective children were more accurate than the impulsive children, while on comparable global problems no

107. Jerome Kagan, Howard A. Moss, and Irving E. Sigel, "Psychological Significance of Styles of Conceptualization," in *Basic Cognitive Processes in Children*, ed. John C. Wright and Jerome Kagan, *Monographs of the Society for Research in Child Development* 28, no. 2 (1963): 73-112.

108. Tamar Zelniker and Wendell E. Jeffrey, *Reflective and Impulsive Children: Strategies of Information Processing Underlying Differences in Problem Solving, Monographs of the Society for Research in Child Development* 41, no. 5 (1976): 1-52.

difference between the groups was found. The difference in information-processing strategies, analytic versus global, or part scanners versus whole scanners, not verbal processes versus imagery, explained the difference in accuracy between the reflectives and impulsives. One important educational implication of Zelniker and Jeffrey's findings is that impulsive children, who are relatively more frequently found in the lower socioeconomic classes, are not always inferior to reflective children in problem-solving ability when a global strategy is appropriate to the solution of the problem. For teaching, the finding implies that we can expect learning to be difficult when a mismatch exists between a child's global cognitive strategy and the analytic organization of many curricula and instructional tasks.

Cohen hypothesized that two incompatible cognitive styles, called analytic and relational styles, develop in cultures emphasizing either shared functions or formal primary social groups, respectively.[109] Children with a relational or nonanalytic style should experience difficulty in schools and on tests where an analytic strategy is needed to succeed. She found that many standardized tests of intelligence and achievement, including nonverbal tests, assess students' analytic cognitive style and field-independent cognitive style. She concludes that relational children in an analytically organized school environment face a cultural conflict, which is not the same as a cultural deprivation.

In an extensive series of studies, Witkin and associates identified a field-independent or differentiated cognitive style and a field-dependent or global cognitive style, which is not unlike but not identical to Kagan's analytic and nonanalytic categories. A field-independent, or field-insensitive, person can locate an embedded figure in a complex background, or ignore a distracting tilted rectangle to align a vertical rod perpendicularly, or position his seated body uprightly although the room he sees before him and his chair have been artificially rotated from their normal upright positions.[110]

109. Rosalie Cohen, "Conceptual Styles, Culture Conflict, and Nonverbal Tests of Intelligence," *American Anthropologist* 71 (1969): 828-56.

110. For a review of the educational implications of field-independent and field-dependent cognitive styles, see Herman A. Witkin et al., "Field-dependent and Field-independent Cognitive Styles and Their Educational Implications," *Review of Educational Research* 47 (Winter 1977): 1-64.

Compared with field-independent people, field-dependent people are more socially oriented, more aware of social cues, better able to discern the feelings of others from their facial expressions, more responsive to a myriad of information, more dependent on others for reinforcement and for defining their own beliefs and sentiments, and more in need of extrinsic motivation and externally defined objectives. Field-independent people are relatively impersonal, individualistic, insensitive to others and their reinforcements, interested in abstract subject matter, and intrinsically motivated. They have internalized frames of reference, and experience themselves as separate or differentiated from others and the environment. They tend to use previously learned principles and rules to guide their behavior.

The relationship between cognitive processes of the brain and Witkin's model of cognitive style is interesting. Field independence-dependence might be related to hemispheric brain processes.

Cohen, Berent, and Silverman report a striking parallel between field-dependence and lateralization of the brain.[111] After electroconvulsive shock to the right cortical hemispheres of twelve patients with epilepsy every patient became less field-dependent. Shock to the left hemispheres of each of twelve other epileptic patients made each one more field-dependent.

In a review of field-independence and extent of brain lateralization, Oltman indicates that degree of lateralization correlates with field-independence, both representing articulated cognitive styles.[112] Although the relations between Witkin's research and the recent research on the human brain are not fully understood, these two lines of research converge on important issues. The recent brain research suggests some of the cognitive processes that may underlie cognitive styles.

Information about the processes that characterize cognitive styles can be useful in matching instruction to individual differences. For example, Pask and Scott classified learners as serialists or holists and

111. Bertram D. Cohen, Stanley Berent, and Albert J. Silverman, "Field-dependence and Lateralization of Function in the Human Brain," *Archives of General Psychiatry* 28 (1973): 165-67.

112. Philip K. Oltman, "Field-dependence and Extent of Lateralization," paper presented at the annual meeting of the American Psychological Association, Washington, D.C., September 1976.

wrote serially ordered and holistically ordered instructional materials to teach a zoological taxonomy.[113] The serialists and the holists learned much better when the instructional materials matched their cognitive styles than when the materials did not match their cognitive styles. The study exemplifies one way instruction can be improved when it is based upon process-oriented cognitive styles that relate to knowledge about the encoding strategies of the brain.

LEARNING DISABILITIES

The recent literature relating learning disabilities, especially reading difficulties and dyslexia, to brain processes is voluminous and provocative. The recent brain research leads to interesting and productive hypotheses about cognitive processes that may underlie disabilities in learning. Often learning disabilities in children are due to deficiences in left-hemispheric, verbal-analytic processes;[114] other times the problems are due to deficiencies of attention.[115] As one example, we will review some of the studies on brain processes in difficulties in learning to read.

Dyslexia, a generic term encompassing a myriad of reading disabilities, refers to reading difficulty in apparently normal individuals given standard reading instruction. Some dyslexic children show atypical brain functions, with bilateral spatial processing which may lead to deficient phonetic, sequential linguistic processing.[116] Other researchers also find weak left-hemispheric specialization of language[117] or serial-ordering deficits among children with

113. G. Pask and B. C. E. Scott, "Learning Strategies and Individual Competence," *International Journal of Man-Machine Studies* 4 (1972): 217-53.

114. B. LaRue Guyer and Morton P. Friedman, "Hemispheric Processing and Cognitive Styles in Learning-Disabled and Normal Children," *Child Development* 46 (1975): 658-68.

115. Sebastiano Santostefano, Louis Rutledge, and David Randall, "Cognitive Styles and Reading Disability," *Psychology in the Schools* 2 (1965): 57-62; Antoinette Krupski, "The Role of Attention in the Reaction-Time Performance of Mentally Retarded Adolescents," *American Journal of Mental Deficiency* 82 (1977): 79-83.

116. Sandra F. Witelson, "Developmental Dyslexia: Two Right Hemispheres and None Left," *Science* 195 (1977): 309-11.

117. Madelyn E. Olson, "Laterality Differences in Tachistoscopic Word Recognition in Normal and Delayed Readers in Elementary School," *Neuro-*

reading difficulties.[118] Yamadori found that a Japanese patient with an occluded left middle cerebral artery could read Japanese ideograms (Kanji), presumably processed mainly in the right hemisphere, but had great difficulty reading Japanese phonograms (Kana), probably processed more in the left hemisphere.[119]

Right-hemispheric processes are also sometimes deficient and cause somewhat different types of reading problems, usually involving spatial functions.[120] The studies of right-hemispheric functions in reading difficulties, however, are at present too involved and divergent to be briefly summarized here.

It seems that there are many types of dyslexia and many possible causes of it. Boder describes an interesting, diagnostically useful model of the basic types of developmental dyslexia.[121] The *dysphonetic* dyslexics read words globally rather than analytically and spell by sight rather than by sound. Especially noticeable are their bizarre spellings of phonetic words. The *dyseidetic* dyslexics read words analytically, but have difficulty learning the appearance of letters and difficulty in seeing the shapes or configurations of previously learned words. They seem to learn each word analytically. They may be letter blind or word blind, and often incorrectly spell words phonetically, the same way they read them. The

---

psychologia 11 (1973): 343-50; Tony Marcel, Leonard Katz, and Marjorie Smith, "Laterality and Reading Proficiency," *Neuropsychologia* 12 (1974): 131-39; Tony Marcel and Paul Rajan, "Lateral Specialization for Recognition of Words and Faces in Good and Poor Readers," *Neuropsychologia* 13 (1975): 489-97; M. E. Thomson, "A Comparison of Laterality Effects in Dyslexics and Controls Using Verbal Dichotic Listening Tasks," *Neuropsychologia* 14 (1976): 243-46.

118. Suzanne Corkin, "Serial-ordering Deficits in Inferior Readers," *Neuropsychologia* 12 (1974): 347-54.

119. Atsushi Yamadori, "Ideogram Reading in Alexia," *Brain* 98 (1975): 231-38.

120. Grace H. Yeni-Komshian, David Isenberg, and Herman Goldberg, "Cerebral Dominance and Reading Disability: Left Visual Field Deficit in Poor Readers," *Neuropsychologia* 13 (1975): 83-94; I. M. Clifton-Everest, "Dyslexia: Is There a Disorder of Visual Perception?" *Neuropsychologia* 14 (1976): 491-94; John T. E. Richardson, "The Effect of Word Imageability in Acquired Dyslexia," *Neuropsychologia* 13 (1975): 281-88.

121. Elena Boder, "Developmental Dyslexia: Prevailing Coneepts and a New Diagnostic Approach," in *Progress in Learning Disabilities*, vol. 2, ed. Myklebust, pp. 293-321.

mixed dyslexic or *alexic* children show symptoms of both phonetic and eidetic problems. Boder's model has educational implications for remediation because it centers upon identification of the cognitive processes used by children with reading disabilities. From an understanding of these processes, teachers or therapists can begin to construct differentiated instructional treatments appropriate for different children. Her categories of dyslexia fit well with cognitive strategies identified by research on the encoding processes of the brain, and summarize well some of the implications of the research for understanding and remediating difficulties in reading.

Educational Implications

We will now comment on some of the possible meanings for education of the findings of the research on the human brain. Some of the possible meanings or implications for educational research are presented first, followed by implications for understanding learning, and then by implications for instruction and teaching.

IMPLICATIONS FOR EDUCATIONAL RESEARCH

In the review of research we discussed recent studies of the cognitive processes of the brain as they related to some studies in psychology and education on learning and instruction. One paradigm for educational research that emerges from these studies in neurology, psychology, and education emphasizes the importance of the mental processes and intellectual backgrounds of learners in determining the learning that occurs during instruction and teaching. Within this paradigm, research in teaching and learning focuses upon understanding the individual student's previous learning and cognitive strategies and upon instruction and teaching that builds upon that learning and those strategies. In this paradigm, the same treatment may mean different things to different learners, and different treatments may be needed to attain the same ends with different learners. The studies described below elaborate and exemplify this paradigm.

Wittrock presented a model of the generative processes of human learning. In the model of generative learning, comprehension is a constructive process.[122] For example, in reading learners are hypothesized to use individualized abstract analytic and specific contextual cognitive processes to generate meaning for the text from their memory of earlier experiences. The sentences in the text are the retrieval cues which initiate the generative processes. In one study of reading one familiar synonym substituted in each sentence for an unfamiliar word doubled children's comprehension of the story and sizably raised their retention of it.[123] In another study a familiar story context doubled story comprehension and sizably increased the learning of undefined, unfamiliar vocabulary words.[124] In a third study instructions to generate elaborative sentences, one per paragraph of text, nearly doubled reading comprehension.[125] Bull and Wittrock found that when children drew simple diagrams to represent the verbal definitions of unfamiliar words their vocabulary scores improved.[126] In all these studies, instruction was designed to induce students to use their experience to generate verbal or imaginal elaborations of the text they read.

To teach children to classify stimuli by two dimensions, rather than by the less complex one dimensional system they used, Wittrock determined the one dimension used by each child.[127] The instruction then taught the child to attend to the second dimension, resulting in nearly errorless two-dimensional classifications.

Another way to study cognitive processes in learning is to relate curricula to information processing strategies. Hartnett studied

122. Merlin C. Wittrock, "Learning as a Generative Process," *Educational Psychologist* 11 (1974): 87-95.

123. Carolyn B. Marks, Marleen J. Doctorow, and Merlin C. Wittrock, "Word Frequency and Reading Comprehension," *Journal of Educational Research* 67 (1974): 259-62.

124. Merlin C. Wittrock, Carolyn B. Marks, and Marleen Doctorow, "Reading as a Generative Process," *Journal of Educational Psychology* 67 (1975): 484-89.

125. Marleen J. Doctorow, Merlin C. Wittrock, and Carolyn B. Marks, "Generative Processes in Reading Comprehension," *Journal of Educational Psychology*, in press.

126. Bull and Wittrock, "Imagery in the Learning of Verbal Definitions."

127. Merlin C. Wittrock, "Developmental Processes in Learning from Instruction," *Journal of Genetic Psychology*, in press.

matches between inductive holistic and deductive analytically organized college curricula, used for years at the University of California, Los Angeles, to teach Spanish as a second language, and right-hemispheric and left-hemispheric cognitive processes.[128] By measuring lateral eye movements in response to thought questions she classified undergraduates according to their preferred cognitive modes. She predicted and found an interaction between hemispheric processes and curricula, with the left and right hemispheric dominant students learning better over one quarter of instruction from the deductive and inductive curricula, respectively.

In the teaching of drawing, Edwards found that beginning students in college often use a stereotyped analytic, linear symbolic approach when they draw human figures.[129] To facilitate a holistic strategy and to discourage naming features of the human form she inverted the picture of a human form and asked the students to draw their representations of it in an inverted orientation. Second, she compared instructions which emphasized the drawing of overall configurations and relations among lines and spaces with instructions which emphasized drawing analytically from the top of the head to the bottom of the legs while naming the human features, for example, eyes, ears, nose. The inverted picture and the holistic instructions sizably facilitated the fidelity of the drawings, probably by replacing an analytic strategy with a holistic strategy. Drawing involves more than motor skill, and the teaching of drawing to beginners at least sometimes involves an understanding of the cognitive strategies they use.

Studies are now beginning to appear in the neuropsychological literature on brain processes and subjects such as geometry and aesthetics. Franco and Sperry found a right-hemisphere superiority for reasoning in geometry, with the proficiency of the left-hemisphere depending upon the four different kinds of geometry and their appropriateness to a detailed, analytic analysis.[130] Levy studied

128. Dayle Hartnett, "The Relation of Cognitive Style and Hemispheric Preference to Deductive and Inductive Second Language Learning" (Master's thesis, University of California, Los Angeles, 1975).

129. Betty Edwards, "An Experiment in Perceptual Skills in Drawing" (Ph.D. diss., University of California, Los Angeles, 1976).

130. Laura Fanco and Roger W. Sperry, "Hemisphere Lateralization for Cognitive Processing of Geometry," *Neuropsychologia* 15 (1977): 107-14.

lateral dominance and aesthetic preference.[131] Dextrals appreciated pictures with the more important content in the right visual field, ostensibly because their activated right hemispheres oriented processing to the left visual field. Pictures which correct this bias are thought to be more aesthetically pleasing. These studies indicate new possibilities for future study of relations between cognitive processes and subjects ranging across the arts and sciences.

For educational research it is clear that people who study learning and instruction cannot afford to remain isolated from the fields of developmental psychology, differential psychology, and neuropsychology. The emerging unity of interests among these fields promises to benefit all of them. It is also clear that paradigms that involve the study of cognitive processes are becoming more feasible and useful for educational research.

IMPLICATIONS FOR UNDERSTANDING LEARNING

Some of the most meaningful educational implications of research studies derive from the models of learning which underlie them. Since ancient times, peoples' understanding of learning and memory influenced education in schools and out of them.

The studies in neurology, psychology, and education reviewed here imply to me that learning is a generative process that is influenced by previous learning and the cognitive and affective attentional and encoding processes and strategies of the brain. The brain actively selects, attends to, organizes, perceives, encodes, stores, and retrieves information. It uses information processing strategies, such as analytic and holistic strategies, to construct organizations and meaning from stimuli.

Sometimes it generates a whole picture from one half of a chimerical stimulus. Other times it analyzes complex spatial patterns into simpler embedded ones. It performs a myriad of functions simultaneously and quickly. A multiplicity of operations, interpretations, and inferences characterizes the complex reality constructed by the brain.

One important educational implication of this model of learning as a generative process then is that learning is not confined to one

131. Jerre Levy, "Lateral Dominance and Aesthetic Preference," *Neuropsychologia* 14 (1976): 431-45.

objective at a time, nor is it only a one dimensional, step-by-step procedure, as it is portrayed in many recent studies of instruction.

The recent research on encoding and on hemispheric processes implies that the brain constructs meaning in at least two different ways, by imposing analytic and holistic organizations upon information. The extensions of this important finding lead into curricular design, the sequencing of instruction, and the learner's elaboration of information by use of different organizational strategies. The finding also implies that instruction organized to induce gestalt-synthetic processes will be different from a linear sequence of information illustrated with pictures. An inductive, or other non-linear, order of information seems more appropriate for inducing a synthetic processing strategy.

Even the most venerable modern concepts in learning acquire new meaning within this framework. Reinforcement, defined either as informational feedback or as an automatic process of learning, that is appropriately designed for one hemispheric strategy may be poorly timed, random, or worse for the cognitive strategy of the other hemisphere. The organized multivariate reality constructed by the brain is far more sophisticated than the one some recent simplistic instructional materials were designed to accommodate.

In addition, attention and motivation also acquire a somewhat different character. From research on the orienting response and other attentional mechanisms of the brain, discrepant, novel, original, and challenging stimulation, whose pattern is not always apparent, seems likely to excite at least transitory attention and perhaps to stimulate differentially one of several encoding strategies. The descending reticular activating system introduces close ties between intentions, plans, and previous experience and motivation or sustained interest. Motivation reflects more than momentary environmental stimulation. In this framework, repetitions of reinforcers and repetitions of behavior seem more likely sometimes to produce habituation and boredom than increased attention and sustained interest.

Whether these implications will prove to be fruitful for understanding learning is not known. But, some of the centrally important concepts in learning will be given new interpretations by the recent research reviewed in this chapter. The customary roles of the learners and teachers may also be changed by the models of learning emerging from the studies reviewed here.

IMPLICATIONS FOR INSTRUCTION AND TEACHING

The brain does not usually learn in the sense of accepting or recording information from teachers. The brain is not a passive consumer of information. Instead, it actively constructs its own interpretations of information and draws inferences from it. The brain ignores some information and selectively attends to other information. One implication from these findings is that instruction should begin with careful observation of learners, their constructive processes and individual differences. Treatments, as we have called them, no longer mean what their names imply. A so-called spatial treatment may be analyzed verbally, for example, or in multiple ways. Instructional procedures should then be related to the cognitive processes of learners and their individual differences.

The individual differences suggested by the research reviewed here emphasize information processing strategies. Instead of age, sex, and intelligence, the strategies of learners, such as analytic and holistic strategies, promise to lead more directly to theoretically interesting instructional procedures. By the same reasoning, studies of student attributions, encoding processes, and attentional and motivational mechanisms may also lead to improved instructional procedures. Instructions to elaborate concepts and issues, in different modes or different strategies, questions about the meanings of subject matter, metaphors, similes, and analogies to induce comparisons, and hypostatizations to represent abstract concepts are all potentially important ways that teachers might facilitate the constructive cognitive processes of the brain.

In sum, the teacher, more than the subject matter, is given new importance and original challenging functions to perform with students. The basic implication for teaching is that teachers need to understand and to facilitate the constructive processes of the learner.

The learner is also given a new, more important active role and responsibility in learning from instruction and teaching. To learn, one should attend to the information and concepts, and construct, elaborate, and extend cognitive representations of them. The teacher can facilitate these processes, but the learner is the only one who can perform them.

These new ideas are as old as Aristotle's model of memory, Simonides' system for recalling information, and Quintilian's suggestions to teachers and students about the facilitation of learning. But these old ideas encourage a new unity of interest among people who study learning, instruction, individual differences, attention, memory, and the human brain.

CHAPTER IV

The Biology of Motivation

SEBASTIAN P. GROSSMAN

Prologue

A discussion of the biological basis of motivation is complicated by the fact that there is little agreement among contemporary psychologists about the functional significance of the theoretical construct "motivation."[1] Some believe that motivational processes serve quite specific "directing" functions essential for the organization of behaviors which are likely to correct a "need" (such as energy, water, and so forth), promote the survival of the individual (that is, avoidance or aggression of a potential enemy) or survival of the species (that is, the location and persuasion of a mate, nest building, rearing of young, and so forth). Presumably, these innate, physiological "drive states" serve as the basis for more complex, motivational influences that are acquired through conditioning. Others argue that motivational mechanisms serve principally or even exclusively "arousal" functions that control the degree of activation in the brain (or some parts thereof). The organization of specific behaviors, according to this view, is a function of cognitive-associative mechanisms which direct behavior in such a way that some critical level of brain activation is maintained but not exceeded (for example, one learns to reduce excessive brain arousal due to starvation-related sensory input from the internal milieu by searching for and ingesting food because only this class of behavior reduces the excessive brain activation under this particular circumstance). Between these extreme theoretical positions

1. The following discussion is based on thousands of research reports Space considerations do not permit the citation of this literature. I shall refer the reader to review articles that summarize (and cite) specific aspects of the literature.

there is the perhaps most commonly accepted notion that the survival of complex biological organisms may require both specific motivational influences which direct behavior toward appropriate goals, and nonspecific arousal which guarantees that the organism is activated and thus capable of responding to aspects of the environment that reduce the sensory input responsible for the arousal of the momentarily dominant motivational state.

Matters are further complicated by the "incentive motivation" that derives from objects which are potentially able to alleviate a particular specific motivational state and/or the associated nonspecific arousal. Incentive motivation obviously interacts with, and to some extent depends upon, specific as well as nonspecific motivational states. A piece of dry bread results in ingestive or related instrumental behaviors only if a strong specific motivational state and the associated suprathreshold arousal exist. The motivational property of particular incentives becomes apparent only when one observes the effects of drastic changes in the quantity or quality of the reinforcement for each behavior (for example, chocolate, cookies, or the smell of a browning steak elicit consummatory or instrumental behaviors even when the level of specific motivation and nonspecific arousal is relatively low).

This is not the occasion for a review of the heated debates that have raged within the field of psychology about the relative importance and relation between what I have called "specific," "nonspecific," and "incentive-motivational" mechanisms. There is empirical evidence for anatomically and perhaps biochemically distinct neural pathways for each of these motivational influences. Before delving into the related theoretical and empirical literature, I would like to emphasize that the following is a selective and personal review of some aspects of an enormous and rapidly growing literature. Each year, literally thousands of scholarly papers appear which deal with some aspect of the biological basis of motivation. It would be sheer folly to attempt a review of this literature in the context of the present chapter. Instead, I intend to highlight some recent developments that are currently reshaping our thinking about motivational mechanisms. The discussion will rely, to an obviously disproportionate extent, on research from my own laboratory, because the questions which gave rise to it (and may, at least in part, have been answered by it) have been instrumental in shaping the general conceptual picture I would like to present. Someone else's review of the current status of these problems might well have arrived at similar (or possibly quite different) conclusions, using examples from other laboratories.

Appetitive Motivation

SPECIFIC MOTIVATIONAL INFLUENCES

The best example of a brain mechanism specifically concerned with the organization of appetitive motivational influences is the hypothalamic control of ingestive behavior in accordance with the organism's energy and fluid needs. Hunger and thirst have been classic models for primary motivational processes for many decades, mainly because eating and drinking are simple, largely unlearned, universal behaviors that are readily monitored. Moreover, constant regulation of the organism's energy stores and fluid balance is so obviously essential for survival that the interplay between physiological need and compensatory behavioral adjustments has provided an irresistible model for primary, specific motivational mechanisms. Although many writers do not specifically credit the relevant experimental literature, most psychological theories of motivation are strongly influenced by the motivational consequences of starvation or water deprivation as studied mainly in the ubiquitous albino rat.

The preeminence of hunger and thirst as biological models for motivational mechanisms was assured by a series of fortuitous experimental observations that gave us what appeared to be a surprisingly clear picture of how the brain organizes motivational functions. The first significant insight occurred in 1943 when Brobeck and his associates reported that damage to a restricted portion of the ventromedial hypothalamus (VMH) resulted in overeating (hyperphagia) and obesity. A few years later, Anand and Brobeck reported that lesions lateral to the VMH produced opposite inhibitory effects on food as well as water intake—the animals neither ate nor drank (that is, they were aphagic and adipsic), and died of starvation and dehydration in the midst of plenty.[2] Figure 1 presents a schematic view of the human hypothalamus. Figure 2 provides a series of cross-sections through the human brain, showing the relationship of the hypothalamus to other cerebral structures.

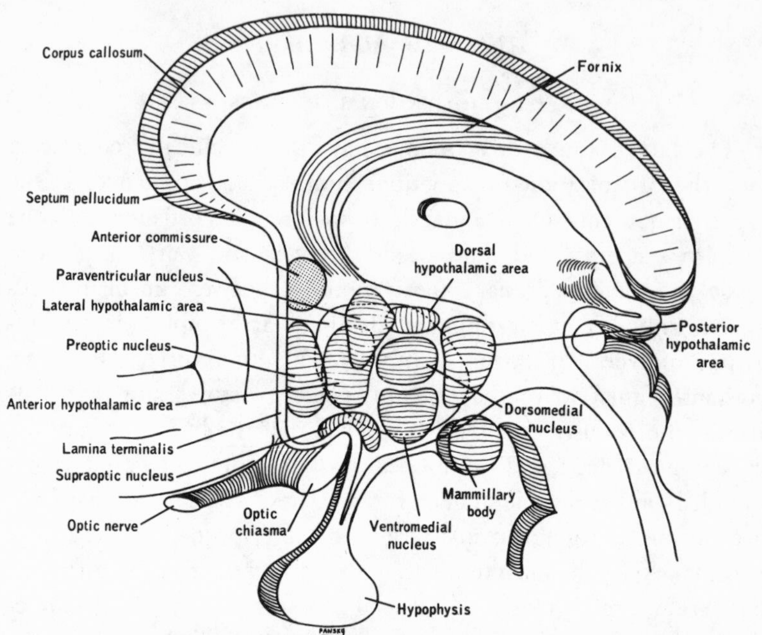

FIG. 1. Schematic view of the human hypothalamus

SOURCE: E. L. House and B. Pansky, *A Functional Approach to Neuroanatomy*, Copyright 1967, McGraw-Hill, Inc. Reprinted with Permission.

These dramatic alterations in behaviors that are essential for survival led Stellar to propose a general physiological theory of motivation.[3] Using hunger as a model, Stellar suggested that appetitive behavior might be controlled by a pair of hypothalamic centers. Both the ventromedial "satiety center" and the lateral "ex-

2. John R. Brobeck, "Regulation of Feeding and Drinking," in *Handbook of Physiology*, Section 1: *Neurophysiology*, vol. 2, ed. John Field, Horace W. Magoun, and Victor E. Hall (Baltimore, Md.: Williams and Wilkins, 1960), pp. 1197-1206.

3. Eliot Stellar, "The Physiology of Motivation," *Psychological Review* 61 (1954): 5-22..

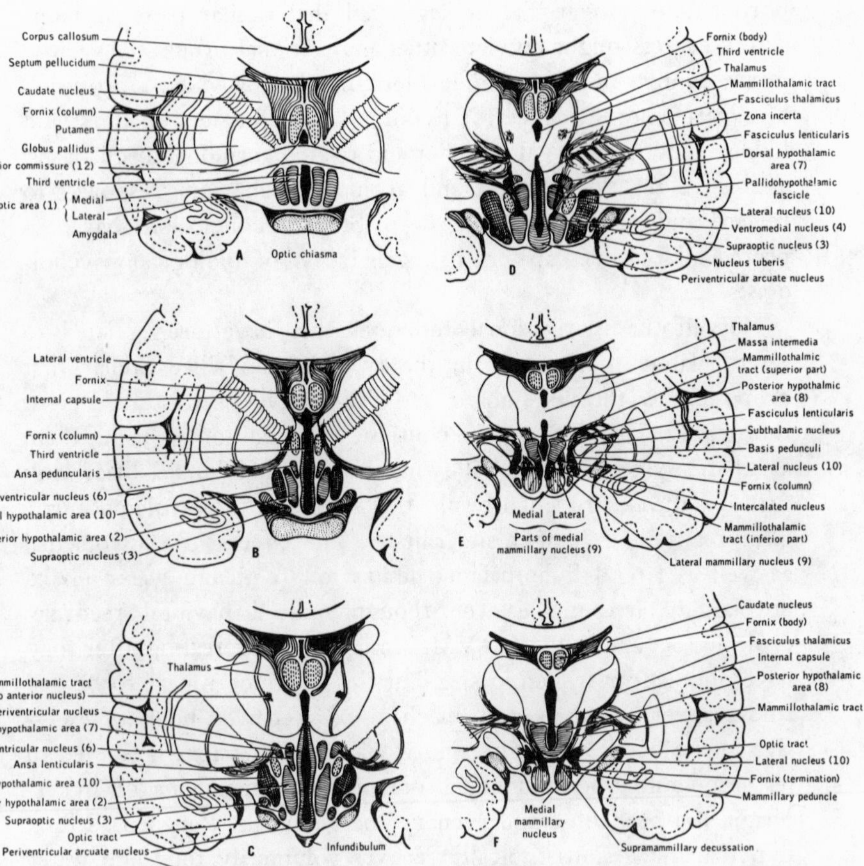

Fig. 2. Serial sections through the human brain, showing the relation between the hypothalamus and other cerebral structures

Source: House and Pansky, *A Functional Approach to Neuroanatomy*. Reprinted with permission.

citatory center" were thought to collect neural as well as extraneural information about the ever-changing state of the organism's energy balance and adjust food intake as well as related instrumental behaviors accordingly. Largely because rats with VMH lesions became aphagic after additional lesions in the lateral hypothalamus (LH), Stellar suggested that the inhibitory satiety mechanism might not affect ingestive behavior directly but exert its influence by modulating the activity of the excitatory center in the LH. The final output of the latter was thought to be directly proportional to hunger. Stellar suggested that similar pairs of interacting centers might regulate other motivational processes. Viewed in the context of an exploding literature that provided a profusion of experimental evidence for hypothalamic influences on thirst and kidney functions, sexual behavior and related hormonal mechanisms, aggressive reactions, escape and avoidance behaviors, responses to reward and punishment, and sleep, Stellar's conclusions have appeared all but inescapable to a generation of biological psychologists.

Of all the motivational functions that have been related to hypothalamic mechanisms in the two decades since Stellar first proposed his theory, hunger and thirst have been studied most thoroughly. I shall therefore continue the tradition of using them as model systems in the following discussion, taking a brief look first at some experimental results that support a hypothalamocentric interpretation of hunger and thirst.[4] The effects of ventromedial as well as lateral hypothalamic lesions on food and water intake are largely irreversible even though some behavioral recovery typically occurs. Rats with VMH lesions stop overeating after they have doubled or tripled in size, but this does not appear to be due to a recovery of the satiety mechanisms. Renewed bouts of excessive intake occur when the animal with VMH lesions is starved to its preoperative weight, and spontaneous reappearance of hyperphagia has been observed even in obese animals. Rats with lateral hypothalamic lesions typically recover voluntarily food and water intake if kept alive by intragastric intubation of food and water for weeks or months, but their ingestive behavior does not appear to be subject to the influences that regulate food and water intake in the intact animal. When deprived of food, the rat that has recovered from LH lesions becomes once again adipsic, suggesting that it drinks only to facilitate the ingestion and perhaps digestion

4. Philip Teitelbaum and Alan N. Epstein, "The Lateral Hypothalamic Syndrome: Recovery of Feeding and Drinking after Lateral Hypothalamic Lesions," *Psychological Review* 69 (1962): 74-90; Philip Teitelbaum, "Motivation and Control of Food Intake," in *Handbook of Physiology*, Section 6: *Control of Food and Water Intake*, vol. 1, ed. Charles F. Code (Baltimore, Md.: Williams and Wilkins, 1967), pp. 319-35; Brobeck, "Regulation of Feeding and Drinking"; Sebastian P. Grossman, "Role of the Hypothalamus in the Regulation of Food and Water Intake," *Psychological Review* 82 (1975): 200-224.

of its dry and salty diet. That this is a correct interpretation is indicated by the fact that the "recovered lateral" does not ingest water in response to experimental treatments which deplete intracellular or extracellular water stores and elicit drinking in the intact animal. It is widely accepted that the water intake that occurs in these animals is motivated primarily by prandial requirements. The food intake of rats that have recovered voluntary ingestive behavior after LH lesions similarly does not appear to be under the control of physiological mechanisms which regulate feeding in the intact rat. Although other, as yet poorly understood, "lipostatic" (that is, regulation of levels of fat) influences seem to contribute to the long-range regulation of food intake, it is widely accepted that the rate of cellular utilization of sugar, as measured by so-called glucoreceptors, is the principal index of energy utilization and energy need. Reducing the rate of cellular glucose utilization experimentally through the administration of either exogenous insulin (which reduces the availability of glucose) or 2-deoxy-D-glucose (which actually increases blood glucose but decreases its intracellular utilization by competing for metabolic pathways) elicits compensatory feeding in intact rats but not in rats which have recovered voluntary ingestive behavior after LH lesions. Since they are hyperphagic when a specially palatable diet is available but eat little or nothing when the taste or texture of their diet is of poor quality or when they are required to work for their keep, it is generally believed that animals with LH lesions are motivated to eat mainly by incentive motivation (that is, the appetite for tasty morsels) rather than by the basic hunger which we assume to be the motivation underlying food seeking and ingesting in intact animals.

The effects of hypothalamic lesions on food and water intake are handsomely corroborated by the results of electrophysiological and neuropharmacological investigations. Electrical stimulation of portions of the lateral hypothalamus of sated animals elicits feeding, drinking, or food- as well as water-rewarded instrumental behaviors.[5] Stimulation of the ventromedial satiety center conversely blocks ingestive behavior in hungry animals.

5. Neal E. Miller, "Motivational Effects of Brain Stimulation and Drugs," *Federation Proceedings* 19 (1960): 846-53; Gordon J. Mogenson, "Hypo-

Microinjections of alpha-adrenergic compounds such as norepinephrine (which acts as an inhibitory neurohumoral transmitter at some synapses) into the perifornical and medial hypothalamus elicit feeding in sated rats possibly by inhibiting satiety-related neurons.[6] Similar injections into the area lateral to the fornix inhibit feeding in deprived animals. Microinjections of pharmacological agents that block the action of this neurotransmitter produce opposite effects both in the medial and lateral hypothalamus.

The presence of cells in the hypothalamus which are specifically sensitive to changes in the availability of glucose or the osmotic pressure of the extracellular or intracellular fluid is indicated by the results of electrophysiological investigations.[7] These studies show that the electrical activity of cells in the medial and lateral hypothalamus is often modified by intravenous or intracranial injections of glucose, or compounds such as insulin or 2-deoxy-D-glucose which affect its intracellular utilization. Other cells respond preferentially to an increase in the osmotic pressure (that is, the salt content) of the fluid of their environment. The presence of glucoreceptors in the medial hypothalamus is further indicated by the results of experiments showing that toxic glucose compounds such as goldthioglucose are preferentially deposited in this area, resulting in a sizable lesion as well as the classic hyperphagia-obesity syndrome.[8]

Even this necessarily cursory review of the available literature makes it easy to understand why the hypothalamocentric theory

---

thalamic Limbic Mechanisms in the Control of Water Intake," in *The Neuropsychology of Thirst*, ed. Alan E. Epstein, Harry R. Kissileff, and Eliot Stellar (Washington, D. C.: V. H. Winston & Sons, 1973), pp. 119-42.

6. Sebastian P. Grossman, "Neuropharmacology of Central Mechanisms Contributing to Control of Food and Water Intake," in *Handbook of Physiology*, Section 6: *Control of Food and Water Intake*, vol. 1, pp. 287-302; Sarah F. Leibowitz, "Brain Catecholaminergic Mechanisms for Control of Hunger," in *Hunger: Basic Mechanisms and Clinical Implications*, ed. Donald Novin, Wanda Wyrwicka, and George A. Bray (New York: Raven Press, 1976), pp. 1-18.

7. Yutaka Oomura, "Significance of Glucose, Insulin, and Free Fatty Acids on the Hypothalamic Feeding and Satiety Neurons," in *Hunger: Basic Mechanisms and Clinical Implications*, pp. 145-58.

8. Norman B. Marshall, Russell J. Barnett, and Jean Mayer, "Hypothalamic Lesions in Goldthioglucose Injected Mice," *Proceedings of the Society for Experimental Biology and Medicine* 90 (1955): 240-44.

of hunger and thirst has enjoyed such widespread popularity in the last two decades. The role of the hypothalamus in other types of behaviors has not been subjected to as much experimental scrutiny, but the results of more limited investigations have, by and large, supported a similar interpretation of other specific motivational influences. The results of recent experiments have nonetheless questioned the elegant simplicity of the hypothalamocentric hypothesis. The principal issues have been the anatomical specificity of the lesions and the behavioral specificity of their effects.

With respect to the first of these problems, we have been led to ask whether the effects of lesions in the lateral or ventromedial hypothalamus might be due to a dysfunction in other parts of the brain due to an interruption of pathways that course through the hypothalamus or immediately adjacent structures but may not synapse in it. When Brobeck and his colleagues first described the effects of hypothalamic lesions on ingestive behavior, he cautioned that the possible involvement of fibers of passage should be considered. However, there was at that time little evidence that other portions of the brain significantly influenced food or water intake and thus no compelling reason to pursue this matter seriously. In the last decade, numerous investigators have reported that lesions in extrahypothalamic structures produce adipsia and aphagia (as well as persisting deficits in responding to glucoprivic [that is, lowered glucose] or hydrational challenges) or hyperdipsia or hyperphagia. Moreover, many of these structures are interconnected by pathways that course through the hypothalamus, often without known synaptic connection to local cells. I have reviewed this literature elsewhere,[9] but a brief discussion of some critical observations may help provide a perspective for this issue.

Morgane first reported in 1961 that lesions in the globus pallidus (the medial portion of the corpus striatum which lies just anterior and lateral to the lateral hypothalamus) resulted in persistent aphagia and adipsia.[10] He suggested that the effects of lateral hypo-

9. Sebastian P. Grossman, "Neurophysiologic Aspects: Extrahypothalamic Factors in the Regulation of Food Intake," *Advances in Psychosomatic Medicine* 7 (1972): 49-72; idem, "Role of the Hypothalamus in the Regulation of Food and Water Intake."

10. P. J. Morgane, "Alterations in Feeding and Drinking Behavior of Rats with Lesions in Globi Pallidi," *American Journal of Physiology* 201 (1961): 420-28.

thalamic lesions might be due to an interruption of components of the pallidofugal fiber system that contains the principal efferent connection of the striatum with lower portions of the brainstem. More recently Ungerstedt and others have described aphagia and adipsia after electrolytic lesions of the substantia nigra which is the source of one of the major afferent pathways to the striatum.[11] This dopaminergic projection to the striatum was further implicated by Ungerstedt's demonstration that microinjections of the neurotoxin 6-hydroxydopamine (6-OHDA), which destroys catecholaminergic neurons and their processes preferentially, also produced aphagia and adipsia. Because the nigrostriatal pathway courses through the lateral hypothalamus and adjacent portions of the internal capsule, Ungerstedt proposed that the effects of LH lesions might be due to interruption of this system and the resulting depletion of dopamine (DA) from the striatum. Since then, other investigators have supported this hypothesis by demonstrating aphagia and adipsia after 6-OHDA injections directly into the lateral hypothalamus, anterior hypothalamus, or globus pallidus.

An interpretation of these results is unfortunately complicated by the fact that the direct application of 6-OHDA to neural tissue damages noncatecholaminergic cells and their processes to some extent, and it has been difficult to assess what role this may play in the etiology of the observed impairments in ingestive behavior. Stricker and Zigmond have attempted to circumvent this problem by injections of 6-OHDA into the cerebral ventricles.[12] When applied in this fashion, 6-OHDA diffuses through the entire brain in much lower concentrations than those typically injected directly into brain tissue. It is generally assumed that this prevents nonspecific tissue damage. (It also, unfortunately, prevents any

11. Urban Ungerstedt, "Adipsia and Aphagia after 6-Hydroxydopamine Induced Degeneration of the Nigro-striatal Dopamine System," *Acta Physiologica Scandinavica*, Supplement 367 (1971): 95-122.

12. Edward M. Stricker and Michael J. Zigmond, "Recovery of Function Following Damage to Central Catecholamine-containing Neurons: A Neurochemical Model for the Lateral Hypothalamic Syndrome," in *Progress in Psychobiology and Physiological Psychology*, vol. 6, ed. James M. Sprague and Alan N. Epstein (New York: Academic Press, 1975); idem, "Brain Catecholamines and the Lateral Hypothalamic Syndrome," in *Hunger: Basic Mechanisms and Clinical Implications*.

localization of the drug's site of action since dopaminergic cells are found in many diverse parts of the brain.) Stricker and Zigmond found that intraventricular injections of 6-OHDA, which deplete the brain of norepinephrine and dopamine in roughly equal proportions, do not produce aphagia and adipsia unless pretreatments are used which protect norepinephrine-containing cells and maximize the drug's toxic action on dopaminergic cells. In fact, persistent aphagia and adipsia (as well as some, but apparently not all, of the regulatory deficits that characterize the "recovered lateral" rat) are seen only when the brain is depleted of all but about 5 percent of its normal store of dopamine. Stricker and Zigmond view their results in the context of studies (above) which demonstrate aphagia and adipsia after intranigral, intrahypothalamic, or intrapallidal injections of 6-OHDA and arrive at the conclusion that a depletion of striatal dopamine probably is responsible for the effects of their intraventricular injections.

My associates and I have investigated the role of hypothalamic and striatal connections in a series of experiments which used a retractable wire knife to surgically transect fibers of passage.[13] Since the diameter of this knife is similar to that of a human hair, the instrument permits the selective interruption of nerve fibers without significant direct damage to nerve cells. In the first of these experiments, we found that a cut along the lateral border of the hypothalamus, which did no direct damage to hypothalamic cells but interrupted all laterally coursing connections of the hypothalamus, produced persistent aphagia and adipsia as well as all of the regulatory deficits that characterize the "recovered lateral" rat. In subsequent studies we have used this instrument to more selectively interrupt striatal afferent and efferent connections with cuts along the medial or lateral surface of the globus pallidus, or adjacent to ventral or dorsal surfaces of various aspects of the striatum. In nearly every case, our cuts produced aphagia and adipsia. The duration of the effects varied systematically as a function of cut size and location from a few days to several weeks or even months.

13. Sebastian P. Grossman and Lore Grossman, "Persisting Deficits in Rats 'Recovered' from Transections of Fibers Which Enter or Leave Hypothalamus Laterally," *Journal of Comparative and Physiological Psychology* 85 (1973): 515-27; Sebastian P. Grossman, "Neuroanatomy of Food and Water Intake," in *Hunger: Basic Mechanisms and Clinical Implications* pp. 51-60.

After most of the cuts, the animals displayed the gradual recovery of voluntary ingestive behavior which is so typical of the animal with lateral hypothalamic lesions, and retained the full complement of persisting regulatory deficits in responding to lowered glucose or hydrational emergencies.

Next, we measured the effects of our cuts on the concentration of dopamine and norepinephrine in the striatum and other portions of the brain and calculated correlations between the severity of the biochemical and behavioral effects. The results of these studies demonstrated significant relationships between the duration of the initial aphagia and adipsia and the extent of dopamine (and, in some cases, norepinephrine) depletion from the striatum and other portions of the forebrain after some, but not all, of our cuts. The overall pattern of results supports the general hypothesis that dopamine depletion from the striatum results in aphagia and adipsia but indicates that other connections of the striatum also play an important role in the control of ingestive behavior. This conclusion is supported by our observation that some cuts which produced only relatively small (30-50 percent) depletions of striatal amines produced inhibitory effects on ingestive behavior that were as severe and persistent as others which reduced striatal (and forebrain) dopamine and norepinephrine much more drastically. (These findings are in very good agreement with reports by others that lateral hypothalamic lesions deplete striatal dopamine only by about 50 percent.) Pharmacologically induced brain dopamine depletions of this magnitude do not produce reliable effects on food or water intake, and even the very severe (95+ percent) depletions achieved in some of Stricker and Zigmond's recent work rarely result in effects which are as persistent or severe as those typically seen after large hypothalamic lesions. The pattern of results that emerges from the different experimental paradigms indicates that severe depletions of brain dopamine produces aphagia and adipsia, and that similar and even more severe impairments in ingestive behavior can be produced by a disruption of other brainstem mechanisms, including various afferent and efferent connections of the striatum.

Our correlational analyses produced an unsuspected result that may be of particular importance in the context of our discussion of behavior specificity (below). Whereas the biochemical effects of some of our cuts correlated significantly with the duration of aphagia and adipsia, there was little indication of a consistent relationship between the residual concentrations of dopamine or norepinephrine in any part of the brain and the severity of most of the persisting regulatory deficits. These observations suggest that the regulatory deficits, which are such a prominent feature of the ingestive behavior of "recovered lateral" rats, may not reflect incomplete recovery of the same neural mechanisms which are responsible for the initial aphagia and adipsia, as has been generally assumed.

The problem of anatomical specificity has also been raised in recent discussions of the ventromedial lesion syndrome because lesions in several other parts of the brain, notably the temporal lobe, the frontal lobe, the septum, the amygdala and the dorsal tegmentum can produce hyperphagia or hyperdipsia. My associates and I have investigated the role of fibers of passage in the ventromedial lesion syndrome and found that cuts anterior, lateral, or posterior to the ventromedial hypothalamic region all produce hyperphagia even though cellular components of the area are intact. Noradrenergic projections to the hypothalamus in particular have been implicated by recent reports of hyperphagia following microinjections of 6-OHDA into regions of the tegmentum that are traversed by the major ascending noradrenergic pathways. Detailed study of the effects of these lesions by Ahlskog and associates has shown that these injections deplete hypothalamic norepinephrine,[14] but the question of a causal relationship between this and the observed hyperphagia remains in doubt. My associates and I have provided relevant information by a correlational analysis of the biochemical and behavioral effects of knife cuts in the area of Ahlskog's 6-OHDA injections and found no evidence of a significant relationship, even though our cuts resulted in marked increases in food intake as well as hypothalamic (and forebrain) norepinephrine depletions. This series of experiments did suggest an association of the behavioral effects with the concentration of the third major biogenic amine (serotonin) in the forebrain. This

14. J. Eric Ahlskog and Bartley G. Hoebel, "Overeating and Obesity from Damage to a Noradrenergic System in the Brain," *Science* 182 (1973): 166-69; J. Eric Ahlskog, Patrick K. Randall, and Bartley G. Hoebel, "Hypothalamic Hyperphagia: Dissociation from Hyperphagia Following Destruction of Noradrenergic Neurons," *Science* 190 (1975): 399-401.

unexpected observation is congruent with recent reports from other laboratories which have described hyperphagia after pharmacologically induced brain serotonin depletion.[15] The negative results of our attempts to correlate food intake and hypothalamic norepinephrine do not, of course, rule out a possibly significant noradrenergic input to ventromedial hypothalamic "satiety" mechanisms, since even a severe depletion in a small portion of the medial hypothalamus would not have been detected by the regional assays used in our work.

Before leaving the general problem of anatomical specificity, I would like to emphasize that none of the observations we have just discussed compels the conclusion that hypothalamic mechanisms are *not* involved in the regulation of hunger or thirst. That lesions in other portions of the brain can produce changes in food or water intake may indicate only that the hypothalamus collects information from a number of potentially critical structures and exercises its effects on behavior in turn by influencing other parts of the brain. Such a picture is entirely compatible with the fact that an interruption of various more or less well-defined pathways into or out of the hypothalamus reproduces the effects of lesions in it, unless it can be shown that these pathways do not synapse there. Moreover, aphagia and adipsia or unresponsiveness to lowered glucose or hydrational emergencies may not reflect a primary disturbance in hunger and thirst. Various sensory, motor, and arousal deficits can interfere with ingestive behavior. The contribution of these influences to the effects of surgical or pharmacological interventions that have been used to modify food or water intake remains to be elucidated (below).

These considerations provide an appropriate introduction to our discussion of behavioral specificity. When Brobeck and associates first reported the effects of hypothalamic lesions on ingestive behavior, it was assumed, somewhat gratuitously, that they reflected primary changes in motivational mechanisms. This assumption has been questioned by the results of many recent investigations that

15. Charles F. Saller and Edward M. Stricker, "Hyperphagia and Increased Growth in Rats after Intraventricular Injections of 5, 7-dihydroxytryptamine," *Science* 192 (1976): 385-87; Stuart T. Breisch, Frank P. Zemlan and Bartley G. Hoebel, "Hyperphagia and Obesity Following Serotonin Depletion by Intraventricular *p*-Chlorophenylalanine," *Science* 192 (1976): 382-84.

have focused on the diversity of the behavioral effects of the electrolytic, surgical, or chemical lesions that modify food and water intake.

Rats with ventromedial hypothalamic lesions overeat and become obese, but it is not clear to what extent an interference with basic satiety signals is responsible for these effects. Significant overeating occurs only when palatable foods are readily available. When the texture or taste of the diet is of poor quality or the animals are required to expend considerable effort to obtain it, rats with ventromedial lesions typically eat *less* and work less hard than intact controls. Rats with ventromedial hypothalamic lesions display this "finickiness" and disinclination to work also when the palatability of their water is lowered or they are asked to work for water rewards, suggesting that these disturbances reflect an impairment of functions that are not specifically related to feeding (even though food-intake may well be affected by them). Rats with VMH lesions overreact to apparently all sensory inputs, and it is possible that at least part of their increased response to palatable food may reflect this as yet poorly understood factor. Finickiness cannot be the sole determinant of hypothalamic hyperphagia and obesity since some lesions produce finickiness without overeating, and obesity itself appears to encourage finickiness, but numerous studies have shown that palatability becomes an extremely important factor after VMH lesions.

The influence of palatability as well as the hyperphagia and obesity itself are, to some extent, sex-linked. Female rats with ventromedial lesions overeat and become obese on a standard laboratory diet. Males with comparable lesions rarely increase their intake and almost never become truly obese unless a very palatable high-fat diet is available. There is considerable evidence that other hormonal disturbances contribute significantly to the hyperphagia and obesity after VMH lesions, but the nature and relative importance of these influences in the etiology of the syndrome are as yet poorly understood. Some animals with ventromedial lesions become obese without display of excessive food intake. Others are hyperphagic until they reach a static phase of obesity but are subsequently capable of regaining this abnormal body weight after a period of starvation without significantly increasing their food intake. Growth- and sex-hormone secretions are disrupted by ventromedial hypothalamic lesions and there is some evidence that the hyperphagia and/or obesity can be modified by appropriate replacement therapy. Yet, these can only be contributory factors since overeating and weight gain have been observed in rats with VMH lesions after hypophysectomy. There are numerous other complications (such as the recent observation that vagotomy abolishes the hyperphagia even though it has only very transient inhibitory effects on food intake in the intact rat) which need not, I trust, be presented here to make the point that a simple decrease in satiety or increase in hunger does not adequately account for the increased food intake seen after VMH lesions.

Behavioral specificity has become even more of an issue with respect to the inhibitory effects of lateral hypothalamic lesions, because recent investigations have shown that the initial period of aphagia and adipsia is characterized by profound sensory, motor, and arousal deficits that may well make it impossible for the animal to eat or drink. For several days after surgery, rats with LH lesions are stuporous and respond sluggishly, if at all, to sensory input. They also display a complex syndrome of motor dysfunctions that includes rigidity and a "waxy immobility" which lead to the assumption and maintenance of bizarre postures. The recovery of normal motor functions has been reported to follow a time course that is different from and often shorter than that of feeding or drinking itself. However, Teitelbaum and associates have presented experimental data indicating that the recovery of sensory responsivity parallels the recovery of ingestive behavior.[16] Teitelbaum has recently suggested that the reappearance of voluntary ingestive behavior (which precedes the reappearance of nutritionally adequate food and water intake by days or even weeks) correlates so well with the gradual recovery of normal responsiveness to environmental stimuli that it is impossible to rule out the possibility that

16. David R. Levitt and Philip Teitelbaum, "Somnolence, Akinesia, and Sensory Activation of Motivated Behavior in the Lateral Hypothalamic Syndrome," *Proceedings of the U. S. National Academy of Sciences* 72 (1975): 2819-23; John F. Marshall, Blair H. Turner, and Philip Teitelbaum, "Sensory Neglect Produced by Lateral Hypothalamic Damage," *Science* 174 (1971): 523-25.

a "lack of endogenous arousal" rather than the absence of hunger or thirst might be the cause of the initial aphagia or adipsia.

Ungerstedt, as well as Stricker and Zigmond, similarly conclude that the aphagia and adipsia seen after 6-OHDA injections into the substantia nigra, lateral hypothalamus, or cerebral ventricles might well be due to somnolence and akinesia. Stricker and Zigmond have recently proposed that depletion of striatal dopamine may interfere with the operation of an arousal mechanism that permits various other parts of the brain to respond to homeostatic signals which reflect changes in the body's energy or fluid balance.[17] Near complete destruction of this system is believed to result in unresponsiveness to all stimuli and, only secondarily, in aphagia and adipsia. The capacity to respond to changes in the internal and external milieu gradually returns according to this hypothesis because a few undamaged components of the catecholaminergic arousal system(s) develop compensatory adjustments (such as denervation supersensitivity of postsynaptic receptors, increased reuptake and capacity to synthesize dopamine in remaining nerve terminals, and so forth). Animals which have recovered voluntary ingestive behavior eat only palatable foods, according to this theory, because the relatively weak signals from the internal milieu cannot, by themselves, produce sufficient arousal to elicit feeding. Only when strong olfactory or taste stimuli are added can the system respond adequately. Similarly, these animals are adipsic or hypodipsic when deprived of food because strong sensations which arise from the mouth and throat during the ingestion of dry and salty foods need to be added to signals from osmo- or volume-receptors to exceed the threshold of the impaired arousal system. The animals are thought to be incapable of responding to the severe lowered glucose or hydrational emergencies which are used experimentally to test regulatory capabilities because the remainder of the catecholamine arousal system(s) cannot cope with stressful situations.

There is general agreement that central injections of 6-OHDA which deplete brain catecholamine stores result in arousal (as well

17. Stricker and Zigmond, "Recovery of Function Following Damage to Central Catecholamine-containing Neurons."

as motor) impairments that may well be responsible for the initial period of aphagia and adipsia typically observed in the first week or two after the injection. What is not as clear is whether the often relatively mild and transient regulatory deficits which have been observed in these animals are due to incomplete recovery of arousal functions. Even more controversial is Stricker and Zigmond's suggestion that their arousal hypothesis also accounts for the typically much more severe and persistent effects of lateral hypothalamic lesions.

NONSPECIFIC INFLUENCES

The hypothesis advanced by Stricker and Zigmond is, in principle, not new. The concept of "generalized activation" or "arousal" strongly influenced the thinking of many physiologists of the first decades of the twentieth century. Duffy introduced the notion to psychology,[18] and arousal theories of motivation have flourished in biological psychology ever since the work of Lindsley and Magoun provided empirical evidence for the existence of an extensive biological substrate for arousal functions.[19]

Lindsley and coworkers demonstrated that electrical stimulation of the diffusely organized central core of the lower brainstem, the so-called reticular formation, produces behavioral arousal as well as activation of the electrical activity of more rostral portions of the brain, and that destruction of portions of the reticular formation results in somnolence and general unresponsiveness to sensory input (even though many major sensory afferents to the brain are intact). The reticular formation also appears to exert facilitatory as well as inhibitory effects on sensory functions and is thus in a position to influence the organism's response to its environment not only by adjusting the responsiveness of cortical, integrative mechanisms but also by selective facilitation or inhibition of specific access routes.

Largely on the basis of these and related observations, Lindsley

18. Elizabeth Duffy, "Emotion: An Example of the Need for Reorientation in Psychology," *Psychological Review* 41 (1934): 184-98.

19. Donald B. Lindsley, "Emotion," in *Handbook of Experimental Psychology*, ed. Stanley S. Stevens (New York: John Wiley and Sons, 1951), pp. 473-516; idem, "Psychophysiology and Motivation," in *Nebraska Symposium on Motivation*, ed. Marshall R. Jones (Lincoln, Neb.: University of Nebraska Press, 1957), pp. 44-105.

proposed a formal arousal theory of motivation which suggested that motivational states may be characterized by (a) general arousal of cortical functions that originates in the midbrain reticular formation and involves mainly extrathalamic projections to cortical structures and (b) a more specific alerting response to those aspects of the external or internal environment that produce the arousal-inducing stimulation.[20] Lindsley proposed to reduce the problem of motivation to an innate tendency to maintain a level of activation at least during waking hours that supports a threshold quantity of neural activity, but does not exceed some upper limit which might result in a disturbance of natural rhythms. According to this theory, environmental conditions which result in excessive sensory input to the reticular formation (and cortical activation) elicit behaviors that are likely to reduce the stimulation. Environmental conditions that fail to provide sufficient stimulation to sustain suprathreshold neural activity instigate behaviors which add sensory input to the system. Ingestive behaviors occur, according to this hypothesis, not because of the activation of specific motivational mechanisms in the hypothalamus or elsewhere but because a combination of stimuli from the internal (that is, glucoprivation or increased input from osmoreceptors) and external (that is, the odor and/or sight of food or water) environment exceed the upper level of cortical arousal. Presumably, the organism learns to select from its response repertoire those behaviors which are most likely to result in the locating and ingestion of food or water.

Lindsley's arousal theory and similar proposals by others neatly account for some experimental observations which have embarrassed proponents of motivational theories that rely exclusively on specific motivational influences. Animals as well as man will work to obtain access to novel and/or interesting environments; do not tolerate prolonged exposure to conditions that sharply limit sensory input; and voluntarily engage in activities that involve certain dangers. A number of theorists have attempted to account for these observations by postulating a specific motivation to avoid boredom.[21] But this comes awfully close to admitting that a minimal

20. Ibid.

21. Daniel E. Berlyne, *Conflict, Arousal, and Curiosity* (New York: McGraw-Hill, 1960).

level of cortical neural activity is at least one of the functions which man and members of many other species attempt to regulate by appropriate adjustments of their behavior.

Lindsley's theory has problems explaining (a) why some stimuli although quite weak result in a great deal of arousal and others, which are much more intense, do not; and (b) what mechanisms permit the identification and classification of particular patterns of sensory input in terms of an indexing system that provides the basis for the selection of the most probably successful remedial behaviors. The most widely accepted answer to the first question involves the concepts of "novelty," "discrepancy," or "incongruity"[22] and is based on the empirical observation that behavioral orienting as well as electrophysiological indices of cortical arousal "habituate" (that is, diminish) with repeated presentations of even intense stimuli (provided they are not themselves harmful or serve as conditioned stimuli for potentially harmful or rewarded events). The second question has received less satisfying replies, including Lindsley's own suggestion that the postulated specific alerting process selectively activates portions of the brain which are in some way relevant to "the satisfaction of a need or want."[23] By the time the mechanisms that exercise this specific alerting function are endowed with sufficient capabilities to discriminate learned as well as unlearned stimulus patterns in such a way that rapid access is gained to appropriate behaviors, it becomes difficult to distinguish these central switching devices from specific motivational influences except in purely semantic terms.

Stricker and Zigmond's recent reformulation of the arousal theory circumvents the problem altogether by proposing specific as well as nonspecific motivational influences. Stimuli from the internal and external environment are thought to have both a specific effect that activates "neurons involved in eliciting some appropriate motivational state" and a nonspecific one that "removes a gate and thereby permits such responses to actually occur."[24] Their applica-

22. Harry Helson, *Adaptation-level Theory* (New York: Harper and Row, 1964).

23. Lindsley, "Psychophysiology and Motivation."

24. Stricker and Zigmond, "Recovery of Function Following Damage to Central Catecholamine-containing Neurons."

tion of this hypothesis to the specific issue of the role of hypothalamic and extrahypothalamic pathways in the organization of ingestive behavior unfortunately fails to offer any suggestions concerning the nature and/or location of the specific motivational influences. The authors seem to assume that "prepotent" stimuli such as those which signal changes in the organism's energy or fluid balance are innately connected directly with overt motivated responses and that related stimuli (such as gustatory and olfactory cues associated with food) facilitate responding by augmenting nonspecific arousal. All of this might work quite well had the proponents of this hypothesis not insisted on demolishing the hypothalamocentric theory, thus eliminating the most likely anatomical substrate for the proposed specific motivational state.

Stricker and Zigmond's objection to the hypothalamocentric theory appears to rest exclusively on their conviction that the impairments in ingestive behavior which are seen after LH lesions can best be explained in terms of a dysfunction of nonspecific arousal mechanisms. In view of the significance that specific motivational mechanisms assume in the framework of their arousal hypothesis, it might be instructive at this point to ask whether other aspects of the complex literature suggesting that the lateral hypothalamus contains neural mechanisms specifically related to hunger or thirst can be reinterpreted in terms of the suggested gating function of a nonspecific arousal mechanism.

One pillar of support of the hypothalamocentric theory is formed by the effects of electrical stimulation of the region on ingestive behavior. There is no doubt that feeding as well as drinking (and other behaviors such as copulation) can be elicited by such stimulation. Many investigators have interpreted this in terms of an activation of hunger- or thirst-related neural mechanisms.[25]

Others have suggested that the stimulation-induced behaviors are often unstable (that is, several different types of behaviors can be evoked from the same electrode site, and animals can be induced to switch from one to the other) and sufficiently different from

25. Mogenson, "Hypothalamic Limbic Mechanisms in the Control of Water Intake"; W. W. Roberts, "Are Hypothalamic Motivational Mechanisms Functionally and Anatomically Specific?" *Brain, Behavior, and Evolution* 2 (1969): 317–42.

deprivation-induced ingestive responses (that is, rats may eat only one type of food during electrical brain stimulation) that alternative interpretations in terms of a nonspecific facilitation of prepotent or stereotyped response patterns or, perhaps, sensory processing, seem more appropriate.[26] Support for such an interpretation has recently come from an interesting series of experiments by Antelman and associates which have shown that: (a) a mild tail-pinch often elicits behaviors (such as feeding) that are appropriate to specific aspects of the environment (such as the presence of food); and (b) these tail-pinch elicited behaviors have many of the peculiar properties previously shown to characterize behaviors elicited by brain stimulation.[27] These observations are particularly relevant to our discussion because Antelman and coworkers have reported that the tail-pinch elicited behaviors are abolished by systemic administration of dopamine antagonists as well as intranigral injections of 6-OHDA. Although the behavioral specificity of these inhibitory effects is in doubt, these observations suggest that tail-pinch elicited behavior may be the result of an activation of the dopaminergic nigrostriatal system which plays such a central role in Stricker and Zigmond's arousal hypothesis. Antelman and his colleagues suggest that the many obvious similarities between tail-pinch and brain stimulation elicited behaviors favor a similar interpretation of the latter in terms of a nonspecific increase in sensitivity to "survival-oriented and/or prepotent stimuli."[28] Such an interpretation cannot readily account for the fact that animals that are trained to perform food or water rewarded instrumental behaviors will perform these arbitrary acts (and consume the rewards) during hypothalamic stimulation, unless one assumes that the act of lever-pressing can itself become a prepotent response in experimental situations where such behavior has been consistently rewarded in the past. It is nonetheless clear that the hypothalamocentric theory

26. Elliot S. Valenstein, "The Interpretation of Behavior Evoked by Brain Stimulation," in *Brain-Stimulation Reward*, ed. Albert Wauquier and Edmund T. Rolls (Amsterdam: North Holland Publishing Co., 1976), pp. 557-76.

27. Seymour M. Antelman, Neil E. Rowland, and Alan E. Fisher, "Stimulation Bound Ingestive Behavior: A View From the Tail," *Physiology and Behavior* 17 (1977): 743-48.

28. Ibid., p. 742.

no longer derives unqualified support from the electrical stimulation literature.

A second area of investigation which has provided some support for the hypothalamocentric hypothesis is chemical stimulation. Microinjections of norepinephrine and related compounds into the hypothalamus elicit feeding in sated rats and related pharmacological blockers reverse the effect or inhibit feeding in deprived animals. Microinjections of cholinergic agents into the same region elicit drinking in sated animals.[29] It is reasonably clear that these effects are due to a drug action on cells which are related to ingestive behavior, but just where these cells are has been the subject of some debate. Norepinephrine elicits feeding when injected into a fairly large portion of the hypothalamus, but the best effects are obtained from medial placements. The lateral hypothalamus contains only few positive sites. This suggests that the feeding effect may be due to an inhibitory action of the neurotransmitter on cells which are part of the satiety mechanism. Leibowitz has obtained inhibitory effects on feeding from injections of beta-adrenergic compounds into the lateral hypothalamus suggesting that catecholaminergic components of that region may also relate to feeding.[30] It is interesting to note in the context of our discussion that pharmacological tests suggest that at least some of these cells may have dopaminergic receptor mechanisms.

Microinjections of cholinergic compounds into the LH elicit drinking, and do so quite specifically. Unfortunately, the effect is not limited to this region but can be obtained from numerous subcortical injection sites, including the ventricular system.[31] Just why this is so is as yet not clear, but it is doubtful that the efficacy of lateral hypothalamic placements provides much tangible support for the hypothalamocentric theory. (The behavioral specificity of the cholinergic drinking effect *does* support the more general no-

29. Grossman, "Neuropharmacology of Central Mechanisms Contributing to Control of Food and Water Intake."

30. Leibowitz, "Brain Catecholaminergic Mechanisms for Control of Hunger."

31. Alan E. Fisher, "Relationship between Cholinergic and Other Dipsogens in the Central Mediation of Thirst," in *The Neuropsychology of Thirst*, pp. 243-78.

tion of a specific motivational mechanism for thirst quite handsomely.)

Electrophysiological investigations have provided rather strong, if indirect, evidence for specific feeding- and drinking-related motivational mechanisms in both medial and lateral hypothalamus. Oomura and his colleagues have shown that cells in both areas respond, apparently selectively, to glucose and substances such as insulin or 2-deoxy-D-glucose which affect its utilization.[32] Some of these cells also respond to free fatty acids (the concentration of which in the bloodstream increases during periods of food deprivation). The presence of cells in the LH and VMH which respond to the two compounds that are thought to be "metered" by the organism's feeding-related control mechanisms supports the hypothalamocentric theory quite well but indirectly since the relation of glucose and free-fatty acids to hunger is itself poorly understood.

Oomura and his colleagues have also shown that neurons in the lateral hypothalamus increase their firing rate before and after food-rewarded lever presses. Rolls similarly has identified neurons in the LH which respond, apparently selectively, to the sight of food and do so only when the animal is hungry.[33] Changes in cellular activity in the presence of food or food-reward do not, of course, compel the conclusion that these cells are part of a specific hunger motivational system unless it can be shown that other potentially arousing stimuli do not affect their discharge rate. Serious attempts have been made in some but not all of these studies to provide such controls.

Before concluding our discussion of the specific and nonspecific contributions of the hypothalamus to ingestive behavior, I would like to discuss briefly some research from my own laboratory. I have already described the effects of various surgical transections of fibers of passage on ingestive behavior and brain chemistry but have reserved discussion of associated changes in sensory and motor capabilities. Some of our cuts, particularly those which parallel the

32. Oomura, "Significance of Glucose, Insulin, and Free Fatty Acids on the Hypothalamic Feeding and Satiety Neurons."

33. Edmund T. Rolls, "The Neurophysiological Basis of Brain-Stimulation Reward," in *Brain-Stimulation Reward*, pp. 65-88.

lateral border of the hypothalamus, produce initial sensory and motor effects which are similar although typically less severe than those seen after LH lesions. However, other cuts result in severe and persistent inhibitory effects on ingestive behavior without interfering significantly with sensory responsiveness or motor capabilities after the first day or two of general surgical trauma. Even the animals that display more persistent sensory or motor deficits almost invariably recover apparently normal capabilities quite some time before voluntary ingestive behavior returns. This may well be due to the fact that many of our cuts that result in severe inhibitory effects on ingestive behavior produce only relatively small depletions of striatal dopamine and norepinephrine.

Unquestionably the clearest case for a specific, ingestion-related motivational mechanism is a preparation which Walsh and I discovered in the course of an investigation of hypothalamic mechanisms.[34] Serendipitously, we noted that knife cuts in the horizontal plane just above the lateral hypothalamus (in the zona incerta) produced exactly the same impairments in ingestive behavior that are typical of "recovered lateral" rats, but absolutely no discernible impairments in sensory reactivity, arousal, or motor dysfunction (and no depletion of striatal dopamine). The animal with zona incerta lesions eats fairly normal quantities of food but is completely adipsic as soon as it is food deprived. That this animal drinks mainly to wash down dry food is further shown by tests of regulatory functions which demonstrate little or no response to experimental treatments that increase the osmotic pressure of the extracellular fluid or decrease its volume. The animals also do not eat in response to experimental treatments that interfere with intracellular glucose utilization.

On balance, I believe that the available evidence favors the conclusion that the lateral hypothalamus (or immediately adjacent portions of the diencephalon) contain neurons which are concerned quite specifically with the control of hunger and thirst. Pathways related to general arousal and motivation-related gating functions as proposed by Stricker and Zigmond are undoubtedly also repre-

34. Linda L. Walsh and Sebastian P. Grossman, "Zona Incerta Lesions Impair Osmotic but Not Hypovolemic Thirst," *Physiology and Behavior* 16 (1976): 211-15.

sented in this part of the brainstem and it will be difficult to tease the influence of the specific and nonspecific mechanisms apart in future investigations. It may, indeed, be impossible to separate the two functions since it appears quite clear that normal ingestive behavior may well reflect the cooperative interaction of both, as so many theorists in this field believe.

Aversive Motivational States

A HISTORICAL PERSPECTIVE

As we saw in the preceding section of our discussion, the accumulation of knowledge often dismantles simple and convenient explanatory schemes long before it provides enough coherent insights to permit the construction of new and more sophisticated theories. In the case of appetitive motivation, some reconstruction has already begun even though the final form of the new theory is as yet uncertain. In the case of aversive motivational states, our knowledge is at a still more rudimentary stage. Here we still count as a major victory the discovery that global explanatory concepts such as "affect," "aggression," and so forth, are probably not very useful when one tries to understand how the intrinsic organization of the brain results in successful responses to aspects of the environment that are potentially destructive.

Not so many years ago, biological psychologists (as well as other scientists interested in the functional organization of the brain) talked about the neural circuit involved in "affective" reactions, a term which includes all escape, avoidance, and aggressive reactions to noxious or threatening stimuli and, by inference, all aversive motivational states. (Strictly speaking, such a circuit might also be an essential aspect of positive reactions to reward or events associated with it.) Most of the early "neurologizing" about the brain mechanisms that organize behavioral as well as experiential responses to noxious or threatening stimuli relied on anecdotal clinical observations or rather crude experimental manipulations, such as surgical removal of all cortical tissues or transection of the brainstem. The clinical observations indicated that patients with tumors or vascular lesions in the thalamus seemed incapable of controlling the most primitive of emotional responses, and this suggested to

Cannon and many of his contemporaries that this region might contain the "seat" of the emotions.[35] In accordance with the tenor of his times, Cannon suggested that the thalamus was normally under the control of "rational" influences from the cortex, which thus maintained a "check" on affective reactions. The meager experimental literature available at the time indicated that at least rudimentary behavioral responses to noxious stimuli could be observed as long as the hypothalamus was connected to the lower brainstem. Since the removal of all brain tissues rostral to the hypothalamus leaves higher mammals in a severely debilitated state by depriving them of nearly all neural mechanisms that process sensory information and organize voluntary responses to it, the behaviors appeared poorly directed and diffuse. This reinforced the a priori conviction of many contemporary investigators that something as complex and human as affect should be organized in phylogenetically young regions of the brain that reach prominence only in man and other complex mammals. Cannon's choice of the thalamus did not fit this requirement, and his proposal that the experience of emotions required cortical mechanisms conflicted with the widely held belief that the neocortical mantle subserved only complex, intellectual functions. Anatomical studies of the rostral connections of the hypothalamus provided a logically acceptable solution to the problem. According to Papez and others of that period, the hypothalamus was considered essential for the organization of behavioral responses to affect-inducing stimuli,[36] but the experience of affect or emotion was believed to depend on projections from the hypothalamus to the cingulate gyrus or other portions of the limbic system (which is made up mainly of relatively simple, phylogenetically older cortical tissue).

The advent of sophisticated experimental procedures has ever so gradually eroded this general picture even though the results of many of the early studies seemed to be in reasonable agreement

35. Walter B. Cannon, *Bodily Changes in Pain, Hunger, Fear, and Rage*, rev. ed. (New York: Appleton, 1929).

36. J. W. Papez, "A Proposed Mechanism of Emotion," *Archives of Neurology and Psychiatry* (*Chicago*) 38 (1937): 725-43; P. D. MacLean, "Psychosomatic Disease and the 'Visceral Brain'," *Psychosomatic Medicine* 11 (1949): 338-53.

with it. Discrete lesions of the ventromedial hypothalamus have been shown to result in sharply increased reactions to previously neutral or noxious stimulation (such as handling, electric shock, quinine adulteration of the diet, and so forth). Rats with VMH lesions also have been reported to learn avoidance responses faster than controls and to display more aggressive reactions to conspecifics.[37] Even today, these lesion effects are often discussed in terms of a possible increase in "affective reactivity" or similar terms. Electrical stimulation of many sites in the hypothalamus elicits apparently affective "rage," "flight," or "aggressive" reactions.[38] Stimulation of ventromedial hypothalamic sites often results in affective attack behavior in distinction to the effects of lateral hypothalamic stimulation, which have been characterized as "stalking" or "predatory" attack.[39] There is reason to believe that hypothalamic stimulation elicits not only behavioral responses appropriate to noxious or threatening stimulation but also related experiential states that we include in our definition of aversive motivational states. Rats readily learn and perform a variety of arbitrary instrumental behaviors (for example, wheel turning, lever pressing, and so forth) to terminate or avoid stimulation of many hypothalamic sites. Interestingly, they do not learn to avoid stimulation of many sites even though they work hard to turn it off, an indication that their subjective experience may have included positive components.[40]

When experimenters began to turn their attention to the limbic system, it quickly became apparent that lesions or electrical stimulation of many extrahypothalamic areas resulted in behavioral effects that were quite similar to those obtained from the hypothalamus itself. A partial list of the structures which have been implicated by this research includes the medial thalamus, septal area, cingulate cortex, frontal cortex, and amygdala. I do not be-

37. Sebastian P. Grossman, "Aggression, Avoidance, and Reaction to Novel Environments in Female Rats with Ventromedial Hypothalamic Lesions," *Journal of Comparative and Physiological Psychology* 78 (1972): 274-83.

38. Walter R. Hess, *The Functional Organization of the Diencephalon*, ed. John R. Hughes (New York: Grune and Stratton, 1957).

39. John P. Flynn, "Neural Aspects of Attack Behavior in Cats," *Annals of the New York Academy of Sciences* 159 (1969): 1008-1012.

40. Miller, "Motivational Effects of Brain-Stimulation and Drugs."

lieve that it would be instructive to present a necessarily cursory review of the voluminous and often contradictory experimental literatures which describe the effects of lesions or stimulation of each of these structures. Instead, I shall select one of them which has been of interest to me because its influences on many behaviors are remarkably similar to those of the hypothalamus itself. I hope to use the literature on the septal area as a model to illustrate how radically our thinking about the role of limbic system structures in the organization of behavioral responses to noxious or threatening stimuli has changed in the course of a few years. I shall not attempt to duplicate the organization used in our discussion of appetitive motivation because the distinction between specific and nonspecific motivational influences has not been a significant issue in the literature on limbic system influences on behavior. This does not so much reflect a disinterest in nonspecific motivation as the widely held belief that stimuli that induce affective reactions invariably increase general arousal, which thus becomes an integral and probably inseparable component of the neural state we must consider when we discuss aversive emotional responses. It is interesting to recall that similar views have recently become prominent in the literature on appetitive motivation.

A MODEL SYSTEM

The septum or parolfactory area occupies a pivotal position in the limbic system, serving as a relay station for pathways that interconnect the hippocampus, amygdala, hypothalamus, and habenula. It is widely believed that the septum becomes a functionless atrophic structure in the course of mammalian phylogenetic development, but this view has recently been challenged by investigators who have argued that the septum actually increases in size in higher primates and reaches its greatest development in man.[41]

Almost all of the research that is directly relevant to our discussion has been done in the albino rat. In this species, the septum is a sizable structure located just anterior to the thalamus and rostro-dorsal to the hypothalamic-preoptic region. Largely on

41. O. J. Andy and H. Stephan, "Septum Development in Primates," in *Advances in Behavioral Biology*, vol. 20, *The Septal Nuclei*, ed. J. F. DeFrance (New York: Plenum Press, 1976), pp. 3-36.

anatomical grounds, it is subdivided into medial, lateral, and triangular nuclei.

Experimental investigations of the behavioral functions of the septum were first undertaken about twenty years ago. The results of the initial experiments supported Papez's contention that this structure might serve as an important relay station in the limbic system circuit that mediates subjective affective reactions. The first fly in the proverbial ointment was discovered by McCleary in experiments which demonstrated that cats with septal lesions were less, rather than more, responsive to punishment.[42] On the basis of this observation and reports by others which indicated that the septum exerted inhibitory effects on various autonomic functions, McCleary proposed that the septum might be the source of general inhibitory influences on behavior. His prediction that septal lesions would have facilitatory effects on all behaviors which are inhibited as a result of nonreward or punishment resulted in a great deal of interest and a veritable flood of reports of related experimental work. In the fifteen years since McCleary's initial report, just about every behavior and/or psychological function imaginable has been related to this nodal point in the limbic system, and it has become increasingly clear that no single functional disorder, affect-related or not, can meaningfully account for the bewildering spectrum of behavioral change that has been documented after septal lesions. I have recently reviewed this literature and some of my own contributions to it and shall not attempt to duplicate this effort here.[43] A brief summary of the principal effects of septal lesions, intraseptal drug injections, and surgical transections of its connections with other portions of the limbic system may, however, help us understand the current "state of the art" (a term which is particularly apt in this context).

More or less complete destruction of the septum of the rat produces rage (that is, the animal objects vigorously to normal han-

42. Robert A. McCleary, "Response Modulating Functions of the Limbic System: Initiation and Suppression," in *Progress in Physiological Psychology* (New York: Academic Press, 1966), pp. 210-72.

43. Sebastian P. Grossman, "Behavioral Functions of the Septum: A Re-Analysis," in *Advances in Behavioral Biology*, vol. 20 (1976) *The Septal Nuclei*, pp. 361-422.

dling), increases its propensity to kill mice, and the probability of an attack on a member of the same species when both animals are exposed to painful shock (shock-induced, or "reflexive" fighting). These effects are compatible with a lowered threshold of responding to painful shock, bright lights, loud noises, and unpleasant tastes. Much to everyone's surprise, all of these quite dramatic changes in behavior have turned out to be only short-lived in contrast to the others on our list. Because aggressive reactions and possibly related responses to strong stimuli are entirely normal two to three weeks after surgery (and thereafter), it appears very unlikely that a general increase in affective reactivity or even plain irritability can be postulated to help us understand other persistent effects of the lesion.

One of the earliest reports of the behavioral effects of septal lesions noted a marked facilitation of acquisition of a shuttle box conditioned avoidance response (CAR). (In the shuttle box, the rat is trained to move from one compartment to another in order to avoid an electrical foot shock delivered through the floor of the compartment. Neither compartment is permanently safe.) This observation has been replicated in many species as soon as five days after surgery and as late as several months afterwards. A simple interpretation of the effect is, unfortunately, impossible because the facilitatory effects of septal lesions appear to be peculiar to this rather common test paradigm. In a variety of other avoidance learning situations, rats with septal lesions typically learn slower than intact controls. This is true even in the shuttle box when the conditions of the experiment are arranged such that the animal is required to learn to avoid painful shock by always running from compartment A to compartment B (rather than by leaving either compartment when the conditioned stimulus is presented as is typical of the shuttle box paradigm).

Another of the very first reports of behavioral dysfunctions after septal lesions has withstood the test of time and frequent replication. Rats with septal lesions acquire and perform a previously learned conditioned emotional response (CER) less well than controls. In the initial studies, relatively primitive measures of behavioral disruption (for example, "freezing," defecation, urination, and vocalization) in response to stimuli (for example, a light or tone) that had been associated with painful shock were used to demonstrate this effect. However, it has held up well in later more sophisticated experiments where the disruption of an ongoing instrumental behavior (such as lever pressing) provided a more objective measure of the CER.

This brings us to the most baffling component of the "septal lesion syndrome"—the sharply reduced response to punishment which is such a prominent feature of animals with septal lesions. The effect tends to be strongest immediately after surgery but is clearly in evidence during the initial postoperative weeks when the animals appear hyperreactive and irritable with respect to all sensory modalities, including shock-induced pain which is used as a punishment in these experiments. There are some indications that the magnitude of the "passive avoidance deficit," as the reduced reactivity to punishment has often been called, may be a function of the amount of preoperative as well as postoperative experience with unpunished responding, but this hardly helps elucidate the nature of the deficit.

The impaired response to punishment indicates that animals with septal lesions may find it difficult to withhold potentially rewarded behaviors. McCleary believed this to be the result of a loss of inhibitory control over punished and nonrewarded behaviors. In recent years, over-responding has been observed in a variety of experimental paradigms which share only the contingency that high rates of behavior are either inefficient (that is, not rewarded) or punished. Classic examples are paradigms which reward instrumental behavior (typically lever pressing) on intermittent schedules of reinforcement. Normal rats which are trained to press a lever for rewards that are delivered according to a fixed interval (FI) schedule (only lever presses that occur at a predetermined and fixed interval after the last reinforcement are rewarded) rapidly learn not to respond immediately after a reward is received and to increase their response rate gradually as the end of the programmed delay period approaches. Rats with septal lesions appear incapable of this simple adjustment to the reward contingencies—they respond at a high rate throughout the delay interval. Even when the conditions are changed so that responses occurring before the programmed delay not only fail to procure rewards but also reset the delay timer (a reward condition known as "differential reward of low rates of responding," or DRL), rats with septal lesions overrespond and earn few if any rewards.

Animals with septal lesions also continue to respond during extinction when rewards are no longer offered and find it difficult to reverse their search strategies (for example, go left instead of right, select black instead of white) when the reward contingencies are reversed in simple discrimination problems. These findings led McCleary to suggest that septal lesions result in "perseveration" in previously rewarded behaviors. Some years ago, my associates and I tested this notion in an experimental paradigm that required the rat to: (a) press a lever in one compartment; (b) wait thirty seconds or longer; (c) run down a runway to a second compartment and press another lever there; and (d) repeat the sequence, ad libitum. The answer we obtained was unequivocal—rats with septal lesions quite specifically failed to inhibit the next correct response and did not perseverate in the behavior that was most recently rewarded.

The focus of most of the research in this field has been on the apparent loss of inhibitory control over nonrewarded or punished responding. However, rats with septal lesions also respond more avidly than controls when each response is reinforced or when rewards are scheduled according to intermittent schedules such as fixed ratio (every n^{th} response is rewarded) that preferentially reinforce high rates of responding. In these instances, it is difficult to see how a loss of inhibitory control might be responsible for the unusual behavior of rats with septal lesion. Other explanatory concepts, such as increased incentive motivation,[44] have been proposed to account for the apparently general increase in positively reinforced behavior.

Some, but not all, septal lesions produce hyperdipsia which is not secondary to impaired pituitary function and unrelated to prandial requirements since food intake is normal. (The latter is, itself, an interesting exception to the rule that septal lesions increase

44. John A. Harvey and Howard F. Hunt, "Effects of Septal Lesions on Thirst in the Rat as Indicated by Water Consumption and Operant Responding for Water Reward," *Journal of Comparative and Physiological Psychology* 59 (1965): 49-56.

the rate of most behaviors.) Septal lesions do produce finickiness and excessive food- or fluid-consumption when the diet or water supply is sweet or slightly salty but lower than normal intake when they are quinine adulterated. Rats with septal lesions also display a peculiar metabolic disturbance which appears to reset the set-point of body weight. Although food intake remains normal, body weight falls precipitously during the first few days after surgery and remains depressed for the rest of the animal's life.

As more and more behavioral dysfunctions were added to the list, it became increasingly difficult to account for the septal lesion syndrome in terms of unitary concepts such as increased affect, decreased inhibitory control, impaired response to punishment and nonreward or increased incentive motivation. Even various combinations of these and related hypotheses fall short of explaining the peculiar constellation of behavioral change seen after septal lesions. A number of investigators therefore began to suspect some years ago that the septal area might contain a number of different neural mechanisms which exert a variety of possibly unrelated functions.

The most straightforward tests of this hypothesis, involving lesions restricted to selected aspects of the septal area, have had only limited success. Many of the behavioral effects of large septal lesions (for example, increased irritability and aggressive reactions, facilitated shuttle box avoidance, hyperdipsia) are seen after damage to many different subdivisions of the area. Others (for example, decreased responsiveness to nonreward or punishment) appear to be related more selectively to some regions, but it has been difficult to relate this to known structural subdivisions, or specific projections to or from the area.

My associates and I have had some success with intraseptal microinjections of neurotransmitters and related blocking agents. In most of these studies, the effects of agonists and antagonists of the cholinergic family were investigated because peripheral injections of anticholinergic compounds produce effects on many behaviors that are quite similar to those seen after septal lesions. Our investigations produced some unambiguous dissociations as well as a few as yet unresolved mysteries. Among the former is the observation that intraseptal injections of anticholinergic compounds (such as atropine) faithfully reproduce the peculiar pattern of effects on avoidance behavior (facilitation in the shuttle box and inhibition in other situations) but no signs of rage, increased reactivity to shock or other stimuli, or change in intra- or interspecific aggressive reactions.

When we asked about the effects of these injections on reactivity to punishment or nonreward, it rapidly became apparent that the response to these two overtly similar experimental procedures may be influenced by different components of the septum. Intraseptal atropine injections produced clearly selective "disinhibitory" effects on nonrewarded lever pressing during periods of extinction and fixed interval reinforcement conditions but no effect on punished responding during other segments of the same experiment (even though all three conditions were presented repeatedly during each daily test). Since then, we have replicated the atropine effect (or, rather, lack thereof) in other punishment situations. The differential effects of these injections on avoidance acquisition and punished responding are particularly interesting because they disprove an ingenious explanation of the paradoxical effects of septal lesions on shuttle box and other avoidance behaviors. According to a suggestion first made by McCleary, animals with septal lesions might perform well in the shuttle box not because of any change in mechanisms specifically related to CAR acquisition, but because of their "passive avoidance deficit" which helps them learn that shock can be avoided in this situation by returning to the compartment where they have most recently been punished or threatened.

As I indicated above, septal lesions increase responding in two overtly quite different test paradigms. In the DRL situation, high rates result in the loss of potentially available rewards. In the unsignaled avoidance paradigm (where the passage of time itself becomes the conditioned stimulus for avoidance responses), responding more often than the schedule requires is not rewarded and wastes effort just as overresponding in the DRL paradigm does. Because the two tests involve quite different motivational states, the similar effects of septal lesions are often cited as evidence of the pervasiveness of the septal influence on inhibitory control. The results of a simple experiment from my laboratory disabused us of such simplistic thinking. In a variation of our normal drug experiments, we first demonstrated overresponding in both situations after systemic injections of an anticholinergic agent. When we then made septal lesions (which themselves increased responding in both paradigms) the drug effect was abolished in the appetitive DRL but unchanged in the avoidance test.

I would like to end our discussion of the behavioral functions of the septum on a positive note and present the results of a recent series of experiments from my laboratory which suggest that we may yet succeed in our quest. These experiments are predicated on the fact that lesions in several anatomically related areas of the brain reproduce selected aspects of the septal lesion syndrome. The septal area is invaded by four major neural pathways which consist mainly of fibers of passage but also contain axons that synapse in or arise from the septal area. The fornix (FX) carries afferent and efferent connections between the subiculum and hypothalamus and between the hippocampus and septum; the medial forebrain bundle (MFB) contains fibers that interconnect the hypothalamus and lower brainstem with the septum and other forebrain structures; the stria terminalis (ST) interconnects the amygdala with the septum and hypothalamus and the stria terminales (thalami) (SM) provides a path between the amygdala, septum, and habenula nuclei of the thalamus. Lesions in the septum undoubtedly interrupt some components of all of these pathways and it seemed important to discover whether specific aspects of the septal lesion syndrome might be due to the interruption of any one of these connections. Using the wire knife described briefly in our discussion of appetitive motivation, we set out to transect each of the four pathways outside the septum itself so that there would be no direct damage to its cellular structure.

We began our investigation by comparing the effects of transections of the fornix or medial forebrain bundle with those of septal lesions. In the shuttle box, both cuts reproduced the facilitatory effects of the lesion, suggesting that this effect may be due to an interruption of hypothalamo-septo-hippocampal connections, which, according to our pharmacological studies, may have a cholinergic synapse in the septum. Fornix transection but not interruption of the MFB reproduced the facilitatory effects of septal lesion on activity—an interesting dissociation because it indicates that activity changes do not significantly contribute to the facilitation of avoidance behavior in the shuttle box as a number of investigators have suggested. We were delighted to find further that neither fornicotomy nor MFB transection produced the inhibitory effects of septal lesions on the acquisition of other avoidance behaviors. This puts to rest a number of hypotheses which have tried to account for the facilitatory and inhibitory effects of septal lesions on avoidance behavior in terms of a common neural dysfunction.

To clarify some of the issues which were raised in the context of our pharmacological studies, we examined the effects of our fornix and MFB cuts on the acquisition of an unsignalled avoidance response in a shuttle box. Rats with septal lesions learn this task faster than controls but perform it inefficiently because they emit potential avoidance responses much more frequently than necessary. We were intrigued to find that fornicotomy but not MFB transection replicated this pattern of effects. To appreciate our interest in this observation, one must remember that both cuts produced comparable facilitatory effects on shuttle box CAR and neither affected the acquisition of other signaled avoidance behaviors.

Since we had, so far, been unable to duplicate the typical inhibitory effects of septal lesions on other avoidance behaviors, we examined the effects of selective cuts across the stria terminalis (ST) or stria medullares (SM) on the acquisition of our standard "one-way" CAR and shuttle box avoidance. Neither of these cuts affected the acquisition of shuttle box CARs. Stria terminalis transections also failed to affect learning in our one-way situation but cutting the stria medullares resulted in unambiguous inhibitory effects that were as severe as any we have ever seen after septal lesions.

Next, we attempted to elucidate the neural pathways that might be responsible for the characteristic effects of septal lesions on reactivity to punishment. This component of the septal lesion syndrome turned out to be elusive. No change was seen after transection of the fornix, MFB, or stria medullares. Only when we cut the stria terminalis, did we find a severe "passive avoidance deficit."

This turns out to be a pleasant confirmation of earlier reports of similar deficits after lesions in the amygdala (which gives rise to the ST).

The very clear separation of the pathways that affect shuttle box avoidance, "one-way" avoidance, and reactivity to punishment, reinforced our belief that quite different functional disturbances appear to be responsible for the apparently paradoxical effects of septal lesions on various types of avoidance behaviors. Clearly, simplistic hypotheses in terms of increased reactivity to noxious stimulation or the threat thereof are no longer tenable.

The next problem area which we examined was the pervasive effects of lesion in the septum on instrumental responding in situations where high rates of behavior are not rewarded. In the initial experiment of this series, we observed that fornicotomy but not transection of the MFB replicated the disinhibitory effects of the lesion in our 2-lever DRL paradigm. Interruption of the ST had no effect and transection of the stria medullares produced only a slight increase in the frequency of anticipatory errors but no change in overall efficiency. That the inhibitory functions of the septum which influence reactions to nonreward may be mediated specifically by the fornix was further suggested by the results of a second experiment using food rewards scheduled according to fixed interval contingencies. In this test, only fornicotomy resulted in a persistent increase in responding, both during the normally quiet postreinforcement pause and during later normally active segments of the interreward interval.

Lastly, we turned our attention to appetitive behaviors. We were interested to find that only MFB transections which interrupt the connections of the septum with the hypothalamus and lower brainstem produced hyperdipsia and the peculiar weight loss typically seen after septal lesions. Both MFB and fornix transections increased the intake of highly palatable foods and the rate of an instrumental response that was continuously reinforced with very palatable rewards.

What, then, is the bottom line to all of these experiments? As I indicated in my introduction to this section, this area of research lags behind in the sense that we have essentially no viable hypotheses concerning the action and interaction of brain mechanisms that organize aversive motivational states. It has been heuristically useful to assume that they exist because many behaviors represent learned or innate responses to painful or potentially harmful aspects of the environment and we "know" introspectively that these overt behaviors do not occur in vacuo but are accompanied, at least in man, by often powerful motivational states. Since much of the behavior which we study in laboratory tests of aggressive and avoidance responses are not simple reflexive reactions to pain but often complex and arbitrary instrumental acts which avoid a potentially painful stimulus, it appears plausible that aversive motivational states exist in infrahuman mammals. What I intended to illustrate in my brief discussion of the septum, is the presently rather obvious fact that we know very little about the neural mechanisms which organize these motivational states. Worse than that, it appears that even our primitive hypotheses do not withstand critical experimental tests. I have concentrated on the septum because it has been the subject of a relatively enormous amount of experimental attention in recent years. Other portions of the limbic system and associated neocortical and subcortical structures have not, as yet, been studied in quite as much detail, but I could have made essentially the same points with regard to any one of them. Each and every one appears to exercise a broad spectrum of influences on behavior that appear to be the result of aversive motivational states. Yet, when one takes a closer look, the deceptively coherent and simple picture breaks apart, various components of the overall syndrome (of lesions, stimulation, and so forth) increasingly assume an independent existence of their own which is less and less compatible with whatever explanatory scheme the investigator may have had in mind when he started. Avoidance deficits and apparently general disinhibitory effects similar to those seen after septal lesions are common throughout the limbic system but our experience with septal lesions as well as our own and similar work of others on other structures indicate that one must be very cautious in interpreting such effects.

In one sense, this is a particularly difficult time to write about the organization of aversive motivational states in the brain because we have torn apart essentially all of the theoretical models which seemed reasonable only a few short years ago and have not yet gained enough new insights to construct better ones. Yet, this may also be a particularly instructive point in the history of our science for a closer look at the plethora of experimental data because it may be time to begin the reconstruction process. I hope that my brief review of the situation has provided the reader with enough ingredients for some constructive thought.

CHAPTER V

Language and the Brain: Relationship of Localization of Language Function to the Acquisition and Loss of Various Aspects of Language

KENNETH M. HEILMAN

Introduction

The purpose of this chapter is to provide the educator with some fundamental understanding of the neuropsychological processes underlying language. Although educators are not likely to be called on to use this knowledge in a clinical setting, I believe an understanding of the neuropsychological processes underlying behavior is essential for teachers. Learning disorders are common problems, and understanding how the brain works has helped investigators develop theories and investigative paradigms that will uncover the pathophysiology of these problems.[1] Understanding brain mechanisms has led to the development of predictive tests that allow early intervention.[2] Lastly, an understanding of the brain mechanisms underlying language may also enable educators to develop educational methods that best use the innate capability of language-processing systems of both normal and abnormal children and adults.

METHODS OF CONDUCTING BRAIN STUDIES

Before any discussion of brain mechanisms underlying language, some comments should be made on the methodology used to study

1. Martha B. Denckla and Rita G. Rudel, "Naming of Object-Drawings by Dyslexic and Other Learning Disabled Children," *Brain and Language* 3 (1976): 1-15.

2. Paul Satz, Eileen Fennell, and Carol Reilly, "Predictive Validity of Six Neurodiagnostic Tests: A Decision Theory Analysis," *Journal of Consulting and Clinical Psychology* 34 (1970): 375-81.

the brain and the implications that can be drawn from these studies. In general, there are two major methods of studying the brain. First, one can vary the stimuli or the reinforcement and observe how manipulation of these variables alter behavior. Alternatively, one can keep the stimuli and reinforcement constant and alter the brain in animals or await natural alterations in man to observe changes in behavior. In general, brain mechanisms underlying language can be studied using either or both of these methods. The former approach can give information about how the brain functions as a unit, but it cannot for the most part provide information as to what specific portion of the brain is responsible for certain processes.

Lashley trained rats to run mazes.[3] To learn which portion of the brain was responsible for mediating this behavior he destroyed different portions of their brains. Lashley found no specific area that when ablated produced a loss of memory for these mazes, but he found that the more brain he ablated the poorer the rodent's performance was. He therefore concluded that specific functions were not processed in a localized area of the brain but that the brain works by mass action. If one accepts Lashley's hypothesis, there would be little need to perform studies that attempt to ascertain which portions of the brain perform certain functions. Even before he made his hypothesis of mass action, it was known that more than 90 percent of right-handers with a loss of language from a stroke have their stroke in their left hemisphere.[4] The observation that in right-handers language is processed in the left hemisphere is inconsistent with Lashley's theory of mass action. In addition to Broca's work,[5] there is overwhelming evidence that Lashley's theory of mass action cannot be applied to human brains.

Since particular portions of the brain may take part in mediating specific language functions, it is important to find a paradigm that allows us to study the particular areas of the human brain. Primarily, the two methods used to study the language area are brain stimulation and ablation. Since the language areas of the brain contain

3. Karl Spencer Lashley, *Brain Mechanisms and Intelligence: A Quantitative Study of Injuries to the Brain* (New York: Hafner Publishing Co., 1963).

4. Paul Broca, "Localisation des fonctions cérébrales siège du langage articule," *Bulletin of Social Anthropology* 4 (1863): 200-204.

5. Ibid.

complex neuronal networks, gross surface stimulation does not induce a physiologic process but rather interrupts ongoing activity and thereby produces speech arrest. Although brain stimulation has been used to study language,[6] most of our knowledge of the neurological basis of language is based on ablation studies.

Since there are no laboratory animals in which language can be studied, investigators have had to observe language in patients with diseases that have destroyed brain tissue (for example, strokes, tumors). The investigators have noted which areas were destroyed (as determined by radiological and postmortem studies) and the type of language disturbance manifested by these patients. From their observations they attempt to induce the function of the damaged area. Hughlings Jackson noted that when an area of brain is destroyed the patient's behavior is not being caused by the damaged area but rather by the remainder of the brain, which is performing in the absence of the ablated area.[7] The function of an ablated region is the difference between normal language function and the abnormal function seen after a lesion in that area. Conclusions based on this formula are indirect but even so the formula provides the best method currently available to study the neurological base of language. Most of the statements made in this chapter will be based on this experimental paradigm.

This chapter will explore many of the basic aphasic syndromes and use the knowledge gained from their study to help build a model of how the brain processes language. This diagrammatic model will be mainly heuristic.

BASIC ANATOMY

Since this chapter will deal with anatomic structures, it may be worthwhile to introduce some anatomic landmarks for the reader who is unfamiliar with neuroanatomy.

In general, the lower portions of the human brain are concerned with processing and programming motor and vegetative functions (for example, respiration, fluid balance). The areas that are im-

6. Wilder Penfield and Lamar Roberts, *Speech and Brain-Mechanisms* (Princeton, N.J.: Princeton University Press, 1959).

7. John Hughlings Jackson, in *Selected Writings of John Hughlings Jackson*, ed. James Taylor (London: Hodder and Stoughton, 1932).

portant in processing language and other higher functions are in the two cerebral hemispheres, each of which has four major lobes: frontal, parietal, temporal, and occipital (see fig. 1). Most of the

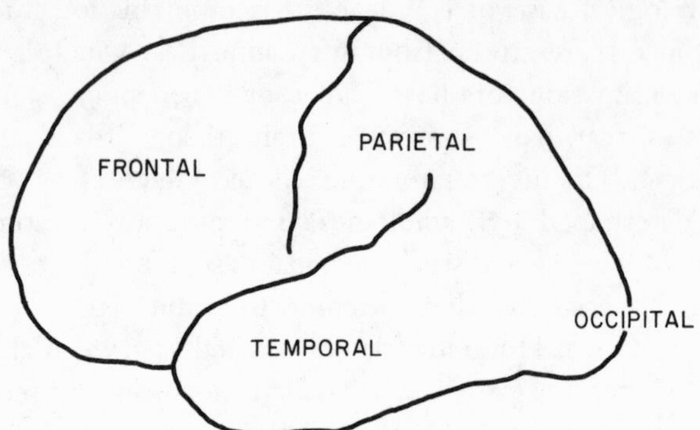

FIG. 1. Lateral view of brain demonstrating major lobes

nerve cells and many of the connections between cells that are close to one another are near the surface of the cerebral hemisphere, which is called the cerebral cortex (see fig. 2). There are several

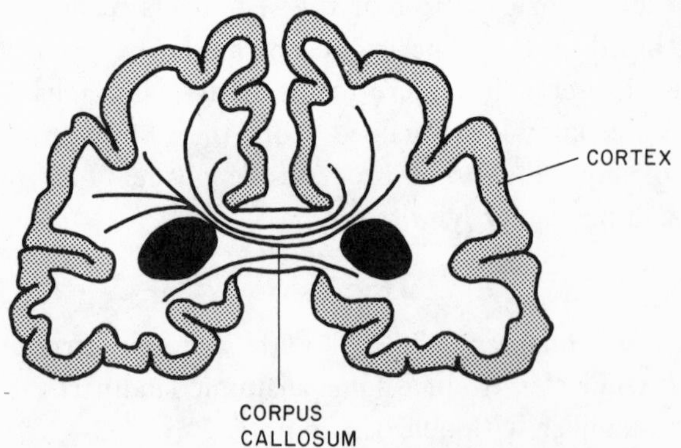

FIG. 2. Coronal section of brain demonstrating cerebral cortex and corpus callosum

connections between the right and left hemispheres. The major connection is the corpus callosum (see fig. 2). Each of the lobes has an area (primary projection area) that contains cells which either receive sensory input or send motor output. The temporal lobe receives auditory input, the occipital lobe visual input, and

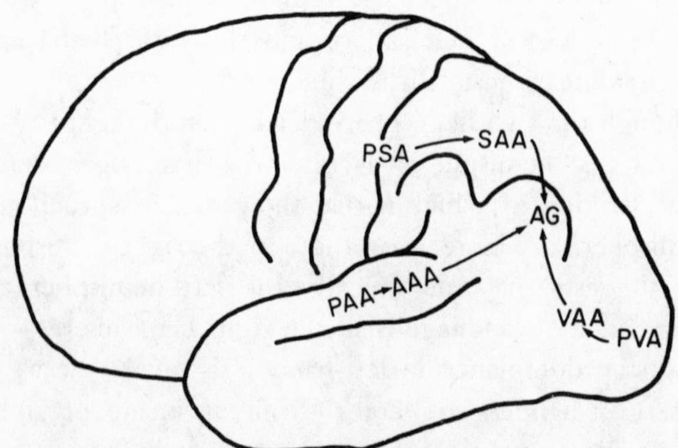

FIG. 3. Left lateral view of brain demonstrating corticocortical projections. PSA, primary somesthetic area; SAA, somesthetic association area; PAA, primary auditory area; AAA, auditory association area; PVA, primary visual area; VAA, visual association area; AG, angular gyrus.

the parietal lobes tactile and kinesthetic input (see fig. 3). These primary areas project only to their association areas, and all these association areas project to the region of the inferior parietal lobule (angular and supramarginal gyrus), as shown in fig. 3.

HANDEDNESS AND LANGUAGE

Broca noted that of eight aphasic stroke patients who were right-handed all had their lesions in the left hemisphere.[8] This suggested to Broca that the left hemisphere of right-handers mediates language. Although there are cases of right-handed patients becoming aphasic from a right-hemisphere lesion, more than 95 percent of right-handers mediate language in their left hemisphere.[9] In right-handers, while the left hemisphere is mediating language the right hemisphere mediates visuospatial,[10] emotional,[11] and other non-

8. Broca, "Localisation des fonctions cérébrales siège du langage articule."

9. Henri Hècaen and Julian de Ajuriaguerra, *Left Handedness: Manual Superiority and Cerebral Dominance*, trans. Eric Ponder (New York: Grune and Stratton, 1964).

10. Robert J. Joynt and M. N. Goldstein, "Minor Cerebral Hemisphere," in *Advances in Neurology*, vol. 7, ed. W. J. Friedlander (New York: Raven Press, 1975), pp. 147-83.

11. Kenneth M. Heilman, Robert Scholes, and Robert T. Watson, "Affective Agnosia with Disturbed Comprehension of Affective Speech," *Journal of Neurology, Neurosurgery, and Psychiatry* 38 (1975): 69-72.

language processes.[12] Bogen views the left hemisphere as the linear, analytic, and logical hemisphere and the right hemisphere as the holistic, nonlinear, gestalt hemisphere.[13]

Although the two hemispheres have been thought to be anatomic mirror images, hemispheric asymmetries have been demonstrated, the most striking of which is that the posterior speech areas of the left hemisphere are larger than those of the right hemisphere.[14] This finding suggests that anatomically the left hemisphere may be a better decoder of language than the right hemisphere.

Language dominance in left-handers is not as clear as in right-handers. Left-handers are not the mirror image of right-handers. Studies of the prevalence of aphasia after stroke in left-handers and in right-handers have demonstrated that aphasia occurs almost twice as often in left-handed patients.[15] This finding suggests that almost twice the amount of brain tissue is mediating language and that in some left-handers both hemispheres are probably processing language. Left-handers, however, are not a homogeneous group and some left-handers probably have only one hemisphere, left or right, that processes language. It is not known whether left-handers are anatomically asymmetrical or whether there are advantages or disadvantages to having less hemispheric specialization.

Aphasias: Language Disorders

BROCA'S APHASIA

The modern era of aphasiology was initiated by Broca's observations of a 51-year-old man who had lost the ability to articulate words and could utter only the word "tan." [16] Comprehension of

12. Brenda Milner, "Laterality Effects in Audition," in *Interhemispheric Relations and Cerebral Dominance*, ed. Vernon B. Mountcastle (Baltimore, Md.: Johns Hopkins Press, 1962), pp. 177-95.

13. Joseph Bogen, "The Other Side of the Brain, I and II," *Bulletin of the Los Angeles Neurological Society* 34 (1970): 73-105, 135-162.

14. Norman Geschwind and Walter Levitsky, "Human Brain: Left-Right Asymmetries in Temporal Speech Region," *Science* 161 (1968): 186-7.

15. I. Gloning et al., "Comparison of Verbal Behavior in Right-handed and Non-Right-handed Patients with Anatomically Verified Lesions of One Hemisphere," *Cortex* 5 (1969): 43-52.

16. Paul Broca, "Nouvelle observation d'aphémie produite par un lésion de la moitié postérieure des deuxième et troisième circonvolutions frontales," *Bulletin de la Société Anatomique de Paris* 36 (1861): 398-407.

spoken and written language had remained intact. On postmortem examination of the patient, a lesion was located in the anterior sylvian region. The center of the lesion was in the third frontal convolution, which has been termed "Broca's area" (see fig. 4).

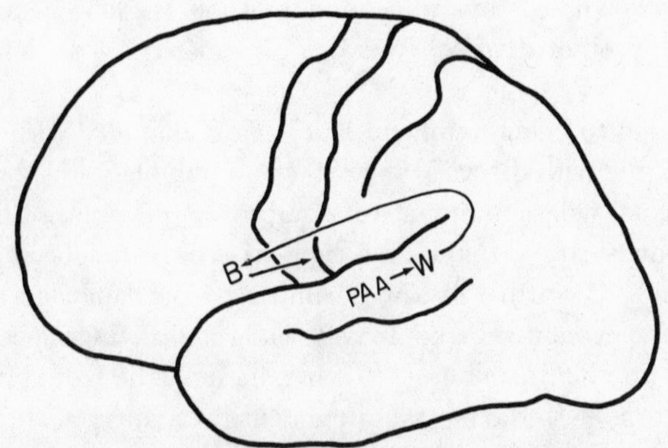

FIG. 4. Left lateral view of brain demonstrating Wernicke's reflex arc. PAA, primary auditory area; W, Wernicke's area; B, Broca's area.

Since comprehension and memory for words was unaffected, Broca thought that this patient had lost the memory for the skilled movements used in expression. Subsequently, he described additional patients with lesions involving the same area of the frontal lobes.[17] Although Goldstein[18] and Mohr[19] have argued that lesions restricted to Broca's area usually produce only a transient dysfluency and that the syndrome called "Broca's aphasia" is usually produced by large lesions, Broca's observation that lesions in the left anterior sylvian region produce a nonfluent aphasia has been firmly established.[20]

Hughlings Jackson noted that patients with nonfluent speech,

17. Broca, "Localisation des fonctions cérébrales siège du langage articule."

18. Kurt Goldstein, *Language and Language Disturbances: Aphasic Symptom Complexes and Their Significance for Medicine and Theory of Language* (New York: Grune and Stratton, 1948).

19. Jay P. Mohr, "Broca's Area and Broca's Aphasia," in *Studies in Neurolinguistics*, vol. 1, ed. Haiganoosh Whitaker and Harry A. Whitaker (New York: Academic Press, 1976), pp. 201-32.

20. D. Frank Benson, "Fluency in Aphasia: Correlation with Radioactive Brain Scan Localization," *Cortex* 3 (1967): 373-94.

similar to that reported by Broca, could use involuntary speech but had difficulty with what he termed "propositional" speech.[21] For example, patients with Broca's aphasia often will curse fluently, sing the words to songs, and count (all nonpropositional speech). Hughlings Jackson postulated that involuntary or nonpropositional speech was being mediated by the nondominant (right) hemisphere, whereas propositional speech was being mediated by the left hemisphere.

In addition to being nonfluent and having difficulty with articulation, patients with Broca's aphasia are agrammatic.[22] Typically, these patients will communicate using only major lexical items (that is, nouns and verbs). This type of speech has been termed "telegraphic" speech because it is similar to the language used in telegrams for economy's sake. It was thought that since speech was so difficult for the Broca's aphasic when he spoke he would pick the word or words with the most content. Zurif, Caramazza, and Myerson, however, asked Broca's aphasics to perform a task that was similar to diagramming sentences.[23] Although the patients did not have to speak to perform this task, they diagrammed sentences agrammatically, which suggested that these aphasics had a central defect in syntactic processing. Heilman and Scholes presented Broca's aphasics with sentences where comprehension depended on their understanding major lexical items and syntax.[24] We used a forced-choice paradigm that allowed an error analysis. Broca's aphasics often poorly comprehended the sentences because they were unable to understand syntactic relationships. Unlike patients with Wernicke's aphasia (to be discussed below), who frequently did not comprehend major lexical items, patients with Broca's aphasia did not have any difficulty with this portion of the task. My colleagues and I have also demonstrated that these patients have

21. Hughlings Jackson, *Selected Writings.*

22. Theodore S. Weisenberg and Katherine L. McBride, *Aphasia* (New York: Hafner Press, 1964).

23. Edgar G. Zurif, Alphonzo Caramazza, and R. Myerson, "Grammatical Judgments of Agrammatic Aphasics," *Neuropsychologia* 10 (1972): 405-18.

24. Kenneth M. Heilman and Robert J. Scholes, "The Nature of Comprehension Errors in Broca's Conduction and Wernicke's Aphasics," *Cortex* 12 (1976): 258-65.

a defect of immediate memory which can also interfere with their comprehension of long and complex sentences.[25] We have proposed that immediate memory is dependent on verbal rehearsal. Broca's aphasics have a decreased ability to repeat or rehearse and therefore have a reduced immediate memory.[26]

WERNICKE'S APHASIA

About a decade after Broca published his papers, Wernicke published a monograph in which he confirmed Broca's observations and in addition postulated that there is a posterior speech area.[27] Patients with lesions in the posterior portion of the superior temporal gyrus (see fig. 4) could neither understand language nor repeat. Wernicke thought that this area, which is adjacent to the auditory area, contains memories of the sound images of words and is important for the decoding of language and for repetition. Patients with Wernicke's aphasia frequently speak in jargon that contains neologisms (new words) and paraphasic errors (wrong words or words where the wrong phonemes are used). Two hypotheses have been proposed to explain the paraphasia associated with posterior lesions. One is that output of normal language requires feedback (servosystem) and patients with Wernicke's aphasia cannot monitor themselves. The second hypothesis states that Broca's area is important in encoding language because it contains the engrams (memory traces) required to program the muscle sequences used in phonemic production but, in order to encode correct language, Broca's area needs direction from Wernicke's area, which contains engrams of word images. Without this direction Broca's area encodes the wrong phonemic sequences.

Support for the latter hypothesis comes from the observation of other patients with a posterior aphasia (conduction aphasia), who are paraphasic but are still able to comprehend language and their own paraphasic errors.

25. Kenneth M. Heilman, Robert J. Scholes, and Robert T. Watson, "Defects of Immediate Memory in Broca's and Conduction Aphasia," *Brain and Language* 3 (1976): 201-8.

26. Ibid.

27. Carl Wernicke, *Der aphasische Symptomenkomplex* (Breslau: Cohn and Weigart, 1874).

Wernicke's aphasia is manifested not only by paraphasic language (with poor comprehension and repetition) but frequently also by logorrhea (excessive verbal output) and anosoagnosia (denial of illness). Both of these latter defects are probably caused because these patients do not understand themselves.

Although patients with Wernicke's aphasia are unable to name objects, Wernicke himself noted that some patients with this disorder were able to recognize objects and knew what the objects were used for. Some of the patients could also communicate through gesture. Wernicke therefore thought that some of them had intact concepts.

CONDUCTION APHASIA

So far, I have described two language areas: Broca's, which contains the memories for movement needed to program muscles for speech output, and Wernicke's, which contains the auditory memories of word images needed to decode language and also needed to guide Broca's area so that it programs muscles to produce the intended words. According to Wernicke, a lesion between these areas would disconnect the decoder from the encoder but leave both intact.[28] Patients with such a lesion should therefore be able to comprehend because the decoding process is intact. Because Broca's area is also intact, they should be able to encode phonemic sequences; however, since the center of auditory word images (Wernicke's area) is disconnected from Broca's area, this area of posterior speech cannot guide Broca's area in producing program sequences that will produce an intended word. Therefore, patients with this disorder, like the Wernicke's aphasics, are paraphasic and have difficulty with repetition. Unlike the Wernicke's aphasics, these patients can decode and they comprehend their own errors and therefore are not logorrheic or anosognostic.

A bundle of nerve fibers (arcuate fasciculus) goes from the posterior to the anterior region of the brain. Konorski and coworkers postulated that this bundle carried information from Wernicke's to Broca's area and is interrupted in conduction aphasia.[29] Although

28. Ibid.

29. J. Konorski, H. Kozniewska, and L. Stepien, "Analysis of Symptoms and Cerebral Localization of Audio-Verbal Aphasia," *Proceedings of the Seventh International Congress of Neurology* 2 (1961): 234-36.

there are lesions that interrupt this bundle, they are almost always associated with cortical lesions of the supramarginal gyrus (see fig. 4).[30]

The conduction aphasia syndrome, in which the patient has fluent paraphasic speech and difficulty with repetition but can comprehend, is most commonly caused by lesions in Wernicke's area rather than by lesions of the arcuate fasciculus or overlying cortex.[31] Since Wernicke's is normally the area that is important in decoding language, decoding in conduction aphasia is probably being performed by another portion of the brain. Kleist proposed that in these cases the right hemisphere may be mediating language.[32] Barbiturates injected into the left hemisphere through the left carotid artery of right-handers anesthetize the left hemisphere and induce speech arrest. Injection into the right hemisphere via the right carotid artery does not produce speech arrest. Kinsbourne injected the left carotid artery of right-handed conduction aphasics who had left-hemisphere lesions.[33] There was no speech arrest. When he injected the right carotid artery of these patients, their speech was arrested, which suggested that it was the right hemisphere that was mediating language and was producing the symptoms seen in conduction aphasia.

PURE-WORD DEAFNESS

Patients who have pure-word deafness are not able to comprehend spoken language or repeat. They are able to comprehend written language, speak normally, and name objects. Although this describes a deaf person, Kussmaul noted that these patients have normal hearing.[34] Many of them can identify meaningful nonlanguage sounds.[35] Lichtheim postulated that patients with pure-

30. D. Frank Benson et al., "Conduction Aphasia," *Archives of Neurology* 28 (1973): 339-46.

31. Ibid.

32. Karl Kleist, *Gehirnpathologie* (Leipzig: Barth, 1934).

33. Marcel Kinsbourne, "The Minor Cerebral Hemisphere as a Source of Aphasic Speech," *Archives of Neurology* 25 (1971): 302-6.

34. Adolf Kussmaul, *Die Störungen der Sprache* (Leipzig: F.C.W. Vogel, 1877).

35. L. Lichtheim, "On Aphasia," *Brain* 7 (1885): 433-84.

word deafness had a lesion that disconnected the auditory impulse on both sides from the center of auditory word images (Wernicke's area).[36] These lesions prevent the primary auditory area, which analyzes sound, from sending impulses to Wernicke's area, which is performing a phonemic analysis. A lesion that destroys both the right and left primary auditory cortex also produces a similar picture; these patients, however, have cortical deafness and are also unable to comprehend meaningful nonlanguage sounds.

GLOBAL APHASIA (MIXED APHASIA)

Patients who have had both Broca's and Wernicke's areas destroyed are nonfluent and cannot comprehend, repeat, or name. These patients are called "global" or "mixed" aphasics.

TRANSCORTICAL SENSORY APHASIA

Four regions where lesions may produce aphasic disturbances have been discussed: (a) Broca's area (the third frontal convolution), (b) Wernicke's area (the posterior portion of the superior temporal gyrus), (c) the supra-marginal gyrus-arcuate fasciculus, and (d) the primary auditory area and its connections with Wernicke's area. These areas with their connections form a loop, Wernicke's reflex arc (see fig. 4). Although patients with lesions in different parts of this loop may have different symptoms, a patient with a lesion in any portion of the loop has difficulty with repetition. Lichtheim described an aphasic patient whose speech was fluent but could neither comprehend nor name objects well.[37] Unlike a Wernicke's aphasic, this patient's ability to repeat was normal. Lichtheim recognized that although Wernicke's reflex arc may be sufficient for simple repetition, one has to use other parts of the brain if intelligence or volition is needed. Lichtheim proposed that there is an area of concepts (semantic field, or *Begriffsfeld*). He also proposed that Wernicke's area projects to this area of concepts, which then projects to Broca's area (see fig. 5). Lichtheim thought this patient had interrupted the connection between Wernicke's area and the semantic area. Because Wernicke's reflex

36. Ibid.

37. Ibid.

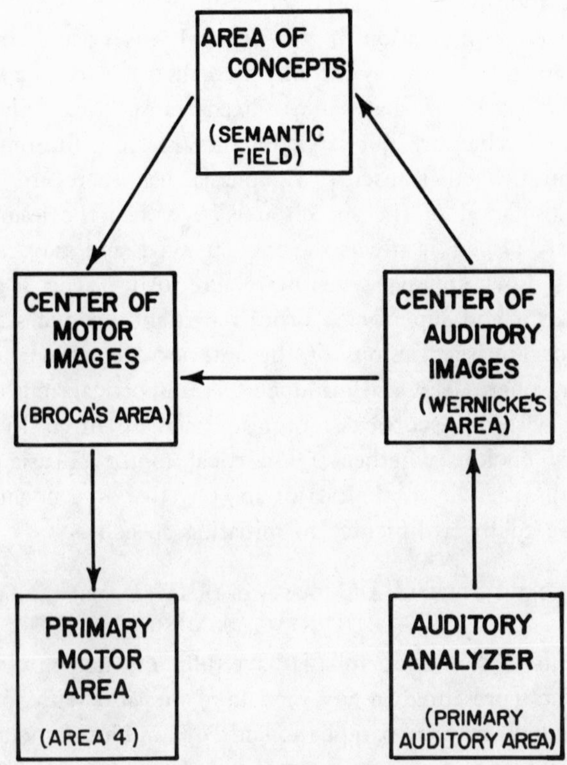

FIG. 5. Lichtheim's schema

arc was intact in the patient, he could repeat; but since the patient could not transfer information from Wernicke's area to the area of concepts he could not comprehend. This type of aphasia was later termed by Goldstein as "transcortical sensory aphasia."[38] Lichtheim reported a patient who was unable to speak spontaneously but was able to comprehend and repeat.[39] Lichtheim thought that the lesion that had disconnected the semantic field from Broca's area would interfere with volitional speech, but since the area of concepts would still be accessible from Wernicke's area comprehension should be intact. Because Wernicke's reflex arc would also be intact, repetition should be unimpaired. Goldstein

38. Goldstein, *Language and Language Disturbances.*

39. Lichtheim, "On Aphasia."

classified such patients as "transcortical motor aphasics."[40] Patients often have a combination of transcortical sensory and transcortical motor aphasia. This syndrome is called "mixed transcortical aphasia."[41] A lesion that causes mixed transcortical aphasia spares Wernicke's reflex arc but separates the arc from the remainder of the brain. Mixed transcortical aphasia has therefore also been termed "isolation of the speech area."[42] When the lesion is more posteriorly placed, it affects the angular gyrus and may cause transcortical sensory aphasia; when more anteriorly placed, it affects the area anterior and superior to Broca's area and produces transcortical motor aphasia. Lesions of the anterior medial portion of the left hemisphere can also produce a transcortical motor aphasia. Patients with transcortical motor aphasia are often hypokinetic, and it is unclear whether transcortical motor aphasia is a true aphasic disorder or an akinesia of speech (that is, a nonaphasic disorder caused by a difficulty in initiating speech).

ANOMIC APHASIA AND TRANSCORTICAL SENSORY APHASIA WITH INTACT NAMING

Patients with anomic aphasia have difficulty not only with naming objects (presented in any modality) but also with spontaneous speech, which may be paraphasic and contain circumlocutions with a decreased use of major lexical items (nouns and verbs). The patients use many clichés and their spontaneous speech may be empty and vague. Comprehension of spoken language and repetition are normal.

The localization of the lesion that causes this aphasic syndrome is similar to the one that causes transcortical sensory aphasia, and these two syndromes often blend together.

Goldstein reported a patient who could not evoke a name for a designated object but the patient would frequently evoke the name spontaneously and could select the correct name if given a multiple choice.[43] This suggested to Goldstein that the patient's

40. Goldstein, *Language and Language Disturbances*.

41. Ibid.

42. Norman Geschwind, F. Quadfasel, and J. Segarra, "Isolation of the Speech Area," *Neuropsychologia* 6 (1968): 327-40.

43. Goldstein, *Language and Language Disturbances*.

word memory was unimpaired but what was impaired was the ability of a concept to be able to retrieve the word. He did not believe in localization of function and thought this defect was being caused by a loss of ability of these patients to assume an abstract attitude.

The mechanism underlying the behavioral abnormalities seen in anomic aphasia cannot be explained by either Wernicke's or Lichtheim's schema. Some investigators thought anomia was a mild form of Wernicke's aphasia.[44] Wernicke himself, however, thought it was a form of transcortical aphasia. Besides being unable to explain anomic aphasia, Lichtheim's schema had another major problem. If voluntary speech went from the area of concepts to Broca's area, patients with lesions in Wernicke's area should have normal spontaneous speech. Although patients with Wernicke's aphasia have fluent speech, their spontaneous speech is abnormal and contains paraphasic errors.

Kussmaul proposed a schema similar to Lichtheim's in which he postulated that the area of concepts instead of going directly to Broca's area had to pass first through Wernicke's area.[45] My associates and I have modified Kussmaul's schema (see fig. 6).[46] In this model, lesions of Wernicke's area (phonemic area) produce abnormalities of spontaneous speech because the area of concepts projects back to Wernicke's area. A lesion that prevents the area of concepts from having access to Wernicke's area should also cause anomic aphasia. With such a lesion, Wernicke's reflex arc is intact, so that repetition should be normal. Since the auditory analyzer has access to Wernicke's area and Wernicke's area has access to the semantic field, comprehension should be normal. Because concepts do not have access to word images (Wernicke's area), these patients are anomic.

If our modification of Kussmaul's schema is correct, aphasia should result when the area of concepts has access to Wernicke's

44. P. Marie and C. Foix, "Les Aphasies de Guerre," *Revue Neurologique* 21 (1917): 53-87.

45. Kussmaul, *Die Störungen der Sprache*.

46. Kenneth M. Heilman, Daniel M. Tucker, and Edward Valenstein, "A Case of Mixed Transcortical Aphasia with Intact Naming," *Brain* 99 (1976): 415-26.

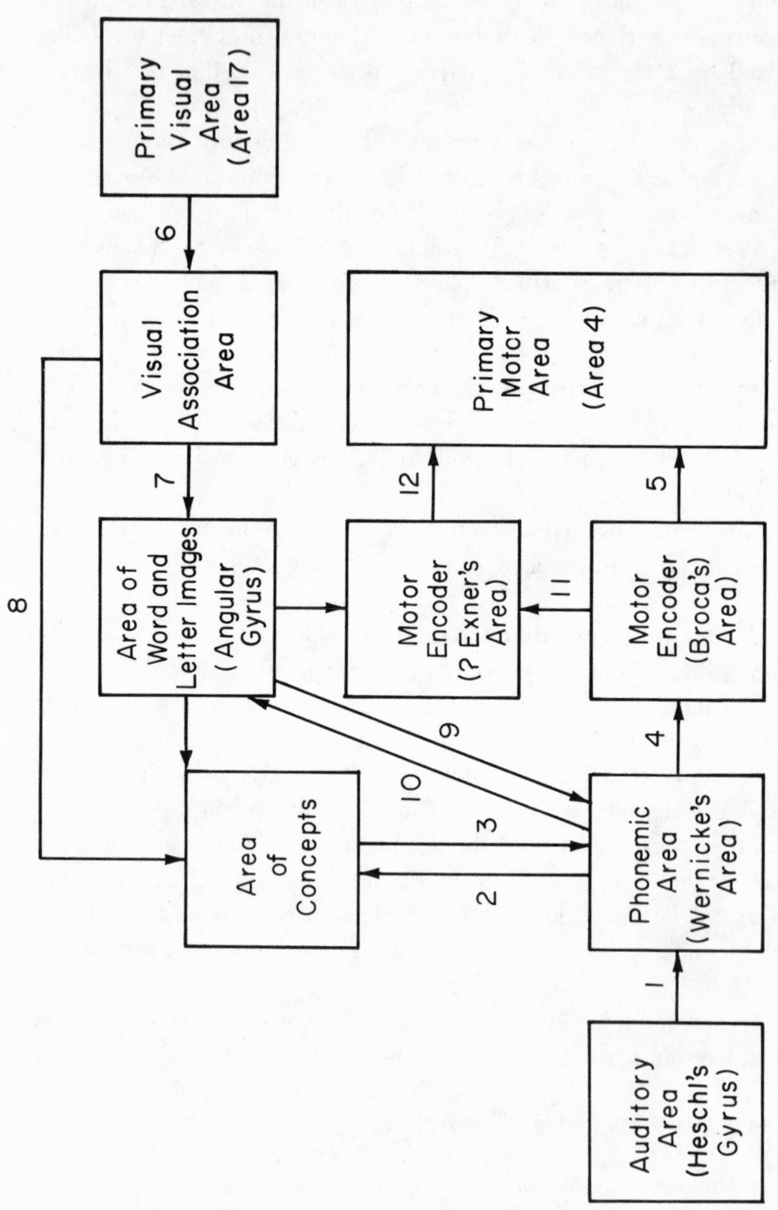
Primary Visual Area (Area 17)
6
Visual Association Area
7
8
Area of Word and Letter Images (Angular Gyrus)
Area of Concepts
9
10
3
2
Primary Motor Area (Area 4)
12
Motor Encoder (? Exner's Area)
11
Motor Encoder (Broca's Area)
5
4
Phonemic Area (Wernicke's Area)
1
Auditory Area (Heschl's Gyrus)

Area of Dysfunction	Functions Impaired	Functions Maintained	Syndrome
Auditory Area (bilateral) (Heschl's gyrus)	Repetition, comprehension of spoken language and of nonlanguage sounds	Naming, spontaneous speech, reading comprehension	Cortical deafness, pure-word deafness, auditory agnosia
Pathway 1	Repetition, comprehension of spoken language	Naming, spontaneous speech, reading comprehension	Pure-word deafness
Phonemic area (posterior portion of superior temporal gyrus)	Repetition, comprehension of spoken and written language, naming, spontaneous speech	None	Wernicke's aphasia
Pathway 2	Comprehension of spoken and written language	Repetition, naming, reading without comprehension	Transcortical aphasia with intact naming
Area of concepts (inferior parietal lobule)	Comprehension of spoken and written language, naming, spontaneous speech	Repetition, reading without comprehension	Transcortical sensory aphasia
Pathway 3	Naming, spontaneous speech	Repetition, comprehension	Anomic aphasia
Pathway 4	Repetition, spontaneous speech	Comprehension	Conduction aphasia
Motor encoder (third frontal convolution)	Spontaneous speech, naming, repetition, reading aloud	Comprehension of spoken and written language	Broca's aphasia
Pathway 5	Spontaneous speech, naming, repetition, reading aloud	Writing, comprehension of spoken and written language	Aphemia
Visual association areas (bilateral) Pathway 6	Reading, recognizing and drawing visually presented objects	Writing and other language functions	Apperceptive agnosia
Pathway 7	Reading aloud and comprehension, naming (e.g., colors)	Normal language except for reading	Alexia without agraphia
Pathway 8	Recognizing visually presented objects	Reading, writing, normal language	Associative agnosia without alexia
Area of word and letter images (angular gyrus) Pathways 9 and 10	Reading aloud and comprehension, writing (spontaneous and to dictation)	Spontaneous speech, comprehension, repetition	Alexia with agraphia
Exner's area (second frontal convolution) Pathways 11 and 12	Writing	All other language functions	Pure agraphia

Fig. 6. Author's revision of Kussmaul's schema

area (phonemic area) but the phonemic area does not have access to the area of concepts, or semantic area. We described a patient who was able to repeat (Wernicke's reflex arc being intact), was able to name (semantic area had access to Wernicke's area), but was not able to comprehend (Wernicke's area did not have access to the semantic area).[47] This aphasic syndrome has been termed "mixed transcortical aphasia with intact naming."

The location of the semantic field has not been well defined; however, Goldstein[48] and Luria[49] believe that it is in the parietal lobes. It is also not known whether the semantic field is in the left hemisphere or both hemispheres.

Theoretically, if a patient has a lesion of Wernicke's area (Wernicke's aphasic) then although he cannot comprehend spoken or written language and cannot express himself, he still may have internal language if he has an intact semantic area (that is, he should be able to categorize and generalize and he should be able to know what objects are used for). Wernicke noted that some patients who could not even comprehend still knew what objects were used for. We also tested patients with mixed transcortical aphasia with intact naming with a categorization test.[50] The patient comprehended poorly but was able to categorize.

CHILDHOOD APHASIA

Freud recognized that aphasia in childhood was comprised of two groups—congenital aphasias and acquired aphasias.[51] This section will deal mainly with the latter.

The nature of an acquired aphasia in childhood depends on age. Young children have a different clinical picture from that of older children whose clinical syndromes are very similar to those aphasic syndromes previously discussed. Although there is a continuum, for

47. Ibid.

48. Goldstein, *Language and Language Disturbances*.

49. Alexander R. Luria, "Language and Brain," *Brain and Language* 1 (1974): 1-15.

50. Heilman, Tucker, and Valenstein, "A Case of Mixed Transcortical Aphasia with Intact Naming."

51. Sigmund Freud, *Die infantile Cerebrallähmung* (Vienna: n.p., 1897).

the purpose of discussion I refer to childhood aphasics as children of eight years or younger. The aphasic disturbance that best characterizes childhood aphasia is nonfluency. Although these patients are often referred to as being shy, withdrawn, or scared, the cause of their behavior is really an aphasic disorder. When these children do speak they show a poverty of words, use small phrase length, and may use agrammatic or telegraphic speech. They usually have little if any paraphasic speech. Many of these children appear to have what in an adult would be called Broca's aphasia. Some of them may also have a comprehension disturbance, and their clinical appearance is similar to the global aphasia seen in adults.

Although the right hemisphere is held to be important in the development of speech, aphasic children, like aphasic adults, mainly have left-hemisphere disease.[52]

In addition to the nonfluent aphasia in children, the other major difference between adult and childhood aphasics is that children are more likely to recover from aphasia than adults are. Several studies have demonstrated that unilateral hemispheric damage in preadolescent children rarely if ever causes permanent aphasia.[53] Although I shall discuss recovery of function in a later section, this observation of recovery is important in understanding congenital aphasia because if congenital aphasia were caused by pathological lesions the lesions would have to be bilateral. One of the few cases of congenital aphasia that came to postmortem examination was reported by Landau and colleagues.[54] Their patient with congenital aphasia had normal hearing and intelligence. Postmortem examination of this patient revealed bilateral lesions in the regions responsible for language. If one eliminated from a group of congenital aphasics all those with mental retardation, hearing defects, emotional diseases and maturational defects, would the remaining children all have bilateral disease of the speech areas? Although

52. Th. Alajouanine and François Lhermitte, "Acquired Aphasia in Children," *Brain* 88 (1965): 653-62.

53. L. S. Basser, "Hemiplegia of Early Onset and the Faculty of Speech with Special Reference to the Effects of Hemispherectomy," *Brain* 85 (1962): 427-60; Eric H. Lenneberg, *Biological Foundations of Language* (New York: John Wiley and Sons, 1967).

54. William Landau, R. Goldstein, and F. Kleffner, "Congenital Aphasia," *Neurology* 10 (1960): 915-21.

many of those remaining would have bilateral lesions, I expect that not all of them would have the congenital aphasia caused by external agents but that some were children not endowed with the neural circuitry required for language processing.

Alexia and Agraphia: Reading and Writing Disorders

READING DISORDERS

The schema developed to help with understanding the brain mechanisms underlying aphasic syndromes can be further developed to aid in understanding disorders of reading (see fig. 6).

Visual stimuli first come to the cortex at the primary visual area. Lesions of the primary visual areas of both hemispheres leave certain brain stem reflexes intact (that is, the pupils will respond to light); however, patients with cortical blindness cannot otherwise see stationary objects or read. Primary areas always project to their association area (Flechig's rule), and the primary visual areas project to the visual association areas. Lesions of the visual association areas do not produce blindness. Defects of the visual association area can produce "apperceptive agnosia." Visual agnosia is a defect in visual recognition not caused by defective sensation (blindness) or unfamiliarity. Patients with apperceptive agnosia cannot name or demonstrate the use of visually presented objects but can recognize objects presented in another manner (for example, touch). Patients with apperceptive agnosia cannot draw the objects they see or pick one out from an array of objects, which suggests a perceptual defect. Patients with apperceptive agnosia usually cannot read.

After visual stimuli are processed by the visual association cortex, they go to the language areas. Patients with lesions in the region of the angular gyrus cannot read or write.[55] This syndrome has been called "alexia with agraphia." These patients cannot recognize letters, cannot write normally, and cannot read if letters are spoken or felt. The region of the angular gyrus possibly contains visual letter or word images, and destruction of this area is re-

55. D. Frank Benson and Norman Geschwind, "The Alexias," in *Handbook of Clinical Neurology*, vol. 4, ed. P. J. Vinken and G. W. Bruyn (Amsterdam: North Holland Publishing Co., 1969), pp. 112-40.

sponsible for both the alexia and agraphia associated with angular gyrus lesions. There are theoretically two possible routes by which the stimuli from the area of visual word images can get to the semantic area. From the angular gyrus, the projections important in reading can go directly either to the semantic area or they can go to Wernicke's area (see fig. 6) and then to the semantic area. The patient previously mentioned with a mixed transcortical aphasia and intact naming had an intact semantic field. This patient was able to name objects presented visually and he was also able to read aloud flawlessly; however, he was unable to comprehend what he had read. If printed words took the same pathway as the objects to be named (that is, from the visual association area to the semantic field), then this patient should have been able to comprehend what he read; but he could not. Wernicke argued that language initially was audibly acquired and that the subsequent acquisition of visual language is by reference to this initial auditory acquisition.[56] Observations of this patient suggest that Wernicke was correct and that the area of visual word images projects to Wernicke's area before projecting to the semantic area. The observation that Wernicke's aphasics cannot comprehend written language also supports this concept. Because Wernicke's aphasics cannot phonemically decode, they also can neither read aloud nor comprehend what they have read.

We have seen two global aphasics and one Wernicke's aphasic who could comprehend written language better than spoken language.[57] Hier and Mohr have reported a case of Wernicke's aphasia who also could comprehend written language better than spoken language.[58] These observations would suggest that some patients have direct access to the semantic area from the area of visual word images or, alternatively, these patients have a combination of pure word deafness and Broca's or conduction aphasia. Perhaps all people have direct access to the semantic area from the area of

56. Ibid.

57. Seymour Wolfson and Kenneth M. Heilman, "Intact Reading and Writing in Global Aphasics," in preparation.

58. Daniel B. Hier and Jay P. Mohr, "Incongruous Oral and Written Naming Evidence for a Subdivision of the Syndrome of Wernicke's Aphasia," *Brain and Language* 4 (1977): 115-26.

word images but most global and Wernicke's aphasics cannot comprehend written language because most lesions which produce global or Wernicke's aphasia also destroy the area of visual images (angular gyrus) or the semantic areas.

Nonfluent aphasics (that is, Broca's, transcortical motor) are not able to read aloud but usually can comprehend. Conduction aphasics may also have difficulty with reading aloud and may or may not comprehend, depending on the position of their lesion.

A lesion that interrupts the visual projection, which goes from the visual association cortex to the angular gyrus region, induces a reading disturbance. Since these patients have normal language areas and an intact area of visual word images, they are not only able to write normally but also may not be aphasic. This syndrome described by Dejerine is called "alexia without agraphia"[59] or "agnostic alexia." Since other sensory areas have access to the language area, these patients can read if letters are spelled aloud or if they can feel letters. Because of the disconnection between visual association areas and speech areas, these patients also cannot name colors, but they can sort colors. Very often they can name objects, numbers, and letters,[60] which suggests that the pathway which carries the information from the visual areas to the speech area is different from the one that carries words and colors (see fig. 6).[61] There have been descriptions of patients with associative agnosia who could not name objects but who could read.[62] These patients probably have a lesion of the pathway that goes from the visual association area to the area of concepts (see fig. 6).

The lesion that most commonly causes alexia without agraphia destroys the left visual cortex or visual fibers coming to the left visual cortex. Patients with this disorder can see because they use their right (nondominant) visual cortex; however, they also have a lesion in the commissure (corpus callosum) which prevents the

59. Benson and Geschwind, "The Alexias."

60. Ibid.

61. Heilman, Tucker, and Valenstein, "A Case of Mixed Transcortical Aphasia with Intact Naming."

62. Martin L. Albert, Avinoam Reches, and Ruth Silverberg, "Associative Visual Agnosia without Alexia," *Neurology* 25 (1975): 322-26.

right visual cortex from transmitting information to the language area on the left side.[63] Lesions under the cortical speech areas can also produce a similar disconnection without destroying any visual cortex or visual fibers.[64]

DISORDERS OF WRITING

Aphasia is a disturbance of language, not speech. Therefore, most of the patients with aphasic disturbances previously discussed also have aphasic writing disturbances. In general, agraphic errors mirror aphasic errors and, as previously mentioned, writing disturbances can be associated with reading disturbances (alexia with agraphia) or syndromes of the angular gyrus. In the absence of language and reading disturbances, loss of the ability to write is unusual. It may be seen in the left hand of patients who have undergone a section of the corpus callosum. Such a lesion separates the left hemisphere, which processes language, from the right hemisphere, which controls the left hand. Pure agraphia has also been reported in patients who developed weakness of their preferred hand and agraphia of their nonpreferred hand.[65] In normals, although the nonpreferred hand is not as skilled as the preferred hand, it is capable of producing normal written language. These patients also had an apraxia of their nonpreferred hand (loss of skilled movements). Analysis of these cases suggested that the hemisphere dominant for language was different from that dominant for ability to perform skilled movements, and that the lesion in the hemisphere dominant for handedness destroyed engrams for complex motor activity and caused the agraphia and apraxia.

In addition to reading and writing, the following defects are often associated with dominant parietal (angular gyrus) lobe lesions: right-left confusion (cannot tell their right from their left), finger agnosia (cannot name their fingers), acalculia (cannot calculate), construction apraxia (cannot draw a cube on command), and anomic aphasia.

63. Benson and Geschwind, "The Alexias."

64. Samuel H. Greenblatt, "Subangular Alexia without Agraphia or Hemianopsia," *Brain and Language* 3 (1976): 229-45.

65. Kenneth M. Heilman et al., "Apraxia and Agraphia in a Left-Hander," *Brain* 96 (1973): 21-28.

Recovery of Function

Aphasic patients with destructive lesions often recover function. Many patients do learn substitution tricks. Nonfluent aphasics may use gestures in lieu of speaking or writing. Anomic aphasics learn to circumlocute and point, and even global aphasics use affective tones, faces, and postures to communicate. Besides substitution, additional forms of recovery take place, and an area of intact brain is assumed to be mediating language function. From phylogenetic studies, language is known to be a species-specific function; it occurs only in man but can be taught to apes. The major differences between man and phylogenetically lower mammals is the development of the human cortex. There are many theories as to the anatomic basis of language. The two major areas of the cortex where the human brain has grown are in the frontal lobes and in the area where the temporal, parietal, and occipital lobes meet. The latter area is a superassociation area, which receives projections from association areas of the various sensory modalities (touch, vision, and hearing) (see fig. 3). Only man and apes can perform intermodal associations, and only those organisms that can perform intermodal associations are able to use language. If, as Geschwind has suggested, intermodal dissociations are responsible for the mediation of language then the areas that would assume function are very limited.[66] In right-handed persons, although language is mediated by the left hemisphere, the right hemisphere also has similar corticocortical projection and should be able to mediate intermodal asssociations. In normal right-handers, the right hemisphere is usually carrying out visuospatial[67] and emotional[68] functions; however, the right hemisphere would appear to be the next likely area to assume function for the left.

Several major observations demonstrate that the right hemisphere mediates language when the left is impaired. Gazzaniga and Sperry showed that the right side is capable of understanding lan-

66. Norman Geschwind, "Disconnexion Syndromes in Animals and Man," *Brain* 88 (1965): 237-94; 585-644.

67. Joynt and Goldstein, "Minor Cerebral Hemisphere."

68. Heilman, Scholes, and Watson, "Affective Agnosia with Disturbed Comprehension of Affective Speech."

guage (mainly nouns).[69] As previously mentioned, Kinsbourne showed that anesthetizing the right hemisphere in patients with left-sided stroke caused language arrest,[70] and some patients who have had left-side hemispherectomy have been able to recover language.[71]

The two major determinants in predicting recovery of aphasia are age and handedness. Younger patients are more likely to recover than older patients, and left-handers and those with a family history of left-handedness are more likely to recover than right-handers.

In regard to handedness, left-handers often have speech in both hemispheres; therefore they not only have more area at risk but also have more area available to process language, thereby improving their chance for recovery.

If children between the ages of two and eight years have a lesion restricted to one hemisphere they almost always recover. Adults with the same sort of lesion often do not recover. It is not clear why children recover and adults do not. Although Geschwind and Levitsky have demonstrated anatomic asymmetries in adults,[72] this cannot explain this discrepancy because similar anatomic asymmetries are seen in infants even before they acquire language.[73] It appears, therefore, that before and during maturation, the cerebral hemisphere is more equipotential than it is after maturation.

How does the right hemisphere know when or when not to acquire language? It is possible that the callosum contains fibers to homotypic areas that may be inhibitory. In normal children, through the callosum the intact left hemisphere can inhibit the right hemisphere from acquiring language (so that it can acquire

69. Michael S. Gazzaniga and Roger W. Sperry, "Language after Section of the Cerebral Commissures," *Brain* 90 (1967): 131-248.

70. Kinsbourne, "The Minor Hemisphere as a Source of Aphasic Speech."

71. Juhn Wada and Theodore Rasmussen, "Intracarotid Injection of Sodium Amytal for the Lateralization of Cerebral Speech Dominance," *Journal of Neurosurgery* 17 (1960): 266-82.

72. Geschwind and Levitsky, "Human Brain: Left-Right Asymmetries in Temporal Speech Region."

73. Wada and Rasmussen, "Intracarotid Injection of Sodium Amytal for the Lateralization of Cerebral Speech Dominance."

visuospatial and other skills). In the absence of left-hemisphere language function or in the absence of the corpus callosum, inhibition is lacking and the right hemisphere acquires language. Support for these hypotheses comes from Sperry and Saul's observation that patients with agenesis (failure of formation) for the corpus callosum do not have the symptoms of callosal disconnection because these patients probably have bilateral speech representation.[74] With maturation of language skills in a normal brain, this transcallosal inhibition grows progressively stronger. Although an adult may have damage to the left hemisphere (which impairs language function) or have a callosal section, by the time this happens the right hemisphere may already be committed to visuospatial and other skills and may not be able to take over language function.

74. Ronald E. Saul and Roger W. Sperry, "Absence of Commissurotomy Symptoms with Agenesis of the Corpus Callosum," *Neurology* 18 (1968): 307.

CHAPTER VI

Cerebral Lateralization and Cognitive Development

MARCEL KINSBOURNE AND MERRILL HISCOCK

Few topics in the neurosciences can match the study of cerebral lateralization in its power to stimulate the imagination of people. Students of a number of disciplines have become captivated by the idea that the right and left halves of the human cerebrum differ in function, and this captivation has led to investigation and to speculation. Some writers have attempted to explain various individual differences among normal people in terms of degree of cerebral dominance or the balance of influence between the hemispheres.[1] It has been suggested that communication between the hemispheres is the basis of creativity, that the right hemisphere plays a special role in certain psychiatric disorders, and that privileged and deprived groups in society can be differentiated in terms of "hemispheric style."[2] It is very tempting to relate a vast number of human characteristics to cerebral lateralization.

Cerebral Lateralization and Learning Disabilities

Education has not gone untouched by this atmosphere of speculation and hypothesis construction. On the contrary, the connec-

1. Robert D. Palmer, "Development of a Differentiated Handedness," *Psychological Bulletin* 62 (1964): 257-72; Luigi Pizzamiglio, "Handedness, Ear Preference, and Field Dependence," *Perceptual and Motor Skills* 38 (1974): 700-702; Paul Bakan, "Hypnotizability, Laterality of Eye Movements, and Functional Brain Asymmetry," *Perceptual and Motor Skills* 28 (1969): 927-32; Wayne Weiten and Claire F. Etaugh, "Lateral Eye Movement as Related to Verbal and Perceptual Motor Skill and Values," *Perceptual and Motor Skills* 36 (1973): 423-28.

2. Joseph E. Bogen and Glenda M. Bogen, "The Other Side of the Brain: III. The Corpus Callosum and Creativity," *Bulletin of the Los Angeles Neurological Society* 34 (October, 1969): 191-220; David Galin, "Implications for Psychiatry of Left and Right Cerebral Specialization," *Archives of General Psychiatry* 31 (1974): 572-83; Joseph E. Bogen (chairman), Symposium on "Aspects of Neurosociology" at the Fifth Annual Meeting of the International Neuropsychology Society, Santa Fe, N.M., February, 1977.

tion of education with cerebral lateralization predates the current popularity of the topic. Fifty years ago, Samuel Orton, a neurologist and neuropathologist, began promulgating a theory relating a number of language disabilities in children to incomplete development of functional superiority in the dominant hemisphere.[3] Orton's formulation, which was destined to have immense influence on the philosophy and practice of special education in North America, rested on the premise that an engram, or physiological representation of a stimulus, is established simultaneously in both cerebral hemispheres. Since the two homologous engrams were thought to be oppositely oriented (that is, to be mirror images of each other), incomplete suppression of the engram in the nondominant hemisphere supposedly results in interhemispheric rivalry which, in turn, results in confusion and inconsistent performance. Thus, developmental language disabilities (termed strephosymbolia, or "twisted symbols") were linked to incomplete left-hemispheric or right-hemispheric dominance. Moreover, Orton pointed out an apparent parallel between the language problems in children with incomplete cerebral dominance and the consequences of damage to the "master" hemisphere in adults. The symptoms of children with developmental strephosymbolia mimicked the symptoms of brain-damaged adults with acquired strephosymbolia, but in the case of the children the underlying mechanism was thought to be physiological dysfunction rather than a brain lesion.

It is difficult to estimate the influence of Orton's model on modern education, although the passage of time has diminished its visibility within the educational research literature. Extreme views regarding incomplete lateralization and its remediation have been discredited and seem to be gradually diminishing in popularity.[4] Nevertheless, belief in an intimate link between cerebral lateralization and cognitive performance persists.[5] As Critchley phrased

3. Samuel T. Orton, *Reading, Writing, and Speech Problems in Children* (New York: Norton, 1937).

4. Gene V. Glass and M. P. Robbins, "A Critique of Experiments on the Role of Neurological Organization in Reading Performance," *Reading Research Quarterly* 3 (1967): 5-51.

5. See Part IV of *The Neuropsychology of Learning Disorders: Theoretical Approaches*, ed. Robert M. Knights and Dirk J. Bakker (Baltimore: University Park Press, 1976).

it, "Although this over-simple hypothesis [that is, Orton's] might not find favor in contemporary thinking, the underlying notion of imperfect cerebral dominance is still acceptable today as one factor of importance [in explaining reading disability]."[6]

The notion that learning disabilities are somehow related to faulty cerebral dominance is an old notion that still is very much alive today. In this chapter, we shall examine that notion and its contribution to education. We shall outline the empirical evidence and point out some of the ambiguities and deficiencies. Then, we shall devote the major portion of this chapter to the assumptions that underlie the various studies, and to the basic research that is relevant to those assumptions.

The Empirical Basis

A large and heterogeneous collection of studies attests to the widespread interest in a possible connection between learning disabilities and anomalies of lateralization. Numerous investigators have sought to establish a statistical association between learning disability and some observable characteristic, such as handedness, that is thought to be related to cerebral dominance. We shall summarize the data by first considering handedness and then discussing studies in which other measures of laterality are examined.

Vernon notes that "no other symptom associated with dyslexia has attracted more attention than has defective *lateralization*; that is to say, the apparent failure to establish superior skill in one or the other hand, or to show strong preference for using one hand rather than the other in performing skilled tasks."[7] Despite the attention afforded handedness, the findings are inconclusive.[8] Many authors have reported an elevated incidence of left-handedness among dyslexic children. Others have reported a high incidence

6. MacDonald Critchley, *The Dyslexic Child*, 2d ed. (London: Heinemann, 1970), p. 66.

7. Magdalen Vernon, *Reading and Its Difficulties* (London: Cambridge University Press, 1971), p. 138.

8. The data are reviewed in the following: Critchley, *The Dyslexic Child*; Magdalen Vernon, *Backwardness in Reading* (London: Cambridge University Press, 1957); Vernon, *Reading and Its Difficulties*; O. L. Zangwill, "Dyslexia in Relation to Cerebral Dominance," in *Reading Disability*, ed. John Money (Baltimore: Johns Hopkins Press, 1962).

of "weak lateralization," or ambidexterity. In fact, reported incidence rates for left-handedness or mixed-handedness (ambidexterity) in samples of learning-disabled children occasionally have reached 75 percent, although most investigators report far more modest statistics. Thus, even though the incidence rates vary markedly, there are numerous claims that deviation from firmly established right-handedness is more common among poor readers than among controls. There also are numerous findings that are contradictory to those claims. Since mixed-handedness is not uncommon among university students, mixed-handedness per se does not necessarily imply cognitive deficit.[9] Especially in the more recent literature, direct comparisons of poor readers and controls frequently fail to reveal any difference in the incidence of left-handedness or strength of handedness.[10]

Many clinicians and researchers, including Orton, have focused their attention on the consistency of handedness, footedness, and eyedness rather than on handedness alone. Orton considered the risk of strephosymbolia to be no greater for strong left-handers than for strong right-handers.[11] The child at risk was the one who, for example, preferred the right hand and right foot but who used the left eye for sighting.

Left-eyedness is far more common than left-handedness. If eyedness is defined in terms of eye preference for sighting, about 30 percent of normal children and adults can be classified as consistently left-eyed.[12] Since no more than 10 percent of the popu-

9. Marian Annett, "A Classification of Hand Preference by Association Analysis," *British Journal of Psychology* 61 (1970): 303-21.

10. For example, see I. H. Balow, "Lateral Dominance Characteristics and Reading Achievement in the First Grade," *Journal of Psychology* 55 (1963): 323-28; Lillian Belmont and Herbert G. Birch, "Lateral Dominance, Lateral Awareness, and Reading Disability," *Child Development* 36 (1965): 57-72; M. M. Clark, *Reading Difficulties in Schools* (Harmondsworth: Penguin Books, 1970); Katrina de Hirsch, Jeannette J. Jansky, and William S. Langford, *Predicting Reading Failure* (New York: Harper and Row, 1966); J. G. Lyle, "Reading Retardation and Reversal Tendency: A Factorial Study," *Child Development* 40 (1969): 833-43; Eve Malmquist, *Factors Related to Reading Disabilities in the First Grade of Elementary School* (Stockholm: Almquist and Wiksell, 1958); and Michael Rutter, Jack Tizard, and Kingsley Whitmore, eds., *Education, Health, and Behavior* (London: Longmans, 1970).

11. Orton, *Reading, Writing, and Speech Problems in Children.*

12. Clare Porac and Stanley Coren, "The Dominant Eye," *Psychological Bulletin* 83 (1976): 880-97.

lation is left-handed, there must be a large number of people who are left-eyed but right-handed.[13] On the basis of their number alone, we would expect most of these people to be free of learning disabilities. However, this group (as well as left-handers who sight with their right eye) might be at greater risk than the rest of the population.

Extensive research into the relationship between eyedness and learning disabilities has failed to produce any substantial agreement.[14] As was the case in studies of deviation from right-handedness, several studies of eyedness report that deviation from the norm is associated with learning disabilities. Even more studies report that inconsistency between eyedness and handedness (crossed dominance, or mixed dominance) is associated with some form of learning problem. Again, however, there is a long list of studies—especially relatively recent studies—that show no relationship between eyedness, or crossed dominance, and learning disabilities.[15]

In recent years, the attention of researchers has shifted from handedness and eyedness to perceptual asymmetries. The study of listening asymmetries, in particular, seemed to be a safe, convenient, and relatively direct means of determining the manner in which speech perception is lateralized in normal and abnormal populations of children and adults.[16] The technique, called dichotic listening, involves the simultaneous presentation of competing sounds to the two ears. A right-ear superiority for speech sounds

13. Robert E. Hicks and Marcel Kinsbourne, "On the Genesis of Human Handedness: A Review," *Journal of Motor Behavior* 8 (1976): 257-66; Vernon, *Reading and Its Difficulties.*

14. Porac and Coren, "The Dominant Eye"; Vernon, *Backwardness in Reading*; idem, *Reading and Its Difficulties.*

15. For example, see Balow, "Lateral Dominance Characteristics and Reading Achievement in the First Grade"; Belmont and Birch, "Lateral Dominance, Lateral Awareness, and Reading Disability"; A. J. Harris, "Lateral Dominance, Directional Confusion, and Reading Disability," *Journal of Psychology* 44 (1957): 283-94; and R. I. Coleman and C. P. Deutch, "Lateral Dominance and Left-Right Discrimination: A Comparison of Normal and Retarded Readers," *Perceptual and Motor Skills* 19 (1964): 43-50.

16. Doreen Kimura, "Cerebral Dominance and the Perception of Verbal Stimuli," *Canadian Journal of Psychology* 15 (1961): 166-71; idem, "Some Effects of Temporal-Lobe Damage on Auditory Perception," *Canadian Journal of Psychology* 15 (1961): 156-65; idem, "Speech Lateralization in Young Children as Determined by an Auditory Test," *Journal of Comparative and Physiological Psychology* 56 (1963): 899-902.

is thought to reflect left-hemispheric representation of language. Visual asymmetries also can be obtained if stimuli are flashed briefly to the right or left of fixation.[17] In this case, a right visual half-field superiority for linguistic material is thought to reflect left lateralization of language.

Satz recently reviewed the studies in which perceptual tasks—dichotic listening in most cases—were administered to children with reading disabilities.[18] The results of those nineteen studies seem to be as variable and as incoherent as the results of the handedness and eyedness studies. Satz points out that very few of the studies actually show reduced asymmetry in the learning-disabled group. In many cases, both the learning-disabled children and their controls showed a significant right-ear advantage; in other cases neither group showed a right-ear advantage.

It seems that even with the aid of modern behavioral techniques it remains impossible to reach any consensus regarding the role of cerebral lateralization in learning disabilities. We agree with Benton's succinct conclusion that "the vast literature on laterality characteristics and reading skill does not lead to any simple generalizations."[19] The literature simply fails to answer the question of whether reading disabilities, or any other kind of learning disabilities, are linked to anomalous lateralization.

To what can we attribute the inconclusiveness of these data? Why has a seemingly straightforward question proven so resistant to solution? As is usually the case, methodological criticisms may be put forth. Handedness has been defined in various ways, some of which are questionable. There are many pitfalls to be avoided in measuring eyedness. Dichotic listening and tachistoscopic (vis-

17. M. P. Bryden, "Tachistoscopic Recognition, Handedness, and Cerebral Dominance," *Neuropsychologia* 3 (1965): 1-8; Doreen Kimura, "Dual Functional Asymmetry of the Brain in Visual Perception," *Neuropsychologia* 4 (1966): 275-85; M. J. White, "Laterality Differences in Perception: A Review," *Psychological Bulletin* 72 (1969): 387-405.

18. Paul Satz, "Cerebral Dominance and Reading Disability: An Old Problem Revisited," in *The Neuropsychology of Learning Disorders*, ed. Knights and Bakker, pp. 273-94.

19. Arthur L. Benton, "Developmental Dyslexia: Neurological Aspects," in *Advances in Neurology*, ed. Walter J. Friedlander, vol. 7 (New York: Raven, 1975), p. 24.

ual) tasks may vary along several dimensions. Different populations of children have been sampled, and the sample sizes vary markedly across studies. It is interesting to note, for instance, that relationships between anomalous laterality and poor reading are often found in clinical studies but not in studies of entire populations of normal children.[20]

Although we shall discuss these sources of variability in greater detail, methodological critique is not our primary objective. The methodological problems are only symptoms of more fundamental problems at the conceptual level. In other words, neither developing a better handedness questionnaire nor increasing sample sizes nor measuring reading skill with greater precision is likely to resolve the question of whether cerebral lateralization and reading ability are related in some manner. Instead of refining our techniques or expending a greater number of resources to repeat an experiment that has already been done several times, we first should seek a more adequate understanding of the question we hope to answer and the various implications of that question. Does the question make sense? Are the concepts sufficiently clear? Can the concepts be operationalized? What are we assuming when we ask the question?

Four Basic Assumptions

Underlying the diverse theoretical positions, experimental methodologies, and criteria for selecting subjects are four assumptions that are explicit or implicit in nearly all studies of lateralization and learning disability.

First, there is the assumption that the term "learning disability" can be defined adequately. Most researchers act as if a learning disability, usually a disability in reading, represents a unitary entity. In other words, one reading disability is the same as any other reading disability. Probably few, if any, researchers actually believe that this is the case. Nonetheless, when they compare reading-disabled children with normal controls on a so-called lateralization task, they are implicitly assuming that reading disability is a mono-

20. William Yule and Michael Rutter, "Epidemiology and Social Implications of Specific Reading Retardation," in *The Neuropsychology of Learning Disorders*, ed. Knights and Bakker, pp. 25-39.

lithic diagnostic category and that children falling into this category resemble each other in brain organization.

Second, postulation of a relationship between cognitive performance and cerebral lateralization implies that the postulator can specify what is meant by cerebral lateralization. In practice, a variety of operations has been used to define the presence or degree of lateralization. Is handedness equivalent to lateralization? Is a composite index of handedness, eyedness, and footedness a better measure? Does a right-sided advantage in a perceptual task define language lateralization? Does the concept of *degree* of lateralization have any meaning?

Third, it is commonly assumed that the most prevalent pattern of cerebral organization (that is, left lateralization of language) is optimal, and that deviations from that norm imply some impairment of function. Thus left-handedness, which until recently was thought to indicate a pattern of cerebral specialization that is the mirror image of the right-hander's pattern, frequently has been regarded as contributing to cognitive inefficiency.[21]

Fourth, the rationale for almost all studies in this area and for their interpretation rests squarely on the assumption that lateralization develops ontogenetically. Thus, learning-disabled children are expected to be "slow to lateralize." Or, to cite a more complex model, clear-cut lateralization has been claimed to be disadvantageous at one level of reading and advantageous at a subsequent level.[22]

Are All Learning Disabilities Alike?

Perhaps it is patently unfair to criticize researchers for behaving as if all learning disabilities were alike. After all, there is a venerable tradition in both psychology and medicine of comparing heterogeneous groups. Psychotics are compared to neurotics. Brain-damaged retardates are compared to familial retardates. Young children are compared to older children. In many cases, these comparisons yield a useful first estimate of a relationship that can be

21. The early view of cerebral organization in right- and left-handers is summarized in Zangwill, "Dyslexia in Relation to Cerebral Dominance."

22. Dirk J. Bakker, "Hemispheric Specialization and Stages in the Learning-to-Read Process," *Bulletin of the Orton Society* 23 (1973): 15-27.

refined and further elucidated by subsequent research. The heterogeneity within each group may not be sufficient to obscure the essential difference between groups, or the heterogeneity may be largely irrelevant to the dependent variable being considered. On the other hand, heterogeneity within groups may completely mask important differences between two groups. Since learning-disabled children and normal controls do not seem to differ in any consistent manner on lateralization measures, the matter of classification must be examined closely.

There are two fundamental aspects to the matter of selecting the "right" children to include in studies of learning disability and cerebral organization. The first aspect is the nontrivial problem of defining the term "learning disability" and translating that definition into selection criteria. This is the problem of mapping the boundaries of the territory with which we are concerned. The second aspect of the classification problem involves subdividing that territory into behaviorally homogeneous sections. The first aspect is universally recognized but difficult and controversial; the second aspect may be equally difficult and important but is almost universally ignored in studies dealing with cerebral lateralization.

DEFINING LEARNING DISABILITY

It should be pointed out that a definition of learning disability found useful in educational practice is not necessarily the most useful definition for the examination of neuropsychological factors in learning disability, although there does seem to be a general consensus among many educators and researchers as to the essential nature of learning disabilities.[23] The core component, according to that consensus, is an unrealized expectancy for a child's school performance. The learning-disabled child is an academic underachiever who fails to perform as well as a specified set of variables would predict. The potential divergence between educationally useful and experimentally useful definitions arises in re-

23. William H. Gaddes, "Prevalence Estimates and the Need for Definition of Learning Disabilities," in *The Neuropsychology of Learning Disorders*, ed. Knights and Bakker, pp. 3-24; Byron P. Rourke, "Brain-Behavior Relationships in Children with Learning Disabilities," *American Psychologist* 30 (1975): 911-20.

gard to the variables included in or excluded from the set of predictors.[24] If all kinds of underachievers can benefit from the same set of special educational programs, then educators might want to define learning disability as underachievement relative to IQ scores and chronological age. Such a definition would fail to exclude learning problems associated with emotional disturbance, environmental deprivation, or known neurological damage. In fact, there may be no reason to exclude children with below-average IQ scores. On the other hand, researchers must be much more exclusive in their definition if they are to learn much about the relationship between learning disability and the brain. Mixing generally dull, emotionally disturbed, environmentally deprived, and brain-injured children with a "purer" core of strictly defined learning-disabled children will not lead to clear and definitive findings.

In any event, as Gaddes has emphasized, learning disability is anything but an all-or-none affliction.[25] Children vary in a roughly Gaussian manner on any dimension of skill. Even if researchers can agree on strict and standard qualitative criteria for defining learning disabilities, the absolute degree of academic impairment and the magnitude of the impairment relative to various predictor variables are free to vary within and between studies. As a practical matter, it is very difficult to control all the selection factors that are potentially relevant to differences in cerebral lateralization and, at present, we do not know the particular factors that need to be controlled.

As difficult as it is to define the realm of learning disabilities, arrival at a satisfactory definition still leaves us far short of the definitional precision needed before we can realistically expect to find neuropsychological correlates. In other words, we may be able to agree on the differentiation of learning-disabled children from other children who perform poorly in school, but we still burden ourselves with the assumption that all learning disabilities are alike. This is the second aspect of the classification problem:

24. Otfried Spreen, "Neuropsychology of Learning Disorders: Post-Conference Review," in *The Neuropsychology of Learning Disorders*, ed. Knights and Bakker, pp. 445-67.

25. Gaddes, "Prevalence Estimates and the Need for Definition of Learning Disabilities."

the issue of subgroups within the population of learning-disabled children.

THE IDENTIFICATION OF SUBGROUPS

Consider the researcher who wishes to test the hypothesis that reading-disabled nine-year-olds differ from other nine-year-olds with respect to cerebral lateralization. Typically, the researcher would select reading-disabled children on the basis of some specified criteria and then select normal readers who are matched for age, sex, and score on an IQ test. The reading-disabled children and their controls would be compared on measures of handedness and eyedness or for ear superiority in dichotic listening. If there are significant differences between groups and if these differences can be replicated for other samples of reading-disabled children, the research could represent an initial step to the understanding of how reading disability is related to lateralization. If, however, the outcome of various studies resembles the pattern of results summarized previously, the question of subgroups should be explored. Perhaps there is more than one kind of reading disability. Perhaps there are several varieties of reading disability, and perhaps some are associated with anomalous cerebral lateralization and others are not.

Since nearly all studies of lateralization in learning-disabled children actually have focused on reading disabilities, there is little need to point out the inadvisability of combining children who are specifically dyscalculic, for example, with those who are specifically dyslexic. There is, however, a greater likelihood of combining specifically dyslexic children with children having a learning disability that includes arithmetic as well as reading.

Beginning with Kinsbourne and Warrington's classification system, several writers have suggested ways of decomposing learning disabilities into subcategories.[26] Spreen summarized six different classificatory schemes that were proposed by contributors

26. Marcel Kinsbourne and Elizabeth Warrington, "Developmental Factors in Reading and Writing Backwardness," *British Journal of Psychology* 54 (1963): 145-56; Helmer Myklebust, *Development and Disorders of Written Language*, vol. 1, *Picture Story Language Test* (New York: Grune and Stratton, 1965); Elena Boder, "Developmental Dyslexia: A New Diagnostic Approach Based on the Identification of Three Subtypes," *Journal of School Health* 40 (1970): 289-90.

to a single conference on the neuropsychology of learning disorders.[27] These schemes include a distinction between "specific reading retardation" and "general reading backwardness"; a taxonomy based on auditory and visual processing deficits; a distinction between groups based on spelling, reading, and IQ criteria; a classification based on reading breakdown at different levels of analysis; a dichotomy between stimulant responders and nonresponders; and a classification system based on arousal level.[28]

The diversity of emphasis within this small group of writers demonstrates that it is no easy matter to find *the* best way of categorizing different kinds of learning disabilities. Indeed, there may be no one best way. Subcategories of learning disabilities may exist primarily in the eye of the beholder. Or, to describe the situation a bit more optimistically, classification systems may have differential utility depending on the purpose of the study. A researcher who focuses on task analysis of the reading process in poor readers is unlikely to profit from a classification scheme that divides children according to their response to medication. Nor are the different classification systems mutually exclusive; but how they relate to each other is not known.

There are at least two ways in which one might attempt to solve the subgroup problem. One approach is theoretical; the other is empirical. The theoretical approach entails dividing learning-disabled children according to criteria that are thought to be related to hemispheric function. For example, there is a commonly assumed association between verbal IQ and left-hemispheric function, and between performance IQ and right-hemispheric function. The empirical basis for these associations is dubious, but the

27. Spreen, "Neuropsychology of Learning Disorders: Post-Conference Review."

28. See the following articles in *The Neuropsychology of Learning Disorders*, ed. Knights and Bakker: Yule and Rutter, "Epidemiology and Social Implications of Specific Reading Retardation," pp. 25-39; Paula Tallal, "Auditory Perceptual Factors in Language and Learning Disabilities," pp. 315-23; Hazel E. Nelson and Elizabeth K. Warrington, "Developmental Spelling Retardation," pp. 325-32; Donald G. Doehring, "Evaluation of Two Models of Reading Disability," pp. 405-11; Paul H. Wender, "Hypothesis for a Possible Biochemical Basis of Minimal Brain Dysfunction," pp. 111-22; and H. Bruce Ferguson, Suzanne Simpson, and Ronald L. Trites, "Psychophysiological Study of Methylphenidate Responders and Nonresponders," pp. 89-97.

argument at least can be pursued for illustrative purposes.[29] Distinctions among learning-disabled children on the basis of discrepancies between verbal and performance IQ have proven useful in a strictly psychological context.[30] Many learning-disabled children have disproportionately low scores on the verbal subtests of an IQ test. This "language-type" of learning disability is associated with letter substitution errors in spelling and other characteristic linguistic deficits.[31] Another group of children with learning disabilities produces a characteristic IQ test profile in which performance IQ is lower than verbal IQ. These children, whose essential deficit seems to involve the processing of sequential information, frequently show so-called Gerstmann syndrome signs (finger agnosia, right-left confusion, difficulty with place values in arithmetic, and spelling difficulty). The spelling errors of these children include a large number of order errors (that is, mislocations).[32] Instead of lumping all learning-disabled children together, it may be more fruitful to examine separately the laterality of each of these two learning-disabled subgroups and to exclude learning-disabled children who do not fit into either category.

The empirical approach offers an alternative to the complexities of theoretically based classification systems. Such an approach would require, first, the testing of learning-disabled children on

29. John Todd, Frederick Coolidge, and Paul Satz, "The Wechsler Adult Intelligence Scale Discrepancy Index: A Neuropsychological Evaluation," *Journal of Consulting and Clinical Psychology* 45 (1977): 450-54; Joseph D. Matarazzo, *Wechsler's Measurement and Appraisal of Adult Intelligence*, 5th ed. (Baltimore: Williams and Wilkins, 1972).

30. Marcel Kinsbourne, "Selective Difficulties in Learning to Read, Write, and Calculate" (Paper presented at the Learning Disabilities Symposium, Chicago, 1976); Kinsbourne and Warrington, "Developmental Factors in Reading and Writing Backwardness"; Steven Mattis, Joseph H. French, and Isabelle Rapin, "Dyslexia in Children and Young Adults: Three Independent Neuropsychological Syndromes," *Developmental Medicine and Child Neurology* 17 (1975): 150-63.

31. Kinsbourne and Warrington, "Developmental Factors in Reading and Writing Backwardness"; Martha Denckla, "Minimal Brain Dysfunction and Dyslexia: Beyond Diagnosis by Exclusion," in *Topics in Child Neurology*, ed. Michael E. Blaw, Isabelle Rapin, and Marcel Kinsbourne (New York: Spectrum, 1977), pp. 243-62.

32. Kinsbourne and Warrington, "Developmental Factors in Reading and Writing Backwardness."

one or more "lateralization tasks." On the basis of previous research, one could expect to find appreciable variability in degree of asymmetry. Thus, children could be categorized according to direction or degree of asymmetry on the so-called lateralization tasks. The performance of "normally lateralized" and "anomalously lateralized" children then could be compared on several cognitive measures in the hope of finding performance characteristics that differentiate the two groups. The empirical approach, however, is not without its own pitfalls. The investigator must identify and measure the "right" cognitive dimensions. That may necessitate an extensive battery of tests, but the use of a large number of measures is conducive to obtaining significant differences by chance. Consequently, any positive findings would have to be cross-validated for an independent sample of learning-disabled children. If a set of measures survives cross-validation, it should prove possible to select subjects on the basis of that set and to demonstrate that one of the two subgroups, but not the other, differs from normal children in performance on so-called lateralization tasks.

Throughout this discussion, there has been an element of devil's advocacy. We have assumed that it is logical to expect a relationship between at least some kinds of learning disability and anomalous, incomplete, or delayed lateralization of language functions. We have assumed that individual differences in lateralization can be measured satisfactorily. In the following sections, we shall turn our attention to assumptions such as these.

What Is Lateralization?

The terms "cerebral dominance" and "cerebral lateralization" often are used interchangeably and without definition or explanation. The imprecise and indiscriminate use of these terms tends to obscure differences among various models, assumptions, and operational definitions regarding brain organization. For instance, lateralization may be regarded as a hypothetical construct or it may be used to refer to a very specific behavioral characteristic such as degree of hand preference.[33] When applied to specific charac-

33. See Satz, "Cerebral Dominance and Reading Disability: An Old Problem Revisited."

teristics, the term is often used in connection with dissimilar operational definitions. Thus, a child may be identified as strongly lateralized on the basis of consistent handedness, footedness, and eyedness or on the basis of marked right-ear superiority in dichotic listening. If the two sets of measures are in agreement, then there may be justification for referring to both as measures of lateralization. But what can one say about lateralization when there is strong right-sided hand, foot, and sighting preference, but left-ear superiority in dichotic listening? The first problem, then, is the ambiguity inherent in common usages of the terms "dominance" and "lateralization." In attempting to answer questions about the relationship between cerebral lateralization and learning disability, it makes a difference whether one defines lateralization as, say, hand preference or whether one considers lateralization as a hypothetical construct that cannot be fully measured by any one operation.

Although the term "lateralization" is commonly regarded as a more modern synonym for the older term "dominance," it is important to recognize an essential difference in meaning between the two terms. Zangwill notes that the dominant hemisphere historically "has been supposed to 'take the lead' in manual skill and in the control of articulate speech."[34] As Zangwill points out, this concept actually comprises two separate but confusable aspects. The first is functional specialization, that is, there is some qualitative or quantitative asymmetry in the representation of certain higher mental functions. For example, one hemisphere has a greater role or a different role in speech than does the other hemisphere. In Zangwill's words, "function is asymmetrically represented in the two halves of the brain so that equivalent unilateral lesions do not produce equivalent effects."[35] This presumed hemispheric specialization is what most writers refer to as cerebral lateralization. The concept of dominance, however, also implies an executive function of one hemisphere that is not implied in the term "lateralization." This is the notion that one hemisphere exerts a mastery or control over the other.[36] Although there is little support for this concept,

34. Zangwill, "Dyslexia in Relation to Cerebral Dominance," p. 104.
35. Ibid., p. 105.
36. Ibid.

it seems very similar to Orton's concept of dominance.[37] The issue is further confused by the term "double dominance," which means that one hemisphere is dominant for some functions and the opposite hemisphere is dominant for others.[38]

We shall set aside these issues temporarily and conclude only that the meanings of the concepts of lateralization and dominance are not self-evident. On the contrary, the concepts require much more thought than they usually receive. In the following paragraphs, we shall analyze the operations used to assess lateralization and dominance and then we shall offer some suggestions about the concepts themselves and how they might be clarified.

HANDEDNESS AND BRAIN ORGANIZATION

Today the relationship between the preferred hand and the linguistic cerebral hemisphere is well documented. A hundred years worth of case reports linking side of brain damage and incidence of aphasia (disruption of language) indicates that the great majority—more than 98 percent—of right-handers are left lateralized for language.[39] A similar conclusion can be drawn from the results of sodium Amytal testing. This procedure, sometimes called the Wada technique, involves injection of a fast-acting barbiturate into the arterial system supplying one side of the brain.[40] The drug incapacitates one cerebral hemisphere for a period of a few minutes. It has been found that left-sided injections, but not right-sided injections, temporarily impair linguistic functioning in more than 95 percent of right-handers.[41] The evi-

37. Orton, *Reading, Writing, and Speech Problems in Children.*

38. Bakan, "Hypnotizability, Laterality of Eye Movements, and Functional Brain Asymmetry."

39. O. L. Zangwill, "Speech and the Minor Hemisphere," *Acta Neurologica et Psychiatrica Belgica* 67 (1967): 1013-20.

40. Juhn Wada and Theodore Rasmussen, "Intracarotid Injection of Sodium Amytal for the Lateralization of Cerebral Speech Dominance: Experimental and Clinical Observations," *Journal of Neurosurgery* 17 (1960): 266-82.

41. Theodore Rasmussen and Brenda Milner, "Clinical and Surgical Studies of the Cerebral Speech Areas in Man," in *Otfrid Foerster Symposium on Cerebral Localization*, ed. K. J. Zulch, O. Creutzfeldt, and G. C. Galbraith (Heidelberg: Springer-Verlag, 1975), pp. 238-57; Gian F. Rossi and Guido Rosadini, "Experimental Analysis of Cerebral Dominance in Man," in *Brain Mechanisms Underlying Speech and Language*, ed. Clark H. Millikan and Frederic L. Darley (New York: Grune and Stratton, 1967), pp. 167-84.

dence, then, very clearly demonstrates that virtually all right-handers are left-lateralized for language. Left-handers, however, appear to be much more heterogeneous in language representation. The aphasia data and results of sodium Amytal testing suggest that the majority of left-handers (as many as two-thirds) have left-lateralized language.[42] In other words, the linguistic hemisphere of most left-handers is not contralateral to the dominant hand. Most of the remaining left-handers appear to be right-lateralized for language, but others seem to have some linguistic capability in both hemispheres.[43]

What, exactly, does hand preference tell us about brain organization? We can be quite sure that right-handers have their language represented in the left cerebral hemisphere. If an adult uses the right hand for everyday unimanual activities (for example, eating with a spoon, throwing a ball, brushing the teeth), there is only a slight chance that that person's language is represented anywhere but in the left hemisphere. We have argued elsewhere that this statement holds for children as well as for adults.[44] How-

42. George Ettlinger, C. V. Jackson and O. L. Zangwill, "Cerebral Dominance in Sinistrals," *Brain* 79 (1956): 569-88; I. Gloning et al., "Comparison of Verbal Behavior in Right-handed and Non-right-handed Patients with Anatomically Verified Lesion of One Hemisphere," *Cortex* 5 (1969): 41-52; Harold Goodglass and F. A. Quadfasel, "Language Laterality in Left-handed Aphasics," *Brain* 77 (1954): 521-48; Henri Hécaen and M. Piercy, "Paroxysmal Dysphasia and the Problem of Cerebral Dominance," *Journal of Neurology, Neurosurgery, and Psychiatry* 19 (1956): 194-201; Henri Hécaen and J. Sauget, "Cerebral Dominance in Left-handed Subjects," *Cortex* 7 (1941): 19-48; M. E. Humphrey and O. L. Zangwill, "Dysphasia in Left-handed Patients with Unilateral Brain Lesions," *Journal of Neurology, Neurosurgery, and Psychiatry* 15 (1952): 184-93; Alexander R. Luria, *Traumatic Aphasia: Its Syndromes, Psychology, and Treatment*, trans., Douglas Bowden (Paris: Mouton, 1970); Wilder Penfield and Lamar Roberts, *Speech and Brain Mechanisms* (Princeton, N.J.: Princeton University Press, 1959); Lamar Roberts, "Aphasia, Apraxia, and Agnosia in Abnormal States for Cerebral Dominance," in *Handbook of Clinical Neurology* vol. 4, ed. P. J. Vinken and G. W. Bruyn (Amsterdam: North-Holland, 1969), pp. 312-26; William R. Russell and Michael L. E. Espir, *Traumatic Aphasia: A Study of Aphasia in War Wounds of the Brain* (London: Oxford University Press, 1961); Zangwill, "Speech and the Minor Hemisphere"; Rasmussen and Milner, "Clinical and Surgical Studies of the Cerebral Speech Areas in Man"; Rossi and Rosadini, "Experimental Analysis of Cerebral Dominance in Man."

43. Rasmussen and Milner, "Clinical and Surgical Studies of the Cerebral Speech Areas in Man."

44. Marcel Kinsbourne and Merrill Hiscock, "Does Cerebral Dominance Develop?" in *Language Development and Neurological Theory*, ed. Sidney J. Segalowitz and Frederic A. Gruber (New York: Academic Press, 1977), pp. 171-91.

ever, if the person shows a preference for the left hand, we can make no safe statement about language lateralization. The best bet still is left-hemispheric representation of language, but the odds are only slightly greater than even.

Thus, the evidence reveals only a rather weak statistical association between hand preference and the likelihood of left-hemispheric language representation. Apart from the possibility of less complete lateralization in at least some left-handers there is no convincing evidence that handedness is related to *degree* of lateralization.[45] This is the very assumption that was made by Orton and is implicit in many contemporary viewpoints: that the degree of behavioral asymmetry or "sidedness" reflects the degree to which language is lateralized.[46]

Orton emphasized the significance of eyedness and, to a lesser degree, the significance of footedness and handedness in the assessment of right- or left-sidedness.[47] In the current era of dichotic listening and tachistoscopic procedures, asymmetrical performance on these tasks can be added to the more traditional indices of sidedness. Sidedness might be defined as the degree of asymmetry on a single measure (for example, degree of handedness), the concordance among different measures (that is, the number of these procedures yielding a right-sided preference or superiority), or as some combination of degree of asymmetry on individual tasks and degree of intertask concordance.

First, we shall consider some of the implications of inferring degree of lateralization from degree of handedness. The measurement of handedness is not a clear-cut matter. Handedness can be conceived of either as hand preference or as a difference between the hands in skill level. Questionnaire measures of hand preference yield bimodal, J-shaped frequency distributions with a large num-

45. K. Conrad, "Über aphasische Sprachstörungen bei hirnverletzten Linkshändern," *Nervenartz* 20 (1949): 148-54; Goodglass and Quadfasel, "Language Laterality in Left-handed Aphasics"; Hécaen and Piercy, "Paroxysmal Dysphasia and the Problem of Cerebral Dominance"; Rasmussen and Milner, "Clinical and Surgical Studies of the Cerebral Speech Areas in Man"; O. L. Zangwill, *Cerebral Dominance and Its Relation to Psychological Function* (London: Oliver and Boyd, 1960).

46. Orton, *Reading, Writing and Speech Problems in Children.*

47. Ibid.

ber of scores at the extreme right-hand pole and a much smaller concentration of scores near the left-hand pole.[48] Right-hand minus left-hand differences on performance measures such as strength and speed form unimodal, approximately bell-shaped frequency distributions.[49] It appears that a small right-hand superiority in skill is sufficient to produce a strong preference for the use of the right hand. In any event, asymmetric hand use and asymmetric hand skill are not the same thing, although there does seem to be an association between these two aspects of handedness.[50]

If a choice is made to measure hand preference rather than asymmetry of manual skill, the investigator must decide how best to sample from the population of manual activities and how to weight each activity. Is hand preference for writing equal in importance to hand used for dealing cards? Does one focus attention on preferences that are likely to be environmentally influenced (for example, writing, eating, using scissors) or does one concentrate on preferences that seem to be independent of cultural and other environmental shaping?[51] Perhaps it is useful to divide subjects into preference groups on the basis of an association analysis so that questionnaire items are weighted according to their correlations with other items.[52]

If the investigator chooses to define handedness in terms of a performance difference between the hands rather than hand preference, some of the problems inherent in the use of handedness questionnaires can be avoided but there will be other problems to replace them. Provins and Cunliffe found statistically significant retest reliability for only two of seven measures of motor-skill

48. R. C. Oldfield, "The Assessment and Analysis of Handedness: The Edinburgh Inventory," *Neuropsychologia* 9 (1971): 97-113.

49. Marian Annett, "The Distribution of Manual Asymmetry," *British Journal of Psychology* 63 (1972): 343-58; T. L. Woo and Karl Pearson, "Dextrality and Sinistrality of Hand and Eye," *Biometrika* 19 (1927): 165-99.

50. Annett, "A Classification of Hand Preference by Association Analysis"; idem, "A Coordination of Hand Preference and Skill Replicated," *British Journal of Psychology* 67 (1976): 587-92.

51. Evelyn L. Teng et al., "Handedness in a Chinese Population: Biological, Social, and Pathological Factors," *Science* 193 (1976): 1148-50.

52. Annett, "A Classification of Hand Preference by Association Analysis."

asymmetry, and one of the two reliable measures was the highly practiced skill of cursive writing.[53] Differences between the hands were unreliable for most tasks despite a short test-retest interval, considerable heterogeneity of hand preference among the (adult) subjects, and adequate retest reliability of performance with the preferred hand. Other studies have produced statistically significant but rather modest estimates of retest reliability for the difference between the hands in motor skill.[54] Perhaps because the individual measures are not very reliable, correlations among measures of manual asymmetry tend to be low and, in some instances, not significantly different from zero.[55] Thus, even if a test of manual performance asymmetry proves to be reliable, one cannot be sure it is measuring a general dimension of sidedness in motor skill. In fact, Fleishman has identified several independent factors of motor and perceptual-motor ability, and it is not clear which are most relevant to differences in cerebral organization.[56] Differential experience with the two hands in everyday life constitutes another problem. Highly practiced skills may yield the most reliable differences between the hands, but the magnitude and reliability of these differences probably reflect, in part, differential practice. Even novel tasks may be influenced by facilitative or interfering transfer from similar aspects of everyday tasks. The investigator must decide whether the definition of handedness to be used is better embodied in a "pure" (that is, completely novel) test of skill or in a task that is confounded by the effects of differential experience or practice. Within the testing situation, practice effects, fatigue effects, order effects, and other task variables may

53. K. A. Provins and Penny Cunliffe, "The Reliability of Some Motor Performance Tests of Handedness," *Neuropsychologia* 10 (1972): 199-206.

54. Marian Annett, P. T. W. Hudson, and Ann Turner, "The Reliability of Differences between the Hands in Motor Skill," *Neuropsychologia* 12 (1974): 527-31; Donald Shankweiler and Michael Studdert-Kennedy, "A Continuum of Lateralization for Speech Perception?" *Brain and Language* 2 (1975): 212-25.

55. Shankweiler and Studdert-Kennedy, "A Continuum of Lateralization for Speech Perception?"

56. Edwin A. Fleishman, "On the Relation between Abilities, Learning, and Human Performance," *American Psychologist* 27 (1972): 1017-32.

exert strong influences on the magnitude of performance differences between the hands.[57]

MIXED DOMINANCE AND BRAIN ORGANIZATION

It is no easy matter to specify the degree to which a person is right- or left-handed. An alternative, as mentioned previously, is to assess the consistency of a person's asymmetry across different pairs of receptors and effectors (for example, hands, feet, eyes). Presumably, inconsistent sidedness, or "mixed dominance," suggests incomplete lateralization.[58] What are the implications and the problems in this approach? Relatively little is known about footedness, except that foot preference tends to be correlated with hand preference.[59] Many of the problems inherent in the measurement of handedness would seem to apply to the measurement of footedness as well. The main issue, though, is the significance of footedness. Does an estimate of hand and foot preference provide more information about brain lateralization than do two measures of hand preference? There is no reason to believe that footedness has any special significance.

Greater claims have been made for the importance of eyedness and the association between crossed eye-hand dominance and cognitive deficit. It is not uncommon today to find clinicians who consider "mixed dominance" of this kind to be a pathognomonic indicator of learning disability. As noted previously, the evidence is unconvincing. There are many normal students who have crossed eye-hand dominance and there are many learning-disabled children who do not. Equally important is the lack of theoretical or empirical basis for linking eye dominance and cerebral lateralization. In their comprehensive review of the eye-dominance literature, Porac and Coren state that "there is little neurological and physio-

57. Robert E. Hicks and Marcel Kinsbourne, "Human Handedness," in *The Asymmetrical Function of the Brain*, ed. Marcel Kinsbourne (New York: Cambridge University Press, 1978), pp. 523-49.

58. Orton, *Reading, Writing, and Speech Problems in Children.*

59. Marian Annett and Ann Turner, "Laterality and the Growth of Intellectual Abilities," *British Journal of Educational Psychology* 44 (1974): 37-46; M. M. Clark, *Left-Handedness* (London: University of London Press, 1957).

logical data to support the presence of any relationship between ocular and cerebral dominance."[60] This statement is based primarily on the lack of an exclusive or preferential relationship between the eye and either cerebral hemisphere. The optic tract is only partially crossed, or semidecussated, on its route from the eye to the cerebral visual reception areas. At the optic chiasm, located in the pathway from the retina to the lateral geniculate nuclei, half of the fibers from each eye proceed toward the right hemisphere and half proceed toward the left hemisphere. Consequently, a preference for visual input from, say, the right eye does not imply a left-hemispheric advantage in processing that input. The information from the right eye is transmitted directly to both hemispheres.

Despite the absence of reasons to expect a correlation between handedness and eyedness, several investigators have looked for such a relationship. Of the twenty investigations cited by Porac and Coren, nine reports claimed associations between the two variables and eleven did not.[61] Porac and Coren argue that the positive findings may be "slightly artifactual" because most people are right-handed and also use their right eye for sighting. Especially when subjects are dichotomized or trichotomized with regard to lateral preference, there may be an apparent association between handedness and eyedness even if the two tendencies in fact are orthogonal.[62] The apparent association disappears when quantitative ratings of strength of lateral preference are used.[63]

PERCEPTUAL ASYMMETRY AND BRAIN ORGANIZATION

In the past ten or fifteen years, researchers have shown less interest in the traditional measures of handedness and eyedness than

60. Porac and Coren, "The Dominant Eye," p. 886.

61. Ibid.

62. R. A. Collins and R. I. Collins, "Independence of Eye-Hand Preference in Mentally Retarded: Evidence of Spurious Associations in Heterogeneous Populations," *American Journal of Optometry and Archives of the American Academy of Optometry* 48 (1971): 1031-33.

63. Stanley Coren and Clare P. Kaplan, "Patterns of Ocular Dominance," *American Journal of Optometry and Archives of the American Academy of Optometry* 50 (1973): 283-92; Clare Porac and Stanley Coren, "Is Sighting Dominance a Part of Generalized Laterality?" *Perceptual and Motor Skills* 40 (1975): 763-69.

in measures of perceptual asymmetry. Presumably, techniques such as dichotic listening and half-field tachistoscopic tasks provide a more direct assessment of cerebral lateralization. If so, why are the results, as summarized previously, so inconsistent? Inconsistent differences between learning-disabled children and control subjects might be attributed to classification problems discussed previously, but the average degree of asymmetry varies considerably among control groups in these various studies.[64]

Some of the variability among dichotic listening studies probably can be attributed to unknown and uncontrolled variations in the acoustical characteristics of the stimulus material. Berlin and his colleagues have demonstrated the importance of stimulus parameters such as signal-to-noise ratio, intensity level, band width, and synchrony of stimulus onset.[65] The comparability of results from different studies is jeopardized when these variables are disregarded. In addition, floor and ceiling effects may influence asymmetry scores to the degree that between-group comparisons become invalid.[66] There is considerable diversity of opinion concerning the appropriate statistical treatment of dichotic listening scores. Of particular relevance to the question of anomalous lateralization in learning-disabled children is the difficult problem of how to compare the size of asymmetry across individuals or groups that differ in overall level of performance. Researchers have a choice of working with raw scores for each ear or transforming the raw data to one of several "laterality indices."[67] Alternatively,

64. Satz, "Cerebral Dominance and Reading Disability: An Old Problem Revisited."

65. Charles I. Berlin and Malcolm R. McNeil, "Dichotic Listening," in *Contemporary Issues in Experimental Phonetics*, ed. N. J. Lass (New York: Academic Press, 1976), pp. 327-87; Charles I. Berlin and John K. Cullen, Jr., "Acoustic Problems in Dichotic Listening Tasks," in *Language Development and Neurological Theory*, ed. Segalowitz and Gruber, pp. 75-88.

66. Kinsbourne and Hiscock, "Does Cerebral Dominance Develop?"; Satz, "Cerebral Dominance and Reading Disability: An Old Problem Revisited."

67. Gary M. Kuhn, "The Phi Coefficient as an Index of Ear Differences in Dichotic Listening," *Cortex* 9 (1973): 450-56; John C. Marshall, David Caplan, and Jane M. Holmes, "The Measure of Laterality," *Neuropsychologia* 13 (1975): 315-21; Michael Studdert-Kennedy and Donald P. Shankweiler, "Hemispheric Specialization for Speech Perception," *Journal of the Acoustical Society of America* 48 (1970): 579-94; Richard Harshman and Stephen

they may prefer to use frequency or rank-order data.[68] Unfortunately it is quite possible that different statistical choices will lead to contradictory conclusions.[69]

PERCEPTUAL TASKS AS A MEASURE OF LATERALIZATION: SOME PROBLEMS

Although methodological problems are troublesome, the difficulty with perceptual tasks as a measure of cerebral lateralization extends beyond the diversity of technical standards or the intractability of scaling problems. The fundamental problem seems to be conceptual rather than methodological; it is the assumption that the magnitude of listening asymmetry or visual-field asymmetry is a direct measure of the degree to which language is lateralized in an individual or a group. This assumption stems from uncritical acceptance of a purely structural model of perceptual asymmetries.[70] The structural model of perceptual asymmetries relies on two facts: (a) that in most people it is the left hemisphere which is specialized for language processing and (b) that there is preferential access to each hemisphere of information coming from receptors on the opposite side of the body. Consequently it is argued that when speech messages of different content are simultaneously presented to the two ears, it is the message arriving at the ear contralateral to the "verbal" hemisphere that gains preferential

---

Krashen, "An Unbiased Procedure for Comparing Degree of Lateralization of Dichotically Presented Stimuli" (Paper presented at the Eighty-third Meeting of the Acoustical Society of America, April, 1972).

68. M. P. Bryden, "Laterality Effects in Dichotic Listening: Relations with Handedness and Reading Ability in Children," *Neuropsychologia* 8 (1970): 443-50; M. P. Bryden and Fran Allard, "Dichotic Listening and the Development of Linguistic Processes," in *The Asymmetrical Function of the Brain*, ed. Kinsbourne, pp. 392-404; J. T. E. Richardson, "How to Measure Laterality," *Neuropsychologia* 14 (1976): 135-36.

69. For example, Sara Sparrow and Paul Satz, "Dyslexia, Laterality, and Neuropsychological Development," in *Specific Reading Disability: Advances in Theory and Method*, ed. Dirk J. Bakker and Paul Satz (Rotterdam: Rotterdam University Press, 1970), pp. 41-60.

70. Kimura, "Cerebral Dominance and the Perception of Verbal Stimuli"; idem, "Some Effects of Temporal-Lobe Damage on Auditory Perception"; idem, "Dual Functional Asymmetry of the Brain in Visual Perception"; idem, "Functional Asymmetry of the Brain in Dichotic Listening," *Cortex* 3 (1967): 163-78.

access to that hemisphere and therefore is better decoded. Those signals which come in through the ear on the same side as the hemisphere dominant for language achieve less priority in processing and therefore are less perfectly recognized. An analogous explanation is used in the visual modality. When verbal information is flashed to one side of the central point of fixation, then if that is the side opposite the hemisphere dominant for language, the information gains direct access to that hemisphere and is dealt with efficiently. If, on the other hand, the information is presented to the visual half-field on the same side as the language-dominant hemisphere, then it is first conducted contralaterally to the hemisphere that is not so specialized and only secondarily is transported, across the corpus callosum that connects the two hemispheres, to the language processing part of the brain. This more indirect path, it is argued, causes the message to lose intelligibility and to be relatively poorly recognized.

If perceptual asymmetries are the direct result of the manner in which the afferent pathways are "wired," it seems reasonable to suggest that variations among people in degree of asymmetry might be associated with variations in degree of cerebral specialization. That is, the direct input of information to a cerebral hemisphere would be advantageous only to the degree that that hemisphere is more adept than its counterpart in processing that information. The model breaks down immediately, however, when applied to dichotic listening. Kimura argued that binaural competition is necessary to demonstrate an ear advantage, because listening asymmetries depend on the "occlusion" of the ipsilateral pathway by the contralateral pathway.[71] Even the partial occlusion suggested by Kimura, however, would not be a sufficient condition to ensure that the ear advantage is a direct index of lateralization. Individual differences could be attributed to differences in the degree of occlusion or the degree to which the contralateral pathway is superior to the ipsilateral pathway. Only in the case of total occlusion of one pathway by the other could individual differences be attributed to differences in cerebral lateralization. In fact, occlusion does not appear to be a factor at all. Various in-

71. Ibid.

vestigators have elicited a right-ear advantage for linguistic material without reliance on binaural rivalry.[72]

Thus, even based on a structural model of listening asymmetry it does not follow that differences in degree of asymmetry can necessarily be regarded as indicating differences in degree of cerebral lateralization of language. Alternatively, such differences might merely reflect variation in the degree to which the pathway from one ear to the language hemisphere is superior to the pathway from the other side as a vehicle for information.[73]

More importantly, there are several grounds on which to question the premise that perceptual asymmetries are, in fact, attributable to structural factors of any nature:

1. Ear difference scores in dichotic listening are less reliable than measures of a fixed, structural property should be.[74] Blumstein et al. reported test-retest reliability coefficients of .21 for vowels,

72. Dirk J. Bakker, "Left-Right Differences in Auditory Perception of Verbal and Nonverbal Material by Children," *Quarterly Journal of Experimental Psychology* 19 (1967): 334-36; idem, "Ear Asymmetry with Monaural Stimulation," *Psychonomic Science* 12 (1968): 62; idem, "Ear Asymmetry with Monaural Stimulation: Task Influences," *Cortex* 5 (1969): 36-42; idem, "Ear Asymmetry with Monaural Stimulation: Relations to Lateral Dominance and Lateral Awareness," *Neuropsychologia* 8 (1970): 103-17; T. G. Bever, "The Nature of Cerebral Dominance in Speech Behavior of the Child and Adult," in *Language Acquisition: Models and Methods*, ed. Renira Huxley and Elisabeth Ingram (London: Academic Press, 1971), pp. 231-61; S. P. Haydon and F. J. Spellacy, "Monaural Reaction Time Asymmetries for Speech and Non-Speech Sounds," *Cortex* 9 (1974): 288-94; Jose Morais and Paul Bertelson, "Laterality Effects in Diotic Listening," *Perception* 2 (1973): 107-11; Jose Morais and C. J. Darwin, "Ear Differences for Same-Different Reaction Times to Monaurally Presented Speech," *Brain and Language* 1 (1974): 383-90; K. A. Provins and M. A. Jeeves, "Hemisphere Differences in Response Time to Simple Auditory Stimuli," *Neuropsychologia* 13 (1975): 207-11; J. R. Simon, "Ear Preference in a Simple Reaction-Time Task," *Journal of Experimental Psychology* 75 (1967): 49-55.

73. Sheila Blumstein, Harold Goodglass, and Vivian Tartter, "The Reliability of Ear Advantage in Dichotic Listening," *Brain and Language* 2 (1975): 226-36; Jose Morais and Paul Bertelson, "Spatial Position versus Ear of Entry as Determinant of the Auditory Laterality Effects: A Stereophonic Test," *Journal of Experimental Psychology: Human Perception and Performance* 1 (1975): 253-62; M. R. Rosenzweig, "Cortical Correlates of Auditory Localization and of Related Perceptual Phenomena," *Journal of Comparative and Physiological Psychology* 47 (1954): 269-76.

74. Blumstein, Goodglass, and Tartter, "The Reliability of Ear Advantage in Dichotic Listening"; Luigi Pizzamiglio, Corradino De Pascalis, and Andrea Vignati, "Stability of Dichotic Listening Test," *Cortex* 10 (1974): 203-5.

.46 for music, and .74 for consonants. When frequency data (that is, the number of subjects showing a right- or left-ear advantage) were analyzed, there was a statistically significant association between test 1 and test 2 only in the case of the musical stimuli. On the consonant and vowel tasks, about one-third of the (adult) subjects shifted ear advantage from test 1 to test 2. There is no reason to believe that the test-retest reliability of children's ear differences should be any better. Quite likely, it is worse.[75] Visual asymmetries appear to be even less reliable than dichotic listening asymmetries.[76] A portion of the unreliability of these measures may be attributed to a statistical limiting factor: the reliability of difference scores decreases as the correlation between their component scores increases.[77] Nevertheless, perceptual asymmetries are remarkably unstable for indices of a fixed brain characteristic. It is particularly difficult to draw inferences about lateralization in people who show a right-sided preference on initial testing and a left-sided preference upon retesting.

2. Perceptual tests underestimate the population incidence of left lateralization of language. For instance, in dichotic listening studies, no more than about 80 percent of a sample of normal, right-handed subjects typically show a right-ear advantage, no matter how small.[78] Blumstein et al. estimated that 15 percent of their right-handed subjects were consistently left-ear dominant for consonants. These estimates stand in contrast to the 95 to 99 percent incidence of left lateralization of language reported for right-handers in both the aphasia literature and the sodium Amytal literature.[79] The significance of this mismatch in incidence esti-

75. Merrill Hiscock and Marcel Kinsbourne, "Selective Listening Asymmetry in Preschool Children," *Developmental Psychology* 13 (1977): 217-24.

76. David Hines and Paul Satz, "Cross-modal Asymmetries in Perception Related to Asymmetry in Cerebral Function," *Neuropsychologia* 12 (1974): 239-47.

77. Ibid.

78. Blumstein, Goodglass, and Tartter, "The Reliability of Ear Advantage in Dichotic Listening"; Bryden and Allard, "Dichotic Listening and the Development of Linguistic Processes."

79. Zangwill, "Speech and the Minor Hemisphere"; Rasmussen and Milner, "Clinical and Surgical Studies of the Cerebral Speech Areas in Man"; Rossi and Rosadini, "Experimental Analysis of Cerebral Dominance in Man."

mates has been pointed out vividly by Satz, who used Baysean statistics to demonstrate the fallacy inherent in making inferences about an individual's language lateralization on the basis of dichotic listening asymmetries.[80] If 95 percent of the population actually have speech represented in the left hemisphere, nearly all subjects in any sample will have left-hemispheric language regardless of dichotic listening score. Accordingly, Satz's analysis shows that, if 70 percent of a sample show a right-ear advantage, the probability of left-hemispheric language is .97 for subjects with a right-ear advantage and .90 for subjects with a left-ear advantage. If a subject has a left-ear advantage, the likelihood of right lateralization is only .10. Thus, the investigator who infers anomalous lateralization from a left-ear advantage may be wrong nine times out of ten with a sample of adult right-handers. There is little reason to believe that the classificatory precision of dichotic listening is better in a sample of children.[81]

3. Asymmetries of perception can be modified by certain situational and experiential factors.[82] Kinsbourne demonstrated that a concurrent verbal task will introduce a rightward bias in visual perception, and recent studies have replicated and elaborated this earlier finding.[83] It has been reported that displacing prisms alter listening asymmetry; if the subject's visual field is shifted to the right, the right-ear advantage is enhanced.[84] Ear symmetry can be

80. Satz, "Laterality Tests: An Inferential Problem."

81. Marcel Kinsbourne, "The Ontogeny of Cerebral Dominance," *Annals of the New York Academy of Sciences* 263 (1975): 244-50; Kinsbourne and Hiscock, "Does Cerebral Dominance Develop?"

82. See Michael Studdert-Kennedy, "Dichotic Studies II: Two Questions," *Brain and Language* 2 (1975): 123-30.

83. Marcel Kinsbourne, "The Cerebral Basis of Lateral Asymmetries in Attention," *Acta Psychologica* 33 (1970): 193-201; Joseph B. Hellige and Pamela J. Cox, "Effects of Concurrent Verbal Memory on Recognition of Stimuli from the Left and Right Visual Fields," *Journal of Experimental Psychology: Human Perception and Performance* 2 (1976): 210-21; Joseph B. Hellige, "Visual Laterality Patterns and Pure vs. Mixed List Presentation" (Paper presented at the Eighty-fifth Annual Convention of the American Psychological Association, August, 1977).

84. L. Goldstein and J. R. Lackner, "Sideways Look at Dichotic Listening," (abstract) *Journal of the Acoustical Society of America* 55, Supplement (1974): S10.

altered by varying the apparent location of the sound source.[85] Consequently, the right-ear advantage actually may be a "right-side-of-space" advantage. Other studies demonstrate that ear asymmetry is modulated by various aspects of the task.[86] Perhaps the most compelling demonstration of contextual factors is the finding of Spellacy and Blumstein that vowel sounds may yield either a right-ear advantage or no asymmetry depending on whether the context in which the sounds were heard is linguistic or nonlinguistic. Other studies suggest that the presence or absence of a right-ear advantage depends, in part, on the subject's previous experience with a particular kind of stimulus. Thus, musicians differ from nonmusicians in perception of dichotic melodies, and Thai speakers differ from English speakers in the perception of certain Thai words.[87]

4. Another argument against the notion of isomorphism between a person's perceptual asymmetry and an underlying dimension of cerebral asymmetry arises from an examination of the manner in which perceptual asymmetries are distributed. The argument is reminiscent of our previous discussion of the distributions of right-left differences in motor measures. The present argument, however, is different insofar as the disparity exists between percep-

85. Jose Morais, "The Effects of Ventriloquism on the Right-Side Advantage for Verbal Material," *Cognition* 3 (1975): 127-39; Morais and Bertelson, "Spatial Position versus Ear of Entry as Determinant of the Auditory Laterality Effects: A Stereophonic Test."

86. Bonnie Bartholomeus, "Effect of Task Requirements on Ear Superiority for Sung Speech," *Cortex* 10 (1974): 215-23; C. J. Darwin, "Ear Differences in the Recall of Fricatives and Vowels," *Quarterly Journal of Experimental Psychology* 23 (1971): 46-62; M. P. Haggard, "Encoding and the REA for Speech Signals," *Quarterly Journal of Experimental Psychology* 23 (1971): 34-45; M. P. Haggard and A. M. Parkinson, "Stimulus and Task Factors as Determinants of Ear Advantage," *Quarterly Journal of Experimental Psychology* 23 (1971): 168-77; Frank Spellacy and Sheila Blumstein, "The Influence of Language Set on Ear Preference in Phoneme Recognition," *Cortex* 6 (1970): 430-39.

87. T. G. Bever and R. J. Chiarello, "Cerebral Dominance in Musicians and Non-Musicians," *Science* 185 (1974): 537-39; D. Van Lancker and V. A. Fromkin, "Hemispheric Specialization for Pitch and 'Tone': Evidence from Thai," *Journal of Phonetics* 1 (1977): 101-9; Peter R. Johnson, "Dichotically-stimulated Ear Differences in Musicians and Nonmusicians" (Paper presented at the Thirty-eighth Annual Meeting of the Canadian Psychological Association, Vancouver, B.C., June, 1977).

tual measures and more direct evidence about cerebral specialization. Indeed, the basic issue is whether the concept of varying degrees of lateralization (in right-handers) has any meaning.

Perceptual asymmetries tend to be small in magnitude, but more direct clinical techniques suggest that lateralization of language in right-handers is marked and unambiguous. Right-ear performance in normal populations seldom exceeds left-ear performance by more than a few percentage points.[88] In contrast, unilateral injection of sodium Amytal into the carotid arteries of right-handers brings about either complete cessation of speech or no change in speech, depending on the side of the injection. It is a very rare case in which left-sided and right-sided injections each produce partial disruption of speech in a right-handed patient or in which neither injection disrupts speech.[89] Similarly, the aphasia data show that in most right-handers damage to right-hemispheric areas homologous to left-hemispheric speech areas produces no measurable deficit in language functions.[90] Probably all normal asymmetries of human performance are distributed along continua.[91] Also, the estimates from clinical data may be biased somewhat by sampling problems and by emphasis on expressive rather than receptive language.[92] Nevertheless, despite these qualifications, it is difficult to relate the continua of dichotic listening

88. Berlin and McNeil, "Dichotic Listening"; Blumstein, Goodglass, and Tartter, "The Reliability of Ear Advantage in Dichotic Listening."

89. Rasmussen and Milner, "Clinical and Surgical Studies of the Cerebral Speech Areas in Man."

90. For example, Zangwill, "Speech and the Minor Hemisphere"; M. Wyke, "Dysphasia: A Review of Recent Progress," *British Medical Bulletin* 27 (1971): 211-17.

91. Annett, "The Distribution of Manual Asymmetry"; Shankweiler and Studdert-Kennedy, "A Continuum of Lateralization for Speech Perception?"; Woo and Pearson, "Dextrality and Sinistrality of Hand and Eye."

92. Marcel Kinsbourne, "Mechanisms of Hemispheric Interaction in Man," in *Hemispheric Disconnection and Cerebral Function*, ed. Marcel Kinsbourne and W. Lynn Smith (Springfield, Ill: Charles C Thomas, 1974) pp. 260-85; Jerre Levy, "Psychobiological Implications of Bilateral Asymmetry," in *Hemisphere Function in the Human Brain*, ed. Stuart J. Dimond and J. Graham Beaumont (London: Paul Elek, 1974), pp. 121-83. The evidence concerning right-hemisphere capacity for receptive language is summarized in Alan Searlemen, "A Review of Right Hemisphere Linguistic Capabilities," *Psychological Bulletin* 84 (1977): 503-28.

and visual asymmetry to the apparently binary distribution of language lateralization reported for right-handers in the clinical literature.

A MODEL FOR HEMISPHERIC SPECIALIZATION

In discussing perceptual asymmetries, we have argued that the size of an ear advantage or of a visual half-field advantage should not be used as an index of degree of cerebral lateralization. We have tried to provide sufficient reason to use caution in drawing inferences about the brain, either for an individual child or for a group of children, on the basis of ear differences or visual half-field differences. We have *not* argued that the existence of perceptual asymmetries in a population is independent of that population's cerebral lateralization. Indeed, we have no doubt that the asymmetrical organization of the brain underlies all perceptual asymmetries.

We believe that cerebral specialization influences perceptual asymmetry in a way that is fundamentally different from that depicted by a structural model. A structural representation of the human (or subhuman) nervous system fails to consider that the organism is more than a preprogrammed, reactive device that responds to environmental stimulation in a largely mechanical fashion. On the contrary, the organism's behavior is characterized by properties we may call selectivity, attention, purposive behavior, expectancy, planning, and so forth.[93] Full recognition of the flexibility and adaptability of human behavior leads to a model of hemispheric specialization that can account for the "inconsistencies" of perceptual asymmetry described above.[94]

This model is based on the proposition that the fundamental

93. Donald O. Hebb, "The Problem of Consciousness," in *Current Status of Physiological Psychology: Readings*, ed. Devendra Singh and Clifford T. Morgan (Monterey, Cal.: Brooks/Cole, 1972), pp. 4-9.

94. Kinsbourne, "The Cerebral Basis of Lateral Asymmetries in Attention"; idem, "The Control of Attention by Interaction between the Cerebral Hemispheres," in *Attention and Performance IV*, ed. Sylvan Kornblum (New York: Academic Press, 1973), pp. 239-55; idem, "Mechanisms of Hemispheric Interaction in Man"; idem, "The Mechanism of Hemispheric Control of the Lateral Gradient of Attention," in *Attention and Performance V*, ed. Patrick M. A. Rabbitt and Stanislav Dornic (London: Academic Press, 1975), pp. 81-97.

role of each cerebral hemisphere is the direction of orientation toward the contralateral side of space. Differential activation of the two hemispheres produces an overt or covert shift of attention away from the side of the more highly activated hemisphere. Although the attentional model has been substantiated primarily by data from visual perceptual tasks and observation of oculomotor activity, it is equally applicable to auditory phenomena.[95] When linguistic stimuli impinge on the neonate, subcortical mechanisms activate the left hemisphere to a greater degree than the right.[96] Consequently, attention is biased to the right. Similarly, in older children and adults, listening to speech, speaking, or thinking verbally tends to bias attention toward the right side of space.[97] The species seems to be additionally preprogrammed so that other classes of stimuli elicit different distributions of activation.[98] The

95. Kinsbourne, "The Cerebral Basis of Lateral Asymmetries in Attention"; Hellige and Cox, "Effects of Concurrent Verbal Memory on Recognition of Stimuli from the Left and Right Visual Fields"; Marcel Kinsbourne, "Eye and Head Turning Indicates Cerebral Lateralization," *Science* 176 (1972): 539-41; Katherine Kocel et al., "Lateral Eye Movement and Cognitive Mode," *Psychonomic Science* 27 (1972): 223-24; David Galin and Robert Ornstein, "Individual Differences in Cognitive Style: I. Reflective Eye Movements," *Neuropsychologia* 12 (1974): 367-76; Rachel E. Gur, "Conjugate Lateral Eye Movements as an Index of Hemispheric Activation," *Journal of Personality and Social Psychology* 31 (1975): 751-57; Gary E. Schwartz, Richard J. Davidson, and Foster Maer, "Right Hemisphere Lateralization for Emotion in the Human Brain: Interactions with Cognition," *Science* 190 (1975): 286-88; Hiscock and Kinsbourne, "Selective Listening in Preschool Children"; Kinsbourne, "The Ontogeny of Cerebral Dominance"; Morais, "The Effects of Ventriloquism on the Right-Side Advantage for Verbal Material"; Morais and Bertelson, "Spatial Position versus Ear of Entry as Determinant of the Auditory Laterality Effects: A Stereophonic Test."

96. Dennis L. Molfese, "Central Asymmetry in Infants, Children and Adults: Auditory Evoked Responses to Speech and Music," *Journal of the Acoustical Society of America* 53 (1973): 363-73; idem, "Infant Cerebral Asymmetry," in *Language Development and Neurological Theory*, ed. Segalowitz and Gruber, pp. 21-35; Dennis L. Molfese, R. B. Freeman, Jr., and David Palermo, "The Ontogeny of Brain Lateralization for Speech and Nonspeech Stimuli," *Brain and Language* 2 (1975): 356-68; Martin F. Gardiner and Donald O. Walter, "Evidence of Hemispheric Specialization from Infant EEG," in *Lateralization in the Nervous System*, ed. Steven Harnad et al. (New York: Academic Press, 1976), pp. 481-500.

97. For example, Kinsbourne, "Eye and Head Turning Indicates Cerebral Lateralization."

98. For example, see Molfese, "Infant Cerebral Asymmetry."

attentional biases may be relatively automatic and inflexible in the neonate, but as the organism matures and the cerebrum becomes prepotent in controlling behavior, attentional biases become modulated to an increasing degree by cortical influence. Situational factors become important determinants of orientation in space. Cognitive variables such as mental set, expectancy, and previous experience influence the manner in which stimuli are interpreted and processed. Thus, ambiguous dichotic stimuli might be interpreted either as linguistic or nonlinguistic material, and the two hemispheres would be activated accordingly.[99] Also, as the individual's nervous system becomes increasingly mature, it enables its owner to become more flexible in the way in which he disposes of his attention. The older child or adult can more readily overcome built-in biases such as that which connects lateral cerebral activation and lateral biasing orientation. This ability voluntarily to override the way in which another system is wired contributes to the lack of perfect correlation between the direction in degree of asymmetry and the presumed lateralization of language in a given individual.

The major arguments regarding the definition and measurement of lateralization can be summarized in a concise manner:

1. None of the common measures of "sidedness" is an adequate index of individual or group differences in cerebral lateralization. The existence of a monotonic relationship between magnitude of hand, foot, eye, ear, or visual half-field asymmetry and hemispheric specialization remains to be established.

2. Clinical evidence suggests that left-lateralization of speech in right-handers is essentially an all-or-none phenomenon. If the concept of varying degrees of lateralization has any meaning for a right-handed population, it would seem to apply to speech perception rather than speech production.

3. Asymmetries of perception can be attributed to (a) hemispheric specialization and (b) attentional biases that result from asymmetries of cerebral activation. Orientational asymmetries are influenced by situational and cognitive factors.

99. Spellacy and Blumstein, "The Influence of Language Set on Ear Preference in Phoneme Recognition."

What Are the Consequences of Deviant Lateralization?

The manner in which higher mental functions are represented in the cerebral cortex can vary among people along two dimensions.[100] One dimension might be called degree of specialization. A given function may be represented in a well-defined, circumscribed region of cortex, or the same function may be more diffusely represented over a larger proportion of the cortical mass. The other dimension of individual differences might be called topography. A function may be represented in the "usual" cortical location or it may be represented elsewhere in the cortex. For instance, functions that are found on the left side in most people may be represented on the right side in a minority of people.

In the previous section, we concluded that our present repertoire of noninvasive investigative techniques is not adequate to detect reliably even gross anomalies in the topography of language representation (for example, right-lateralization of language). The right-hander with speech represented in the right hemisphere is a potential source of data concerning the effects of anomalous topography, but these people are rare and we do not have the means to pick them out from the general population. Similarly, the study of normal right-handers, at present, can tell us little about the importance of degree of specialization. The clinical evidence suggests that cerebral specialization for speech in right-handers is seldom, if ever, so diffuse that speech is represented in both hemispheres.[101] Consequently, we can learn very little about the ramifications of "deviant" lateralization by studying the general population of right-handers.

Left-handers, however, are a group with diverse cerebral representation of language. Consequently, the careful study of left-handers may shed some light on the significance of anomalous topography and, ultimately, on the significance of unusually diffuse representation of language. We shall begin by discussing what

100. Marcel Kinsbourne, "Cerebral Dominance, Learning, and Cognition," in *Progress in Learning Disabilities*, vol. 3, ed. Helmer R. Myklebust (New York: Grune and Stratton, 1975), pp. 201-18.

101. Rasmussen and Milner, "Clinical and Surgical Studies of the Cerebral Speech Areas in Man."

is known about language lateralization in left-handers. Then we shall present evidence regarding the intellectual characteristics of left-handers and draw some conclusions. The label, "left-handers," will be used to include ambidextrous people, as well as those showing a clear preference for the left hand, since the pattern of speech lateralization in the two groups appears to be similar.[102]

LANGUAGE LATERALIZATION IN LEFT-HANDERS

As we pointed out earlier, clinical evidence indicates that most left-handers have left-lateralized language but the proportion of left-handers with right lateralization far exceeds the proportion of deviant right-handers. The best estimate from aphasia cases and from use of the sodium Amytal technique is that one-quarter to one-third of left-handers have right-hemispheric speech.[103] One of the best single sources is Rasmussen and Milner's report of the results of sodium Amytal testing administered to 140 right-handers and 122 non-right-handers.[104] Of the right-handers, none had bilateral speech and only six (4 percent) had right-hemispheric speech. In contrast, eighteen (15 percent) of the left-handers and

102. Charles Branch, Brenda Milner, and Theodore Rasmussen, "Intracarotid Sodium Amytal for the Lateralization of Cerebral Speech Dominance: Observations on 123 Patients," *Journal of Neurosurgery* 21 (1964): 399-405; Brenda Milner, Charles Branch, and Theodore Rasmussen, "Observations on Cerebral Dominance," in *Ciba Foundation Symposium on Disorders of Language*, ed. A. V. S. de Reuck and Maeve O'Connor (London: Churchill, 1964), pp. 200-214.

103. Ettlinger, Jackson, and Zangwill, "Cerebral Dominance in Sinistrals"; Gloning et al., "Comparison of Verbal Behavior in Right-handed and Non-right-handed Patients with Anatomically Verified Lesion of One Hemisphere"; Goodglass and Quadfasel, "Language Laterality in Left-handed Aphasics"; Hécaen and Piercy, "Paroxysmal Dysphasia and the Problem of Cerebral Dominance"; Hécaen and Sauget, "Cerebral Dominance in Left-handed Subjects"; Humphrey and Zangwill, "Dysphasia in Left-handed Patients with Unilateral Brain Lesions"; Luria, *Traumatic Aphasia: Its Syndromes, Psychology and Treatment*; Penfield and Roberts, *Speech and Brain Mechanisms*; Roberts, "Aphasia, Apraxia and Agnosia in Abnormal States of Cerebral Dominance"; Russell and Espir, *Traumatic Aphasia: A Study of Aphasia in War Wounds of the Brain*; Zangwill, "Speech and the Minor Hemisphere"; Rasmussen and Milner, "Clinical and Surgical Studies of the Cerebral Speech Areas in Man"; Rossi and Rosadini, "Experimental Analysis of Cerebral Dominance in Man."

104. Rasmussen and Milner, "Clinical and Surgical Studies of the Cerebral Speech Areas in Man."

ambidextrous patients had right hemispheric speech and another eighteen showed evidence of some speech representation in each hemisphere. Data obtained from patients after unilateral electroconvulsive therapy (ECT) provide further basis for inferring a markedly elevated incidence of right-hemispheric language among left-handers.[105] In normal populations, the average magnitude of the right-ear advantage in dichotic listening and the right half-field advantage in visual tasks frequently tends to be smaller among left-handers than among right-handers.[106]

INTELLECTUAL CHARACTERISTICS OF LEFT-HANDERS

Ideally, neurologically intact left-handers with deviant lateralization of speech would be identified and then compared to other left-handers and to right-handers on a variety of psychological measures. Such comparisons would provide a powerful means of determining the intellectual consequences, if any, of having a topographical arrangement unlike that of the majority. Unfortunately, we have no proven noninvasive means of distinguishing among subcategories of left-handedness, although one possible method has been suggested.[107] Consequently, we are forced to capitalize on the rather loose statistical relationship between handedness and the probability of right-lateralization of language. It is clear that any representative sample of left-handers will include a substantial proportion of people with deviant language lateralization. If there is some advantage associated with the norm of left-lateralized language, then a judiciously selected test battery

105. J. J. Fleminger, D. J. de L. Horne, and P. N. Nott, "Unilateral Electroconvulsive Therapy and Cerebral Dominance: Effect of Right- and Left-Sided Electrode Placement on Verbal Memory," *Journal of Neurology, Neurosurgery, and Psychiatry* 33 (1970): 408-11; R. T. C. Pratt and Elizabeth K. Warrington, "The Assessment of Cerebral Dominance with Unilateral E. C. T.," *British Journal of Psychiatry* 121 (1972): 327-28; R. T. C. Pratt, Elizabeth K. Warrington, and A. M. Halliday, "Unilateral E. C. T. as a Test for Cerebral Dominance with a Strategy for Treating Left-handers," *British Journal of Psychiatry* 119 (1971): 78-83; Elizabeth K. Warrington and R. T. C. Pratt, "Language Laterality in Left-handers Assessed by Unilateral E. C. T.," *Neuropsychologia* 11 (1973): 423-28.

106. See Hicks and Kinsbourne, "Human Handedness."

107. Jerre Levy and Marylou Reid, "Variations in Writing Posture and Cerebral Organization," *Science* 194 (1976): 337-39.

should differentiate our sample of left-handers from a sample of right-handers. Specifically, the left-handers should show (a) poorer average performance and (b) greater variability.

In simplest terms, then, the objective is to discover whether left-handers, on the average, are less intelligent than right-handers. Indirect evidence suggests that this may be the case. It has been reported that left-handers are overrepresented not only among learning-disabled children but also among the mentally retarded and among children with various language disorders.[108] Although some of the data from normal samples support the hypothesis that left-handers are less intelligent than right-handers, those findings are suspect on the basis of sampling problems. For instance, the two studies that reported a selective deficiency in nonverbal ability among left-handers involved small and highly selected groups of university students.[109] Subsequent studies, using larger samples of university students or of the general population, have not found any notable intellectual deficit in left-handers.[110] Perhaps the last word on the subject has been provided by the authors of a U.S. Government National Health Survey, who reported psychometric data for more than 6000 right-handed children and more

108. H. Bakwin, "Psychiatric Aspects of Pediatrics: Lateral Dominance, Right- and Left-handedness," *Journal of Pediatrics* 36 (1950): 385-91; Cyril Burt, *The Backward Child*, 3d ed. (London: University of London Press, 1950); E. A. Doll, "Psychological Significance of Cerebral Birth Lesions," *American Journal of Psychology* 45 (1933): 444-52; H. Gordon, "Left-handedness and Mirror Writing Especially among Defective Children," *Brain* 43 (1920): 313-68; Robert E. Hicks and A. K. Barton, "A Note on Left-handedness and Severity of Mental Retardation," *Journal of Genetic Psychology* 127 (1975): 323-24; M. O. Wilson and L. B. Dolan, "Handedness and Ability," *American Journal of Psychology* 43 (1931): 261-68; M. E. Morley, *The Development and Disorders of Speech in Childhood*, 2d ed. (Baltimore: William and Wilkins, 1965); Zangwill, *Cerebral Dominance and Its Relation to Psychological Function.*

109. Jerre Levy, "Possible Basis for the Evolution of Lateral Specialization of the Human Brain," *Nature* 224 (1969): 614-15; E. Miller, "Handedness and the Pattern of Human Ability," *British Journal of Psychology* 62 (1971): 111-12.

110. Gary G. Briggs, Robert D. Nebes, and Marcel Kinsbourne, "Intellectual Differences in Relation to Personal and Family Handedness," *Quarterly Journal of Experimental Psychology* 28 (1976): 591-601; Freda Newcombe and Graham Ratcliff, "Handedness, Speech Lateralization, and Ability," *Neuropsychologia* 11 (1973): 399-407; C. Hardyck, L. F. Petrinovich, and R. D. Goldman, "Left-Handedness and Cognitive Deficit," *Cortex* 12 (1976): 266-79.

than 750 left-handed children between the ages of six and eleven years.[111] Despite the unusually large sample size and the careful sampling technique, the right- and left-handed children were almost identical in average performance on verbal and nonverbal tests.

TWO POSSIBLE ETIOLOGIES FOR LEFT-HANDEDNESS

How can these seemingly contradictory findings be reconciled? How is it that left-handedness is associated with various kinds of pathology and, at the same time, left-handers in the general population are as intelligent as their right-handed counterparts? The paradox can be resolved by postulating two distinct etiologies for left-handedness.

Normal variation. Most people are left-handed as the result of normal variation. Whether that variation is genetic, environmental, or the result of an interaction between genotype and environment is not entirely clear. Left-handedness clearly "runs in families"; several studies have reported parent-child correlations for hand preference.[112] Although family studies fail to isolate genetic factors from the effects of common environmental variation, other sources of evidence support a genetic explanation.[113] Nevertheless, cultural factors can alter the expression of hand preference and the proper genetic model for the inheritance of handedness remains unde-

111. Jean Roberts and Arnold Engel, *Family Background, Early Development, and Intellegence of Children 6-11 Years: United States,* National Center for Health Statistics, *Vital and Health Statistics: Data from the National Health Survey, Series* 11, no. 142, DHEW Publication no. (HRA) 75-1624 (Washington, D.C.: U.S. Government Printing Office, 1974).

112. Marian Annett, "Handedness in Families," *Annals of Human Genetics* 37 (1973): 93-105; idem, "Handedness in the Children of Two Left-handed Parents," *British Journal of Psychology* 65 (1974): 129-31; Paul Bakan, Gary Dibb, and Phil Reed, "Handedness and Birth Stress," *Neuropsychologia* 11 (1973): 363-66; H. D. Chamberlain, "The Inheritance of Left-handedness," *Journal of Heredity* 19 (1928): 557-59; Arthur Falek, "Handedness: A Family Study, *American Journal of Human Genetics* 11 (1959): 52-62.

113. Annett, "Handedness in Families"; Robert E. Hicks and Marcel Kinsbourne, "Human Handedness: A Partial Cross-Fostering Study," *Science* 192 (1976): 908-10; Robert E. Hicks and Marcel Kinsbourne, "On the Genesis of Human Handedness: A Review," *Journal of Motor Behavior* 9 (1976): 257-66.

termined.[114] At present, we can only conclude that most left-handers are left-handed for natural reasons, and we are unable to specify in detail the mechanism or mechanisms that produce this deviation from the norm.

Pathological left-handedness. The second category of left-handedness may be called pathological left-handedness.[115] In other words, some left-handers have become left-handed as a result of lateralized brain insult. Early left-sided damage (probably prenatal or perinatal), even if subtle, may be sufficient to shift handedness from right to left. Of course, right-sided damage would cause left-handers to become right-handed, but there are two reasons why a shift in this direction occurs far less frequently. The main reason is simply that the pool of left-handers susceptible to this kind of a handedness shift is much smaller than the pool of right-handers who are susceptible to shift from right to left-handedness. Even if there is equal probability of left- and right-sided injury, the number of pathological left-handers will exceed the number of pathological right-handers by a wide margin. Since the baseline population of left-handers is relatively small, the pathological left-handers will constitute a substantial proportion of left-handers relative to the pathological right-handers, whose number will be minuscule among the vast right-handed population. The second reason for the disparity in number between pathological left- and right-handers is that the probability of injury to the two hemispheres is not equal. On the contrary, the frequency of pathological left-handedness may be elevated because of the special vulnerability of the left hemisphere to injury.[116] Left occipito anterior presentation of the

114. Teng et al., "Handedness in a Chinese Population: Biological, Social, and Pathological Factors"; Marian Annett, "A Model of the Inheritance of Handedness and Cerebral Dominance," *Nature* 204 (1964): 59-60; Jerre Levy and Thomas Nagylaki, "A Model for the Genetics of Handedness," *Genetics* 72 (1972): 117-28; P. T. W. Hudson, "The Genetics of Handedness—A Reply to Levy and Nagylaki," *Neuropsychologia* 13 (1975): 331-39; Hicks and Kinsbourne, "On the Genesis of Human Handedness: A Review."

115. H. Gordon, "Left-handedness and Mirror Writing Especially among Defective Children," *Brain* 43 (1920): 313-68; Paul Satz, "Pathological Left Handedness: An Explanatory Model," *Cortex* 8 (1972): 121-35; idem, Left-Handedness and Early Brain Insult: An Explanation," *Neuropsychologia* 11 (1973): 115-17.

116. Kinsbourne, "Cerebral Dominance, Learning, and Cognition."

fetal head during childbirth, which is the most common presentation, places maximal pressure on the left side of the head and thus increases the likelihood of left-sided damage. In addition, because the left carotid artery supplies the left hemisphere in a relatively indirect fashion, the left hemisphere is more susceptible than the right to damage due to vascular insufficiency.

The distinction between "natural" and pathological left-handedness resolves the paradox stated above, but the concepts must be used cautiously. One cannot assume that sporadic, or nonfamilial, left-handers in the general population are brain-damaged. Although Bakan has claimed that left-handedeness is associated with adverse birth circumstances, other investigators have been unable to substantiate this claim.[117] Moreover, there is specific evidence that the Wechsler IQ scores of sporadic left-handers are not lower than those of right-handers or familial left-handers.[118] The concept of pathological left-handedness should be applied only to populations known to be deviant on grounds other than handedness.[119]

Although we have emphasized the question of anomalous topography of specialization and its consequences, if any, the data concerning left-handers likewise could be used to address the question of anomalous degree of specialization and its consequences, if any. There is reason to believe that, irrespective of the side to which language is lateralized, the individual left-hander is likely to be less thoroughly lateralized than a right-handed counterpart. The prognosis for recovery from aphasia due to unilateral insult is reported to be better for left-handers than for right-handers.[120] Other char-

117. Paul Bakan, "Birth Order and Handedness," *Nature* 229 (1971): 195; Bakan, Dibb, and Reed, "Handedness and Birth Stress"; G. I. Hubbard, "Handedness Not a Function of Birth Order," *Nature* 232 (1971): 276-77; Murray Schwartz, "Left-handedness and High-risk Pregnancy," *Neuropsychologia* 15 (1977): 341-44; Teng et al., "Handedness in a Chinese Population: Biological, Social, and Pathological Factors."

118. Briggs, Nebes, and Kinsbourne, "Intellectual Differences in Relation to Personal and Family Handedness."

119. See Annett, "A Classification of Hand Preference by Association Analysis"; Annett and Turner, "Laterality and the Growth of Intellectual Abilities."

120. Luria, *Traumatic Aphasia: Its Syndromes, Psychology, and Treatment*; A. Subirana, "The Prognosis in Aphasia in Relation to Cerebral Dominance and Handedness," *Brain* 81 (1958): 415-25.

acteristics of language disorder also suggest a more diffuse representation of language in left-handers than in right-handers.[121] In addition, as noted previously, the testing of left-handers after unilateral sodium Amytal injection has revealed bilateral speech representation in a significant proportion (about 15 percent).[122] With some of these patients, injections to either side failed to arrest speech; with other patients, the duration of speech arrest was shorter than usual. In about half of Rasmussen and Milner's bilateral patients, one hemisphere seemed to be responsible for naming and the opposite hemisphere seemed to be responsible for serial recitation.

If there were differences between the intellectual skills of normal right- and left-handers, those differences might be attributable to differences in either the topography or the degree of cerebral specialization. Since there appear to be no reliable intellectual differences between the two handedness groups, we can conclude that neither anomalous topography nor anomalous degree of specialization is a sufficient condition to produce a performance deficit. If a group of left-handers shows a deficit in some skill, that deficit is not necessarily a result of the anomalous manner in which the brains of many left-handers are organized. It is more likely that both the anomalous lateralization and the performance deficit are the result of previous insult of some kind to the developing brain.

If deviant states of brain organization are thought of as consequences rather than causes, the inconsistent association between left-handedness and learning disability becomes easier to understand. The young brain is vulnerable to various kinds of subtle insult. The insult may or may not produce a left-handed child and it may or may not lead to cognitive defects serious enough to affect the child's school performance. One might speculate that, especially in cases of learning disability that are brought to the

121. Hécaen and Piercy, "Paroxysmal Dysphasia and the Problem of Cerebral Dominance"; Hécaen and Sauget, "Cerebral Dominance in Left-handed Subjects"; Roberts, "Aphasia, Apraxia, and Agnosia in Abnormal States of Cerebral Dominance": P. Marcie, "Writing Disorders in 47 Left-handed Patients with Unilateral Cerebral Lesions," *International Journal of Mental Health* 3 (1972): 30-37.

122. Rasmussen and Milner, "Clinical and Surgical Studies of the Cerebral Speech Areas in Man."

attention of the psychological or medical practitioner, there is a substantial number of children whose early insult has produced (pathological) left-handedness *and* circumscribed intellectual impairment.

Does Cerebral Lateralization Develop?

Inherent in the incomplete lateralization hypothesis of learning disability is the assumption that cerebral specialization develops over time. Thus, cognitive deficits are thought to be related to delayed or incompletely established lateralization of function.[123] This developmental emphasis does not preclude congenital factors; in fact, Orton believed that genetic dispositions underlie the putatively incomplete dominance of strephosymbolic children.[124] The presumed critical feature of learning-disabled children, however, is that during maturation their cerebral hemispheres fail to become specialized at the usual rate or to the usual degree. The importance of the developmental dimension of cerebral lateralization is underlined by writers who postulate that the role of each hemisphere in reading differs as a function of the child's age or of the child's stage of reading acquisition.[125]

What if lateralization does not develop? What if the neonate is fully lateralized from the moment of birth? In that case, it would make no sense to speak of delayed lateralization, nor to intervene in the hope of somehow accelerating the course of lateralization. If lateralization is not a developmental phenomenon, it is likely that learning-disabled children are either as fully lateralized as their nondisabled classmates or that learning-disabled children are destined to progress throughout life without ever acquiring the usual form of brain organization. It is clear that the acceptance or rejection of the "progressive lateralization hypothesis" changes quite markedly the way in which one conceptualizes

123. Zangwill, "Dyslexia in Relation to Cerebral Dominance."

124. Samuel T. Orton, "Visual Functions in Strephosymbolia," *Archives of Ophthalmology* 30 (1943): 707-13.

125. Bakker, "Hemispheric Specialization and Stages in the Learning-to-Read Process"; Dirk J. Bakker, Tine Smink, and Piet Reitsma, "Ear Dominance and Reading Ability," *Cortex* 9 (1973): 301-12; Sparrow and Satz, "Dyslexia, Laterality, and Neuropsychological Development."

the relationship between cerebral lateralization and learning disorders. In this section we shall review the arguments for and against the notion of progressive lateralization.[126]

THE PROGRESSIVE LATERALIZATION HYPOTHESIS

The idea that cerebral lateralization develops during childhood appeals to common sense. Neurological development and behavioral development both adhere to principles of growth, differentiation, and organization.[127] Since the highly complex language of the adult develops from a nonlinguistic neonatal state, it seems reasonable that the lateralized adult cerebrum develops from a functionally symmetrical neonatal cerebrum.

Lenneberg constructed an argument for early equipotentiality that quickly gained widespread popularity.[128] On the basis of his own clinical experience as well as published case reports (primarily those of Basser[129]), Lenneberg described the typical course of recovery from aphasia in children at various ages. He noted two important differences between aphasia in children and in adults: (a) unilateral aphasia-producing cerebral insult in early childhood seldom, if ever, leaves permanent impairment, and (b) right-hemispheric damage produces some language impairment in children much more frequently than in adults. These observations led Lenneberg to conclude that the two hemispheres are equally good substrates for language at the beginning of language acquisition and that language gradually becomes lateralized in the left hemisphere as the child matures. In other words, language is bilaterally represented at first, but there is a progressive decrease in the role of the right hemisphere until, at puberty, language is fully lateralized to the left.

126. Kinsbourne, "The Ontogeny of Cerebral Dominance"; Kinsbourne and Hiscock, "Does Cerebral Dominance Develop?"

127. Ernest Gardner, *Fundamentals of Neurology*, 5th ed. (Philadelphia: W. B. Saunders, 1968); W. R. Thompson, "Development and the Biophysical Bases of Personality," in *Handbook of Personality Theory and Research*, ed. E. F. Borgatta and W. W. Lambert (Skokie, Ill.: Rand McNally, 1968).

128. Eric H. Lenneberg, *Biological Foundations of Language* (New York: Wiley, 1967).

129. L. S. Basser, "Hemiplegia of Early Onset and the Faculty of Speech with Special Reference to the Effects of Hemispherectomy" *Brain* 85 (1962): 427-60.

There is another way to interpret Lenneberg's observations. First, we shall consider the observation that aphasias of childhood are less severe and more transitory than those of adulthood. In this case, it is possible that the observation itself is incorrect. It is almost impossible to ascertain that brain damage in small children is comparable to that sustained by adults because the brains are so different in size and because the common causes of injury are quite different. Nevertheless, Lenneberg's observation may be correct. If so, the reported mild and transitory nature of childhood aphasias can be attributed simply to the plasticity of the immature brain. The right hemisphere of the young child (or alternative areas within the left hemisphere) may be able to subserve speech quite adequately in the event of injury to the left-hemispheric speech regions. The concept of neural plasticity in the immature organism is a well-established principle of physiology.[130] In contrast, Lenneberg's concept of a gradually shrinking brain base for a given function is a novel and untested notion.

We shall turn now to Lenneberg's second observation, namely, that right-hemisphere damage frequently disrupts language in children. This observation supported Lenneberg's belief that both hemispheres of the child are involved in language processing. Again we would begin by questioning the accuracy of the observation itself. After examining the case studies on which Lenneberg founded his claims, Krashen concluded that the development of language lateralization is complete by the age of five years.[131] Language disturbance after right-hemisphere lesions does not seem to be more frequent in children above five years of age than in adults. If it were not for the relatively sparse data for children below the age of five years there would be no suggestion at all of an elevated incidence of language disturbance after right-hemisphere insult, and these data can be discounted on several grounds.[132]

130. Patricia S. Goldman, "Developmental Determinants of Cortical Plasticity," *Acta Neurobiologica Experimentalis* 32 (1972): 495-511; *The Neuropsychology of Development*, ed. Robert Isaacson (New York: Wiley, 1968).

131. Stephen D. Krashen, "Lateralization, Language Learning, and the Critical Period: Some New Evidence," *Language Learning* 23 (1973): 63-74.

132. Basser, "Hemiplegia of Early Onset and the Faculty of Speech with Special Reference to the Effects of Hemispherectomy"; Henri Hécaen, Ac-

There are two kinds of sampling problems associated with case reports such as those compiled by Basser.[133] First, there is a probability that the noteworthy cases (for example, aphasia after right-hemispheric damage) will be reported more often than the commonplace cases (for example, aphasia after left-hemisphere damage and absence of aphasia after right-hemisphere damage). Thus, the high incidence of language disturbance after right hemisphere insult may be an artifact of selective reporting. Second, children who suffer brain damage may not be representative of the general population of children. Many of the causes of brain damage in children with right-sided aphasias may be inflated by inclusion of children who switched language lateralization from left to right as a result of earlier damage to the left hemisphere.

In addition to the sampling problems, there are important definitional problems. There is the problem of defining the lesion. It is necessary to know that the lesion is restricted to one hemisphere but, in many cases and especially trauma cases, it is difficult or impossible to be sure that the damage does not extend to the opposite hemisphere. Thus, bilateral damage frequently cannot be ruled out in cases of apparently right-sided aphasia. The other definitional problem involves the behavioral definition of aphasia. In some cases, the criteria for reporting aphasia are so loose or ambiguous that emotionally traumatized children, for instance, might be classified as aphasic simply because they refuse to talk to the clinician.

Even if there is an elevated incidence of right-sided aphasia among young children, this would establish only that language is represented in the right hemisphere and not that language is bilaterally represented. Complete redundancy of language in the two hemispheres would imply that language would be unaffected by unilateral damage, regardless of side. Alternatively, if both hemispheres

---

quired Aphasia in Children and the Ontogenesis of Hemispheric Functional Specialization," *Brain and Language* 3 (1976): 114-34; Kinsbourne and Hiscock, "Does Cerebral Dominance Develop?"; Marcel Kinsbourne, "Changing Patterns of Childhood Aphasia: Discussion," *Transactions of the American Neurological Association*, in press.

133. Basser, "Hemiplegia of Early Onset and the Faculty of Speech with Special Reference to the Effects of Hemispherectomy."

are necessary for language, aphasia would be equally likely in the event of insult to the left or right hemisphere. We cannot firmly establish the bilaterality of speech unless we can study both hemispheres of the same child. Even if we attribute a generous degree of validity to Lenneberg's data base, we find his inference concerning the bilateral basis of language in young children to be unjustified.[134]

EVIDENCE AGAINST PROGRESSIVE LATERALIZATION

In the ten years since the publication of Lenneberg's influential book, a great amount of evidence pertinent to the equipotentiality hypothesis has been compiled.[135] This evidence shows clearly that the human cerebral hemispheres are specialized at a very early age. The evidence is summarized below:

1. Anatomical asymmetries in the adult cerebrum are matched by similar asymmetries in the neonatal cerebrum.[136] In particular, the temporal speech region usually is larger on the left side than on the right. Although structural differences do not necessarily imply functional differences, the neuroanatomical findings are suggestive, and they contradict early observations of structural identity between the two hemispheres.[137]

2. When average evoked potentials—stimulus-dependent patterns of electrical activity—are recorded from the infant brain,

134. Eric Lenneberg, *Biological Foundations of Language.*

135. Ibid.

136. Norman Geschwind and Walter Levitsky, "Human Brain: Left-Right Asymmetries in Temporal Speech Region," *Science* 161 (1968): 186-87; D. Teszner et al., "L'asymetrie droite-gauche du planum temporale: À Propos de l'etude anatomique de 100 cerveaus," *Revue Neurologique* 126 (1972): 444-49; Sandra F. Witelson and Wazir Pallie, "Left Hemisphere Specialization for Language in the Newborn: Neuroanatomical Evidence of Asymmetry," *Brain* 96 (1973): 641-46; Juhn Wada, Robert Clarke, and Anne Hamm, "Cerebral Hemispheric Asymmetry in Humans," *Archives of Neurology* 32 (1975): 239-46; Grace H. Yeni-Komshian and Dennis A. Benson, "Anatomical Study of Cerebral Asymmetry in the Temporal Lobe of Humans, Chimpanzees, and Rhesus Monkeys," *Science* 192 (1976): 387-89.

137. Note, for instance, the viewpoint of Pierre Maria, which is summarized in Maureen Dennis and Harry A. Whitaker, "Hemisphere Equipotentiality and Language Acquisition," in *Language Development and Neurological Theory*, ed. Segalowitz and Gruber, pp. 93-106.

the amplitude of the response from each hemisphere depends on the nature of the auditory stimulus.[138] In infants, as in older children and adults, left-hemispheric responses to speech stimuli tend to be greater than right-hemispheric responses, but left-hemispheric responses to music and noise tend to be smaller than right-hemispheric responses. In fact, the asymmetries were reported to be greater in infants than in adults. Other researchers, using a different technique, also have found early electrophysiological asymmetries in response to speech and music.[139]

3. Infants display asymmetries of posture and head-turning. The tonic neck reflex, which involves the head and all four limbs, is an inherently asymmetrical posture. Infants, even premature infants, exhibit the tonic neck reflex, and the majority orient to the right.[140] In other words, the head is turned to the right and the right hand is extended. This posture suggests an early prepotency of the left brain. Similarly, other observers have noted that neonates turn their heads spontaneously to the right much more often than to the left, and that they show a rightward bias when bilaterally stimulated.[141] In fact, Siqueland and Lipsitt found it difficult to study the conditioning of right-turning simply because infants tend to turn to the right spontaneously.[142]

4. A right-hand preference has been demonstrated in infants

138. Molfese, "Central Asymmetry in Infants, Children, and Adults: Auditory Evoked Responses to Speech and Music"; idem, "Infant Cerebral Asymmetry"; Molfese et al., "The Ontogeny of Brain Lateralization of Speech and Nonspeech Stimuli."

139. Gardiner and Walter, "Evidence of Hemispheric Specialization from Infant EEG."

140. Arnold Gesell and Louise B. Ames, "The Development of Handedness," *Journal of Genetic Psychology* 70 (1947): 155-75.

141. E. R. Siqueland and L. P. Lipsitt, "Conditioned Head Turning in Human Newborns," *Journal of Experimental Child Psychology* 4 (1966): 356-57; Gerald Turkewitz, B. W. Gordon, and M. G. Birch, "Head Turning in the Human Neonate: Effect of Praudial Condition and Lateral Preference," *Journal of Comparative and Physiological Psychology* 59 (1968): 189-92; J. Liederman, "Lateral Head-Turning Asymmetries in Human Neonates: Hereditary, Organismic, and Environmental Influences" (doctoral diss. University of Rochester, 1977).

142. Siqueland and Lipsitt, "Conditioned Head Turning in Human Newborns."

only three months of age.[143] The infants retained an object in the right hand significantly longer than in the left hand. Previous failures to find very early hand preference can be attributed to inappropriate choice of response measures.[144] Since infants tend to reach with both hands and since they usually fail to reach across the midline, reaching tasks are ill-suited for demonstrating early handedness.

5. Infants show perceptual asymmetries that are similar to the perceptual asymmetries observed in older children and adults. During the past few years, it has been established that infants are able to discriminate among speech sounds.[145] Consequently, it makes sense to ask if there is an ear advantage associated with the detection of speech. In other words, if pairs of sounds are presented in dichotic competition, do infants show a right-ear advantage for the detection of transitions from one speech sound to another? Entus used a measure of recovery from sucking habituation to demonstrate a right-ear advantage for speech and a left-ear advantage for music in infants as young as fifty postnatal days.[146] Glanville, Best, and Levenson reported similar ear asymmetries in a study that used recovery from cardiac habituation as a measure of auditory perception.[147]

In addition to the various kinds of experimental evidence against the equipotentiality hypothesis, there is some suggestive clinical

143. Paula J. Caplan and Marcel Kinsbourne, "Baby Drops the Rattle: Asymmetry of Duration of Grasp by Infants," *Child Development* 47 (1976): 532-34.

144. Gesell and Ames, "The Development of Handedness."

145. P. D. Eimas et al., "Speech Perception in Infants," *Science* 171 (1971): 303-6; A. R. Moffitt, "Consonant Cue Perception by Twenty to Twenty-Four-Week-Old Infants," *Child Development* 42 (1971): 717-31; Sandra E. Trehub and M.S. Rabinovitch, "Auditory-Linguistic Sensitivity in Early Infancy," *Developmental Psychology* 6 (1972): 74-77.

146. Anne K. Entus, "Hemispheric Asymmetry in Processing of Dichotically Presented Speech and Nonspeech Stimuli by Infants," in *Language Development and Neurological Theory*, ed. Segalowitz and Gruber, pp. 63-73.

147. Bradley B. Glanville, Catherine T. Best, and Robert Levenson, "A Cardiac Measure of Cerebral Asymmetries in Infant Auditory Perception," *Developmental Psychology* 13 (1977): 55-59.

evidence.[148] The lateralization of early damage does not seem to affect the child's ultimate full scale IQ, verbal IQ, or performance IQ in any reliable manner, but specific linguistic or visuospatial tasks do elicit the expected pattern of deficits.[149] One way to interpret these data is to conclude that crude or global criteria, such as clinically obvious aphasic signs or IQ scores, are not sufficient to show reliable differences between the right- and left-hemispheres as substrates for language development. Carefully selected tasks, however, may show specific deficits that differ according to the hemisphere that is damaged.

Refutation of the equipotentiality hypothesis does not preclude the possibility that the degree of hemispheric specialization increases during childhood, and some investigators have suggested that it does increase.[150] Thus, we are faced again with the issue of degree of lateralization and all the ambiguities and problems associated with that concept. In addition, the question of ontogenetic change is a very difficult one. Methodologies appropriate for infants may not be appropriate for slightly older children. Even electrophysiological measures change quite markedly from infancy to adulthood.[151] The nature and level of skills change so dramatically during development that the same task may be accomplished in fundamentally different ways at different age levels. As discussed

148. Bruno Kohn and Maureen Dennis, "Selective Impairments of Visuo-Spatial Abilities in Infantile Hemiplegics after Right Hemidecortication," *Neuropsychologia* 12 (1974): 505-12; Maureen Dennis and Bruno Kohn, "Comprehension of Syntax in Infantile Hemiplegics after Cerebral Hemidecortication: Left Hemisphere Superiority," *Brain and Language* 2 (1975): 747-52; Dennis and Whitaker, "Hemispheric Equipotentiality and Language Acquisition."

149. Marian Annett, "Laterality of Childhood Hemiplegia and the Growth of Speech and Intelligence," *Cortex* 9 (1973): 4-33; Matarazzo, *Wechsler's Measurement and Appraisal of Adult Intelligence*; James C. Reed and Ralph M. Reitan, "Verbal and Performance Differences among Brain-injured Children with Lateralized Motor Deficits," *Perceptual and Motor Skills* 29 (1969): 747-52; Dennis and Whitaker, "Hemispheric Equipotentiality and Language Acquisition."

150. M. P. Bryden and Fran Allard, "Dichotic Listening and the Development of Linguistic Processes"; Paul Satz et al., "Developmental Parameters of the Ear Asymmetry: A Multivariate Approach," *Brain and Language* 2 (1975): 171-85.

151. Gardiner and Walter, "Evidence of Hemispheric Specialization from Infant EEG"; Molfese, "Infant Cerebral Asymmetry."

previously, it is difficult to compare the magnitude of asymmetries when performance levels are widely disparate.

Moreover, the claims that lateralization increases with age are based primarily on dichotic listening data. Consequently, the claims are founded on the questionable assumption that the magnitude of ear asymmetry reflects the magnitude of cerebral lateralization. In this case, the validity of that assumption is a moot point, for most of the data indicate that the ear advantage does not increase with increasing age.

Several investigators have demonstrated a right-ear advantage for linguistic material in preschool children.[152] In fact, children as young as two and one-half years of age show the right-ear advantage, and there is no reason to believe that even younger children would not show a similar asymmetry if an appropriate means of testing them were devised.[153] The issue in question, then, is whether the magnitude of the right-ear advantage increases from early childhood to the time of puberty. Longitudinal data are not available, but cross-sectional data, in general, show no increase in the magnitude of listening asymmetry across this age range.[154] A minority of studies, however, do suggest that the size of the right-ear advantage

152. M. Nagafuchi, "Development of Dichotic and Monaural Hearing Abilities in Young Children," *Acta Otolaryngologica* 69 (1970): 409-14; Bever, "The Nature of Cerebral Dominance in Speech Behavior of the Child and Adult"; John H. V. Gilbert and I. Climan, "Dichotic Studies in 2 and 3 Year Olds: A Preliminary Report," *Speech Communication Seminar, Stockholm*, vol. 2 (Upsala: Almquist and Wiksell, 1974); D. Ingram, "Cerebral Speech Lateralization in Young Children," *Neuropsychologia* 13 (1975): 103-5; Hiscock and Kinsbourne, "Selective Listening in Preschool Children"; Kinsbourne and Hiscock, "Does Cerebral Dominance Develop?".

153. Bever, "The Nature of Cerebral Dominance in Speech Behavior of the Child and Adult"; Gilbert and Climan, "Dichotic Studies in 2 and 3 Year Olds: A Preliminary Report."

154. Charles I. Berlin et al., "Dichotic Right Ear Advantage in Children 5 to 13," *Cortex* 9 (1973): 394-402; Kimura, "Speech Lateralization in Young Children as Determined by an Auditory Test"; idem, "Functional Asymmetry of the Brain in Dichotic Listening"; Carol Knox and Doreen Kimura, "Cerebral Processing of Nonverbal Sounds in Boys and Girls," *Neuropsychologia* 8 (1970): 227-37; Harold Goodglass, "Developmental Comparison of Vowels and Consonants in Dichotic Listening," *Journal of Speech and Hearing Research* 16 (1973): 744-52; Kinsbourne and Hiscock, "Does Cerebral Dominance Develop?"; Merrill Hiscock and Marcel Kinsbourne, "Selective Listening in Children" (Paper presented at the Thirty-eighth Annual Meeting of the Canadian Psychological Association, Vancouver, B.C., June, 1977).

increases with increasing age.[155] The contradictory evidence may reflect differences among studies in subject selection criteria, stimulus material, technical standards, difficulty level, or statistical treatment.[156] The question of ontogenetic changes in the ear advantage remains open and deserving of further research, but the best answer at present is that the right-ear advantage does not increase with increasing age.

The argument for constant asymmetries of performance across the childhood years is bolstered by evidence from the study of verbal-manual time sharing in children. It has been shown that, in right-handed adults, speech interferes with right-hand activity more than it interferes with left-hand activity.[157] This asymmetry of interference is attributed to left lateralization of speech and the predominantly contralateral control of the limbs.[158] Left-lateralized speech and skilled right-hand movement both require processing within the left hemisphere and, since the amount of "cross-talk" between two motor systems is proportional to the "functional proximity" of their respective cerebral representations, speech should interfere more with right-hand activity than with left-hand activity (which requires processing within the right hemisphere).[159]

155. M. P. Bryden, "Laterality Effects in Dichotic Listening: Relations with Handedness and Reading Ability in Children," *Neuropsychologia* 8 (1970): 443-50; Bryden and Allard, "Dichotic Listening and the Development of Linguistic Processes"; Satz et al., "Developmental Parameters of the Ear Asymmetry: A Multivariate Approach."

156. Robert J. Porter, Jr., and Charles I. Berlin, "On Interpreting Developmental Changes in the Dichotic Right-Ear Advantage," *Brain and Language* 2 (1975): 186-200; Satz et al., "Developmental Parameters of the Ear Asymmetry: A Multivariate Approach."

157. Marcel Kinsbourne and Jay Cook, "Generalized and Lateralized Effects of Concurrent Verbalization on a Unimanual Skill," *Quarterly Journal of Experimental Psychology* 23 (1971): 341-45; Robert E. Hicks, "Intrahemispheric Response Competition between Vocal and Unimanual Performance in Normal Adult Human Males," *Journal of Comparative and Physiological Psychology* 89 (1975): 50-60; Marcel Kinsbourne and Robert E. Hicks, "Functional Cerebral Space: A Model for Overflow, Transfer, and Interference Effects in Human Performance," in *Attention and Performance VII*, ed. J. Requin (Hillsdale, N.J.: Erlbaum, 1977).

158. J. Brinkman and H. G. Kuypers, "Split-Brain Monkeys: Cerebral Control or Ipsilateral and Contralateral Arm, Hand, and Finger Movements," *Science* 176 (1972): 536-39; Michael S. Gazzaniga, *The Bisected Brain* (New York Appleton-Century-Crofts, 1970).

159. Gary G. Briggs and Marcel Kinsbourne, "Cerebral Organization as Revealed by Multilimb Tracking Performance," unpublished manuscript.

Of course, the asymmetrical interference would not be expected to occur unless speech is lateralized. Thus, asymmetrical time sharing in preschool children demonstrates that speech is lateralized in these children.[160] More importantly, we have shown that the magnitude of the asymmetry remains constant between the ages of three and eleven years.[161]

The traditional concepts of hemispheric equipotentiality and progressive lateralization have become very questionable in the light of a recent and rapidly expanding body of experimental evidence.[162] Despite a few inconsistencies and lacunae in the data, it appears that brain function is lateralized from birth, if not earlier, and that language does not become increasingly lateralized as the child matures. If there is a connection between lateralization and learning disability, apparently the underlying mechanism cannot be a simple delay in the lateralization process. Rather, any anomalous state of cerebral organization existing in learning-disabled children would have to be present at a very early age, and it would persist into adulthood. Since very few right-handed adults have anomalous representation of language, the number of right-handed learning-disabled children whose disability results from anomalous lateralization would have to be limited to those few children who will have right-hemispheric speech as adults.

Conclusions

For fifty years, researchers have been attempting, without success, to document a reliable association between deviant "laterality" and certain cognitive deficiencies. Failures were met with additional attempts and, sometimes, with improved or novel methods. Until recently, everyone seemed to think that the question was straightforward and "researchable," and no one seemed to question the

160. Marcel Kinsbourne and Julie McMurray, "The Effect of Cerebral Dominance on Time Sharing between Speaking and Tapping by Preschool Children," *Child Development* 46 (1975): 240-42.

161. Merrill Hiscock and Marcel Kinsbourne, "Ontogeny of Cerebral Dominance: Evidence from Time-Sharing Asymmetry in Children," *Developmental Psychology*, in press.

162. *Language Development and Neurological Theory*, ed. Segalowitz and Gruber.

logic of the task. As we have pointed out, however, the attempt to link a learning disorder and anomalous lateralization presupposes certain notions about the nature of the learning disorder, the nature of lateralization, and the implications of departure from the norm. We have attempted to demonstrate that those notions (assumptions) are unfounded. There is no reason to believe that all learning-disabled children should suffer from the same aberration of cerebral organization. The evidence does not justify the assumption that individual differences in cerebral organization can be measured by noninvasive behavioral techniques. We have seen that there is no reason to expect an association, in a normal population, between deviant lateralization and cognitive ability. The presumed progressive nature of language lateralization during childhood is contradicted by a number of studies that have been conducted in the past few years. In short, each of the major assumptions that we examined was found wanting.

Our critique of the literature has both retrospective and prospective implications. In evaluating the extensive literature on cerebral lateralization and learning disabilities, it is now easier to understand why the results have been so inconsistent. For instance, differences between clinical studies and population studies might be attributable to the greater likelihood of finding pathological left-handers in the clinical samples. Studies of perceptual asymmetries might very well produce heterogeneous results if attentional strategies and various situational variables contribute substantially to the outcome.

Proper interpretation of the existing literature is important insofar as it facilitates the development of concepts and conclusions that, in turn, will lead to more productive research in the future. Our analysis of the information currently available leads us to conclude that the laterality of language representation probably has no relevance to language performance. In making this statement, we are not ruling out the possibility of delayed left-hemisphere maturation in children with language disorders of some kind. It is important to note the distinction between the concept of delayed left-hemisphere maturation, which may be one component of a general developmental delay, and the concept of delayed (or incomplete) lateralization. Delayed lateralization implies only that the language processor is spread thin across both hemispheres, but there is no necessary implication with respect to how efficiently it functions. Delayed left-hemisphere maturation implies only that the language processor in the left hemisphere is deficient; there is no implication that language processing is being accomplished elsewhere in the brain.

Part Three

CHAPTER VII

Minimal Brain Dysfunction

MARTHA BRIDGE DENCKLA

History of the Term "MBD"

The term "minimal brain dysfunction" (MBD) is now in its midteens and viewed anthropomorphically it is indeed experiencing the turmoil and controversy appropriate to adolescence. Since I am a neurologist, I may be accused of bias toward the term, with "brain" the stressed word, out of enlightened self-interest alone; or it may be objected that the issue of terminology is undeserving of much attention except to neurologists, famous for their obsessive-compulsive personalities. Yet in this volume on education and the brain, with other chapters devoted to specific behavior-brain relationships, it would appear that my mandate is to be less a basic scientist and more a clinician who has to communicate with educators and parents, so that terms used in everyday communication assume practical importance as directives toward action. Moreover, I would argue that terms come to affect basic scientific approaches, particularly when we are all in the rather early stages of research into education and the brain, so that behavioral descriptors influence what we test or measure. I will begin, therefore, by reviewing the history of the term "minimal brain dysfunction" before discussing what is bad or good about the term at present and where it may be leading us in the future.

It was in 1962 that, by virtue of publications, the christening took place. In England the somewhat more formal (but restrictive) word "cerebral" occupied the stressed position in the monograph by Bax and MacKeith.[1] Also in 1962, Clements and Peters pub-

1. Martin Bax and Ronald MacKeith, *Minimal Cerebral Dysfunction*, in *Clinics in Developmental Medicine*, no. 10 (London: William Heinemann, 1962).

lished an article using essentially the same term, but with the third word written in the plural ("dysfunctions").[2] That article was published in an American psychiatry journal and was a ringing manifesto when set against its historical context of overwhelmingly psychodynamic interpretations of behavior. This pioneering American work contributed to the formal, official definition of minimal brain dysfunction in a 1966 publication of a task force sponsored by the U.S. government.[3] It is of note that the plural form is dropped in this definition and that the term "learning disabilities" appears in parentheses after "minimal brain dysfunction." It was clear that "learning disabilities," without any modifying adjective, was considered a general category synonymous with "minimal brain dysfunction" and that "specific learning disability" was intended to refer to one of the major manifestations of (that is, was subsumed under) "minimal brain dysfunction."

The roots of the 1962 publications on either side of the Atlantic—MBD (American) and MCD (English)—were similar but not identical in data base and orientation. As already indicated, the Americans were working in the field of child psychiatry and promoting MBD as an antidote to the prevalent psychogenicity bias, "a wide and false dichotomy . . . in terms of only psychogenesis or only organicity."[4] Clements and Peters were striving to make further and more subtle extrapolations from the primary point of reference bequeathed to them from the 1940s, that is, the "brain damage behavior syndrome" (hyperkinetic syndrome, organic brain syndrome, hyperkinetic-impulse disorder) of Strauss and co-workers.[5] Clements and Peters clinically perceived the overlap between the more easily recognized Strauss syndrome and the specific developmental dyslexia syndrome described even ear-

2. Sam D. Clements and John E. Peters, "Minimal Brain Dysfunction in the School-age Child," *Archives of General Psychiatry* 6 (1962): 185-97.

3. Sam D. Clements, *Minimal Brain Dysfunction in Children: Terminology and Identification*, U.S. Public Health Service Publication no. 1415 (Washington, D.C.: U.S. Department of Health, Education, and Welfare, 1966).

4. Clements and Peters, "Minimal Brain Dysfunction in the School-age Child," p. 196.

5. Alfred A. Strauss and M. A. Lehtinen, *Psychopathology and Education of the Brain-injured Child* (New York: Grune and Stratton, 1947).

lier. They used the term "minimal brain dysfunctions" (always careful to preserve the plural) as a convenient placeholder for the variety of overlaps that in fact clinically outnumber "pure" or "specific" presentations. They were quite clear about the level of implication of MBD as "an honest blank . . . reserved in our thinking for the inclusion of as yet unnamed subtle deviations arising from genetic factors, perinatal brain insults, and illnesses and injuries sustained during the years critical for the development and maturation of those parts of the nervous system having to do with perception, language, inhibition of impulses, and motor control."[6] Our current understanding is but little advanced over theirs of 1962. Their plea that we recognize the role of the brain in the child's capacity to interact with the environment is the historical thrust of the term "minimal brain dysfunction" in the United States.

The British "minimal cerebral dysfunction" was by contrast less polemic and more positive in its genesis. Echoes and reminiscences, fragmentary syndromes or *formes frustes* of well-known major chronic handicaps of childhood, were brought together under the MCD category, apparently as a way of focussing upon use of existing facilities in Great Britain for more subtle, minor developmental disabilities. The "clumsy child" was a pale version of a child with cerebral palsy; the dyslexic was a restricted slow learner (that is, a child with a *specific* mental deficiency); the impulsive child with a dysrhythmic EEG was reminiscent of the unmanageable epileptic. The tone of the 1962 monograph was that "MCD" as a label was a beginning of awareness, a starting point for full assessment and for help for subtly disordered children by virtue of bringing together and organizing the different professional services under some common umbrella.

It should be emphasized once more that both MBD (American) and MCD (British) were introduced in 1962 as modest, presumptive, and hypothetical categorizations, not as diagnoses or terms of closure. Basically, the Americans were saying, "Remember the brain!" and the British were saying, "Isn't this clinical picture reminiscent of some major brain disorder for which we have some

6. Clements and Peters, "Minimal Brain Dysfunction in the School-age Child," p. 185.

therapeutic approach?" The Americans have been more aggressive, resulting both in more rapid development of treatment programs and in more abuse of the clinical terminology (see below), while the British have been rather more thoughtful, deliberate, and epidemiologically elegant over the past decade,[7] but lag in getting programs together.[8]

ARGUMENTS AGAINST THE TERM "MBD"

Within the last five years there has been considerable disillusionment with the term "MBD." No less an authority than Ingram, a Scottish pediatrician who has made enormous contributions to clinical knowledge of developmental speech and reading disabilities, moved to abandon "MBD" by saying, "It is not a diagnosis; it is an escape from making one."[9] Wolff, a careful clinical observer of the choreiform syndrome, reported his data after deploring the "hypostatization" of the "MBD" label.[10] What was started as a beginning has become a premature closure, an empty signature. Seduced into thinking that we have said something with an operational referent just because we can generate a grammatical utterance with the words "minimal brain dysfunction" as subject or object, we may have forgotten why there was a plural (dysfunctions) and the very broad, loose, presumptive nature of the "brain" label that was originally intended.

I believe that the misuse of "MBD" has come about for both the best and the worst of reasons (although, as an amateur psycholinguist, I believe the human mind incapable of resisting the pull of singular nominative terms unless constantly corrected). The best of reasons—the good intentions—came via another psychiatrist with many of the same urgent messages that Peters pro-

7. Michael Rutter, Philip Graham, and William A. Yule, *A Neuropsychiatric Study in Childhood*, in *Clinics in Developmental Medicine*, nos. 35/36 (London: William Heinemann, 1970).

8. Unsigned editorial, *The Lancet*, September 1, 1973.

9. T. T. S. Ingram, editorial in *Developmental Medicine and Child Neurology* 15 (1973): 527.

10. Peter H. Wolff and Irving Hurwitz, "Functional Implications of the Minimal Brain Damage Syndrome," in *Minimal Cerebral Dysfunction in Children*, ed. Stanley Walzer and Peter H. Wolff (New York: Grune and Stratton, 1973), pp. 105-15.

claimed but of a generation brought up on the biochemical basis of medicine. This was Wender, whose widely read 1971 book was entitled *Minimal Brain Dysfunction in Children* and who was motivated by the desire to find a single underlying biochemical abnormality common to the diverse behavioral manifestations subsumed under "MBD."[11] Because he was a psychiatrist and was not working closely with an educator, Wender tended to give little attention to the book-learning disabilities and their neuropsychological correlates. Because he was profoundly influenced by the successes of molecular biology of his own training years (a *Zeitgeist* I shared), Wender rather brilliantly pushed toward a unitary biochemical explanation, wedded to the behavioral concept of "anhedonia" (hence insensitivity to conditioning), for the poorly socialized behavior of children with hyperactive syndrome. Wender also succeeded in overidentifying the hyperactive syndrome with MBD rather than regarding that syndrome as one subtype of MBD. (Psychiatrists, who naturally see more children with annoying or upsetting social-emotional deviations, generally tend to equate MBD with the hyperactive syndrome; but Wender, from the best of medical intentions, went the step further from description to mechanism.) As yet there is no confirmation of any biochemical deficiency in *any* MBD child; ironically, this may result from premature lumping together of syndromes.

Unfortunately, the worst of reasons—the commercial promotion of stimulant medications—also fostered the unitary, singular identification of the MBD child. Advertisements and elaborate handouts from pharmaceutical firms tend to generalize, noting only in fine print the existence of other subtypes of MBD that are *not* troubling by virtue of motility or attentional deficits. In defense of the industry, one representative has noted that even a 1971 report of a Department of Health, Education, and Welfare panel "clearly equates minimal brain dysfunction with hyperkinetic behavioral disturbances."[12]

Thus, as a result of a natural evolutionary process seen repeat-

11. Paul H. Wender, *Minimal Brain Dysfunction in Children* (New York: Wiley-Interscience, 1971).

12. Howard D. Cohn, letter in *New England Journal of Medicine* 285 (November 11, 1971): 1150.

edly in the history of science, MBD has been (a) overidentified clinically with one common subtype, (b) overidentified with one proposed biochemical deficiency, and (c) overidentified with one type of probably nonspecific drug therapy. This is bad enough from a clinical point of view, but from a research point of view (ironically, even for Wender's research with a biochemical orientation) the lumping together of diverse syndromes under one loose term and then reporting findings on "them" (when their variance within MBD is greater than the variance among normal controls) is worse than useless—it is actually misleading. Indeed, there is no such entity as MBD. The term is like the entrance into an apartment building rather than the door into a room.

There are also valid objections to the modifier "minimal." Benton has pointed out that there may be massive brain abnormality in a young child but only minor apparent deficiency, so that "minimal" does not apply to the brain substrate for the behavior.[13] As for the dysfunction being minimal, the life consequences of seemingly subtle dysfunction, if integrated over time, are often far from minimal.[14]

But should we discard the term? Would we gain anything by adopting "neurologically-based learning disabilities," except that the latter is harder to say and even worse to abbreviate? Or could we, out of deference to the pioneers who published in 1962, restore the term "MBD" to its place-holding, beginning-to-investigate, "loose organic line" status?

ARGUMENTS IN FAVOR OF THE TERM "MBD"

Obviously, I am a cautious defender of the term, otherwise I would have refused to write a chapter such as this one with the title so stated. The best model we have, both for terminology and for the future of the field medically, is that of epilepsy or seizure disorders. (Note at once the older singular and the more modern plural term.)

13. Arthur L. Benton, "Minimal Brain Dysfunction from a Neuropsychological Point of View," in *Minimal Brain Dysfunction*, ed. Felix F. de la Cruz, Bernard H. Fox, and Richard H. Roberts, *Annals of the New York Academy of Sciences* 205 (1973): 29-37.

14. Dennis P. Cantwell, *The Hyperactive Child: Diagnosis, Management, Current Research* (New York: Spectrum Publications, 1975).

When a patient is referred to a seizure clinic it is because the medical question is "Does this patient have a seizure disorder?"—a question that recognizes the possibility that the patient has had episodes that may or may not be seizures. The *history* of the episodes is the single most important data base for the diagnostic process, the first decision being whether we are dealing with seizures or with migraine, fainting spells, breath-holding spells, temper tantrums, malingering, hysteria, and so forth. Other important data come, for example, from physical examinations, electroencephalograms, and blood tests. But frequently it is by virtue of history that we know whether or not the seizure clinic is an appropriate place for the patient ever again to appear. The diagnosis of epilepsy (or, more specifically, a certain kind of epilepsy) is much further down the line. Thus, we demonstrate intellectual honesty as well as deference to the patient's feelings when we do not call the clinic an "epilepsy clinic." "Seizure disorder" is somewhere in the middle, not just a chief complaint but not yet a diagnosis. We will dismiss from seizure clinic those who do not have seizures but who have some borderline overlap (for example, migraine). Also, we will send elsewhere (for example, to a neurosurgeon) those whose seizures are symptomatic of some larger or deeper medical problem (tumor, vascular, malformation, calcium imbalance) where the seizures are only the tip of the iceberg. Our seizure clinic follow-up enrollment, therefore, consists of those patients who have chronic, intermittent, fluctuating epilepsies—a variety of manifestations and a variety of causes. We are only just beginning to match up certain manifestations with certain causes (for example, "true" *petit mal*). On the whole, knowing more about which drug treatment matches which manifestation, we admit of an array of causes for each seizure type: genetic, biochemical, anatomical dysgenesis, perinatal or postnatal injury or illness, and so forth. We continue to follow and treat in a seizure clinic all these various chronic conditions, all of which have in common (a) the nature of their symptoms at the point of entry into the system and (b) the nonprogressive, not specifically treatable nature of the underlying physical problem, that is, whatever ultimate microscopic chemical or anatomical cause exists for periodic perturbations of the electrical-physiological activity of the brain.

I submit that analogous statements can be made about learning disabilities clinics and about generating diagnoses subsumed under minimal brain dysfunction(s). The patient enters with the question asked by parents and/or teachers: "Is this a case of a learning disability?" As in the first step of separating seizure from migraine, breath-holding, or other condition, the first step in taking a patient's history (including perusal of school referral material) is separating out mental retardation or incorrect perception or evaluation of the child by the home or school (an exaggerated example being the child who is getting "B's" when his mother thinks he should be getting "A's"). Although it is not always easy to decide upon the validity and reliability of measurement of a given child's intelligence, at least in principle the definitions of either learning disabilities or minimal brain dysfunction agree that normal intelligence is a prerequisite for group membership.

Once past this step of excluding those who do not "pass" the entrance examination, we begin to collect data, from both history and physical examination, with which to address the further issue, "Is this a learning disability in the production of which *brain* factors are implicated?" Here is where we admit freely that we deal in guilt by association. We do not prove brain mechanisms are operative; we indict them by circumstantial evidence. The same is true for most of the epilepsies; despite the scientific look of the electrodes and equipment, the EEG is a physiological test from which are extracted correlates of the behavioral complaints called seizures. Rarely is a seizure observed during clinical examination. Diagnosis depends more on history and on the limited time sample of physiology, an intermittent perturbation caught on moving EEG paper, than on the clinical evaluation of learning disabilities. In neither field are we looking directly at underlying causes; in both fields we are using statistically significant recurring clusters of associated historical and examination facts to arrive at diagnoses, which are really working hypotheses: "This looks like a case of ________________; let's try the usual treatment for __________ and see how it works." The important attitude is the willingness to abandon the first choice of working hypothesis and move on to another if treatment does not in fact prove helpful.

Thus I have come to think of minimal brain dysfunction, like epilepsy, as a middle-line resting place in the diagnostic process, a pause (not a closure) before going on for more specific syndrome diagnosis: which kind of MBD, which kind of epilepsy? There are even some useful generalities that can be derived at this middle level of categorization (although never the "bottom line" generating specific therapy). For example, in epilepsy the principles of minimizing stress, irregularity of sleep and eating, avoidance of certain provocative situations, and so forth obtain for virtually every form, independent of the different anticonvulsants appropriate for each form. Similarly, there are certain general principles, to be discussed later in this chapter, derived from experience at the middle level of diagnostic categorization "minimal brain dysfunctions."

Thus I would argue that we have little to gain by discarding "MBD" or "epilepsy," but much to gain by sharpening our distinctions *within* each category and by constant vigilance against "hypostatization"[15] or reification. We must remind each other frequently that the use of the term "minimal brain dysfunction" means no more than "Caution: brain factors at work here."

Two final points demand clarification before ending this affirmative section. One relates to the question of substituting "neurologically-based learning disabilities syndrome" for MBD on the grounds that the former is more flexible and less frightening than the latter. I agree that "neurologically-based" is more flexible in that it gets rid of the troublesome adjective "minimal," leaving open the degree of deficiency or the extensiveness of the underlying pathology. I do not agree, however, that "neurologically-based" is less frightening to patients and parents. Having tried it out, I have found its impact far more suggestive of medical disease than the simple term "brain." In fact, "brain" seems rather more flexible and broad, allowing us to get away from restricted disease or damage models and to include brain variations in our concept of minimal brain dysfunction. The best part of the term is the word "brain," for it reminds us not only that the brain is the organ of the mind but also that variations in the organizations of brains underlie temperaments, cognitive styles, talents, and habits.

A second point is that the term "MBD" should no longer be regarded as part of a differential diagnosis of learning disability in

15. Wolff and Hurwitz, "Functional Implications of the Minimal Brain Damage Syndrome."

the either-or sense of neurologically-based versus psychiatrically-based. Since the brain, the organ of the mind, is an organ designed to assimilate experience and be modified by it, there really is no such thing as a learning disability which, by the time it comes to clinical attention, is *not* substantially psychiatrically-based. The speed with which difficulty in mastering a task becomes an emotional block for a person faced with that task is astounding; it happens in the kindergarten. It is my position, therefore, that we look for MBD as an archaeologist might look for an ancient city under the rubble and ruins of the surface. Again, we are looking for correlates (multivariate, not univariate), risk factors, uncompensated-for imbalances ("Caution: brain factors at work"). Our research papers may have to dichotomize for the sake of purity. In clinical practice we deal constantly with double and triple losers in early life, children whose learning disabilities are overt and handicapping because cultural, social, and emotional deprivations have not provided them with compensations for intrinsic brain dysfunctions. It is my contention that we shall probably find that MBD is more common in the emotionally disturbed and the culturally deprived than in control populations and that what we learn from the exclusively defined "MBD-learning disabled" will serve to sharpen the tools with which we dig under the more complex surfaces of emotional and cultural disturbances to reveal MBD risk factors.

I will now turn to the clinical syndromes that actually are seen and categorized under the term I have decided to live with—"minimal brain dysfunctions." Here we have even less consensus as to nomenclature and must fall back upon phenomenology.

Phenomenology: Classification of Syndromes Subsumed under "Minimal Brain Dysfunctions"

There are two ways in which it is useful to categorize clinical syndromes: (a) by chief complaint, for example, headache with characteristic histories and signs and (b) by underlying causes, for example, vascular disease. We know so little of the causes in this adolescent field that the first approach (classification by histories and signs) deserves most of the emphasis. In fact, whenever statistical analysis has addressed the issue of the one-to-one relationship between chief complaint and presumptive causes, even in the broadest sense derived from history, no such neat sorting out has emerged. As with the epilepsies, any one clinical complaint seems to have at least several correlates of history. Dyslexia turns out to have much the same neuropsychological profile (and educational implications) in familial as in high-risk perinatal cases.[16] Table 1 shows the clusters presenting as correlates of dyslexia and table 2 shows the clusters presenting as correlates of the hyperactive syndrome. Some of these clusters will be discussed in each of the following sections.

TABLE 1

CLINICAL SYNDROMES PRESENTING WITH CHIEF COMPLAINT OF DYSLEXIA ALONE (5 PERCENT OF MBD)

1. Language disorder, global or mixed
   a. All or most language tests below average
   b. Verbal IQ (below 90) significantly lower than performance IQ
2. Speech disorder (articulatory-graphomotor)*
   a. Usually associated with fine motor disorder*
   b. Often associated with some degree of language disorder overshadowed by speech
3. Anomic-repetition disorder
   a. Circumlocutory errors on confrontation naming
   b. Sentence and digit repetition span short
4. Dysphonemic-sequencing disorder
   a. Poor ear for phonetic/phonemic detail
   b. Sentence and digit span normal but internal sequence incorrectly reproduced
5. Verbal memorization disorder: slow verbal learning curve
6. Correlational (sequential-spatial) disorder
7. Right hemisyndrome with any of the above

* See Steven Mattis, Joseph H. French, Isabelle Rapin, "Dyslexia in Children and Young Adults: Three Independent Neuropsychological Syndromes," *Developmental Medicine and Child Neurology* 17 (1975): 150-63.

16. Steven Mattis, Joseph H. French, and Isabelle Rapin, "Dyslexia in Children and Young Adults: Three Independent Neurological Syndromes," *Developmental Medicine and Child Neurology* 17 (1975): 150-63; Martha B. Denckla, "Minimal Brain Dysfunction and Dyslexia: Beyond Diagnosis by Exclusion," in *Topics in Child Neurology*, ed. Michael Blaw, Isabelle Rapin, and Marcel Kinsbourne (New York: Spectrum Publications, 1977), pp. 243-62.

TABLE 2

CLINICAL SYNDROMES PRESENTING WITH CHIEF COMPLAINT OF HYPERACTIVITY ALONE (10 PERCENT OF MBD)

1. Immaturity syndrome
    a. Acts young for age
    b. Coordination (fine more than gross) by history and office examination young for age
2. Episodic loss of control
    a. EEG often paroxysmally slow or shows other intermittent borderline epileptiform abnormalities
    b. Moody and brooding temperament usually
3. Underactivated (underaroused) syndrome
    a. EEG often shows persistently slow area, paradoxical sleep patterns in waking, rare spike/wave
    b. Often oculomotor or cerebellar signs on examination ("patchy" but classic signs of eye movement or other coordination deficiency)
4. Prechtl's choreiform syndrome
5. Left hemisyndrome combined with immaturity syndrome; immaturity, but more conspicuously a social failure with peers (possibly right frontal correlate)

I would like to discuss separately one particular grouping, with implications of acquired causation, because of the didactic value of the distinction. This group, which I have called "pastel classics," shows subtle but classical neurological deviations in examination findings which implicate lateralized or even more restricted focal acquired brain damage or dysgenesis.

PASTEL CLASSICS: "D" AS IN "DAMAGE" OR "DYSGENESIS"

In this instance the "D" in MBD is hardened by the combination of a history of events in the context of which the brain is at risk and a set of signs indicative of abnormality. Before describing these syndromes I must note two major concepts: (a) soft signs (as contrasted with hard signs) on neurological examination and (b) signs as useful markers in the nervous system for neurobehavioral (that is, neuropsychological) syndromes. These signs are the unique contribution of the examination performed by a neurologist and contribute heavily to the middle-level categorization that MBD is implicated in a given case. Yet the significance of these signs in terms of brain mechanisms or in terms of educational relevance is rarely delineated.

Soft and hard signs. In checking recent articles by prominent pediatric neurologists[17] I found that soft signs were either mentioned but not defined, or described as "subtle, mild, or equivocal," or consisted of a listing of a mixture of classical abnormalities and failures to meet milestones. Going back to 1969, I found an important article from Birch's group listing some classical abnormalities as "hard," others as "soft," and age-referenced signs intermingled with the "soft."[18] No rationale for this division was given, although a trained neurologist would guess from the list that the hard signs were more inter-examiner-reliable and less difficult to demonstrate from one occasion to another (that is, they were reproducible by the same examiner). For example, sensory signs are always softer than motor signs. Thus, we find a persistent confusion of usage on the hard-soft issue, the lines being drawn at times along a dimension of degree (for example, not bad enough to call cerebral palsy or consider a tumor diagnosis), or examinability (reliable and reproducible), and, finally, along lines of qualitative distinction.

Giving in to tradition and designating as hard those classic signs that are unquestionable in degree and examinability, I have been influenced by two major theoretical giants (Kinsbourne and Rutter)[19] to divide soft signs into two types: first, "mild and subtle" but absolutely classical neurological abnormalities with focal or

17. Richard Schain, *Neurology of Childhood Learning Disorders*, 2d ed. (Baltimore: Williams and Wilkens, 1977); J. Gordon Millichap, *The Hyperactive Child with Minimal Brain Dysfunction: Questions and Answers* (Chicago: Yearbook Medical Publishers, 1976); Arnold P. Gold, "The Neurological Examination and MBD," in *Learning Disabilities and Related Disorders: Facts and Current Issues*, ed. J. Gordon Millichap (Chicago: Yearbook Medical Publishers, 1977), pp. 33-37.

18. Margaret Hetzig, Morton Bortner, and Herbert D. Birch, "Neurologic Findings in Children Educationally Designated as 'Brain Damaged'," *American Journal of Orthopsychiatry* 39 (1969): 437-46.

19. Rutter, Graham, and Yule, *A Neuropsychiatric Study in Childhood*; Marcel Kinsbourne, "Minimal Brain Dysfunction as a Neurodevelopmental Lag," in *Minimal Brain Dysfunction*, ed. de la Cruz, Fox, and Roberts, pp. 268-73.

system-localizing implications—soft signs that suggest mechanisms in terms of brain space; second, developmental soft signs that are subnormal, that is, either failures to achieve certain competencies in time (age-referenced) or failures to outgrow certain primitive characteristics in time. Thus, I have come to think of soft signs as subtle indicators of how the brain is organized in terms of space and in terms of time. Under "pastel classics" I discuss organization in terms of space, and under "D" for developmental I shall discuss implications of localizing in time. (See table 3.)

TABLE 3

TWO CLASSES OF SOFT SIGNS: PASTEL CLASSICS AND DEVELOPMENTAL-ONLY

A. Pastel classics from basic neurological examination: asymmetry always most convincing of abnormality versus subnormality
1. Reflex increase or decrease from normal
2. Pathological reflex (best example: Babinski or upgoing toe on plantar stimulation)
3. Weakness (even if subtle)
4. Tone increase or decrease from normal
5. Pathological postures or gait patterns
6. Tremors
7. Cerebellar-type incoordination*
8. Fixed or complex squints (that is, nonparalytic failures of parallel or conjugate eye movements)
9. Nystagmus (wobbling of eyes)
10. Dysarthria* (not simply articulatory immaturity)
11. Deficiencies in sensation and sensory discrimination (rare)

B. Developmental-only
1. Looks/performs like a younger child with respect to any one of the following: stance, gaits, postures, rapid movements of limbs, fingers, articulatory muscles, eyes*, *or*
2. Shows excess overflow (synkinetic, including mirror movements) for age, *or*
3. Below age on sensory discrimination tests

* Most difficult to describe but qualitatively different

Signs as useful markers. The second general point about any sort of neurological sign reported is that of relevance—what has it to do with the chief complaint? Earlier I directed attention to the correlative, as opposed to the explanatory, nature of most diagnoses in this field. At best, we are at the level of behavior-behavior or function-function chains of causality. The strictly neurological signs, which Arthur Benton calls the "infrabehavioral signs," are further removed from such complaints as poor concentration, poor reading, and poor peer relations than are the neuropsychological clusters. Aphasia explains dyslexia far more relevantly than does right-sided paralysis. Yet on their own the neuropsychological syndromes may provide less compelling evidence for the inclusion of that brain factor in our diagnostic formulation. It is the patient with Wernicke's aphasia, free of any motor signs and talking nonsense, who is erroneously confined to a psychiatric ward. He lacks the infrabehavioral markers of familiar signs. If it may be said that psychiatry is neurology without *physical* signs, then the overlap of the two fields in "mental status" is clearly the area of most potential confusion; and "where we are so ignorant, we cannot afford to throw away information."[20] The diligent search on the part of a neurologist for subtle classic signs is not oriented toward treatment for those signs. Obviously, motor handicaps so subtle that they take such detective work to find are neither limiting factors to the child nor reasons for referral for physical or occupational therapy. Rather, as Touwen and Prechtl point out in their still unsurpassed monograph on the examination of the child for minor neurologic dysfunction,[21] a cluster of soft classic signs (three or more) to make a hemisyndrome makes us look more closely at and take more seriously an associated neuropsychological cluster. Our understanding of brain mechanisms is better when we do get a case which fits a familiar pattern. Even then, of course, we must put the whole interpretation in quotation marks, because our models are derived from consequences of damage to brains of right-handed adults. (Non-right-handers and children with pastel classics probably do not have the same clinical-anatomical correlations; but, taken by analogy, the "as if" serves amazingly well to predict the behavior-behavior or function-function relationships relevant to education.)

20. Norman Geschwind, personal communication.

21. Bert C. L. Touwen and Heinz S. R. Prechtl, *The Neurological Examination of the Child with Minor Nervous Dysfunction* (London: William Heinemann, 1970).

Children who come to a learning disabilities clinic turn out to have pastel classics in about one-tenth of cases. The most common is the only syndrome in our field with an eponym, "Prechtl's Choreiform Syndrome." Briefly, these children present with histories of hyperactivity syndrome, most markedly the components of impulsivity, mood lability, and low frustration threshold. (See table 2 for context.) Often they are poor readers, but their general maladjustment to the social constraints of home and school, even in the face of high intelligence, dominates the presenting picture. As the mother of one such boy put it, "He just cannot seem to flow into civilization." Having the patient stand with eyes closed and upper limbs and tongue held straight out ahead of him ("Keep those muscles as still as you can," says the examiner) brings out irregular, short, shock-like or piano playing-like lapses of muscle groups. The child looks "twitchy." Handwriting and drawing reveal sudden displacements from lines, also caused by these twitches or lapses of posture. The term for the mild involuntary movement is "choreiform," whereas in major form but with the same quality the name is "chorea."

I think that Prechtl's choreiform syndrome in fact looks and acts like a pastel version of the classic "Huntington's chorea." In both there is involuntary movement (same quality) and a behavioral syndrome in which impulsivity, lability, and lack of goal-oriented persistence are prominent features. Prechtl's syndrome allegedly improves with age; Huntington's, sadly, definitely deteriorates. But, again, direct treatment of the movement disorder may worsen the behavioral-mental state; the marker is not the worst part of the problem. (Early in the course of Huntington's disease, chorea may be absent or hard to detect but the patient is committed to a mental institution.) Conversely, medications intended to ameliorate mental status may worsen the involuntary movements. I have seen stimulants (given to combat the hyperactive syndrome, the behavioral problem) worsen choreiform movements and even provoke a transition into a syndrome of multiple tics, a more disfiguring involuntary movement disorder.[22]

22. Martha B. Denckla, Jules Bemporad, and Mary MacKay, "Tics Following Methylphenidate Administration: A Report of Twenty Cases," *American Medical Association Journal* 235 (1976): 1349-51.

From an orientation of research into causes, this pastel classic would appear to be worthy of singling out from among all the hyperactive syndromes as a candidate for study of dopamine and other biogenic amines. Intriguingly, it sometimes occurs in two or three siblings, again suggesting a biochemical brain deviation, since it can hardly be argued that choreiform movements are a learned family style. (But the syndrome also occurs in babies with low birth weight, prematurity, perinatal distress, and other sporadic brain risk factors.) Even if there are several causes for Prechtl's choreiform syndrome, all causes may act through some common disruption of aminergic balance; if so, rational and useful treatment awaits biochemical research on this kind of pastel classic hyperactive child.

Another pastel classic is the child with right hemisyndrome (three or more right-side-of-body signs, like distal weakness, hypotonia, and increased reflexes) implying that the left hemisphere of the brain is damaged or dysgenetic (malformed). The associated relevant neuropsychological syndrome is most often that of some form of language disorder, but sometimes there is deficiency of nonlanguage, "left-hemisphere-style" (note again the analogy, not anatomy, symbolized by the quotation marks) systems alone, or disorder of both language and nonlanguage together. Such children behave to a striking degree like mild or subtle versions of adult aphasia and/or related disorders. Their test protocols reveal the workings of a lopsidedly right-brained approach to tasks.[23] They respond in the holistic, big configuration, simultaneous-sensitive manner of the "strong right brain," relatively speaking, and have difficulty balancing this style with the detail-attentive, sequential, analytical, linguistic style of the left brain that is so important academically. I have found children with left-brain damage (right hemisyndrome) to be the best route finders of a group of neurologically impaired children with normal intelligence.[24]

23. Please refer to chapter 6 in this volume by Marcel Kinsbourne and Merrill Hiscock for explanations and theoretical implications of lateral asymmetry of cerebral functions.

24. Martha B. Denckla, Rita G. Rudel, and Melinda Broman-Petrovics, "Spatial Orientation in Normal, Learning-Disabled and Neurologically Impaired Children," in preparation.

The prognosis for reading disability is that it will almost certainly occur in children with a right hemisyndrome and an associated left-hemisphere-deficient neuropsychological profile. It is with the severity of the latter, not with presence or absence of the right hemisyndrome, that the severity of the dyslexia correlates. The neurologist's interest in finding the motor abnormalities, usually so subtle as to have gone undetected even in classes in the gymnasium, is to use these as markers for where there is trouble in this patient's brain and, if the history affords evidence as to when the hemisyndrome was acquired, to gather information relevant to understanding issues of plasticity and reorganization of brain systems after early interference with development.[25] There is one sense in which talking of "nonlanguage but left-hemisphere-system" disorder, even with the disclaimer of anatomical specificity of the "left," has a useful immediate implication: that is, within the visual modality imbalanced operation of right hemisphere contribution can be understood, resolving the seeming paradox of the child who builds model airplanes "visually" but is unable to read the model airplane directions "visually." The neurological frame of reference, even if the "right/left" vocabulary is analogical shorthand, not anatomical explanation, gives us a brain model for insight into the different contributions of *process* factors rather than *modality* factors. This has been a great step forward, rendering obsolete certain time-wasting perceptual training programs.

We are just beginning to collect cases of the third pastel classic on my list, namely the child with a left hemisyndrome (three motor system markers asymmetrically implicating right-brain impairment). The neuropsychological profile of these children, especially with longitudinal follow-up, has revealed again the oversimplification of older assumptions that verbal functions do not suffer from imbalance if right hemisphere contribution is deficient. In fact, these children often have mildly delayed speech and reading, then become good enough speakers and readers but fail to develop normally in verbal reasoning (as measured, for example, by the "similarities" test on the Wechsler Intelligence Scale for

25. Please refer to chapter 8 in this volume by Rita Rudel for a full discussion of the subject of neural plasticity, sparing of function, and functional reorganization after early insults.

Children [WISC]), in use of inferential higher-order language (for example, double meanings, puns, humor, metaphor), and in socio-linguistics (that is, what to say to whom and in what context). Study of these children has made us realize that the attribution of the substrate of language to the left brain and visuospatial to the right brain was a crude kind of dichotomy and true only at low levels. Further deficits seen in association with left hemisyndrome are (a) mathematics disability, dyscalculia above the rote arithmetic level; (b) geographical disorientation, worse in real life than on maps; (c) disability in the processing of meaning conveyed by facial and vocal expression, a kind of affective agnosia that has profound psychiatric consequences; and (d) a high rate of prevalence of poor social-emotional control, a social foolishness on the output side which compounds the social obtuseness (affective agnosia) on the intake side. This perhaps correlates with recent evidence from improved skull X-rays (computer-assisted tomography) indicating that normally there should be more frontal lobe tissue on the right than on the left (in right-handers).[26] In short, higher-order verbal skills, spatial orientation skills, mathematical understanding, and normal give-and-take of social-emotional expressions all appear vulnerable to loss of the right hemisphere contribution. Since the social-emotional learning disability is a relatively new and freshly explored one, it illustrates the importance of the neurological markers of motor involvement in the pastel classics subsumed under MBD, giving us entrance rights, as it were, into the consideration of brain mechanisms underlying complex behavior. Thus, as the history of the "minimal field" has moved from *brain damage* to *brain dysfunction* to *brain differences*, the behavioral correlates with educational implications are even now expanding as follows: from "b's and d's" to "do's and don't's" to "mad, sad, and glad." I reemphasize that the motoric phenomena are least important educationally but most important in the process of inference when the same neuropsychological profile presents itself without the motor markers of involuntary twitches or hemisyndrome. This process of reasoning by extra-

26. Marjorie LeMay, "Morphological Cerebral Asymmetries of Modern Man, Fossil Man, and Non-Human Primate," *Annals of the New York Academy of Sciences* 280 (1976): 349-66.

polation leads us to the next section. It may be that we are on the verge of feasible use of X-ray and EEG markers to reassure us of the brain basis for motor-free neuropsychological profiles, but as of this writing such evidence is not available.

DEVELOPMENTAL-ONLY SOFT SIGNS: "D" AS IN "DYSFUNCTION/DELAY"

When no classical neurological examination findings exist, when often recurring patterns of referral history, risk context (perinatal or family history), and developmental-only soft signs fit together, we infer minimal brain dysfunction. Indeed, when two of the best described developmental pictures (developmental dyslexia and developmental hyperactivity) coincide and overlap we have the best continuing rationale for use of the economical label "MBD."[27] See tables 1 and 2 to recall that there is no homogeneity in hyperactivity or in dyslexia unless further specified. "Dysfunction" is a deliberately vague word, an honest admission that we simply do not know causes when neither classic signs nor more physical laboratory tests exist. I wish to emphasize, however, that this deliberate vagueness is not a counsel of good cheer but is neutral with respect to prognosis. There is at present no reason to give a better prognosis for developmental-only descriptions of dysfunction or delay than for pastel classics. Set in the context of other good abilities, such that the basal normal IQ criterion is met, the neuropsychological correlates, classic signs or not, may carry the same outlook. Until we separate groups by type of signs and type of history (risk factors), which has rarely been done, we must have the courage and honesty to say the prognosis is unknown.

The term "delay," or "maturational lag," must be understood as a truthful description of a neuropsychological profile of which one could say that if the child had been younger, the findings would have been regarded as normal. As Kinsbourne has noted:

> It appears that any influence that is deleterious to neurons can, if it has impact on developing brain, retard the pace of some aspect of brain development. Whether the insult leads to developmental lag or frank

27. John E. Peters, J. S. Romine, and Roscoe A. Dykman, "A Special Neurological Examination of Children with Learning Disabilities," *Developmental Medicine and Child Neurology* 17 (1975): 63-78.

neurological deficit depends on the distribution and severity of this impact.[28]

The terms "delay" or "lag" do not carry a guarantee of catch-up. In other words, subnormality is not necessarily more benign than abnormality; for example, mental retardation is not necessarily less handicapping than cerebral palsy.

The terms "delay" or "lag" and the appearance of behavior "just like a normal child, only younger," not only engender unwarranted optimism but also encourage programs of training designed to bring the child up to readiness level in whatever area a lag is shown. This appears to be not only misguided optimism (implicit assumption that training can fix brain circuits or hurry up maturation) but also a waste of the child's limited time. Unless the lag in question is in some behavior that is sufficiently important in and of itself, such as speaking clearly, there is no evidence to support the notion that once a child speaks like a six-year-old he or she will, without further assistance, go on to read like a six-year-old. Lags in skipping, hopping, moving eyes independent of head, and so forth (see table 3) are even less worthy of training to an age criterion, whereas bicycle riding and handwriting merit educational attention. Many developmental-only signs are, like pastel classics, most valuable as markers, as next-door neighbors to the substrate of constructs like attention, memory, and self-control for which we have inadequate examination correlates. In the absence of pastel classic signs, with their implied localization in brain space, the developmental-only signs are evidence for the failure of some integrated brain mechanisms to appear in time. Thus the educator must still deal with a child whose brain at this time has certain lacks or dysfunctions. In the frame of reference of the present still largely lockstepped school years, "lacks" or "lags," "lates" or "nevers" must be taught with the same sorts of compensatory strategies.

Table 4 lists several developmental-only syndromes in order of frequency of presentation to a clinic. "Developmental-only" is a

28. Kinsbourne, "Minimal Brain Dysfunction as a Neurodevelopmental Lag," p. 268.

description and not a statement about cause or a prognosis. The listing in table 4 should not be viewed as definitive, because some further astute clinical observation, some subtle and sophisticated EEG or CAT-scan reading will cull out of the developmental-only category at least one of the syndromes listed. Even now, a neurologist, neuropsychologist, or neurolinguist familiar with adult aphasia will object that, motor markers and diagnostic tests aside, several of the dyslexia syndromes in tables 2 and 4 are strikingly like the classic abnormalities of aphasic syndromes.[29] Qualitative analysis of the error patterns of dyslexic children's naming indeed

TABLE 4

CLINICAL SYNDROMES PRESENTING AS DEVELOPMENTAL DYSFUNCTIONS, LISTED IN ORDER OF FREQUENCY SEEN IN A LEARNING DISABILITIES CLINIC

1. Combined dyslexia/hyperactivity
   a. Syndromes 2, 3, 4 from table 1 plus syndrome 1 from table 2 (speech and/or language plus immaturity)
   b. WISC profile low points on Digit Span, Digit Symbol Coding, and Arithmetic
   c. Approaches 60 percent of MBD-LD prevalence
2. Immaturity syndrome of hyperactivity (that is, developmental hyperactivity)
3. Dysphonemic-sequencing syndromes of dyslexia
4. Language disorder syndrome of dyslexia
5. Speech disorder syndrome of dyslexia
6. Anomic-repetition disorder syndrome of dyslexia
7. Combined dyslexia/hyperactivity with speech/language deficit and Prechtl's choreiform syndrome
8. Developmental Gerstmann syndrome
   a. Arithmetic deficiency
   b. Spelling deficiency
   c. Right-left and finger disorientation
   d. Other spatial-sequential association deficiencies
9. Verbal memorization syndrome of dyslexia
10. Correlational (sequential-spatial) syndrome

29. Please refer to chapter 5 in this volume by Kenneth Heilman for a description of aphasic syndromes.

reveals differences from controls that cannot neatly be described as those of normal younger children.[30] These are preliminary findings of a research endeavor, however, and this chapter is dedicated to a clinical overview. I reemphasize the caution that the absence of infrabehavioral classic signs tells us nothing about the nature of the brain mechanism underlying a learning disability; it is only a convenient "first cut" in a sorting procedure.

The list of developmental-only syndromes is headed by the hyperactive-dyslexic mixture for which Clements and Peters felt the need of a new name. Again, the mixture is not even a single syndrome, for it includes three syndromes mentioned in table 1 and one mentioned in table 2. I shall return to this combination of speech/language and behavior/attention problems when discussing minimal brain differences. Here I want to refer to the frequently noted profile on the WISC: low scores on Arithmetic, Digit Span, and Digit Symbol Coding.[31] I would submit that a combination of language (automatic level) and attentional deficiency explains this triad as well as does the more widely popular explanation based on an "anxiety" factor. (I am not arguing that the latter *never* explains the triad; in fact, it often does, sometimes even in combination with the former. Life is rarely simple.)

Since this is an overview chapter, I will pause to describe only the last three items on the list in table 4. (The reader will recall some descriptions under the heading "damage" above, as well as summaries of salient findings in tables 1 and 2.) "Developmental Gerstmann Syndrome" has been described by distinguished neurologists[32] and thus deserves our attention even though it is rare; I see perhaps two cases each year. These children speak early and

30. Rita G. Rudel and Martha B. Denckla, "Word Finding under Varying Stimulus Conditions in Normal and Learning-Disabled Children," in preparation.

31. Jean S. Symmes and Judith L. Rapoport, "Unexpected Reading Failure," *American Journal of Orthopsychiatry* 42 (1972): 82-91; Freya W. Owen et al., *Learning Disorders in Children: Sibling Studies, Monographs of the Society for Research in Child Development*, vol. 36, no. 4 (Chicago: University of Chicago Press, 1971).

32. Marcel Kinsbourne, "Developmental Gerstmann Syndrome," *Pediatric Clinics of North America* 15 (1968): 771; D. Frank Benson and Norman Geschwind, "Developmental Gerstmann Syndrome," *Neurology* 20 (1970): 293-98.

well, read well, do not have behavioral, attentional, or general athletic coordination deficiencies. They have difficulty with arithmetic and spelling, typically getting both numerals and letters out of order. They also have finger agnosia (trouble with names or other organizational schemes for ordering the fingers) and right-left disorientation. In arithmetic, they have particular difficulty utilizing place value of numerals and confuse the columns (ones, tens, hundreds, and so forth) as they carry out arithmetic operations. I have found that their copying of designs and their map skills are often poor. Although there is as much controversy over the unitary explanation of the Developmental Gerstmann Syndrome as there is with respect to the acquired adult form, there are basically two schools of thought. Some (like Kinsbourne[33]) view the underlying problem as one of sequencing, whereas others (like myself) see it as a spatial-sequential mapping or a matching problem. Probably each school is correct for some cases. Complicating the controversy are (a) the rarity of pure cases with convincingly strong intellectual assets and (b) the frequency with which all the Gerstmann characteristics occur in conjunction with poor reading (dyslexia). Is the rare Gerstmann Syndrome just a "dyslexia, compensated," subsumed under another syndrome? Put another way, is the "dysphonemic-sequencing" form of dyslexia just the Gerstmann Syndrome, compensated perhaps by unusually high spatial ability? The seemingly academic controversy assumes a neuropsychological frame of reference. If left-hemisphere-mediated sequencing abilities are low *or* if the left-right connections between hemispheres are poor, can we differentiate between dysphonemic-sequencing dyslexia and Gerstmann Syndrome on the basis of level (high, average, or low) of right-hemisphere-mediated spatial abilities? This, I submit, is the way to ask questions about learning disabilities in the future.

"Correlational dyslexia," an even rarer syndrome (I see one each year), is susceptible to description and analysis in similar terms. This kind of child has reading and spelling troubles. Depending on age (age is an important clue, for age ten is the critical divider if one follows these cases longitudinally) the child will

33. Kinsbourne, "Developmental Gerstmann Syndrome."

also fall down on tests in which sequential output/simultaneous input have to be integrated. Examples would be design copying, map walking (route walking), or matching tapped rhythms to spatial representations of the sequences. Otherwise, this is the child who is at risk for a psychogenic interpretation, because his WISC scores show no obvious spreads or scatters. Only his vacillating style, or lack of harmony between analytic and holistic approaches, will be of note to a developmental neuropsychologist *within* subtests. If seen after age ten, this child may show nothing but poor (that is, ungifted) spelling. It is my guess that only the vicissitudes of English spelling can outlive the ceiling effect implicit in design copying, map walking, and even reading.

My thoughts, for which there is no evidence other than circumstantial, as to the mechanism of correlational dyslexia are that connections between right- and left-brain (myelination of corpus callosum and/or relevant collosal association areas) are either deficient or delayed. Again, since these are rare cases, it is difficult to build up a series of them; and since such subtle anatomy cannot be demonstrated in living people, we cannot yet do anything but attempt a physiological study, such as spectral analysis of EEG in which we look for inter- and intrahemispheric coherence functions during different states, such as rest and performance. This idea has not yet been tested with correlational dyslexic children. I would like to do so.

Finally, "verbal memorization syndrome" merits some description. It illustrates the concept of contexts of a disability, both the biological and the educational context. The description here is that of a slow verbal learner, one who takes a more than average number of trials to memorize verbal paired associates or rote verbal series. This child differs from the anomic or general language disorder case in that his problem is not inconsistent retrieval of memorized items (so that scores dependent on multiple-choice items very far exceed scores on direct recall items, beyond the usual expected recognition-ratio gap that is true for all of us). Instead, the slow verbal learner creeps and crawls along the way to criterion and then consistently retrieves hard won verbal information. In a long-term educational context, then, the slow learner may well outperform the language-disabled child, as is well known to be the case in reading.[34] Equally important to understand, however, is that the slow verbal learner may test psychometrically and perform academically very much like a more global slow learner. This is because of the high verbal loading shared by IQ tests and academic learning. There is a danger in overextending the predictive power of IQ testing from school to life; that dangerous extrapolation is best exemplified by the case of the slow verbal learner who may, if only we think to test him or her, perform normally or better on tests of visual-configurational, mechanical, and other nonverbal life skills. The slow verbal learner challenges us to come up with such nonverbal, nonacademic tests of ability to learn, or at least to heed the history of nonacademic competence, which all too often is dismissed as parental wishful thinking such as denial of mental retardation. The life prognosis of the slow verbal learner may be better than either that of the bright but aphasia-like, language-disordered child or that of the more global mentally slow child, since slowly but surely the slow verbal learner may emerge as both literate and competent. These children are rare in pure developmental-only form but are extraordinarily rewarding examples of the need for both broad (life outside the school) and long-term (life after school) perspectives on learning disabilities.

Many other combinations of developmental-only as well as pastel classic syndromes are occasionally seen. I have emphasized those which are either most common or, if rare, illustrate some concept of central importance.

VARIATIONS IN CEREBRAL ORGANIZATION: "D" AS IN "DIFFERENCES"

Just as it is impossible to deny sociocultural relativism in the determination of who comes to a learning disabilities clinic (for example, the tone-deaf and the unathletic are usually not referred), so also it is undeniable that normal variation or extreme positions on a normal distribution curve of a certain trait overlap the concept of minimal brain dysfunction. It is impossible to discuss here all the neuropsychological variations for which there are hints

34. William Yule and Michael Rutter, "Epidemiology and Social Implications of Specific Reading Retardation," in *The Neuropsychology of Learning Disorders: Theoretical Approaches*, ed. Robert M. Knights and Dirk J. Bakker (Baltimore: University Park Press, 1976), pp. 25-40.

or clues. I shall settle for overviews of two correlates of variation more obvious than others: sex and handedness (preference manifestations). I shall start with the debating society proposition that "school favors the right-handed female."

Why right-handed? I shall expand "handed" to "preferring," so as to admit foot and eye preference to the debate on manifestations of cerebral organization. Preference is not synonymous with dominance, but is one outward manifestation thereof; and preference is not synonymous with lateralized greater skill on every task at every age.[35] Non-right-preferring children appear to be at risk for learning disabilities, although learning disabilities cannot be said to be caused by whatever minimal brain differences underlie left- or mixed-preference patterns. My own experience, year after year, of disproportionately great numbers of right-handed, right-footed, but left-eyed (RRL) children constituting 65 percent of the learning disabled must be tempered by the fact that 35 percent of all others in the world are RRLs. Left-handers (particularly straight LLL types) are not so conspicuously overrepresented among our patients but are among their immediate relatives, again suggesting that different brain factors, other than observable preference patterns, put these children at risk for learning disabilities. Another anomaly we have noted but have not yet submitted to statistical scrutiny is that of the allegedly and observably right-preferring child who nonetheless demonstrates greater left-sided skill on timed motor tasks. Such subtle mismatches between the expected and the observed are probably clues to central connections about which we can only speculate. There are data, however, which indicate that children with preference patterns other than RRR did score less well than the RRR group on speech and language tests at ages four, six and a half, and nine years.[36] Young adults with strong, congruous right-preferring patterns also tend to have more neatly verbal specialization for left hemisphere and

35. Martha B. Denckla, "The Neurological Basis of Reading Disability," in *Reading Disability*, ed. Florence G. Roswell and Gladys Natchez, 3d ed. (New York: Basic Books, 1977), pp. 25-47.

36. Annetta K. McBurney and Henry G. Dunn, "Handedness, Footedness, Eyedness: A Prospective Study," in *Neuropsychology of Learning Disorders*, ed. Knights and Bakker, pp. 139-47.

higher-level performance on visual-verbal tasks.[37] Such tasks are the stuff that school is made of, so that even in adult life certain types of brains seem more favorable for school-related challenges. It is of interest, however, that in the same study the better performers on a spatial task were those with mixed preference, poorly lateralized.[38] This is an excellent example of how brain differences, even those persisting into adult life, put people at risk for school difficulty but may have some hidden (in school) selective advantage as the other side of the coin. The person with a high level of spatial ability may have such a gift for object constancy that for him or her, as a child, "b" equals "d." In the adult, this gift makes the person a creative architect.

Another way in which mixed preference or left preference may put a child at risk is by conflict between the required left-right direction of scanning written English language and a natural right-to-left scan preference (which is what "left-eyed" probably means, a manifestation of right-hemisphere-programmed oculomotor scan). Although not enough as a single determinant to cause reading disability, such right-to-left scan preference could interact unfavorably with attentional and linguistic imperfections to hamper reading. Thus might several minor risk factors add up to a learning disability.

At present, the best way to summarize the evidence on the non-right-preferring population (left-preferring persons being the storm center of particularly heated controversy in today's literature) is to state that in them the underlying cerebral organization is not one of such neat or clean lateralization of function, that is, verbal subserved by left and spatial by right. This less dichotomous specialization of left and right brain halves seems to correlate with some sacrifice of automatic verbal efficiency but some possible gains in other skills.

What about femaleness? This controversial issue—sex and the brain—cannot be avoided by a learning disabilities clinician. Despite frequent use of the "his or her" format throughout this

37. Anthony W. H. Buffery, "Sex Differences in the Neuropsychological Development of Verbal and Spatial Skills," in *Neuropsychology of Learning Disorders*, ed. Knights and Bakker, pp. 187-205.

38. Ibid.

chapter, I am really concerned here mostly about "his" problems because of differences. Female brains are 20 percent more mature than male brains from twenty weeks gestational age (the time at which the mother feels life in the womb) until just past puberty (a variable occurrence). Females pass through the early phase of preverbal, right-hemisphere-preponderant learning style faster than do males; greater percentages of females are strictly right-preferring and are thus more neatly sorted out than are males. (Again, there is controversy on lateral asymmetry in females, largely due to issues involving interpretation of data.)[39] All of those left-hemisphere-mediated styles and strategies—linguistic, automatic, sequential, analytical—are more firmly and maturely possessed by a greater proportion of girls than of boys. This does not mean that girls are either permanently or globally superior to boys, but rather that for school-related functions, the sex differences favor girls. Thus being a boy is a risk factor, because both the timing of maturation and the ultimate mature organization of the male brain seem better suited to life beyond school. For example, coordination matures more slowly in boys than in girls, so that for most of the elementary school years handwriting is less precise and more painful for boys. The plateau for coordination comes in adolescence for girls, shortly thereafter for boys, so that no significant difference persists in adults. On the other hand, it is after puberty that boys begin to surpass girls in spatial ability, and this difference persists into adult life. Although minimally useful in school, spatial ability is critical for success in certain technical and artistic careers.

It becomes clearer why timing alone places boys in jeopardy if we look at normal brain maturation and at that most common mixed developmental learning disability, the hyperactive/dyslexic subsyndrome of MBD. Brain connections from back (posterior association) to front (anterior association) areas of cortex are next to last on the within-hemisphere maturation waiting list. These connections, particularly in the left hemisphere, are the "hear it—speak it" and "see it—copy it" circuits. Last to mature are the

39. Sandra F. Witelson, "Sex and the Single Hemisphere: Specialization of the Right Hemisphere for Spatial Processing," *Science* 193 (1976): 425-27.

very far front brain connections that reciprocate both with the previously described association areas and with the deeper, murkier, primitive emotional parts of the brain. By analogy with what we know of the adult, these last maturing connections, linking what we know to what we want through some inhibitory/delay system, probably subserve the capacities for self-control, selective attention, and work so necessary for education. Deficiency relative to age (and grade) expectations would be more common among boys, who are 20 percent less mature than girls, particularly with respect to the next to last and the very last connections developing in the brain. Often it is said by parents that their so-called hyperactive son is just an exaggerated extreme boy, and to some extent I agree. Add to this the relative imprecision of "hear-say" and "see-copy" functions in males compared to females of the same age, and the mimicry of the most common MBD syndrome, a combined speech/language and attention/behavior syndrome is close, indeed. A practical implication is that boys with birthdays in the months of September through December, brilliance notwithstanding, are at risk in elementary school.

The best example of the recent shift in thinking toward MBD as in "differences" is the nondeficit hypothesis with respect to pure (unexpected) dyslexia. As first set forth by Symmes and Rapoport, unexpected reading failure is a consequence of overspecialization of the brain (presumably genetic, with some selective advantage) for spatial ability.[40] Although such overspecialization is seen as inconvenient for school, it is viewed favorably in a biological context; neurological correlates, such as relate to cerebral dominance or lateral asymmetry, are not discussed. The neuropsychological experiments of Witelson, involving right-handed dyslexic boys, suggested overcommitment of both brain halves to spatial/simultaneous processing strategies at the expense of linguistic/analytic style.[41] It has been pointed out that there may be a selection artifact in studies of dyslexic boys matched for normal IQ with controls, for in order to be designated as average in

40. Symmes and Rapoport, "Unexpected Reading Failure."

41. Witelson, "Abnormal Right Hemisphere Specialization in Developmental Dyslexia," in *Neuropsychology of Learning Disorders*, ed. Knights and Bakker, pp. 233-55.

intelligence the dyslexic boy's lower verbal ability would have to be offset by higher spatial ability. This would tend to make almost a foregone conclusion of the different brain, spatial specialized concept. Factor-analyzed IQ groupings, especially if scores of nondyslexic but otherwise learning-disabled controls cluster differently than do scores of dyslexic children, might meet this objection. Comparing dyslexic children with normals will not resolve the issue. Tasks neither too easy nor too hard for the groups studied might increase the meaningfulness of the lateral asymmetries found, since right/left score differences do not imply the same things about underlying hemispheric specialization at various points on a spectrum of task difficulty.[42] At any rate, the concept of different types of brains, of a biological variation model rather than a disease model, opens an exciting era for MBD.

Therapy: Educational Implications and Recommendations

The reader will by now have concluded correctly that MBD is a collection of hints, clues, hypotheses, and circumstantial evidence which point, "This way to the brain." In truth, what we have to offer education is the outstretched hand of a fellow empiricist, the physician whose art is not yet a science. Thus much of this section should be read in the spirit of "let us try this out together."

MEDICAL TREATMENT

It is to be anticipated that when specific syndromes, that is, each one of the minimal brain dysfunctions, are traced to causes, there will be specific physical treatments (or, hopefully, preventive measures) for at least some of them. We do not yet have such rationales for diets, allergy desensitizations, detoxifications, vitamin or hormone supplements, or even pharmacological agents.[43] All that a physician can say is, "Perhaps, but there is no evidence" with respect to almost every one of the possible physical treatments

42. Paul Satz, "Cerebral Dominance and Reading Disability: An Old Problem Revisited," in *Neuropsychology of Learning Disorders*, ed. Knights and Bakker, pp. 273-94.

43. Panel discussion, "Diets and Other Unknown Remedies," in *Learning Disabilities and Related Disorders: Facts and Current Issues*, ed. Millichap, pp. 155-62.

mentioned. The physician is in the position right now of stating cautiously, "Minimal brain dysfunctions are physically based but not physically treated." Education and environment are the present-day treatments of choice and emphasis.

With respect to the stimulant medications, particularly methylphenidate (Ritalin), some special remarks are warranted. Feelings run high when stimulants are discussed, and even among reputable medical researchers there are diametrically opposed opinions. I would advise the reader to listen to such arguments with caution, noting (a) whether stimulants are being recommended as adjuncts to a total environmental treatment program or as the central, singly emphasized critical element in treatment and (b) whether objections to stimulants are directed at lack of benefit of stimulants, overuse of stimulants to the exclusion of environmental therapy, or side effects of stimulants, that is, the risk-benefit ratio is unacceptable, even while accepting benefits.

I think it is fair to state that at present there is no evidence to indicate that even a single subgroup of MBD represents a case of the kind of demonstrable chemical deficiency syndrome for which stimulants are a replacement. Certainly the reflex level of association of "diagnosis: MBD" with "treatment: stimulants" is unjustified. Even "diagnosis: hyperactive syndrome" does not mean "treatment: stimulants." I can go further and state that even the purest of the hyperactive group (see syndrome 1 in table 2) rarely responds to stimulants alone. Within this group only a handful of children—those who are unusually bright and fortunate in their families and schools—are cured by stimulants. Most of the time the stimulants, where appropriately addressed to the issues of concentration and inhibition (benefits), are symptom-relievers like aspirin. By analogy, I often explain that aspirin is marvelous for the fever and aches and pains caused by an infection, but aspirin is no substitute for appropriate antibiotics. The physician need not spurn symptomatic treatment but surely does not confuse it with total or even essential treatment.

On the other hand, I wish to emphasize the relatively good record of stimulants in terms of risk-benefit ratios. Stimulants are blessedly free of side effects outside of those acting on the nervous system. Remarkably, they rarely cause allergic reactions; and because of short duration of action they can be stopped quickly or timed within day or within week to suit the needs of symptomatic treatment without buildup of a drug in the patient's body. I am willing to use stimulants on a trial basis fairly often because of the low-risk nature of these drugs, not because the drugs are either indispensable, necessary, or sufficient. Why not try to help with symptoms to make people feel better or function better if the risk is in fact acceptably low?

For certain children, for example, those with involuntary movements, which means one whole subgroup of the hyperactive syndrome, those with Prechtl's choreiform syndrome, the risks of ill effects on the central nervous system seem higher and the risk-benefit ratio thereby unfavorable. For other children, side effects such as interference with sleeping or eating patterns may develop unpredictably for any individual and fail to respond to manipulations of dosage or timing of administration. One common reason for abandoning stimulant treatment, however, is that overly inhibited, sad, worried, depressed, or zombie reactions are mistakenly perceived as side effects rather than as the results of an overdose. Going down to amazingly tiny doses in such cases can benefit self-control and concentration. There is no right dose for everyone, and the physician can work closely with home and school to make fine-tuned adjustments.

My most common reason for withholding stimulant symptomatic treatment for hyperactive children is overeagerness or over-expectation for such therapy at school or in the home. I often explain that stimulants are less than one-quarter of the treatment program and that until the other three-quarters are in progress in home and school it will not even be possible to perceive and/or report the benefits of that one-quarter treatment. Such a perspective on stimulants is a middle-of-the-road position: stimulants are useful adjuncts but not decisive or exclusive cures.

THERAPIES OUTSIDE THE SCHOOL

Another dispute faced by the physician making the diagnosis of one of the MBD syndromes is that of home versus school, each party responding to the emphasis on environmental treatment by shouting at the other party, "You are not doing enough!" This reciprocal blame game, often an outlet for guilt feelings, is at least one step better than blaming the child for laziness, naughtiness, and the like, but beyond that can only retard or impede treatment. I reemphasize that the question implying dichotomy ("Is this an emotionally based or a neurologically based learning disability?") is a source of misleading oversimplification, since coexistence of brain and environmental factors is the rule rather than the exception. Parents often feel that schools would like to call the problem "all emotional" and say that it is all the parents' fault. Before recommending therapies involving the family and the child with identifiable mental health resources, therefore, it is usually necessary to make it clear that the school will not thus be relieved of its responsibilities to address the special needs of the child. A conference in which findings and recommendations are discussed with both parents and school professionals is useful in making explicit the position that referral for mental health help is a "not only, . . . but also" cotherapy linked to school programming. Parents often need a private conference in which to discuss the indications for and nature of therapy; clearly the school must accept a certain degree of exclusion from the discussion of what goes on within the family, settling for openness about matters which are at the home-school interface (for example, policy about completion of homework).

Almost all families with learning-disabled children should have counseling for at least a short period of time. The counseling should be educational, so that they can rehearse the diagnosis as more questions arise; it should enable them to gain knowledge of what to do and how to do it; and it should be only partially ventilatory, to allow them to let out grief, disappointment, anger, worry, mutual blame. There is often a problem in getting well-informed counselors for parents, as knowledge of minimal brain dysfunctions and learning disabilities is not such a routine part of the training of the mental health professionals. Some good books exist, primarily on the child-rearing approach to the hyperactive child,[44] but there are a great many inadequate or inaccurate books with the right titles but the wrong content. There is a great need

44. Mark Stewart and Sally Olds, *Raising A Hyperactive Child* (New York: Harper and Row, 1973).

for building counseling into our treatment programs, as a medical-educational collaboration in order to enlist parents (and siblings) in the treatment of MBD children.

More disturbed families or family members should, of course, be advised to seek appropriate forms of therapy. Yet the "engineering" approach of counseling focussed upon the special needs of one child need not await the lengthy process of independent therapy dealing with other significant problems. The child's life is short, and a parent may well have to learn to "assume a virtue if (you) have it not." Put another way, counseling as environmental engineering for the child may be thought of as what to do until the insight comes.

Psychotherapy for the child is a more variable matter, depending upon the complicating environmental issues as well as the age of the child. Sometimes I would like to see a depressed child get individual therapy but I will hold that recommendation "on the back burner" because other therapies more germane to the child's mastery of skills are higher priorities. Families, like schools, cannot be asked to spend time and money in too many directions at once; and a child cannot spend his entire life rushing from one therapy to another. I am very much impressed by the adolescent's need for psychotherapy. Traditional approaches, however, suffice only for the clearly secondary neurotic complications. I see the need for a whole new set of "socialization teaching" psychotherapies for such MBD problems as self-control, social imperception, difficulty in conversing with peers or in picking up slang words used by peers, and so forth, which come to the fore in adolescence. At present, such therapies (and therapists) are but promises on the horizon.

Over the life span of the child, therapies outside the school are as important as therapies in school. Both parents and teachers should understand this collaboration and refuse to play the blame game. Perhaps this is where the physician who is following the child can be of most help.

THE TEACHER AS CLINICIAN

I am going to say nothing at all about materials, methods, books, physical arrangements, or classrooms, or one-to-one teaching. I believe that the implications of each of the MBD syndromes for education are philosophically enormous: the teacher must become a clinician treating each child, rather than a teacher who knows a certain age group developmentally or a certain body of subject matter. Just as notes of pulse, blood pressure, temperature, and progress of a patient are kept on a hospital chart, so must a clinician-teacher be explicitly aware of the specific MBD child's case. The materials and methods listed above are like the surgeon's clamps, sponges, and other operating equipment; nobody outside the operating room, including the surgeon, can tell exactly which ones of these pieces of equipment are going to be used as the needs of the moment dictate. Thus, by analogy I am personally unwilling to tell a clinician-teacher which reading method to use, where to put the child's desk, or whether one-to-one is better than one-to-four teaching. But I will come forth very emphatically with general principles and syndrome-specific guidelines. There are three general principles that apply in dealing with almost any child with brain-based learning disabilities:

1. Do not be (or at least act) angry with the child. The child is not a case of moral turpitude. Waves of negative feeling do not work well. If you get angry, you can back off and apologize or explain the loss of self-control; your imperfection gives you something in common with the MBD child.

2. Do not ask for speed. Deficit areas are compensated for by utilization of alternate paths or mechanisms of less than optimal efficiency. Although the "express train" or "highways" are not available the local train or backroads are open, but take longer. There is no magic answer here. Give more time or give less work.

3. Be explicit and precise. Go step-by-step, not only in teaching a skill but also in shaping a social behavior. In their various deficit areas, MBD children need explicitness where others make use of implicit signals or information.

Corollaries to these principles are (a) that positive reinforcement is the most effective, although the visions of cash rewards, candies, or even token chips conjured up by the label "behavior modification" are rarely necessary and smiles and checkmarks are remarkably rewarding; and (b) that emphasis upon finding and bringing out what is good about the child will promote and support the child's motivation and effort in the long, hard task of plugging away at learning for which he is not naturally gifted. Willingness to change course or approach as the child grows and changes is another important attitudinal characteristic of the clinician-teacher. What I fear most about "diagnosis" and "prescriptive teaching" is that, as happens in medical settings, frozen thinking grips the user of these terms. I think that each child deserves reevaluation and renewed planning at least once a year. Like most of my recommendations for the child with some form of MBD, this last one is very expensive, for in the last analysis my most universal prescription involves "people power."

EXAMPLES OF GENERAL APPROACHES

What follows is a series of guidelines on specific MBD issues. Each has been written for and used in the setting of a clinic devoted to children with learning disabilities. Each of these short "essays" has been sent out to schools along with the detailed report about a child who exemplifies the issue or problem discussed in that essay.

Spoken language problems of many dyslexic children: a subtle challenge in the "mainstream" classroom. Within the past five years, there has been growing recognition of the relationship of most reading disability (dyslexia) to subtle but demonstrable disabilities of spoken language or verbal memory.[45] Beyond the consequence of this research in the straightforward application to the teaching of reading in general and remedial reading in particular, and particularly important in the growing movement away from visual-perceptual training, there are slowly growing applications to school in the larger context beyond the books. The well-behaved, often well-coordinated, intelligent child who needs special reading instruction is known to have needs beyond that, projected in time to the successively greater language demands of doing written work and tackling a foreign language. But what about classroom instruction and discussion? Increasingly it is apparent that successful mainstreaming is dependent upon the regular classroom teacher's

45. Mattis, French, and Rapin, "Dyslexia in Children and Young Adults"; Denckla, "The Neurological Basis of Reading Disability."

awareness of the adjustment necessary if the child who goes out for special help is to survive in school. It is in this respect that the subtle language deficits of many dyslexic children are not sufficiently clarified for the teacher. First, there is the issue of rate. Many dyslexic children process incoming language slowly and, if bombarded with too much too fast, may "blow a fuse." As is the case when one overloads a circuit with too many appliances, the entire circuit is broken and all appliances on that circuit will not operate. Thus, excess information load can lead to total lack of comprehension of everything the teacher has said, not just the last bit, and to the accusation, "You're not listening." Repeating questions or instructions more slowly and in shorter chunks will bring great relief to this child. Second, on the expressive side, many dyslexic children are verbal, talking on and on as they wander through associations to cue themselves to the exact words. If ridiculed or impatiently pushed, they may stutter or withdraw into silence and become habitual "I don't know" responders. A third problem is that of the good thinker and poor memorizer, who learns slowly and is therefore seen as stupid, or who, conversely, is harshly judged as not working up to capacity when his IQ test results indicate good thinking ability. Such a child is at once a slow learner and smart, affording a dramatic example of the lack of unity of intelligence. This split condition requires understanding in the classroom discussion situation.

Comprehension, word-finding, and word-learning problems all create difficulties in peer relations and thus explain some gymnasium, playground, and corridor phenomena as well as deficiencies in the three Rs. Some of the secondary behavior problems are not results of frustrations with book learning. The same is true for misdiagnosed hyperactivity. Rather, there are direct social-emotional behavior consequences of verbal deficits, quite aside from the dyslexia that is the dramatic index symptom. Use of physical aggression because one cannot find the right words that never harm, retreat from or disruption of games when rules are linguistically too complex and too quickly or lengthily explained for the child to grasp, withdrawal into shy, quiet stupidity—all these are direct effects of subtle verbal deficiencies. By being aware of these factors the teacher may in a patient manner be a language therapist and a "translator," as well as a special sort of social-emotional therapist for the child so often narrowly perceived as dyslexic. Furthermore, failure to thrive at the junior and senior high school levels, despite excellent progress in reading and spelling skills, deserves a closer look to find a realistic ceiling for academic performance imposed upon such young people by disabilities in spoken language or in verbal memory.

Needs of the bright child who is seriously delayed in reading. Any successful school program for a brighter than average child, typically over the age of nine, who is seriously delayed in reading must confront the two simultaneous problems of low self-esteem and depression (expectation of failure and a despairing resistance to hard work). Such children need to be surrounded by a peer group of similarly bright and learning-disabled children so that they can see that they are not the only ones with this combination of high and low points. They need small classes with all of the staff surrounding them trained and sensitive to the emotional as well as to the specific textbook needs of learning-disabled children. And they need a teaching approach in classes that allows them to learn subject matter through experiential learning, "hands-on," outside of books. Positive experiences in nonacademic skills should be provided, such as woodworking, nature, camping, sculpture, music, and so forth. Without these total milieu components no amount of tutoring in reading can be expected to be successful, for motivation to keep plugging away will not be maintained.

Cognitive-perceptual factors in social-emotional problems of some MBD children. Within the last decade there has been a growing awareness of the role of the "other" or nondominant side of the brain in skills involving "mazes, spaces, and faces."[46] Ironically, emphasis on visual-perceptual factors has faded with respect to the explanation of reading disabilities, only to reappear in our recognition of the important role of such factors in other, nondyslexic learning disabilities. Most easily recognized are those children who have some classical left-side-of-body weakness, tone and/or reflex deviations. But even without such motor markers children may show dysfunction on spatial subtests of psychometric and psycho-

46. Joseph Bogen, "The Other Side of the Brain: An Appositional Mind," *Bulletin of the Los Angeles Neurological Society* 34 (1969): 135-63.

educational tests such as Block Design, Object Assembly, Mazes, Raven's Colored Progressive Matrices, Frostig's Spatial Relations, Money's Road Map. Academic disabilities include mathematics (spatial concepts, place value of numbers), writing (trouble with spacing and organization on page), and map skills in geography.

Less obvious but more important are the disabilities of these "perceptually-spatially" deficient children in social, emotional, and behavioral adjustment. School may terrify them because they get lost (literally "lost in space") in the corridors. On the playing field, they may run to third base instead of running to first. Such a child may wet his pants rather than risk getting lost en route to the bathroom. He may cling to the teacher on the shortest of trips and refuse to participate in games at recess. Such behaviors are, descriptively, "social-emotional problems." But the roots in *brain dysfunction*, rather than in disturbed early experiences with significant persons, lead to different therapeutic attitudes and approaches, including the teacher's reaction.

Inability to perceive the subtle gradations of facial expression and vocal intonation patterns (also found in adults who suffer strokes injuring their right hemispheres) may impair peer relations and response to adults. Hearts full of affection and good intentions do not prevent the right-brain-dysfunctional children from social rejection. Such children may touch or "bear-hug" other children too much, chatter on in class when the others are bored with their "show and tell" report, and may fail to note the gathering storm clouds of irritation or disapproval on the face of the teacher. The socializing feedback and reinforcers (positive or negative) obtained from facial and/or vocal reactions of others fail to reach the right-brain-dysfunctional child, who is overly verbal and overly dependent upon verbal rules and regulations. The child needs remediation directed toward "mad, sad, and glad." Explicit training in the deficit area, just as one would do for reversal of "b's" and "d's," would for these children mean patient, repeated pointing out of facial and vocal patterns. Use of the compensatory strength would mean explicit verbal labelling of such patterns and explicit verbal rehearsal of social contingencies.

It would be desirable to have individual and group psychotherapy resources to which such children could be referred for the type of social-emotional teaching sketched above. At present, such resources are not widely available. Talking about feelings may actually worsen the situation for the group of children described here. Teachers and other school professionals have an important therapeutic role in taking the learning disabilities attitude and a remedial approach to these socially and emotionally disabled children. Positive patience must be combined with explicit explanations, rather than either moralizing or psychologizing.

Principles of education and discipline for the hyperactive child. Approximately 85 percent of the children referred to a clinic for learning disabilities have a significant component of what we call the "hyperactive syndrome." The most important features of this syndrome, in spite of its name, are not those of physical restlessness, which in fact constitute only two of ten leading characteristics of the syndrome. The most important parts of the syndrome are impulsivity and difficulty with attention span. The child has this learning disability twenty-four hours a day. A broad perspective rather than a narrow focus on specific methods or modalities of instruction is therefore essential to the education and to the rearing of such a child at home.[47]

The basic ingredients, both in school and at home, for the best environmental treatment of the hyperactive child are those summarized by the words "supervision and supportive structure." The basic characteristic of hyperactive children is not their physical restlessness but the fact that they cannot organize their own activities without outside help. Thus they are capable of doing many things as long as someone else serves as the monitor and the attention-focusser for them. Thus, the mother of a seven-year-old recently commented, "At least he can dress himself, but I still have to stand in the room." A father recently remarked, "If you tell him to pick up his socks, you must stay there until he does it." These comments illustrate the hyperactive child's need for the presence of an adult supervising person.

One may ask why we include such a child under the broad category of specific learning disability. The child may not have any difficulty learning specific school subjects, but I argue strongly

47. Stewart and Olds, *Raising a Hyperactive Child.*

that he is learning disabled for twenty-four hours a day, or perhaps sixteen hours if one leaves out the hours of sleep for the tired parents. This is because he has trouble learning the "do's" and "don't's" of life in every situation—in school, at home, on the playing field, and in social groups. He is a child who has difficulty in responding in terms of social regulations, constraints, and limits rather than in terms of what attracts and interests him. This is why he is so often frustrating to parents and teachers who say, "He can do it if he wants to." He seems inconsistent because one day he reads and the next day he does not. Unless one stops to take note of the interest level of the material he reads or the fact that perhaps something more interesting than reading is catching his attention on one day whereas on another day the reading is the best that life has to offer him, one does not realize that he lacks the control to focus himself narrowly and to selectively attend to the task upon which other authority persons wish him to work.

It is difficult to communicate to those who are not experienced with neurological patients the fact that a large part of the human nervous system is devoted to the processes of control, selective inhibition, selective attention, and organization of responses. In fact, so widespread are such systems of the brain that it is currently impossible for us to point to a particular part of the nervous system as being responsible for the existence of the large number of children who have difficulties with this part of their mental development.

There is no way in which a particular workbook, a resource room, a particular sensory modality, or any of the other special kinds of approaches to learning are going to address the really big issue of education for the hyperactive child. Even if we adopt the new name for this syndrome (attentional deficit syndrome) and get away from the apparent emphasis on physical restlessness we are left with the fact that it is "people power" that is really needed rather than these very narrowly focussed kinds of special approaches. "People power" is what these children need and although that is very expensive, the conclusion is unavoidable. A warm, supportive, "cheerleader" kind of supervision is needed and must be provided by the major teacher in a resource room or in the mainstream classroom. It takes teacher time. It takes teacher effort. It takes teacher training on how to remain firm without sounding angry. The worst kind of approach to the child with this problem is to become irritated, sarcastic, punitive, in short, negative. The old song, "you have to accentuate the positive and eliminate the negative," is highly appropriate to what we know about optimal environmental treatment of these children. One must stop responding to them as though they were "bad" and take the whole issue out of the realm of moral turpitude. These are children who have a deficiency in the system in the brain which inhibits, controls, organizes, selects. One nine-year-old recently said to me, "My mind is like a television set on which someone is always switching the channels." Each teacher who deals with children with special needs has to become fully empathic with this kind of experience of mental hyperactivity.

This does not mean that we respond, "Oh, you poor cripple" and simply fail to teach such children. Rather we have to give a part of ourselves, as parents and teachers, to the tasks of being the supervisor, the organizer, the monitor, the attention-focusser to provide the framework and structure within which these children often can perform very well, sometimes brilliantly. Just as important as providing them the means to success is the bleaching out of our own irritations, anger, rejection, and exclusion which lead to the high rate of emotional disturbance in children with this problem. Admittedly, they are not as easy to live with as our more fully and evenly matured children. On the other hand, our enlightened self-interest must tell us that if we do not make the effort to deal with them as children we will unfortunately have to deal with them as disturbed adults. The issues here are much larger than those of learning how to read, write, or do arithmetic. The issues are those of learning how to live in a society with other people. Habit training, character training, and explicit social teaching (for example, what you say when John says ________) are part of the broad program needed for this very large chunk of the learning disabilities population. The importance of specific teaching methods for those who have additional specific language or perceptual problems is not being underestimated by this writer, but rather is being placed into some perspective. To focus upon writing an educational plan in terms of a specific methodology while neglecting the child's total need for adult supervision would be like discussing the use of a bandaid for a person who is dying from a massive bleeding wound.

I would argue that the whole concept of mainstreaming is meaningless if we continue to insist that poorly organized children go in and out of resource rooms that, when compared to an old-fashioned self-contained classroom, are almost like Grand Central Station. We are demanding navigational and organizational skills from the very children who most lack such skills. There is no way to avoid the need for more adult supervision and more adult time and effort in the treatment of these children. Stimulant medication is a useful adjunct, but it provides only a child who is available to the teaching of the adult and does not provide a substitute for that teaching. Stimulant medication may be compared to aspirin: it makes the symptoms less severe, but it does not cure the underlying disease or condition.

The classroom teacher and the parents of such a child have to have intensive training, indeed counseling, to help them understand that their presence is required frequently to look over the shoulder at the child's half-finished paper and say, "Come on, let's finish it; we know we can do it." This positive "cheerleader" but time-consuming kind of adult presence is to the best of my knowledge the greatest need of the many special needs children who have attentional and organizational deficits.

The child with fine motor difficulties because of developmental motor deficits. Children who have mild deviations in central nervous system functioning, whether these are developmental-only or secondary to some subtle acquired insult to the nervous system, often have difficulty with the skill of handwriting. Although there are differences among these groups of children, one thing they all appear to have in common is difficulty working under the pressure of time. It takes little more than simple common sense to realize that when something is hard to do it is doubly difficult to do it quickly. Often, however, we have to communicate to teachers the middle-of-the-road position, which is that such children are not like cerebral palsied children who cannot do certain things, nor are they like normal children who can be expected to do things with full steam ahead. Children with the minor motor handicaps of which we are speaking, broadly subsumed under the title "learning disabilities," are children who can do tasks like handwriting but with certain special dispensations and when given enough compensatory time. One simply has to counsel the teacher that such a child cannot do neat handwriting and fast handwriting at the same time, that there is a trade-off between speed and accuracy which no doctor can do anything to change. The child must either be given fewer things to write in a given unit of time or a longer period of time in which to write the same number of things as the rest of the class. These recommendations may appear less than glamorous but they are the only ones in the present state of our knowledge that are applicable if children with learning disabilities are to be kept in mainstream classrooms. With respect to homework, it is possible to break down the task into component parts. When writing a book report, for example, a child can first dictate what he wants to say onto a tape recorder, then act as his own secretary by transcribing what he is listening to onto a piece of paper, and then work out the spelling and handwriting as later parts of the assembly line production. Of course, this will also take more time, but we know no way to avoid the unpleasant and tough truth that a person who has trouble doing something must simply take more time and more pains to get it done. The fact that he can get it done at all, however, if he is encouraged patiently to plod forward and do so, often serves as a positively reenforcing factor when he does produce something worthy of praise and productive of satisfaction with himself. Breaking down the task into making the tape recording, making the transcription, and then dealing with the mechanics of spelling and handwriting has an added benefit. Many children, little boys in particular, enjoy fiddling around with tape recording equipment, which in itself can be a reinforcing feature of the experience of doing a book report in this interesting manner. Close supervision is often needed, however, since many of our learning-disabled children have a notorious tendency to go off on tangents and restrict themselves to playing with the equipment rather than getting on with the report.

Within the classroom setting, when these routines of breaking down the tasks are not possible or would interfere with the functioning of others, the teacher simply has to give the child more time or less work. There is no way to get around this trade-off. Whenever possible, oral reports in social studies, science, and literature classes should be allowed and accepted for children who have difficulty with handwriting. One cannot altogether dispense with handwriting but one can certainly lighten the load by giving the child credit for good performance and by not constantly placing him in double jeopardy because what he has to say is not going to be communicated since he cannot control his handwriting adequately. Examinations should be graded leniently with respect to the amount produced or, if essay questions are used, oral testing could be employed for a child who has a particular handwriting problem.

Concluding Statement

The implications of minimal brain dysfunctions for educational policy are exemplified by the very existence of this volume. A book entitled *Education and the Brain* is an open response to those in education who urge us to ignore the whys and wherefores (mechanisms) and get on with the business of teaching the basics, and to those in medicine who urge us to leave school to the educators. A book recently published in Scotland expresses my position exactly in its Foreword: "Health is determined by the interaction between the child, his environment, and the society in which he lives and is not a measurable quantity independent of this relationship."[48] My own neurological training gives me the mandate to be the person on the team who focusses on the child's brain, but I hope it is clear that the thing furthest from my mind is to allow my focus to be used to blame the child. On the contrary, I see MBD (if that "D" is stretched to encompass the full range from damage to difference) as generating a set of environmental engineering or person-to-program matching approaches with ongoing collaborations between medicine and education. I believe that such collaboration would broaden and elevate the callings of parent and teacher while restoring to the physician the educational role implicit in the title of "Doctor."

48. *Child Health in the Community: A Handbook of Social and Community Pediatrics*, ed. Ross G. Mitchell (Edinburgh: Churchill Livingstone, 1977).

CHAPTER VIII

Neuroplasticity: Implications for Development and Education

RITA G. RUDEL

"Neuroplasticity" is a term that has been used to refer to the capacity of the brain to recover from the effects of damage. One could reasonably include under neuroplasticity changes that underlie learning or adaptation to rearrangement, but as Teuber[1] has stated, "there is trouble enough with the concept of plasticity as defined by claims for repair or readjustment of central connections postnatally in mammals."[2] At the human level, it is often difficult to define "damage," let alone the determination of the effects of damage on recovery. The site and size of lesions and the age at which they are inflicted determine the limits and extent of recovery in humans as they do in other mammals. But human lesions are never experimental, rarely neatly circumscribed, and their effects also vary to some extent, depending upon their cause, that is, whether they are the result of penetrating injury, tumor, or stroke. The cause of damage in the child is rarely known and its presence is often inferred from behavioral or neurological signs, making comparisons with the adult particularly difficult. Animal studies are therefore crucial for our understanding of recovery from damage, but provocative as the results from these studies may be, they have limitations in their applicability to the effects

1. This chapter is dedicated to the memory of my late teacher, mentor, friend, and collaborator, Hans-Lukas Teuber. After our first series of papers almost twenty years ago, in which we compared the effects of early and late brain damage, we talked about eventually doing another together. That is now impossible. I hope he would at least have been pleased with my lonely effort.

2. Hans-Lukas Teuber, "Neural Plasticity: Extent and Limits," invited keynote address to the Ninth Winter Conference on Brain Research, Keystone, Colorado, January 18, 1976.

of human brain damage and could never, for example, provide us with a comparative aphaseology.

One might feel impelled to inquire why one bothers with the issue of neuroplasticity at all considering its many imponderables. Whatever its complexity, the problem is nonetheless there: What is the extent of recovery of function in the brain and how and in what way does that recovery differ for organisms of different sex and at different stages of development? The answers to these questions may provide us with patterns of symptoms that signal previous damage, alteration, or difference in particular cerebral organizations. They may tell us, for example, whether we must always expect sensory or motor deficits to accompany dysfunction in more complex activities like reading or face recognition. In adults, certain sensory deficits are correlates of perceptual deficits. Is this also true in the child? And if not, why not? What may one expect instead? This is not to imply that dysfunction in more complex activities like reading must be due to brain damage, but it has to be due to some different arrangement of synaptic connections which makes that activity impossible for an otherwise intelligent human. These altered synaptic arrangements, as we shall see, may be the consequence of damage, genetic differences, deprivation, or poor early training. Yet none of these preconditions may be in evidence at the time the child is old enough to be expected to read or to find his way about. It is hoped that an exploration of some of the parameters of recovery of function in young and old, animal and man, male and female, will provide us with a more complete picture of development, both normal and not entirely normal. Determining what, if anything, can alter the inexorable consequences after diagnosis of early damage (however incurred) will make that the beginning rather than the end of our responsibility.

Since adult and child lesions are rarely comparable, neuroplasticity in humans has to be approached, at least at present, in terms of relative alterations of functional systems rather than in terms of recovery from damage of equal extent at identical sites. There are by now considerable data on the relative effects of early and late damage on (a) sensory-motor functions, (b) cognitive functions, and (c) language and intelligence. After a brief look at some of the problems as well as some of the possible consequences of early damage and recovery of function, we shall examine each of these areas in turn.

Defining Damage: Three Possible Consequences of Early versus Late Damage

The neuropsychological search for brain-behavior relationships does not always begin with the brain nor is "damage" always attributable to an observable lesion. At the animal level, studies have demonstrated that rearing in isolation or with early sensory deprivation produces developmental changes from the norm comparable to those following experimental ablation.[3] The extent to which altering the visual world of the neonatal cat changes his repertory of responses is currently a central and controversial issue.[4] Children reared in isolation and those reared in institutions do not develop adequately. Autism has been ascribed to early traumatic experience or to "affective deprivation"[5] and some learning disabilities to "cultural deprivation." No lesions have been demonstrated as a consequence of these early deprivations but implicit in all such claims, at the animal or human level, are altered synaptic arrangements. One would have to conclude that the neonatal brain is simultaneously very sensitive to environmental inadequacies and very resistant to recovery from their damaging effects.

Paradoxically, conclusions drawn from experimental and clinical studies of recovery of function from early brain damage are in sharp contrast, the immature brain apparently being capable of

3. Leo Ganz and Margaret Fitch, "The Effect of Visual Deprivation on Perceptual Behavior," *Experimental Neurology* 22 (1968): 638-60; Edward Geller, "Some Observations on the Effects of Environmental Complexity and Isolation on Biochemical Ontogeny," in *Brain Development and Behavior*, ed. M. B. Sterman, Dennis J. McGinty, and Anthony M. Adinolfi (New York: Academic Press, 1971), pp. 277-96; Richard Held and Joseph A. Bauer, "Visually Guided Reaching in Infant Monkeys after Restricted Rearing," *Science* 155 (1967): 718-20.

4. Teuber, "Neural Plasticity: Extent and Limits"; Colin Blakemore and Richard C. Van Sluyters, "Innate and Environmental Factors in the Development of the Kitten's Visual Cortex," *Journal of Physiology* 248 (1975): 663-716.

5. Leo Kanner, "Autistic Disturbances of Affective Contact," *Nervous Child* 2 (1943): 217-50. See also, Patricia S. Goldman, "The Relationship between Amount of Stimulation in Infancy and Subsequent Emotionality," *Annals of the New York Academy of Sciences* 159 (1969): 640-50.

considerable restitution of function. The experimental monkey studies of Goldman provide instructive insight into the interacting effects of early damage and early experience.[6]

Beginning with the work of Kennard,[7] the outlook for recovery after early damage has been cheerfully optimistic. To quote Teuber:

> The late Margaret Kennard counseled us to have our brain injuries, if we had to have them, as early as it could possibly be managed, since early damage, in her view, was quite generally less disruptive of function than similar injuries sustained later in life.[8]

Bilateral motor cortex removals in adult macaques resulted in total loss of postural control or movement while the same ablations in infant monkeys were followed by recovery of postural and locomotor functions. Kennard did note that these early-operated monkeys showed some adverse effects later in life, such as exaggerated tendon responses and eventually spasticity, but reports of these subsequent difficulties were lost sight of in the more simply stated principle that early damage is less disruptive of function than damage sustained later in development. Taken together, however, Kennard's work does provide two possible consequences of early damage: (a) some effects may be minimal or even transient and therefore less disabling than comparable damage to the adult, and (b) other effects may not appear until later in life.

Rudel et al. studied seventy-two children who ranged in age from five to eighteen years and who were suffering from congenital cerebral palsy. A comparison of this group with matched controls suggested that the question of early versus late damage

6. Patricia S. Goldman, "The Role of Experience in Recovery of Function Following Orbital Prefrontal Lesions in Infant Monkeys," *Neuropsychologia* 14 (1976): 401-11.

7. Patricia S. Goldman, "Developmental Determinants of Cortical Plasticity," *Acta Neurobiologica Experimentalis* 32 (1972): 495-511; idem, "An Alternative to Developmental Plasticity: Heterology of CNS Structures in Infants and Adults," in *Plasticity and Recovery of Function in the Central Nervous System*, ed. Donald G. Stein, Jeffrey J. Rosen, and Nelson Butters (New York: Academic Press, 1974), pp. 149-74; Patricia S. Goldman and H. Enger Rosvold, "The Effects of Selective Caudate Lesions in Infant and Juvenile Rhesus Monkeys," *Brain Research* 43 (1972): 53-56.

8. Teuber, "Neural Plasticity: Extent and Limits."

had no single answer.[9] Instead, the extent of relative impairment appeared to depend upon the test employed and the age of testing. Depending upon these conditions, there are effects of damage which (a) appear early and disappear, (b) are apparent at all ages after early or late lesions, or (c) are apparent only after a delay.

DISAPPEARANCE OF SYMPTOMS WITH EARLY DAMAGE

The early appearance and eventual disappearance of a symptom could be accounted for if the damaged area of the immature brain, committed to a particular function, were to make new synaptic connections. Such rearrangements in circuitry could lead to amelioration of symptoms but also to anomalous connections and to poor survival mechanisms. Thus, Schneider has shown that the retino-tectal fibers of hamsters with early lesions of the superior colliculus grow to the region of the missing colliculus.[10] If the unaffected eye of these animals is occluded, the animal turns in the wrong direction when offered food. The capacity of one part of the brain to "take over" for another depends upon its own functions not yet being fully specified. There is the possibility that the region taking over and causing the early symptoms to "disappear" will subsequently be unavailable for the function to which it eventually should become committed.

"GENERAL" EFFECTS OF DAMAGE: EARLY AND LATE

Those symptoms that are apparent at all ages after early or late lesions have not been adequately explored. These are "general" effects of damage rather than alterations of specific functions, and are characteristic of adults and children with brain damage regardless of the site or size of lesion. For example, brain damage

9. Rita G. Rudel et al., "Localization of Auditory Midline and Reactions to Body Tilt in Brain-damaged Children," *Journal of Nervous and Mental Disease* 131 (1960): 302-9; Hans-Lukas Teuber and Rita G. Rudel, "Behavior after Cerebral Lesions in Children and Adults," *Developmental Medicine and Child Neurology* 4 (1962): 3-20.

10. Gerald E. Schneider, "Mechanisms of Functional Recovery Following Lesions of Visual Cortex of Superior Colliculus in Neonate and Adult Hamsters," *Brain Behavior and Evolution* 3 (1970): 295-323; idem, "Early Lesions of Superior Colliculus: Factors Affecting the Formation of Abnormal Retinal Projections," *Brain Behavior and Evolution* 8 (1973): 73-109.

at any age seems to lead to a slowing of reaction time.[11] Slowness on tests of language,[12] visual information store,[13] and repetitive movements[14] have been demonstrated in children with a variety of developmental anomalies, including dyslexia.

In psychophysical judgments, for example, in judging the midpoint of a line, the extent to which those judgments are spread out or close together may constitute another parameter of "general" level of functioning. According to Rosenberger, the generalization gradient of judgment of the midpoint of a line is broader in adult patients with brain damage than in normal controls.[15] This lack of precision in judgments of an auditory midline, a tendency to stay with the starting point of the stimulus, was shown for brain-damaged adults as well as for children with cerebral palsy.[16] Impairment of any one of several activating systems could be responsible for this loss of neural efficiency or precision. It may also be the price paid for "take-over" of function by a less direct, less competent, and therefore slower and less precise neural substrate than the one genetically specified.

DELAYED EFFECTS OF EARLY DAMAGE

Delayed effects of damage may result if the damaged structure is itself not functionally mature and not utilized. Only when the function becomes dependent upon the damaged neural sub-

11. Harold E. Blackburn and Arthur L. Benton, "Simple and Choice Reaction Time in Cerebral Disease," *Confinia Neurologica* 15 (1955): 327-38.

12. Martha B. Denckla and Rita G. Rudel, "Rapid 'Automatized' Naming (R.A.N.): Dyslexia Differentiated from Other Learning Disabilities," *Neuropsychologia* 14 (1976): 471-79; Carl Spring and Carolyn Capps, "Encoding Speed, Rehearsal, and Probed Recall of Dyslexic Boys," *Journal of Educational Psychology* 66 (1974): 780-86.

13. Gordon Stanley, "Visual Memory Processes in Dyslexia," in *Short Term Memory*, ed. Diana D. Deutsch and J. Anthony Deutsch (New York: Academic Press, 1975), pp. 181-94.

14. Martha B. Denckla and Rita G. Rudel, "Motor Anomalies in Dyslexic Children," in preparation.

15. Peter B. Rosenberger, "Discriminative Aspects of Visual Hemi-inattention," *Neurology* 24 (1974): 76-79.

16. Teuber and Rudel, "Behavior after Cerebral Lesions in Children and Adults"; Rudel et al., "Localization of Auditory Midline and Reactions to Body Tilt in Brain-damaged Children."

strate does the impairment become apparent. Obviously, the effects of damage to those structures essential for reading could not be observed in the neonate for many years thereafter. The delay with which a symptom appears may even differ for males and females, a point demonstrated in the research of Goldman[17] and possibly relevant to sex differences in developmental dyslexia.

One need not always invoke structural take-over, however, to explain the absence or disappearance of symptoms. Klüver cautioned against the assumption that recovery of function involves the establishment of new pathways when the possibility exists for the evolution of new strategies to solve old problems.[18] Normal development consists to a large extent of changing strategies. Children under the age of ten, for example, rely heavily on language in the performance of nonlanguage, spatial tasks,[19] and it is precisely before the age of ten that dyslexic children perform poorly relative to normal readers on route finding and other visuo-spatial tasks.[20] This may reflect the reliance on language of both groups, but dyslexic children have been found to be deficient in language use.[21] By age ten, when normal as well as dyslexic children have begun to use nonverbal strategies, the poor readers are equal to[22] or even superior to normal readers on such tasks.[23]

17. Patricia S. Goldman et al., "Sex-dependent Behavioral Effects of Cerebral Cortical Lesions in the Developing Rhesus Monkey," *Science* 186 (1974): 540-42.

18. Heinrich Klüver, "Functional Significance of the Geniculo-striate System," *Biological Symposia* 7 (1942): 253-59.

19. Susan Carey, Rhea Diamond, and Bryan T. Woods, "The Development of the Ability to Recognize Faces: A Maturational Basis?" *Journal of Experimental Child Psychology*, in press.

20. Martha B. Denckla, Rita G. Rudel, and Melinda B. Petrovics, "Spatial Orientation in Normal, Learning-disabled, and Neurologically Impaired Children," unpublished manuscript.

21. Isabelle Y. Liberman and Donald Shankweiler, "Speech, the Alphabet, and Teaching to Read," in *Theory and Practice of Early Reading*, ed. L. Resnick and P. Weaver (Hillsdale, N.J.: Erlbaum Associates, forthcoming).

22. Karen Sobotka et al., "Some Psychological Correlates of Developmental Dyslexia," *Journal of Learning Disabilities* 10 (1977): 363-69.

23. Denckla, Rudel, and Petrovics, "Spatial Orientation in Normal, Learning-disabled, and Neurologically Impaired Children."

It would be gratuitous to assume that such improvement in performance is due to axonal reorganization.

Ten years is the age at which the corpus callosum completes myelination,[24] allowing adequate or even superior spatial ability to become apparent. What appears to be the overcoming of a symptom (poor spatial ability) may actually be a normal structural change that permits an intact system to perform a task previously poorly performed by a damaged system. Such maturation of neural substrate is not always advantageous to the child with early damage. An epileptogenic focus in one hemisphere is also more readily conveyed to the other side after myelination of the corpus callosum.

One can account for the absence or disappearance of effects of early brain damage through structural rearrangement, synaptic connections with unaffected areas, the take-over of function by one area for another, or the development of new structures that permit the evolution of different strategies. Much of the difference between early and late damage would appear to depend upon the "uncommitted" structures in the immature brain and a reorganization of cerebral pathways. Kennard accounted for the evidence of recovery in the motor system of infant monkeys by assuming some capacity in the animals for dendritic rearrangement, implying a difference in the nature of recovery for mature and immature animals.

Tsang, a student of Lashley, demonstrated that the difference between the consequences of early and late damage may instead be one of degree rather than of kind.[25] Cortical ablation of the brain of infant rats had to be proportionally larger to produce deficits in maze running comparable to the deficits in adult rats. This would mean that maturation involves, to some extent, a decrease in the amount of cortical tissue committed to a particular function and that this less restricted localization in the infant brain accounts for some of the difference between the effects of

24. Paul I. Yakovlev and André-Roch Lecours, "The Myelogenetic Cycles of Regional Maturation of the Brain," in *Regional Development of the Brain in Early Life*, ed. Alexandre Minkowski (Oxford: Blackwell, 1967), pp. 3-70.

25. Yü-Chüan Tsang, "Maze Learning in Rats Hemidecorticated in Infancy," *Journal of Comparative Psychology* 24 (1937): 221-54.

early and late damage. In fact, Massopust and Daigle, using an evoked potential method, have shown that cortical sensory regions of the infant cat are 25 percent larger in both ipsilateral and contralateral hemispheres than in the adult cat, indicating more widespread sensory representation.[26] If it takes a larger lesion in the infant brain than in the adult brain to produce equivalent deficits, so-called "minimal brain dysfunction" may in fact involve rather maximal lesions.[27] Whatever the relationship between lesion and behavioral manifestation, there is ample evidence that early brain damage has little or no effect on the development of sensory functioning, that is, sensory function is spared following early damage.

Sensory and Motor Functions

Following bilateral removals of somatosensory cortex in newborn kittens, no deficit could be detected six months later on a series of roughness discriminations.[28] The same ablation in the mature cat rendered it incapable of making any of these discriminations. Doty has made a similar claim for the visual system of the cat.[29] Ablation of the striate cortex in the mature animal destroys pattern vision, but in the newborn kitten, pattern vision is retained unless the ablation also includes extra-striate foci on the lateral aspects of both hemispheres. Similar findings for the auditory system have been made by Diamond and Neff[30] and by

26. Leo C. Massopust, Jr. and H. J. Daigle, "Cortical Projection of the Medial and Spinal Vestibular Nuclei in the Cat," *Experimental Neurology* 2 (1960): 179-85.

27. Arthur L. Benton, "Developmental Dyslexia: Neurological Aspects," in *Advances in Neurology*, vol. 7, ed. Walter J. Friedlander (New York: Raven Press, 1975), pp. 1-47.

28. R. M. Benjamin and R. F. Thompson, "Differential Effects of Cortical Lesions in Infant and Adult Cats on Roughness Discrimination," *Experimental Neurology* 1 (1959): 305-21.

29. Robert W. Doty, "Functional Significance of the Topographical Aspects of the Retino-Cortical Projection," in *Neurophysiologie und Psychophysik des visuellen Systems*, ed. Richard Jung and Hans Kornhuber (Berlin: Springer, 1961), pp. 228-45.

30. Irving T. Diamond and W. D. Neff, "Ablation of Temporal Cortex and Discrimination of Auditory Patterns," *Journal of Neurophysiology* 20 (1957): 300-15.

Scharlock, Tucker, and Strominger,[31] all pointing to the relative resilience of animal sensory systems to early damage.

Sixty-three children, who were ambulatory and were presumed to be educable and who had early perinatal or prenatal brain damage, were found on neurological examination to have extensive motor but very little concomitant sensory impairment. Thus, fifty-eight had abnormal alternating movements and fifty-two had oculomotor deficits, but only two had visual field defects (on confrontation testing) and none had elevated light touch thresholds.[32] The motor deficits were more subtle than those found in children with cerebral palsy, but they were nonetheless pervasive. However, no somatosensory deficits could be found independent of low mental age, that is, in children too retarded to respond appropriately to the instructions for discrimination of two tactile points or of passive movement. This very low incidence of somatosensory deficit is in sharp contrast to the incidence in adults who sustain injury at maturity. Out of 124 adults with penetrating brain wounds, 66 were reported to have defective sensation when tested with the same methods used in the study of children.[33] Eight of the children had extremely low light touch as well as two-point discrimination thresholds on thumbs and palms.[34] This enhanced sensitivity was associated with particularly marked avoiding responses and incoordination. Behaviorally, they were clumsy, handling objects as if they were "hot potatoes," and they also had extreme difficulty with handwriting. One suspects an excessive sparing of sensory function at the cost of fine motor coordination, or the sparing of gross motor functions with a delayed deficit in fine motor control. At the infrahuman level, in the rhesus monkey, there is no loss of gross motor coordination with early damage to

31. Donald P. Scharlock, Thomas J. Tucker, and Norman L. Strominger, "Auditory Discrimination by the Cat after Neonatal Ablation of Temporal Cortex," *Science* 141 (1963): 1197-98.

32. Rita G. Rudel, Hans-Lukas Teuber, and T. E. Twitchell, "A Note on Hyperesthesia in Children with Early Brain Damage," *Neuropsychologia* 4 (1966): 351-66.

33. Josephine Semmes et al., *Somatosensory Changes after Penetrating Brain Wounds in Man* (Cambridge, Mass.: Harvard University Press, 1960).

34. Rudel, Teuber, and Twitchell, "A Note on Hyperesthesia in Children with Early Brain Damage."

the frontal precentral cortex but there is a delayed deficit in fine control of digits, which appears at two years when such control is complete in normal animals.[35]

The absence of sensory deficits in these children did not mean that they were free of impairments on tasks at more complex levels, impairments associated in the adults with sensory deficits, for example, recognition of objects by touch,[36] performance of body scheme tests,[37] and route-finding tasks.[38] These deficits of perception and of personal and extrapersonal orientation do not appear to depend, as they do in the adult, upon any disturbance of sensory input. One must not rule out the possibility that sensory impairment is one of those consequences of early brain damage which "appear early and disappear." These children were all tested at school age, possibly too late for the detection of sensory deficits but not too late to find their sequelae in impaired performance of more complex tasks.

Their designation as "brain-damaged" was based upon impaired motor functions. These ranged from persistent avoiding responses[39] to difficulty in performing repetitive alternating movements.[40] The relationship of these motor symptoms to perceptual and cognitive difficulties is still unclear, but from evidence of work with developing animals motor deficits may result in impaired feedback.[41]

35. D. G. Lawrence and D. A. Hopkins, "Developmental Aspects of Pyramidal Motor Control in the Rhesus Monkey," *Brain Research* 40 (1972): 117-18.

36. Rudel, Teuber, and Twitchell, "A Note on Hyperesthesia in Children with Early Brain Damage."

37. Rita G. Rudel, Hans-Lukas Teuber, and T. E. Twitchell, "Levels of Impairment of Sensori-motor Functions in Children with Early Brain Damage," *Neuropsychologia* 12 (1974): 95-108.

38. Rita G. Rudel and Hans-Lukas Teuber, "Spatial Orientation in Normal Children and in Children with Early Brain Injury," *Neuropsychologia* 9 (1971): 401-7.

39. T. E. Twitchell, "Minimal Cerebral Dysfunction in Children: Motor Deficits," *Transactions of the American Neurological Association* 9 (1966): 353-55.

40. Rudel, Teuber, and Twitchell, "Levels of Impairment of Sensori-motor Functions in Children with Early Brain Damage."

41. Richard Held and Sanford J. Freedman, "Plasticity in Human Sensorimotor Control," *Science* 142 (1963): 455-62.

This would appear to be particularly true for children with oculomotor disturbances who are selectively impaired on visual or haptic shape perception[42] as well as on route-finding tasks.[43] A retrospective analysis of data on more than 100 children indicates that congenital oculomotor disturbance (a bilateral sign) tends to be associated with indications of right hemisphere damage.[44] The relationship recalls Hebb's suggestion that eye movements around contours develop a schema of spatial coordinates.[45]

In summary, sensory functions appear to be spared with early brain damage in animal or man. This sparing may occasionally lead to hyperesthesia (excessively low thresholds) and does not mean an absence of losses at more complex levels of functioning which, in the brain-injured adult, are associated with sensory deficits. In the child, they tend instead to be correlates of impaired fine motor, and particularly oculomotor, disturbances.

Cognitive Functions

The sparing of sensory functions demonstrated in animal and child recalls the proposal by Vygotski that early injuries of the brain tend to leave elementary functions relatively intact while precluding or impairing the development of more complex aspects of performance.[46] This has already been suggested in the preceding section: the sparing of sensory functions in children does not spare perceptual capabilities which, in the adult, appear to depend upon sensory intactness. One might add to Vygotski's

42. Rita G. Rudel and Hans-Lukas Teuber, "Pattern Recognition within and across Sensory Modalities in Normal and Brain-injured Children," *Neuropsychologia* 9 (1971): 389-99.

43. Denckla, Rudel, and Petrovics, "Spatial Orientation in Normal, Learning-disabled, and Neurologically Impaired Children"; Rudel, Teuber, and Twitchell, "Levels of Impairment of Sensori-motor Functions in Children with Early Brain Damage."

44. T. E. Twitchell, personal communication.

45. Donald O. Hebb, *The Organization of Behavior: A Neuropsychological Theory* (New York: Wiley, 1949). See also, Joseph Bauer and Richard Held, "Comparison of Visually Guided Reaching in Normal and Deprived Infant Monkeys," *Journal of Experimental Psychology: Animal Behavior Processes* 1 (1975): 298-308.

46. L. S. Vygotski, "Development of Higher Mental Functions," *Izvestija Akademii Pedagogicheskikh Nauk*, RFSR, Moscow (1960).

proposition that sparing is least in evidence the more complex the function tested. Thus, children with congenital absence of interhemispheric commissures do not exhibit anything like the severe disconnection in the adult,[47] but one suspects certain other losses. These children display preponderantly low intelligence quotients, suggesting that early absence of commissural connections between the hemispheres might interfere less with information flow between hemispheres than disconnection later in life. It might, however, carry another penalty in a general reduction of intelligence.

Sparing of function with early damage remains the same for lesions that encroach on the "limbic" structures. Following bilateral hippocampectomies, kittens performed as well as controls on two tasks but on a third, which interposed a ten-second delay after each bar press, the operated animals were inferior to controls.[48] That ten-second delay made the test as sensitive to early lesion as to those inflicted on the mature animal. Recent research, which compares reading-disabled children to controls, has similarly noted that even a brief delay between presentation of a stimulus array and a choice response results in impaired performance by the dyslexic group. If choice is made immediately on a variety of stimuli, there is no difference between the groups.[49] Memory for an event after a delay presupposes a more complex level of cognitive organization.

Few animal studies have invaded subcortical structures in the search for effects of early damage, although precisely these structures are likely to be involved in congenital or prenatal injury. A combined frontal-caudate lesion, inflicted in the neonatal monkey,

47. M. A. Jeeves, "Psychological Studies of Three Cases of Congenital Agenesis of the Corpus Callosum," in *Functions of the Corpus Callosum*, ed. E. G. Ettlinger (Boston: Little, Brown and Co., 1965), pp. 74-94; Roger W. Sperry, "Brain Bisection and Consciousness," in *Brain and Conscious Experience*, ed. John C. Eccles (New York: Springer, 1966), pp. 298-313.

48. Robert L. Isaacson, Arthur J. Nonneman, and Leonard W. Schmaltz, "Behavioral and Anatomical Sequelae of the Infant Limbic System," in *The Neuropsychology of Development*, ed. Robert L. Isaacson (New York: Wiley, 1968), pp. 41-78.

49. Frederick J. Morrison, Bruno Giordani, and Jill Nagy, "Reading Disability: An Information Processing Analysis," *Science* 196 (1977): 77-79.

abolishes delayed response capacity entirely, according to a study by Kling and Tucker.[50] More significantly, perhaps, animals with such lesions become hyperactive and unmanageable. Hyperactivity has long been known as a consequence of caudate lesions in adult monkeys,[51] but its delayed onset after early lesions is of considerable interest since it provides a parallel to clinical phenomena seen after early head injury in children.[52] There are hyperactive children without any history of head injury who nonetheless have "developmental" (slow for age) signs, particularly excessive synkinetic movement (overflow).[53]

Both Hebb[54] and Russell[55] have suggested that early damage in frontal areas (that is, the caudate nucleus and/or frontal cortex) might be more disabling in the child than in the adult. Frontal damage in the adult monkey impairs its ability to perform a variety of delayed response tasks but the infant monkey with a bifrontal lobectomy does not develop such a deficit. On a more complex task (an "oddities learning set"), however, Harlow has shown that there is impairment with damage inflicted at any age.[56] There is, then, a subtle interaction of age of damage and task complexity in recovery of function. The work of Kling and Tucker, Harlow,

50. Arthur Kling and Thomas J. Tucker, "Effects of Combined Lesions of Frontal Granular Cortex and Caudate Nucleus in the Neonatal Monkey," *Brain Research* 6 (1967): 428-39.

51. G. D. Davis, "Caudate Lesions and Spontaneous Locomotion in the Monkey," *Neurology* 8 (1958): 135-39.

52. P. Black, "Post-traumatic Syndrome in Children," in *The Late Effects of Head Injury*, ed. Arthur E. Walker, Macdonald Critchley, and William F. Caveness (Springfield, Ill.: Charles C Thomas, 1969), pp. 142-49.

53. Martha B. Denckla and Rita G. Rudel, "Anomalies of Motor Development in Hyperactive Boys," *Annals of Neurology*, in press.

54. Donald O. Hebb, "The Effect of Early and Late Brain Injury upon Test Scores, and the Nature of Normal Adult Intelligence," *Proceedings of the American Philosophical Society* 85 (1942): 275-92.

55. W. Ritchie Russell, *Brain Memory Learning: A Neurologist's View* (Oxford: Clarendon Press, 1950); Paul Fedio, Ina Samuels, and Nelson Butters, Short-term Memory Disorders Following Temporal Lobe Removals in Humans," *Cortex* 8 (1972): 283-98.

56. Harry F. Harlow et al., "Effects of Induction Age and Size of Frontal Lobe Lesions on Learning in Rhesus Monkey," in *The Neuropsychology of Development*, ed. Isaacson, pp. 79-120.

and Goldman[57] makes it apparent that a third critical factor affecting this interaction is the age at which the function appears in the course of normal development.

Goldman has complicated the age factor further by demonstrating (a) sex differences in maturation rates and (b) an effect on recovery of function of experience with the test.[58] We shall take these up in turn: the effect of age at maturation of the function, sex, and experience.

EFFECTS OF AGE

The gamut of possibilities for the effects of age on recovery of function emerges in the work of Schneider with the Syrian golden hamster.[59] This animal has a gestation period of only sixteen days and is born with a very immature nervous system. The brain reaches full size in only three months. Ablation of the visual cortex (area 17) in the adult hamster was sufficient in many cases to cause a failure to learn a simple pattern discrimination, a choice between horizontal and vertical stripes. When tested on the same problem at three months of age, most of the animals with early lesions were able to learn the discrimination even though their lesions were larger than in the adult-operated animals. These animals operated on as neonates were deficient in their performance only in that they were slower than normal controls in learning the task. On an instrumental conditioning procedure, however, which required merely that the animal open the doorways to obtain a reward, animals with lesions inflicted early in life were unable to perform while those with lesions acquired as adults had no dif-

57. Patricia S. Goldman, "Maturation of the Mammalian Nervous System and the Ontogeny of Behavior," in *Advances in the Study of Behavior*, vol. 7 (New York: Academic Press, 1976), pp. 1-90.

58. Patricia S. Goldman, "Age, Sex, and Experience as Related to the Neural Basis of Cognitive Development," in *Brain Mechanisms in Mental Retardation*, ed. Nathaniel Buchwald and Mary A. B. Brazier (New York: Academic Press, 1975), pp. 379-92.

59. Gerald E. Schneider, "Neuroanatomical Correlates of Spared or Altered Function after Brain Lesions in the Newborn Hamster," in *Plasticity and Recovery of Function in the Central Nervous System*, ed. Stein, Rosen, and Butters, pp. 65-109.

ficulty. This reverses the more common outcome of early and late damage, which usually demonstrates greater sparing of functions the earlier the damage.

Despite this negative evidence, there still is no question that for most parts of the brain and for most functions the "Kennard principle" (as Teuber has called it) is operative, that is, there is more recovery after early lesions than late. "Early" does not always mean neonatal and one might, in fact, amend the principle to say "the earlier the lesion the greater the degree of functional recovery." Hurt and Teuber examined 167 patients twenty years after they sustained penetrating brain wounds during the Korean campaign.[60] These men ranged in age from seventeen to over twenty-six years at the time of injury and were first examined within one week after injury. Their examination protocols immediately and twenty years later noted the presence of motor, somatosensory, visual field deficits, and dysphasia. At all ages, in all categories, there was some symptom disappearance, but the youngest group, seventeen to twenty years of age at the time of injury, showed the highest rate of improvement and those twenty-six years of age or older the lowest. The consistent proportionality of patients' age at the time of wounding and subsequent recovery is all the more remarkable considering the very restricted age range. There was a much greater degree of improvement in visual field defects (67 percent) than in amount of residual dysphasia (29 percent) among even the youngest patients. Here the Vygotski principle appears operative: less recovery of function the more complex the function.

The change in neuroplasticity with age may reflect the level of maturation of the neural substrate at the time of injury. Bilateral ablation of the dorsolateral frontal cortex in rhesus monkeys less than two months old does not interfere with their performance on spatial delayed alternation tasks while the identical lesion in adult monkeys totally abolishes this capacity,[61] a finding in com-

60. Reported in Hans-Lukas Teuber, "Effects of Focal Brain Injury on Human Behavior," in *The Nervous System*, vol. 2, *The Clinical Neurosciences*, ed. Donald B. Tower (New York: Raven Press, 1975), pp. 457-80.

61. Goldman, "The Role of Experience in Recovery of Function Following Orbital Prefrontal Lesions in Infant Monkeys."

plete accord with the Kennard principle, the sparing of function with early lesions. Studies of degenerating fiber systems to and from the dorsolateral prefrontal cortex indicate virtually none at two months of age, some at six months, and the complete complement by twenty-four months.[62] At least part of the functional circuits are not structurally differentiated in the infant animal and therefore spared with early ablation. According to Goldman,

> The capacity to perform delayed response tasks with adult proficiency is not present in the neonate and develops gradually over an extended postnatal period. In the monkey, it is doubtful whether fully adult-level delayed response abilities are attained within the first two years of life.[63]

Sparing of function after ablation may be evident only very early in life, in some instances only within the first year. When neonatally operated monkeys are tested after the second year, they exhibit increasing evidence of deficiency in the performance of delayed response tasks compared with unoperated controls of the same age. Prior to that age, some other structure or structures are apparently sufficient to mediate the type of delayed response performance expected of the very young animal.

Essentially this research tells us that there may be sparing with early lesions because the excised structure does not become functional until later in the animal's life. Until then, other structures are capable of mediating the function at a level comparable to the performance of unoperated control animals of the same age. When the structure in question becomes functional in the unoperated animals, allowing for more complex performance, a deficit in the operated animals becomes apparent.

These demonstrations, along with the fiber degeneration studies, have provided an experimental, neurophysiological basis for the clinical observation that children with early brain damage often "look better" at earlier ages when their repertory of abilities meets age expectations. As functional requirements become more complex (when, in monkey terms, the task goes from "delayed response" to an "oddities learning set," or a ten-second delay is in-

62. Ibid.

63. Goldman, "Maturation of the Mammalian Nervous System and the Ontogeny of Behavior," p. 34.

terposed in an object discrimination task), the deficit becomes apparent. Deficits after early damage may not only be delayed but never become noticeable as long as the appropriate demands are not made, that is, until one poses an adequate functional challenge to the impaired late-developing neurostructure. The study referred to earlier, in which children with cerebral palsy were compared with their own age controls as well as with brain-injured adults, found that effects of early damage depended on the test employed as well as on the age of testing.[64] That Hurt and Teuber's subjects were young adults at the time of injury, and still showed so much functional recovery, is not surprising in the light of Yakovlev and Lecours's evidence that myelination in the human continues into the third decade of life.[65]

SEX DIFFERENCES

The rate of neurophysiological maturation so crucial in determining the effect of early damage, may indeed differ for the sexes. Beyond obvious reproductive functions, sex differences are generally ascribed to cultural demands and expectations. There is, however, increasing evidence that certain cognitive abilities develop earlier in one sex than in the other. Language functions are said to develop earlier in girls[66] and some so-called right-hemisphere functions are said to develop earlier in boys. Boys achieve left-ear superiority earlier than girls for discrimination of environmental sounds[67] and left-hand superiority earlier for discrimination of Braille patterns.[68] It seems rather unlikely, even far-fetched, that

64. Teuber and Rudel, "Behavior after Cerebral Lesions in Children and Adults."

65. Yakovlev and Lecours, "The Myelogenetic Cycles of Regional Maturation of the Brain."

66. Anthony W. H. Buffery, "Sex Differences in the Development of Hemispheric Asymmetry of Function in the Human Brain," *Brain Research* 31 (1971): 364-65.

67. Carol Knox and Doreen Kimura, "Cerebral Processing of Nonverbal Sounds in Boys and Girls," *Neuropsychologia* 8 (1970): 227-37.

68. Rita G. Rudel, Martha B. Denckla, and Elinor Spalten, "The Functional Asymmetry of Braille Letter Learning in Normal, Sighted Children," *Neurology* 24 (1974): 733-38; Rita G. Rudel, Martha B. Denckla, and Susan Hirsch, "The Development of Left-Hand Superiority for Discriminating Braille Configurations," *Neurology* 27 (1977): 160-64.

this ontogenetically earlier functional lateralization in boys in any way relates to the much greater incidence of early brain damage among them. Depending on the source, there would appear to be at least five times as many boys as girls with "minimal brain dysfunction,"[69] dyslexia,[70] and cerebral palsy.[71]

And yet, in the rhesus monkey a relationship has been suggested between earlier maturation of orbital prefrontal cortex of males and their greater vulnerability to effects of neonatal damage. A lesion inflicted at fifty days of age produces a deficit in object discrimination as well as a delayed response deficit in male monkeys, but not in females. The operated males make more errors and take longer to learn than unoperated males, but operated females perform at the same level as unoperated females. As would be expected on the basis of the Kennard principle, adult male and female monkeys with the same lesion could not perform the task at all[72] and, as expected on the basis of the animal literature, there are no sex differences in the effect of lesion inflicted at maturity. While the operated infant males were immediately inferior on these tasks to unoperated controls, the deficit did not become apparent in females until they were fifteen to eighteen months old.[73] However, when infant female rhesus monkeys received postnatal injections of testosterone propionate and were then subjected to ablation of the orbital prefrontal cortex, they gave evidence of a deficit in performance at seventy-five days of age, as did the males, rather than at fifteen to eighteen months as did the unoperated, unandrogenized females. Goldman states:

69. Paul H. Wender, *Minimal Brain Dysfunction in Children* (New York: Wiley, 1971).

70. Paul Satz and G. K. Van Nostrand, "Developmental Dyslexia: An Evaluation of a Theory," in *The Disabled Learner: Early Detection and Intervention*, ed. Paul Satz and J. Ross (Rotterdam: University of Rotterdam Press, 1973), pp. 212-48.

71. Abraham Towbin, *The Pathology of Cerebral Palsy* (Springfield, Ill.: Charles C Thomas, 1960).

72. Goldman et al., "Sex-dependent Behavioral Effects of Cerebral Cortical Lesions in the Developing Rhesus Monkey."

73. Goldman, "Age, Sex, and Experience as Related to the Neural Basis of Cognitive Development."

The results thus provide further and more direct evidence that cortical mechanisms may be sexually dimorphic and that such dimorphism may account in part for the broad spectrum of social, psychological, and cognitive traits that differentiate the sexes.[74]

Goldman suggests that the slower development of the orbital cortex in female monkeys may confer a functional advantage, for not only are they less vulnerable to immediate effects of early lesions but there is some evidence that adult female monkeys are superior to males on the delayed response task.[75]

It is difficult to extrapolate from this to the human condition except for confirmation of the greater vulnerability of the male to early damage. Although girls develop some right-hemisphere functions somewhat later than boys, they are not superior to them. Their performance on spatial tasks is less impaired with right hemisphere damage incurred at maturity inasmuch as they rely more heavily on verbal strategies in their performance.[76] Evidence of earlier "lateralization" of a function does not necessarily reflect earlier structural maturity. We probably need a more reliable behavioral index than degree of functional asymmetry of the cerebral hemispheres.

THE EFFECTS OF EXPERIENCE

There is no question that early experience is crucial in determining development, from the simple observation that a child never spoken to can learn no language[77] to the subtle effects of imprinting on certain birds.[78] Early stimulation has been shown to

74. Goldman, "Maturation of the Mammalian Nervous System in the Ontogeny of Behavior," pp. 62-63.

75. Goldman, "Age, Sex, and Experience as Related to the Neural Basis of Cognitive Development."

76. Jeannette McGlone and Wilda Davidson, "The Relation between Speech Laterality and Spatial Ability with Special Reference to Sex and Hand Preference," *Neuropsychologia* 11 (1973): 105-13; Denckla, Rudel, and Petrovics, "Spatial Orientation in Normal, Learning-disabled, and Neurologically Impaired Children."

77. Victoria A. Fromkin et al., "The Development of Language in Genie: A Case of Language Acquisition beyond the 'Critical Period'," *Brain and Language* 1 (1974): 81-107.

78. Wladyslaw Sluckin, *Imprinting and Early Learning* (Chicago: Aldine, 1965).

be vital to emotional responsiveness[79] and there are undoubtedly critical periods for stimulation after which certain functions no longer develop normally. Early traumatic experiences or deprivations have been said to be the cause of a variety of developmental abnormalities, but such a causal relationship has never been established. In fact, as we have seen, the immature nervous system may be *less* affected by early adversity in the form of brain trauma. In a study of Guatemalan children Kagan found that their intellectual competence survived intact as much as one or two years of social or physical deprivation.[80] This survival, however, depended upon remedial help following the period of deprivation. The question arises as to how experience alters or ameliorates the effects of early brain damage.

Again, we must turn to the remarkable work of Goldman[81] and to lesions of the orbital prefrontal cortex which affect delayed response performance in male rhesus monkeys at seventy-five days and in females not until fifteen to eighteen months. By that time, as we have seen, both males and females exhibit full-blown impairments comparable to those seen in adult monkeys sustaining injury as adults, and these impairments persist on testing at two or three years of age. If these early-operated animals receive extensive test experience between the ages of one and one-and-a-half years, however, they are able to do the delayed alternation task by the time they are two or three, even though at the time they receive the test experience they are unable to do the task at all. Monkeys operated on at the same time in infancy, and not given the testing experience at between twelve and eighteen months, never regain the ability to perform the task. Without the test experience, they have a permanent abolition of the function even after 2000 testing trials as demonstrated with ablation of the prefrontal orbital cortex in adult monkeys.

79. Patricia S. Goldman, "The Relationship between Amount of Stimulation in Infancy and Subsequent Emotionality," *Annals of the New York Academy of Sciences* 159 (1969): 640-50.

80. Jerome Kagan, "Resilience and Cognitive Development," *Ethos* 3 (1975): 231-47.

81. Goldman, "Age, Sex, and Experience as Related to the Neural Basis of Cognitive Development"; idem, "The Role of Experience in Recovery of Function Following Orbital Prefrontal Lesions in Infant Monkeys."

Recovery of function in this instance clearly results from test experience and not from the sheer passage of time or neuronal maturation. Goldman notes:

> It is worth pointing out that the prior test experience in the present studies was effective in promoting recovery even though in most instances the monkeys gave no evidence of having successfully learned the delayed alternation task in their initial encounter with it.[82]

Whether such test experience promotes recovery of function through the development of specific learning, through the alerting of attentional mechanisms, or simply through a generalized "enriching" of experience is not known.

The lesson to be drawn from Goldman's data is very clear. Recovery of function after brain damage is enhanced by experience which, at the time it is being offered, does not appear to be having any effect. "Unsuccessful training at one stage of development may ultimately be of decisive benefit to these children at later stages." [83] The slowly evolving nervous system provides alternate routes for learning. Neuronal structures still not functionally committed may be able to take over the process intended for the ablated or damaged structure, but this "learning" may not occur until the alternate structure is itself mature. At the very least, training or test experience may help the child develop compensatory processes or alternative strategies. The effectiveness of such practice may not become apparent until alternative neural substrates are functionally ready.

In summary, the effects of early lesions on cognition depend not only upon the age at which they are inflicted but also upon the age at which one tests for the function, the sex of the animal or child, the intervening experience, and the test one applies. A delayed deficit at the motor, perceptual, or cognitive levels may never become apparent unless one tests for the impaired function. Prenatal or neonatal lesions, sparing more elementary functions,[84] may

82. Goldman, "The Role of Experience in Recovery of Function Following Orbital Prefrontal Lesions in Infant Monkeys," p. 410.

83. Ibid.

84. Rudel, Teuber, and Twitchell, "Levels of Impairment of Sensori-motor Functions in Children with Early Brain Damage"; idem, "A Note on Hyperesthesia in Children with Early Brain Damage."

not have effects, or may have very minimal effects, until the time when more complex functions emerge later in life. It is precisely because the nervous system develops and myelinates slowly that one can have seemingly paradoxical effects of early brain damage: delayed deficits particularly of more complex functions as well as a remarkable degree of functional recovery, even in young adults. Earlier maturation of a particular cortical area in the male monkey predisposes him to earlier effects of brain damage. Possibly sex differences in rates of cortical maturation have the same effect at the human level, making the male more vulnerable to early damage. Interposing practice or test experience between the time of damage and the emergence of a function makes performance of that function possible, even though at the time of test exposure there is no evidence of improvement. The lesson in this for remediation of developmental anomalies is self-evident. Children with evidence of early damage, or those genetically or otherwise at risk for dyslexia, should be given extra help with language, sequential ordering, and memorization before reading is ever required of them. A lack of improvement in these related functions may not necessarily mean that the capacity for reading is not thereby being strengthened. The Goldman paradigm suggests that the teaching of reading, for example, ought to be continued even with those children who appear to be impervious to the instruction. As we have seen, a deficit early in life may disappear with the maturation of alternative neural structures, but early experience with the task is crucial for the establishment of structure-function relationships.

Language and Intelligence

It is here that we abandon models provided by animal studies with their neat comparability of site and size of lesions. Data on the resilience of language and intellectual functions after brain damage are nonetheless challenging for they suggest that however plastic the young brain, however many "escape" routes to sparing it may find, alterations of behavior after early damage follow a pattern familiar from the studies of the effects of damage at maturity. There are, as we shall see, the aphaseoid errors of language disturbances, the correlative impairments of dyslexia, and the patterns of functional hemispheric asymmetry. There is, of course, considerable overlap between language and intelligence; one cannot evaluate the one without the other serving as a point of reference, and language functions constitute a considerable part of most tests of intelligence. For the sake of bringing some order into a very complicated area, we shall endeavor to separate them.

LANGUAGE

If ever there was a faculty that resisted effects of brain damage, it is unquestionably the human faculty of speech. Phylogenetically unique, it emerges in the face of complete excision of the speech area, and is spared with total left hemispherectomy.[85] Partial lesions of the left hemisphere, which would produce severe aphasia in the adult, leave the child able to speak and comprehend language. With left hemispherectomy or with a lesion encroaching directly upon the speech area, language in the child is taken over by other areas.[86] This need not be ascribed to a shift of language function to the other side, but rather as a release of a latent potential for language in the right hemisphere, a potential inhibited in the course of normal speech development in the left hemisphere. What is the language capacity of the right hemisphere?

Language in the right hemisphere and aphasia

The adult. By temporary incapacitation of the adult left hemisphere through the Wada technique, one can elicit response to language but not speech from the right hemisphere. Letters of the alphabet are recognized by either hemisphere by touch[87] or vision[88] and Braille letters by the left hand (and by inference, the right

85. L. S. Basser, "Hemiplegia of Early Onset and the Faculty of Speech with Special References to the Effects of Hemispherectomy," *Brain* 85 (1962): 427-60.

86. B. Milner, "Sparing of Language after Unilateral Brain Damage," *Neuroscience Research Program Bulletin* 12 (1974): 213-17.

87. Lauren J. Harris, Nancy M. Wagner, and Jean Wilkinson, "Cerebral Hemispheric Specialization in Braille Discrimination: Evidence from Blind and Sighted Subjects," paper presented at the Twenty-first International Congress on Psychology, Paris, 1976.

88. G. Barlucchi et al., "Simple Reaction Times of Ipsilateral and Contralateral Hand to Lateralized Visual Stimuli," *Brain* 94 (1971): 419-30.

hemisphere) of blind adults.[89] Globally aphasic patients have residual semantic knowledge but no syntactic or grammatical ability. The most controlled, provocative studies of right-hemisphere language have been undertaken by Zaidel, who is able with a complex lens arrangement to lateralize input to one visual half-field at a time, permitting prolonged exposure. In this way, either the left or right disconnected hemisphere of patients with commissurotomy can be tested independently. Working with such patients and with others who have nothing but a right hemisphere (following left decortication), Zaidel has reported an auditory single word recognition vocabulary of the right hemisphere at between eight and sixteen years, with a mean at eleven years, seven months.[90] On the deRenzi Token test, however, the right hemisphere of these patients fails to decode linguistic multiple reference messages that lack redundancy or context. Word meanings can be processed individually but in limited sequences, suggesting to Zaidel a "short-term sequential memory" deficit. In contrast, the average aphasic patient with residual left-hemisphere capabilities, processes the sequence of the instruction more adequately than the patient with a disconnected or isolated right hemisphere but gets a smaller share of the message. This would imply that the right hemisphere provides a better "hold" function and the left a more adequate sequencing or serial order function.[91]

Zaidel's data do not support the notion that the language capacity of the right hemisphere stops developing all at once, at any given time, upon suppression by the left. The "linguistic age" of the right hemisphere depends upon the type of language function demanded of it. This turns out not to be equivalent to the linguistic age of a four- or five-year-old, as would be the case with uniform inhibition of right-hemisphere language functions

89. Beate Hermelin and Neal O'Conner, "Functional Asymmetry in the Reading of Braille," *Neuropsychologia* 9 (1971): 431-35.

90. Eran Zaidel, "Unilateral Auditory Language Comprehension on the Token Test Following Cerebral Commissurotomy and Hemispherectomy," *Neurospychologia* 15 (1977): 1-18.

91. Rita G. Rudel and Martha B. Denckla, "Relation of Forward and Backward Digit Repetition to Neurological Impairment in Children with Learning Disabilities," *Neuropsychologia* 12 (1974): 109-18.

after establishment of language dominance by the left. Evidence thus far points to different types of language processing in the two hemispheres. They do not duplicate each other; they function in complementary fashion in the intact child or adult.

The right hemisphere alone, however, has poor access to motor expression of its linguistic competence. When cut off from access to the right hand the adult patient manifests an ideomotor dyspraxia,[92] indicating a right-hemisphere weakness of association between verbal comprehension and motor channeling.

The child. As noted, the right hemisphere cannot speak unless the left is removed or there is a lesion of the critical speech area in the left hemisphere very early in life, from most reports before the age of five years. Prior to that age a lesion in either hemisphere will induce temporary aphasia; after age five only a lesion in the left will have that effect.[93] Whether it is in terms of speech or writing or a hand movement to carry out a verbal command, the left hemisphere has the unique capacity to perform the motor acts necessary to implement language, to communicate.[94] It is only with left hemispherectomy or damage to the language zone on the left, prior to the age of five years, that the right hemisphere acquires (or is allowed to exercise) that essential verbal-motor linkage.

While the shift of language to (or disinhibition of language in) the right hemisphere spares speech, a price is paid both in the ultimate development of language capacity (including speaking, reading, writing) as well as in the capacity to perform those functions generally attributed to the right hemisphere. The sparing of language, however, particularly of speech, with early left-hemisphere damage or even removal makes it abundantly clear that only a bilateral lesion inflicted prior to the age of five years can produce mutism or gross aphasia in the child, while a discretely placed lesion in the left hemisphere can do the same for the adult. The neuroplasticity of the developing central nervous system is responsible

92. Dahlia Zaidel and Roger W. Sperry, "Some Long-term Motor Effects of Cerebral Commissurotomy in Man," *Neuropsychologia* 15 (1977): 193-204.

93. Jason W. Brown and Joseph Jaffe, "Note: Hypothesis on Cerebral Dominance," *Neuropsychologia* 13 (1975): 107-10.

94. Zaidel and Sperry, "Some Long-term Motor Effects of Cerebral Commissurotomy in Man."

for this vast difference. A study by Dennis and Kohn indicates that language does not develop equally in the two brain halves.[95] They tested matched groups of left and right hemiplegics whose pathology, leading to hemi-decortication, dated from the first year of life. At the time of testing (mean age, twenty years), although free of clinical signs of aphasia, they showed different levels of comprehension of four types of spoken sentences: active voice affirmative and negative as well as passive voice affirmative and negative. Those hemiplegics functioning with a left hemisphere made more correct responses at shorter latencies. A capacity to deal with the most difficult type of sentence, the passive negative, was developed in the intact left hemisphere by age nine years. The strategy finally developed much later in life by the intact right hemisphere to cope with more complex syntax required much longer time for processing, thus slowing down comprehension. Neither the absence of aphasia in groups of children with either left or right hemispherectomy nor their similar IQs means that they are functioning identically. The child with impairment on the left, although not aphasic as an adult would be, functions linguistically at a disadvantage compared with the child whose impairment is on the right.

As a consequence of functional sparing of speech, total aphasia in young children is relatively rare except in the context of some more global disturbance such as mental retardation or autism. Children with milder disturbances of language abound, however, and in many of them there are alterations from the normal which resemble right-hemisphere rather than left-hemisphere language, that is, slowed input processing of words or phonemes,[96] slower word retrieval,[97] weak syntactic and grammatical ability,[98] limited

95. Maureen Dennis and Bruno Kohn, "Comprehension of Syntax in Infantile Hemiplegics after Cerebral Hemidecortication: Left-Hemisphere Superiority," *Brain and Language* 2 (1975): 472-82.

96. Jon Eisenson, "Developmental Aphasia: A Speculative View with Therapeutic Implications," *Journal of Speech and Hearing Disorders* 33 (1968): 3-13; Arthur L. Benton, "Developmental Aphasia and Brain Damage," *Cortex* 1 (1964): 40-52.

97. Martha B. Denckla and Rita G. Rudel, "Naming of Object Drawings by Dyslexic and Other Learning-disabled Children," *Brain and Language* 3 (1976): 1-15.

98. Ruth Pike, "Memory for Words and Reading Ability," paper presented at the biennial meeting of the Society for Research in Child Development, New Orleans, 1977.

sequencing ability,[99] and impaired short-term memory.[100] Performance in these children is also more deficient if one requires that they respond with a motor act, that is, by speaking[101] or copying[102] rather than by choosing or matching stimuli. This is not to imply that all language-disturbed children are "speaking out of their right hemispheres," but rather that language disturbance in children manifests itself with very much the same inadequacies that are characteristic of right-hemisphere language. Possibly an impaired left hemisphere fails to suppress language sufficiently on the right, or a left hemisphere impaired very early in life functions very much like an intact right, at least in its processing of language.

Language and temporal processing

Latency of response appears to be increased, as we have noted before, in the adult or child with brain damage inflicted at any age. While this is believed to be a general effect, not specific to the location of the lesion, it may be more apparent with damage on the left than on the right. Thus, reaction time is faster following stimulation of the right rather than the left ear.[103] Lackner and Teuber have shown that there is a *bilateral* slowing down of click perception following unilateral damage of the left but not of the right hemisphere. With damage on the left, clicks stimulating both ears have to be more separated in time to be discriminated as two rather than as a single click.[104] Such an effect may be a factor in

99. Joel A. Stark, "A Comparison of the Performance of Aphasic Children on Three Sequencing Tests," *Journal of Communication Disorders* 1 (1967): 31-34.

100. Donald G. Doehring, "Visual Spatial Memory in Aphasic Children," *Journal of Speech and Hearing Research* 3 (1960): 138-49.

101. Rita G. Rudel, Martha B. Denckla, and Melinda B. Petrovics, "Rapid Silent Response to Repeated Target Symbols by Dyslexic and Nondyslexic Children," *Brain and Language*, in press.

102. Freya W. Owen et al., *Learning Disorders in Children: Sibling Studies, Monographs of the Society for Research in Child Development*, vol. 36, no. 4 (Chicago: University of Chicago Press, 1971).

103. J. Richard Simon, "Ear Preference in a Simple Reaction-Time Task," *Journal of Experimental Psychology* 75 (1967): 49-55.

104. James R. Lackner and Hans-Lukas Teuber, "Alterations in Auditory Fusion Thresholds after Cerebral Injury in Man," *Neuropsychologia* 11 (1973): 409-15.

faulty word comprehension or "word deafness," which may follow left hemisphere damage. Albert and Bear have analyzed the dysfunction in an adult "which allows for processing of linguistic acoustic events only at abnormally low speaking rates" and have related it to abnormal processing of even nonverbal temporal events.[105] Tallal and Piercy have demonstrated that aphasic children are similarly incapable of processing nonverbal auditory information at a normal rate and that this deficit underlies their language impairment.[106] These children were not, however, different from normal controls on sequences of visual (also nonverbal) information. Slowness of processing may, then, be specific to a single system, with early damage or late, and related disorders of sequencing and resolution of acoustic stimuli may be effects of slowed response latency. As we shall see, there is considerable response slowing with another language disturbance—dyslexia, developmental or acquired.

Dyslexia—developmental and acquired

A lesion in the left hemisphere of an adult that interferes with the flow of visual information to the verbal area will disturb reading. An added lesion of the splenium sufficient to prevent the flow of visual information from the right occipital (visual) area to the left verbal area will abolish the capacity to read altogether.[107] The ability to write, however, may remain intact, producing a condition in which the patient can write but cannot read what he has written or anything else for that matter. Obviously, there is no comparable effect with early damage. A child who cannot learn to read does not learn to write.

A lesion confined in the adult to the left occipital (visual) cortex will slow down reading even if the printed message does not fall

105. Martin L. Albert and D. Bear, "Time to Understand: A Case Study of Word Deafness with Reference to the Role of Time in Auditory Comprehension," *Brain* 4 (1974): 373-84.

106. Paula Tallal and Malcolm Piercy, "Developmental Aphasia: Impaired Rate of Nonverbal Processing as a Function of Sensory Modality," *Neuropsychologia* 11 (1973): 389-95.

107. Norman Geschwind, "Disconnexion Syndromes in Animals and Man," *Brain* 88 (1965): part I, 237-94; part II, 585-644.

within the area of blindness.[108] Damage that additionally impinges on the verbal area without causing any apparent dysphasia will result in a disturbance of reading, or dyslexia. In three patients followed now for several years, there is some recovery of reading, but the capacity to read rapidly or easily has never returned. Denckla and Bowen have reported on one of these patients,[109] and another is reported by Holtzman, Rudel, and Goldensohn.[110] In these cases of late damage the nature and location of the lesions are known and we have such information as well for a single case of developmental dyslexia. Until prospective studies of human infants are undertaken, we cannot know the antecedents of the condition in most children nor the extent of recovery of function which may have spared sensory input and speech but eventually resulted in the inability to learn to read. It is apparent, however, that the concomitants of dyslexia are virtually the same whether they appear as the result of an acquired lesion or as a developmental deficit of unknown origin. The functional requirements for reading are, after all, identical in the child or the adult and correlative deficits are therefore similar in the developmental or acquired condition.

A brief look at one of the cases of acquired dyslexia in the context of clinical and research data on developmental dyslexia may shed light on the condition as well as on the limits of neuroplasticity, for damage to the language system that spares speech appears to have other consequences.

Neuroanatomical evidence. Dyslexia has been demonstrated in an adult as a consequence of compression of the angular gyrus in the left hemisphere. The same cortical association area in the left hemisphere has been implicated in a case of developmental dyslexia. Recent EEG and evoked potential studies of children with dyslexia point to less interhemispheric and greater intrahemispheric activity

108. Ernst Pöppel and Stefanie R. Shattuck, "Reading in Patients with Brain Wounds Involving the Central Visual Pathways," *Cortex* 10 (1974): 84-88.

109. Martha B. Denckla and Florry P. Bowen, "Dyslexia after Left Occipito-temporal Lobectomy: A Case Report," *Cortex* 9 (1973): 321-28.

110. Robert N. Holtzman, Rita G. Rudel, and Eli S. Goldensohn, "Paroxysmal Alexia," *Cortex*, in press.

among them compared to children who read.[111] Alexia in the adult similarly involves interference with interhemispheric activity.

Sensory-motor status. In the adult a preoperative visual field defect was gone one year after surgery and there were no other signs of sensory loss or motor impairment pre- or postoperatively.

One very rarely finds sensory or motor losses in children with developmental dyslexia. A recent retrospective study shows that there are some "slow-for-age" developmental signs in a selected dyslexic population, particularly on rapid repetitive or alternating movements of the lower limbs.[112]

Intelligence test profile in relation to reading. The adult patient was tested ten days after surgery and again one year later. His reading level, at the fifth-grade level after surgery and at the seventh-grade level one year later, could not have been predicted on the basis of his superior verbal, performance, or full scale IQ scores on the Wechsler Adult Intelligence Scale (WAIS), which one year postoperatively were 126, 133, and 130 respectively. His lowest subtest scores were Digit Span, Arithmetic, and Digit Symbol (Coding, on the Wechsler Intelligence Scale for Children [WISC]).

It is precisely the discrepancy between normal or above-normal intelligence test scores and low reading scores that defines developmental dyslexia. As in the adult patient, reading age is not related to mental age. Symmes and Rapoport, reporting on a series of dyslexic boys without neurological or intellectual signs of impairment, cite the identical WISC profile, lowest scores on the Digit Span, Arithmetic, and Coding subtests, as evidence for a short-term memory deficit in dyslexia.[113]

Memory. Aside from these indications of memory difficulties on the WAIS, the adult patient had trouble recalling stories read to him or learning new verbal paired associates on the Wechsler

111. Bernard Sklar, John Hanley, and William W. Simmons, "A Computer Analysis of EEG Spectral Signatures from Normal and Dyslexic Children," *IEEE Transactions on Biomedical Engineering*, BME vol. 20, no. 1 (1973): 20-26.

112. Denckla and Rudel, "Motor Anomalies in Dyslexic Children," p. 197.

113. Jean S. Symmes and Judith L. Rapoport, "Unexpected Reading Failure," *American Journal of Orthopsychiatry* 42 (1972): 82-91.

Memory Scale. His drawings (Benton Visual Retention Test) from memory were excellent except for a tendency to reverse left-right orientation of small parts, an error that resembles letter reversals. The difficulty that dyslexic children have with learning verbal paired associates has been demonstrated by Vellutino and his collaborators.[114] These children are no different from normal readers in their ability to learn which pairs of abstract forms are associated. Wherever learning and recall of a sequence is involved, however, the memory difficulty can be demonstrated for verbal or nonverbal material.[115]

Naming. When required rapidly to name repeated visual representations of objects, colors, or letters, our patient was slow, as are dyslexic children when they are compared to nondyslexic learning-disabled children.[116] He would occasionally reverse lower-case letters, calling a "p" a "q" and then correctly calling it a "p"; he would misname an object named correctly just seconds before. Letter reversals and such a momentary "loss" of the correct name have also been noted in dyslexic children.

Our patient was very superior on the Oldfield-Wingfield test of object naming, a test sensitive to residual dysphasia in adults.[117] This test, however, is sensitive to dyslexia in children who tend to name fewer objects correctly and make characteristic "aphaseoid" errors: circumlocutions, paraphasias, and errors of dysphonemic sequencing.[118] Our patient made phonemic errors only under the stress of reading, not speaking. If we accept the Kennard principle, the damage to or alteration of the neural substrate of children with specific dyslexia is greater than the damage in our adult patient. This developmental dysfunction, which is at a complex level, ap-

114. Frank R. Vellutino et al., "Verbal vs. Nonverbal Paired-Associate Learning in Poor and Normal Readers," *Neuropsychologia* 13 (1975): 75-82.

115. Suzanne Corkin, "Serial-ordering Deficits in Inferior Readers," *Neuropsychologia* 12 (1974): 347-54.

116. Denckla and Rudel, "Rapid 'Automatized' Naming (R.A.N.): Dyslexia Differentiated from Other Learning Disabilities."

117. R. C. Oldfield and A. Wingfield, "Response Latencies in Naming Objects," *Quarterly Journal of Experimental Psychology* 17 (1965): 273-81.

118. Denckla and Rudel, "Naming of Object Drawings by Dyslexic and Other Learning-disabled Children."

pears only with delay and possibly expresses itself differently and at different ages in males and females. The work of Goldman suggests that it is possible to find a critical type of early experience which would allow the child at risk for dyslexia to learn to read.[119]

It is worth noting that our understanding of dyslexia in childhood has greatly benefited from clinical adult "models." As Teuber has stated, "clinical and experimental approaches are not mutually exclusive." [120] Indeed, the clinical insights of adult neuropsychology can inform and guide our understanding of developmental dysfunction. Teuber has noted that the scotoma gives us access to the role of specific pathways in visual function—"blindness illuminating sight." In the same way, studies of dyslexia help unravel the complex nature of reading.

INTELLIGENCE

Intelligence, defined as whatever it is that is tested by intelligence tests, is not always impaired with brain damage inflicted at maturity. Using maze learning, Lashley noted that the performance adequacy of adult rats decreased in proportion to the amount of brain tissue removed and that the size, not the site, of the lesion was crucial. His student, Tsang, as we have noted, showed that even this was true only for the adult rat; hemidecortication of the infant rat did not impair its maze-learning capacity. Lansdell, however, obtained very different results when he constructed a "rat intelligence test" out of a series of simpler acts, many of which were familiar from the complex environment in which the animals were reared.[121] Site of damage was important in that some lesions produced no impairment and Lashley's principle of "mass action" held for one part of the brain but not for another. While there was less impairment following early damage than late damage, it could nonetheless be demonstrated that, as in the human, deficits depended upon the site and size of the lesion and the task requirements.

119. Goldman, "The Role of Experience in Recovery of Function Following Orbital Prefrontal Lesions in Infant Monkeys."

120. Teuber, "Effects of Focal Brain Injury on Human Behavior."

121. Herbert C. Lansdell, "Effect of Brain Damage on Intelligence in Rats," *Journal of Comparative and Physiological Psychology* 46 (1953): 461-64.

Human intelligence tests are not always sensitive to the effects of brain damage and for that reason they are often useful in providing an index of the premorbid level of performance. This is particularly true, for example, of the vocabulary subtest of the Wechsler scales. The human faculty for language, however, complicates the issue of "intelligence." Weinstein and Teuber reported finding that only patients with lesions in the left temporo-parietal lobe suffered significant losses, if one compared their pre- and postmorbid scores on the Army General Classification Test (AGCT).[122] There are at least two possible explanations of this phenomenon. First, it may be due to the fact that such patients are suffering some residual dysphasia that is picked up by a test employing a set of highly verbal tasks. Second, it may reflect left-hemisphere processing of a nonverbal intellectual component.

Teuber and his colleagues tested their patients with a completely nonverbal instrument, an adaptation of the Gottschaldt hidden figures task, in which the subject is required to find and trace a simple geometric figure embedded in a larger geometric complex.[123] This test turned out to be very sensitive to penetrating brain injury in any lobe and in either hemisphere. Patients who had once been dysphasic as a result of their injuries, however, scored significantly lower than any others. The identical results have been reported for other types of adult brain damage, neoplastic or vascular lesions.[124] Similarly, Basso et al. have reported that the Raven Matrices test, which requires no verbal response, is performed poorly by patients with left-hemisphere damage.[125] One may question whether there are not other pre- or nonverbal components to left-hemisphere functioning, an elusive "g" or general factor of intelligence, or

122. Sidney Weinstein and Hans-Lukas Teuber, "Effects of Penetrating Brain Injury on Intelligence Test Scores," *Science* 125 (1957): 1036-37.

123. Kurt Gottschaldt, "Über den Einfluss der Erfahrung auf die Wahrnehmung von Figuren," *Psychologische Forschung* 8 (1926): 261-317; 12 (1929): 1-87.

124. M. Russo and L. A. Vignolo, "Visual Figure-Ground Discrimination in Patients with Unilateral Cerebral Disease," *Cortex* 3 (1967): 113-27.

125. A. Basso et al., "Neuropsychological Evidence for the Existence of Cerebral Areas Critical to the Performance of Intelligence Tasks," *Brain* 96 (1973): 715-28.

possibly the sort of executive function implicit in the old concept of hemisphere "dominance." A look at the evidence in cases of early damage is instructive.

There is no question that intelligence test scores of children with early or congenital impairment depend upon the sparing of language, even though, as we have seen, speech is spared whether damage is on the left or right. Lansdell has found that the earlier the damage to either side the more sparing of language there is, as reflected in the discrepancy between good verbal and poor nonverbal scores.[126] This might mean that early damage destroys the generally accepted distribution of functions of the two sides of the brain.

Some lateralization of function resists very early damage. In 1961, McFie reported that, on the whole, Wechsler subtest scores were in the same direction in unilaterally brain-damaged children as in adults.[127] In a retrospective study of 292 children with early (mostly congenital) brain damage, Rudel and Denckla showed that those without neurological signs, like those with bilateral signs, had little or no difference between verbal and performance IQs.[128] Those with left-sided signs (right-hemisphere impairment) had a higher verbal than performance IQ ($p < .002$) and those with right-sided signs (left-hemisphere impairment) had a lower verbal than performance IQ ($p < .05$). This seems symmetrical indeed except that the *degree* of difference is not the same. Left-hemisphere damage (inferred from right-sided signs) tends to lower both verbal and performance scores while right-hemisphere impairment (inferred from left-sided signs) tends to lower only scores on nonverbal tasks. In a study of sixty-three brain-damaged children, Rudel, Teuber, and Twitchell showed that those with right-hemisphere damage had a significantly higher verbal than performance

126. H. C. Lansdell, "Verbal and Nonverbal Factors in Right Hemisphere Speech: Relation to Early Neurological History," *Journal of Comparative and Physiological Psychology* 69 (1969): 734-38.

127. John McFie, "The Effects of Hemispherectomy on Intellectual Functioning in Cases of Infantile Hemiplegia," *Journal of Neurology, Neurosurgery, and Psychiatry* 24 (1961): 240-49.

128. Rudel and Denckla, "Relation of Forward and Backward Digit Repetition to Neurological Impairment in Children with Learning Disabilities."

IQ, while those with left-hemisphere damage had depressed verbal and performance IQ scores.[129] Woods and Teuber selected twenty-five children with right and twenty-five children with left hemiplegias of early onset.[130] Language in all had been spared, at a price, including depressed nonverbal scores in those with left-hemisphere damage. To quote Teuber:

> Thus many early left-hemisphere lesions ultimately depress performance not only on sufficiently taxing verbal tasks (though in the absence of any true aphasia) but also, and significantly, on various nonverbal (right-hemisphere) tasks such as those involving construction, picture recognition, and certain aspects of spatial orientation.[131]

There is no symmetry of sparing and the functional asymmetry of the hemispheres expresses itself as well in the extent to which each resists the effects of early damage. Right-hemisphere lesions do not, in complementary fashion, depress language but, rather, hinder the development of those functions that depend upon the integrity of the right hemisphere, as they do in the adult. Teuber sees this asymmetrical effect as a consequence of language development having "precedence." It is "as if reliance on the atypical (right) side for linguistic tasks exerted a crowding effect on that side compromising its normal function."[132]

Such a "demographic" explanation in terms of "crowding," however, does not take into account that the adult with left-hemisphere damage does not have a shift of language to the right hemisphere, but is nonetheless impaired on certain nonlanguage tasks. There is, as we have seen, the poor performance of such patients on an embedded figures task as well as on the Raven Matrices. Taken together, it would seem that the left hemisphere must serve some crucial nonlanguage functions and/or some "executive" function that guides or assists the right. Nor can one com-

129. Rudel, Teuber, and Twitchell, "Levels of Impairment of Sensorimotor Functions in Children with Early Brain Damage."

130. Bryan T. Woods and Hans-Lukas Teuber, "Early Onset of Complementary Specialization of Cerebral Hemispheres in Man," *Transactions of the American Neurological Association* 98 (1973): 113-17.

131. Teuber, "Effects of Focal Brain Injury on Human Behavior," p. 475.

132. Ibid.

pletely rule out the possibility that even so-called nonlanguage tasks are more competently performed with subvocal language. There is evidence for all three possibilities.

To begin with the last, it has been shown that subvocal rehearsal aids children in learning and that, in fact, dyslexic children employ such rehearsal less than do children who read well.[133] The slower performance of young girls on spatial orientation tests suggests that they verbalize the "moves" before they make them.[134] More compelling, however, is the evidence for a concomitant nonverbal factor in left-hemisphere processing. Bogen has cited the "analytic" functions of the left hemisphere, its capacity to seek out details.[135] Such a capacity would appear to be useful, for example, in finding the embedded simple geometric part of a complex figure. Many of the Raven patterns require a matching of linear details and others require analysis of pattern relationships. Without invoking "verbalization," these are functions that are better served by the left hemisphere and they may be impaired with early or late damage that spares language.

Many functions that eventually emerge as right-hemisphere processes are at first better performed by the left. Carey and her collaborators have shown that prior to the age of ten, children use left-hemisphere "tactics" in face recognition. They attend to details rather than to configurations, to "paraphernalia" rather than to the face as a whole.[136] Braille, which is discriminated more efficiently by the left hand (right hemisphere) than by the right (left hemisphere), is learned more easily if the right hand precedes the left on the learning task.[137] It is as if the left hemisphere were

133. Joseph Torgesen and Tina Goldman, "Verbal Rehearsal and Short-term Memory in Reading-disabled Children," *Child Development* 48 (1977): 56-60.

134. Denckla, Rudel, and Petrovics, "Spatial Orientation in Normal, Learning-disabled, and Neurologically Impaired Children."

135. Joseph E. Bogen, "The Other Side of the Brain: VII. Some Educational Aspects of Hemispheric Specialization," *UCLA Educator* 17 (1975): 24-32.

136. Carey, Diamond, and Woods, "The Development of the Ability to Recognize Faces: A Maturational Basis?"

137. Rudel, Denckla, and Spalten, "The Functional Asymmetry of Braille Letter Learning in Normal, Sighted Children."

superior at learning how to do the task and could pass this information to the right. Zaidel and Sperry have shown commissurotomy patients could overcome the apraxic performance of the left hand to verbal command if the same response was first made correctly by the patient's right hand.[138]

The many demonstrations of functional asymmetry of the hemispheres must take into account as well this complementary influence of one hemisphere on the other, which results to some extent in producing a bilateral effect with unilateral injury on the left but a unilateral effect with injury on the right. In the absence of a language deficit, damage to the left hemisphere not only results in subtle changes on tests of language competence but may impair a more generalized learning capacity, eventually impeding the emergence of certain right-hemisphere skills. Evaluation of the effects of early damage on intelligence awaits further work on the ontogeny of functional asymmetry and on the more general "executive" factor which, in the left hemisphere, seems to be dissociable from language.

Concluding Statement

There are lessons to be drawn from the clinical and experimental data on plasticity of the central nervous system. One is struck first of all with the notion that nature abhors a vacuum; neural pathways prevented from taking their genetically appropriate route will find some other. This makes recovery of function predictably uncertain, for it is possible to find sparing of function immediately or delayed, transiently or permanently, with deficits delayed or overcome, and perhaps most enigmatically the rearrangement may be maladaptive, with those structures called upon to "take over" prevented from developing the functions for which they were genetically intended. Recovery of function varies also depending upon the tests used to evaluate extent of impairment and whether or not the necessary structures are mature at the time of injury. Maturation time may be different for males and females, the latter appearing to be less vulnerable to early effects of damage. Some types of experience, particularly early deprivation, may have

138. Zaidel and Sperry, "Some Long-term Motor Effects of Cerebral Commissurotomy in Man."

similar effects as brain injury, while well-timed early encounters with the task requirements may prevent the appearance of a deficit in spite of an early lesion.

There is no question that the developing human nervous system has greater potential for recovery than the mature one, particularly of sensory input and speech. The sparing of elementary functions may give the child an appearance of normalcy until more complex activities are expected of him, and to some extent sparing makes whatever symptoms he has more subtle than they are in the adult. The fact that the child can speak, however, does not preclude an impairment of language or of those nonverbal capacities of the left hemisphere: serial ordering, analytic attention to detail, the capacity to set a rapid pace of response or to enhance performance of the right hemisphere.

Dysphasia and dyslexia, seen clinically and experimentally, appear to have the same concomitant disturbances in the adult and child, whatever their diverse antecedents. The prognosis for recovery after early damage would be more optimistic were an appropriate early intervention found to compensate for impairment of the neural substrate, a possibility suggested in experimental animal work on neuroplasticity. The experimental search for the limits and extent of neuroplasticity provides clinical insight just as clinical evidence for recovery of function may provide the direction for further experimental search.

Part Four

CHAPTER IX

A Mind of Three Minds: Educating the Triune Brain

PAUL D. MAC LEAN

Introduction

On the basis of what the brain knows of itself, it is the most complicated and remarkable instrument in the known universe. It is therefore surprising that in this age of machines and computers we give so little thought to educating ourselves about the structure and functions of the brain. To call attention to this deficiency in our education is not to point a reproving finger at our educators. We do not need to blame anyone. Since the brain accounts for everything we do, the blame lies clearly with the brain!

An interest in the brain requires no justification other than a curiosity to know why we are here, what we are doing here, and where we are going. The same questions would be appropriate for an article on the brain and education. Having no ready answers, however, I shall deal instead with the question, "Where have we been?"—pointing out that in the course of evolution we seem to have acquired a mind of three minds.[1]

THE TRIUNE BRAIN

The main thrust of the rest of this article can be summarized in a few words. In its evolution the human forebrain has expanded to a great size while retaining the basic features of three formations that reflect our ancestral relationship to reptiles, early mammals, and recent mammals (see fig. 1). Radically different in structure and chemistry, and in an evolutionary sense countless genera-

1. Paul D. MacLean, "A Triune Concept of the Brain and Behavior," in *The Hincks Memorial Lectures*, ed. Thomas J. Boag and Dugal Campbell (Toronto: University of Toronto Press, 1973), pp. 6-66.

tions apart, the three formations constitute a hierarchy of three brains in one, or what may be called for short a *tri*une brain.[2] Such a situation indicates that we are obliged to look at ourselves and the world through the eyes of three quite different mentalities.[3] As a further complication, there is evidence that the two older mentalities lack the necessary neural machinery for verbal communication. But to say that they lack the power of speech does not belittle their intelligence, nor does it relegate them to the realm of the "unconscious." Educationally, these are significant considerations because it is usually assumed that we are dealing with a single

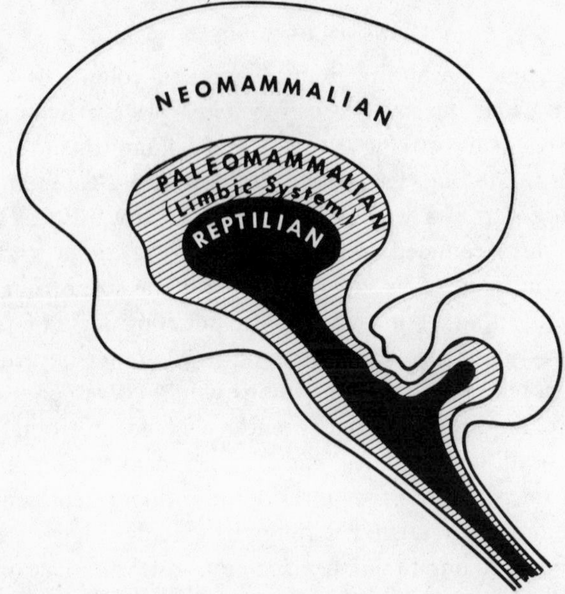

FIG. 1. Showing evolution of the human forebrain. The human forebrain expands in hierarchic fashion along the lines of three basic patterns that may be characterized as reptilian, paleomammalian, and neomammalian.

SOURCE: Paul D. MacLean, "The Brain in Relation to Empathy and Medical Education," *Journal of Nervous and Mental Disease* 144 (1967): 374-82.

2. Paul D. MacLean, "A Triune Concept of the Brain and Behavior"; idem, "The Triune Brain and Scientific Bias," in *The Neurosciences Second Study Program*, ed. Francis O. Schmitt (New York: Rockefeller University Press, 1970), pp. 336-49.

3. Paul D. MacLean, "On the Evolution of Three Mentalities," in *New Dimensions in Psychiatry: A World View*, vol. 2, ed. Silvano Arieti and Gerard Chrzanowski (New York: John Wiley and Sons, 1977), p. 309.

intelligence. How much weight should we give to intelligence tests that largely ignore two of our everpresent personalities because they cannot read or write?

In teaching rhetoric, the Greeks placed emphasis on personal appeal, emotional appeal, and intellectual appeal. In what is to follow, one might say in corresponding terms that we shall be looking for the evolutionary and neural roots of a triune intelligence comprised of a primal mind, an emotional mind, and a rational mind. For our expedition, we should carry along a simple brain model, as well as a few definitions of unfamiliar behavioral terms.

A LIVING BRAIN MODEL

On the average, the human brain occupies a volume of a little over one and a half quarts. We can quickly place a living brain model in our hands by making two fists and holding them together with our fingers lined up. Each fist corresponds to a cerebral hemisphere. Raising our fists with the two thumbs towards us, let us next imagine them rounded out by a pair of gray winter gloves. Now we have in front of us something almost the size of our own brain and representing, as it were, a soft, pulsating mass of protoplasm. The gray gloves would correspond to the outer covering of gray matter known as cortex. Our thumbs would correspond to the front of our brain, including the recently evolved prefrontal cortex that will be discussed at the end of this chapter. Our middle knuckle and the adjacent part of the middle finger represent the area of our motor cortex. In wiggling the middle finger, we can visualize the part of our brain that accounts for voluntary movements, with the face and mouth represented near the knuckle, the leg and foot near the first joint, and the rest of the body in between. The auditory cortex may be visualized as located on the back of the hand just below the middle knuckle, while the area overlying the little finger would correspond to the visual cortex. All of the structures mentioned thus far belong to the so-called "new" cortex. Later, when considering the "old" cortex associated with early mammals, we will pull our fists apart and look at the previously hidden surface, while a view of the counterpart of the reptilian part of the brain will require us to unclench our fists and peer at the palm.

Nerve cells. Primitive peoples use the tree as a symbol of the human body and its limbs. Here we may picture nerve cells as both people and trees. In structure, nerve cells are like trees, having branches that reach up to receive information and an extensive root system for intercommunication. In function, nerve cells are like people with special jobs to do. Like citizens, they are constantly called upon to make decisions and to vote on this and that. The brain with its several billion nerve cells[4] can continue to function with large masses of its population destroyed. But with continued destruction a point is reached when a single nerve cell —casting a single vote—may make all the difference between function and nonfunction.

COMMUNICATION OF MENTAL EMANATIONS

If you have ever held the soft protoplasm of brain in your hands, you realize that a substantial replication of your surroundings can no more exist in such a spongy mass than can the evening news exist in your television set. Kick the floor and ask yourself how that hurting sense of hardness can be generated by the soft substance of the brain. Perceptions ranging from the firm pavement underfoot, to the cold, hard facts of science are all derivatives of a soft brain.

Emanations of the mind, just as other forms of information, have no material substance. To quote the cybernetician, Norbert Wiener, "Information is information, not matter or energy."[5] If psychological information is without substance, how do we put a handle on it for scientific and other purposes? Here we are saved only by the empirical evidence that there can be no communication of information without the agency of what we recognize as physical, behaving entities, no matter how large or small. This invariance may be considered a law of communication.

VERBAL AND NONVERBAL COMMUNICATION

Human communicative behavior may be described as verbal and nonverbal. Like P. W. Bridgman, the physicist-philosopher,

4. Samuil M. Blinkov and Il'ya I. Glezer, *The Human Brain in Figures and Tables: A Quantitative Handbook* (New York: Basic Books, 1968), p. 201.

5. Norbert Wiener, *Cybernetics, or Control and Communication in the Animal and the Machine* (New York: John Wiley and Sons, 1948), p. 155.

people usually assume that "most communication is verbal."[6] Behavioral scientists, however, are beginning to place greater emphasis on nonverbal communication in day-to-day human activities. Many forms of human nonverbal behavior show a parallel to behavioral patterns of animals. Since it is inappropriate to refer to nonverbal communication of animals, another term is needed to refer to such behavior. I have used the word "prosematic," applying to rudimentary signalling, to refer to communication involving any kind of nonverbal signal—vocal, bodily, chemical.[7]

As ethologists have shown, prosematic behavior, like verbal behavior, has meaning (semantics) and orderly expression (syntax).[8] Somewhat comparable to words, sentences, and paragraphs, prosematic communication becomes meaningful in terms of its components, constructs, and sequences of constructs.[9] Because of the need for experimentation much of our knowledge of brain mechanisms underlying prosematic behavior must be derived from work on animals. The relevance of such research to human affairs becomes evident in the light of the three evolutionary developments of the brain that have been considered.

Looking at our brain model again, let it be emphasized that the forebrain (forming the bulk of our two fists) is the part of the nervous system that makes us aware of our environment and gives direction to all of our activities. In that sense it could be compared to the driver of a vehicle. The vehicle (lower brain stem and spinal cord) would correspond to the rest of the nervous system which, somewhat like an automobile, contains all the controls for starting, steering, accelerating, braking, and so forth.[10] A fundamental difference with respect to the analogy is that in the course of evolution the brain has acquired three drivers, all seated up front and all of different minds. Let us look first at the reptilian driver.

6. Percy W. Bridgman, *The Way Things Are* (Cambridge: Harvard University Press, 1959).

7. MacLean, "On the Evolution of Three Mentalities," pp. 311-12.

8. *Non-Verbal Communication*, ed. R. A. Hinde (Cambridge, England: The University Press, 1972).

9. MacLean, "On the Evolution of Three Mentalities," p. 312.

10. In terms of our brain model, the lower brain stem and spinal cord would be represented by the wrists and forearms, but greatly reduced in size.

THE R-COMPLEX

The physical counterpart of the reptilian "driver" is found in a large fist of ganglia at the base of our forebrain. Since there is no name that applies to all of these ganglia, I shall simply refer to them as the R-complex.[11] In ganglia the nerve cells are heaped up in large clumps, whereas in cortex they are arranged in layers. Turning to our brain model again, let us separate and partially unclench our fists. Looking at our palms, we may imagine that we are peering into the ventricles of the brain that hold the cerebrospinal fluid. The bulges of the palm just below the first two fingers and above the thumb would correspond to the largest part of the R-complex (corpus striatum and globus pallidus). The nerve cells contained in these bulges might be imagined as Stone Age cliff dwellers, finding shelter in a honeycomb of caves and tunnels.

Thanks to recent anatomical and histochemical techniques, the three basic evolutionary formations of the forebrain stand out in

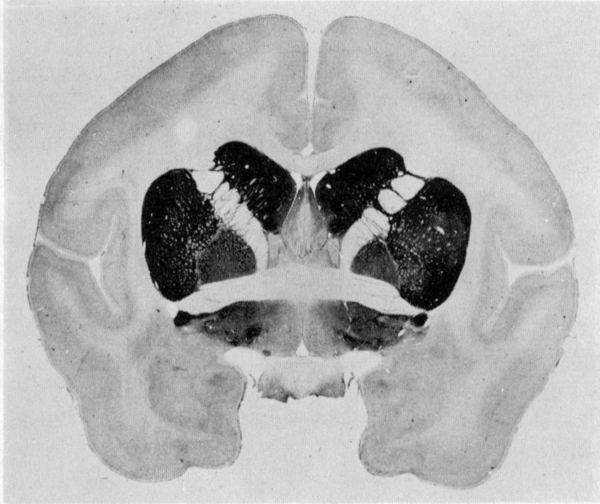

Fig. 2. Section from the brain of a squirrel monkey. The section shows how the greater part of the R-Complex is selectively colored (black areas) by a stain for cholinesterase.

Source: Paul D. MacLean, "Cerebral Evolution and Emotional Processes: New Findings on the Striatal Complex," *Annals of the New York Academy of Sciences* 193 (1972): 137-49.

11. Paul D. MacLean, "The Brain's Generation Gap: Some Human Implications," *Zygon: Journal of Religion and Science* 8 (1973): 114.

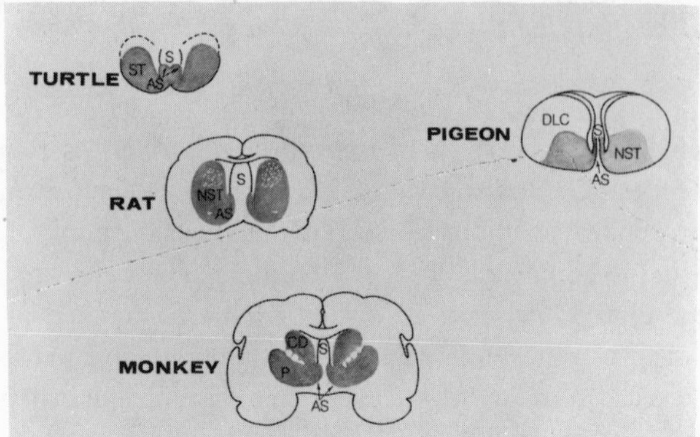

FIG. 3. R-Complex in animals ranging from reptiles to primates. Shaded areas indicate how a stain for cholinesterase distinguishes the greater part of the R-Complex in animals ranging from reptiles to primates. Birds are an offshoot from the *Archosauria* ("ruling reptiles").

SOURCE: Paul D. MacLean, "The Brain's Generation Gap: Some Human Implications," *Zygon: Journal of Religion and Science* 8 (1973): 114. Adapted from André Parent and André Olivier, "Comparative Histochemical Study of the Corpus Striatum," *Journal für Hirnforschung* 12 (1970): 75-81.

clearer detail than ever before. The black areas in figure 2 show how a stain for cholinesterase sharply demarcates the R-complex in the monkey's brain. Figure 3 illustrates how the same stain distinguishes the R-complex in animals ranging from reptiles to man. In using the histofluorescent technique of Falck and Hillarp,[12] it is striking to see the greater part of the R-complex glow a bright green because of large amounts of dopamine, a neural sap that seems to be necessary for setting into motion the total energies of the organism. Parts of the R-complex have recently been found to be rich in opiate receptors.[13]

THE MAMMAL-LIKE REPTILES

Recently, books covering a range of subjects (including one on education) have appeared in which the triune brain concept has been discussed.[14] With the growing awareness of the reptilian

12. Bengt Falck and Nils-Ake Hillarp, "On the Cellular Localization of Catecholamines in the Brain," *Acta Anatomica* 38 (1959): 277-79.

13. Candace B. Pert and Solomon H. Snyder, "Opiate Receptor: Demonstration in Nervous Tissue," *Science* 179 (1973): 1011-14.

14. On education: Leslie Hart, *How the Brain Works* (New York: Basic Books, 1975); on psychology: Robert L. Isaacson, *The Limbic System* (New York: Plenum Press, 1974), chap. 6; on environmental design: B. B. Greenbie,

roots of the mammalian brain, there seems to be some confusion about specific ancestors. Some people seem to be under the false impression that we can trace our lineage to the serpent, while others would say we are of dinosaur stock. People generally are unfamiliar with the mammal-like reptiles presumed to be the antecedents of mammals.

During Permian and Triassic times—for a period of about 100 million years—the mammal-like reptiles covered the face of the earth. Today their remains are found on every continent including Antarctica, suggesting that there may once have existed one massive continent called Gondwanaland.[15] Robert Broom calculated that there must be at least 800 *billion* skeletons of mammal-like reptiles in the Karroo beds of South Africa.[16] There were two main varieties of these animals—carnivores and herbivores. Reminiscent of the Serengeti Plain, some of the carnivores are believed to have preyed on herds of herbivores.

What were these animals like? Some of the advanced carnivores are believed to have resembled dogs and wolves. Unlike their waddling predecessors, they had gotten up off their bellies and with legs supporting the body from underneath, were able to run swiftly. The jaws and teeth were beginning to acquire mammalian characteristics. Did these animals lay eggs? Did they care for their young? Or like the contemporary Komodo lizard, did the young have to escape to the trees to avoid being cannibalized? Vocalization and hearing are indispensable for parent-offspring relationships of mammals. Could the mammal-like reptiles vocalize or were they dumb like many of today's lizards?

Late in Triassic times the mammal-like reptiles mysteriously became extinct. Ferocious and possibly cannibalistic as they were, it

---

Design for Diversity. Planning for Natural Man in the Neo-Technic Environment: An Ethological Approach (Amsterdam: Elsevier Scientific Publishing Co., 1976); on evolution: Arthur Koestler, *The Ghost in the Machine* (London: Hutchinson and Co., 1968); Robert Ardrey, *The Social Contract* (New York: Atheneum Press, 1970); Carl Sagan, *The Dragons of Eden* (New York: Random House, 1977), pp. 51-79.

15. Edwin H. Colbert, "Antarctic Fossils and the Reconstruction of Gondwanaland," *Natural History* 81 (1972): 71.

16. Robert Broom, *The Mammal-like Reptiles of South Africa and the Origin of Mammals* (London: H. F. and G. Witherby, 1932), p. 308.

is probable that they did not bring about their own destruction. Rather, it is presumed that a swifter, more ferocious kind of reptile began to outnumber and destroy them.[17] Such carnage, together with severe climatic changes, must have made it a terrible period in which to be alive. Some of the smaller reptiles "went underground" and slowly became mammals, keeping their young nearby so that they too would not be gobbled up. Other animals escaped to the trees and gradually became birds, with nests for the young representing an extension of the amnion.

REPTILIAN PRIMAL BEHAVIOR

There are no existing reptiles directly akin to the mammal-like reptiles. Present-day lizards, particularly the Komodo dragon, would probably come closest to resembling the mammal-like reptiles. Lizards and other reptiles provide illustrations of complex patterns of behavior commonly seen in mammals, including human beings. One of the surprising results of studying a variety of terrestrial animals is to discover how boringly few kinds of behavior are typical of each and all. In table 1 I have listed twenty-four types of behavior seen among reptiles that involve self-preservation and the preservation of the species. Some of those listed may seem unfamiliar at first, but when illustrated they are immediately recognized, as, for example, "place preference behavior" described in terms of Archie Bunker's chair.

First and foremost of the listed activities, are those that involve the establishment and defense of territory. It requires no reminder that the will-to-power became the heart of Nietzsche's philosophy. He regarded the will-to-power as the basic life force of the entire universe. "Thus life taught me," he wrote.[18] Nietzsche's writings on this subject may yet earn him recognition as a foremost ethologist and authority on human, reptilian behavior!

Regardless of interpretation, one will hardly find the will-to-power more dramatically expressed than in the behavior of some lizards. To see Rainbow male lizards (*Agama agama*) striving for

17. Edwin H. Colbert, *Evolution of the Vertebrates* (New York: John Wiley and Sons, 1955).

18. Friedrich Nietzsche, "Thus Spoke Zarathustra," in *The Portable Nietzsche*, trans. Walter A. Kaufman (New York: Viking Press, 1954), p. 226.

TABLE 1

Primal Patterns of Behavior

1. Selection and preparation of homesite
2. Establishment of territory
3. Trail making
4. "Marking" of territory
5. Showing place-preferences
6. Patrolling territory
7. Ritualistic display in defense of territory, commonly involving the use of coloration and adornments
8. Formalized intraspecific fighting in defense of territory
9. Triumphal display in successful defense
10. Assumption of distinctive postures and coloration in signalling surrender
11. Foraging
12. Hunting
13. Homing
14. Hoarding
15. Use of defecation posts
16. Formation of social groups
17. Establishment of social hierarchy by ritualistic display and other means
18. Greeting
19. "Grooming"
20. Courtship, with displays using coloration and adornments
21. Mating
22. Breeding and, in isolated instances, attending offspring
23. Flocking
24. Migration

dominance, is like returning to the days of King Arthur. These animals have beautiful colors and like many lizards use headbobbing and pushups in their territorial and courtship displays. In a contest, once the gauntlet is thrown down, the aggressive displays give way to violent combat, and the struggle is unrelenting. Twice we have seen dominant males humiliated in defeat. They lost their majestic colors, lapsed into a kind of depression, and died two weeks later.

EXPERIMENTAL FINDINGS

Heretofore, virtually no experiments have been performed on reptiles in an attempt to identify forebrain structures involved in prosematic forms of behavior. Recently, we have conducted experiments on the small, green anole lizard that indicate that the R-complex is requisite for the organized expression of its challenge display when defending its territory.[19]

In contrast to reptiles, the R-complex in mammals has been subjected to extensive investigation, but, curiously enough, 150 years of experimentation have revealed little specific information about its functions. The finding that large destructions of the R-complex may result in no impairment of movement, speaks against the traditional clinical view that it is primarily involved in motor functions. As with reptiles, we are conducting experiments on mammals, testing the hypothesis that the R-complex plays a basic role in prosematic behavior. Thus far, crucial findings have turned up in work on New World primates called squirrel monkeys because they are about the size of squirrels. Showing a remarkable parallel to reptiles, these animals have a naturally occurring challenge display that is somewhat similar to the one used in courtship. In each situation, the male vocalizes, spreads one thigh, and directs the erect phallus towards the other animal.[20] The display is also used as a form of greeting. I have described one variety of squirrel monkeys that will regularly perform a greeting display upon seeing its reflection in a mirror.[21] We refer to the mirror displaying monkey as the "gothic-type" because the ocular patch forms a peak over the eye like a gothic arch, whereas we call the other variety "romans" because the patch is round like a roman arch.

I have used the mirror display test as a means of learning what parts of the brain are involved in display rituals. In experiments involving more than 100 monkeys, I have found that extensive destruction of parts of the new mammalian and old mammalian formations may have no effect, or only a transitory effect, on the display. Incomplete destruction of the pallidal part of the R-

19. Neil B. Greenberg, L. F. Ferguson, and Paul D. MacLean, "A Neuro-ethological Study of Display Behavior in Lizards," *Society for Neuroscience* 2 (1976): 689.

20. Detlev W. Ploog and Paul D. MacLean, "Display of Penile Erection in the Squirrel Monkey (*Saimiri sciureus*)," *Animal Behavior* 11 (1963): 32-39.

21. Paul D. MacLean, "Mirror Display in the Squirrel Monkey (*Saimiri sciureus*)," *Science* 146 (1964): 950-52.

complex,[22] however, or interruptions of its pathways,[23] result in a profound alteration or elimination of the display.

COMMENT ON EXPERIMENTAL FINDINGS

The results of the experiments on monkeys are of special interest because of the demonstration for the first time in a mammal that the R-complex plays a special role in behavior. Together with the experiments on lizards, the findings indicate that in animals as widely separated as reptiles and primates, the R-complex is basically implicated in the organized expression of prosematic behavior of a ritualistic nature.

Before further comment, it is worth noting that thanks to John Locke's "tabula rasa,"[24] it is commonly believed that the human brain begins its existence as a clean slate on which all manner of experience can be written, remembered, and communicated. Pavlov's work on conditioned reflexes, with its main emphasis on the "new" cortex, has reinforced this belief.[25] Consequently, there is a prevailing view that, except for the basic biological functions, human behavior depends on the cultural transmission of knowledge and customs from one generation to the next. Almost the entire emphasis is on learning and verbal communication. One textbook in psychology, for example, begins by saying, "All human behavior is learned."[26] Well, if all human behavior is learned, why is it that in spite of all our intelligence and culturally determined behavior, we continue to do all the ordinary things that animals do?

Earlier we mentioned headbobbing and pushups used by some

22. Paul D. MacLean, "Effects of Pallidal Lesions on Species-typical Display Behavior of the Squirrel Monkey," *Federation Proceedings* 32 (1973): 384; idem, "Effects of Lesions of Globus Pallidus on Species-typical Display Behavior of Squirrel Monkeys," *Brain Research*, in press.

23. Paul D. MacLean, "Role of Pallidal Projections in Species-typical Display Behavior of Squirrel Monkey," *Transactions of the American Neurological Association* 100 (1975): 25-28.

24. John Locke, *An Essay Concerning Human Understanding*, ed. Alexander C. Fraser (London: Oxford Press, 1894).

25. Ivan Pavlov, *Lectures on Conditioned Reflexes*, trans. W. Horsley Gantt (New York: International Publishers, 1928).

26. Neal E. Miller and John Dollard, *Social Learning and Imitation* (New Haven: Yale University Press, 1941), p. 1.

lizards in their territorial challenge display. Components of such displays are also used in the so-called signature display and in courtship. Teachers are used to seeing such displays, both inside and outside the classroom. Social hierarchies among lizards are maintained by the repeated performance of signature and challenge displays. It is of interest that once the dominant lizard has the others bowing to him, they will nevertheless join him in attacking a strange lizard entering their domain.[27] Lizards caged together will gang up on a stranger.[28] Mindful of the claim that all human behavior is learned, one might ask, "Do schoolboys and collegians learn to haze and bully by reading accounts of the ganging up of lizards on a newcomer?"

Imitation. Since the mirror display that has been described involves isopraxic factors, the experimental findings also indicate that the R-complex is implicated in natural forms of imitation. "Isopraxic" refers to behavior in which two or more individuals engage in, and communicate by, the same kind of activity.[29] In circular language, one might define a species as a group of animals that has genetically acquired the perfect ability to imitate itself.[30] It cannot be overemphasized that isopraxis is basic for maintaining the identity of the species or a social group. The autistic child exemplifies the devastating effects of an inability to imitate. Mentally retarded children, on the contrary, may show a considerable disposition to imitate, and advantage has been taken of this proclivity to teach them skills.

OTHER PRIMAL BEHAVIOR

Isopraxis is one of five major interoperative behaviors seen in reptiles and higher forms that serve to bring into relation a number

27. Llewellyn T. Evans, "Field Study of the Social Behavior of the Black Lizard, *Ctenosaura pectinata*," *American Museum Novitates* 1493 (1951): 1-26.

28. Llewellyn T. Evans, "Cuban Field Studies on Territoriality of the Lizard, *Anolis sagrei*," *Journal of Comparative Psychology* 25 (1938): 97-125.

29. Paul D. MacLean, "The Imitative-Creative Interplay of Our Three Mentalities," in *Astride the Two Cultures: Arthur Koestler at 70*, ed. Harold Harris (London: Hutchinson, 1976), p. 191.

30. Ibid., p. 200.

of the activities listed in table 1. The other four such behaviors may be referred to as (a) perseverative, (b) reenactment, (c) tropistic, and (d) deceptive.[31] Without defining them, I shall simply say that in human activities they find expression in slavish conformance to routine and old ways of doing things; personal day-to-day rituals and superstitious acts; obeisance to precedent, as in legal and other matters; ceremonial reenactment; responding to partial representations, whether alive or inanimate; and all manner of deception. Before giving some illustrations it is necessary to say a word about the nature of proclivities.

The nature of proclivities. It should be pointed out that many people contend that proclivities do not exist in human beings. They would argue, for example, that if there were a natural territorial proclivity, why do not all people show it? Impulses and compulsions may be construed as variations of proclivities. It is one of the frustrating aspects of the subjective life that unlike emotional feelings and thoughts, we are either oblivious to, or cannot find the words to express, mental states connected with proclivities. Even the most gifted writers flounder in this area and are hardly better off than the reporter who describes a child beater as being "driven as if by a singular compulsion." How does one translate the subjective state of the young man who, acting under a compulsion, cut open the chest of a companion and ate his heart? It was as though proclivities were like an itch-without-an-itch. Thanks to the rational mind there are as many ways of dealing with an itch as there are human beings: one may do the natural thing and scratch; seek a faith healer or dermatologist; apply one's own remedies; wear special clothing; or simply ignore the itch. Our proclivities and manner of dealing with them might be considered in such terms. Left to its own devices, the metaphorical reptile does what it has to do.

Routine, precedent, and ritual. Later, after considering the two other metaphorical "drivers," mention will be made of experiments indicating that the predisposition to routine has its roots in the older parts of the forebrain. In the meantime, it should be noted that observations of reptiles reveal that they are slaves to routine,

31. MacLean, "On the Evolution of Three Mentalities," pp. 315-16.

precedent, and ritual. Such conformance behavior often has survival value. If, for example, a particular crevice served as an escape from a predator on one occasion, it may do so again. If a roundabout path proved to be safe in arriving at a source of food on one occasion, why risk returning to the same place by a shorter route? We are well aware of our own propensities to follow favorite routes to one place or another or to engage in particular acts that were successful in getting out of bad situations. In legal and other matters, endless time is spent in searching for precedents.

Through time, many of the things we do become established as rituals and are incorporated into our daily routine. An outside observer might regard such rituals as superstitious acts. Scientists have the reputation of looking down their noses at ordinary people who do superstitious things, among which some would include religious observances. But who in a research setting has not seen scientists perform useless pet maneuvers in trying to replicate an experiment? Who has not seen them consume numerous magical wafers as a protection against colds or some other possible evil?

The familiarity that breeds contempt often boils down to a familiarity with a person's tiresome and annoying "rituals" (obsessive-compulsive acts). It is possible that some marital and other interpersonal relationships could be helped if the parties involved were aware of the protective nature of rituals and accordingly learned to develop a tolerance of them.

The constitutional part of us that enforces routine has a powerful means of making it known when there has been a break in routine. As anyone knows who has suggested a change in curriculum, there is hardly anything more sure to upset the emotional and rational minds than the alteration of a long established routine. It was as though the whole sky would fall. In like vein, anything that reinforces routines may have a reassuring, calming effect. Ceremonial reenactments, precirculation of agenda, and so forth, represent cultural measures for preserving a semblance of routine and dissipating anxiety. T. P. Nunn, in considering the role of "instincts" in education, discussed the value of routine in the classroom and elsewhere.[32]

32. Thomas P. Nunn, *Education and Its Data and First Principles* (New York: Longmans, Green and Company, 1920), chap. 6.

Displacement activity. Ethologists have given much attention to "displacement" activity of animals—an expression used to refer to behavior that seems inappropriate for a given situation, as exemplified by an animal's grooming or preening when threatened or otherwise under stress.[33] One may see the same kind of behavior following brain stimulation that induces stressful reactions. It would appear that under both natural and experimental conditions there is spillover excitation, suggesting that there is a reciprocal innervation of mechanisms of stress and of repair that compares to the reciprocal innervation of muscles.[34] After eating, procreating, or the fighting that precedes, their needs follow a cleaning-up (grooming) process. A student's displacement reactions during uneasy moments become more manageable when recognized for what they are—picking (cleaning) the nose, biting nails, scratching the head, rubbing the face or hands, clearing the throat, spitting, and so forth. Helped and abetted by the rational mind, displacement propensities may take the form of such time-honored procedures as appointing a committee when a tough situation arises. In an educational institution it seems to be well understood that the level of anxiety can be gauged by the number of existing committees.

Deceptive behavior. Ever since predation became a way of life, deceptive tactics have been important to both hunter and hunted. Almost nothing is known about brain mechanisms underlying deceptive behavior, but it is probable that the basic circuitry will be found in the R-complex. In the attempted assassination of George Wallace, Arthur Bremer stalked his victim for days at a time, and if he was not around, went for bigger game. Resorting again to reptilian rhetoric, one may ask, "Do present-day assassins learn to stalk by reading Auffenberg's account of the predatory and deceptive behavior of the giant Komodo lizard?"[35] These animals,

33. Nikolaas Tinbergen, *The Study of Instinct* (London: Clarendon Press, 1951).

34. Paul D. MacLean, "The Limbic System with Respect to Self-Preservation and the Preservation of the Species," *Journal of Nervous and Mental Disease* 127 (1958): 1-11.

35. Walter Auffenberg, "Komodo Dragons," *Natural History* 81 (1972): 52-59.

growing up to ten feet in length, will relentlessly stalk a deer for days at a time or wait in ambush for hours, activities that require a detailed knowledge of terrain and a good sense of time. Waiting for just the right moment, the huge lizard will lunge at the deer, cripple it with a slash of the achilles tendon, and bring it to an agonizing death by ripping out its bowels.

No mention can be made of deceptive behavior without being reminded that white-collar criminality has never been so much in the news as during the past few years. If we have learned through our culture that "honesty is the best policy," why is it that people are willing to take enormous risks to practice deception? Why do the games we teach our young place such a premium on deceptive tactics and terminology of deception? How can pupils be expected to come off the playing fields and not use the same principles in the competition and struggle for survival in the classroom?

Tropistic behavior. Tropistic behavior refers to an animal's positive and negative responses to partial or complete representations of animate or inanimate objects. An uncovering of the underlying neural mechanisms promises to be a task as difficult as any facing neurophysiology. Tropistic behavior may overlap with imitative (isopraxic) behavior. In regard to questions of interest to educators, it applies to such matters as different "receptive periods" in a child's or student's development (analogous to "imprinting"), sexual identification, fetishes, fads and fashions (as typified by hairstyles and the ubiquitous "Levis"), and migrational tendencies. As opposed to the seasonal migrations of some reptiles, birds, and mammals, there is usually no ready explanation of what triggers nonperiodic migrations of people. Some ecologists attribute today's restless movements of people to overpopulation and crowding. The flocking of young people to music festivals has been compared to abortive migrations. Since the forebrain is essential even for the schooling of fish,[36] it will not be surprising if the thermostat for migrational fever proves to be located in the R-complex.

36. G. K. Noble, "Function of the Corpus Striatum in the Social Behavior of Fishes," *Anatomical Record* 64 (1936): 34.

The Old Mammalian Brain (Limbic System) and the Emotional Mind

With the evolution from mammal-like reptiles to mammals, there appears to have come into being a primal commandment stating: "Thou shalt not eat thy young or other flesh of thine own kind." Of equal headline importance in the evolution of mammals is the progressive attention and care that they give to their young. As already mentioned, it is doubtful whether or not the mammal-like reptiles took care of the young. Of existing reptiles, only the crocodilia and a few skinks show any interest in their young, which come into the world prepared to do everything that they have to do except to procreate. Among mammals the parental concern for the young eventually generalizes to other members of the species, a psychological development that amounts to an evolution of a sense of responsibility and what we call conscience. It was also mentioned how dependent parent-offspring relationships are on vocalization and the sense of hearing. Under conditions of obfuscation existing in the grounds of a forest, the auditory sense would provide the most reliable means of communication. Separation of offspring from the mother is calamitous. We can divine in this situation the evolutionary roots of unity of the family, unity of the clan, unity of larger societies, as well as the emotional intensity of feelings attending separation, isolation, and the threat of annihilation.[37]

THE LIMBIC SYSTEM

Reptiles have a perfect memory for what their ancestors have learned to do over millions of years, but there are behavioral indications that the reptilian brain is poorly equipped for learning to cope with new situations. The reptilian brain has only a rudimentary cortex. In the lost transitional forms between mammal-like reptiles and mammals, it is presumed that the primitive cortex ballooned out and became further differentiated. The primitive cortex might be imagined as nature's device for providing the animal a better means of viewing the environment and learning to survive.

37. Consider also the strong emotional feelings that may be generated by musical and other sounds.

Turning to our hand model again, we separate our fists and see the location of the old cortex. Our fingernails correspond to the white matter connecting the two hemispheres (the corpus callosum). The surrounding area formed by the knuckles and adjacent palm corresponds to the ring of cortex representing our inheritance from lower mammals. As illustrated in figure 5, in all existing mammals the old cortex is found in a large convolution which Broca in 1878 called the limbic lobe because it surrounds the brain stem.[38] This lobe is a common denominator in the brains of all mammals. In 1952, I suggested the term "limbic system" as a designation for the limbic cortex and the structures of the brain stem with which it has primary connections.[39] Through its strong connections with the hypothalamus it has a much more direct influence than the new cortex on visceral and endocrine functions. Clinical and experimental findings of the past forty years indicate that the limbic brain derives information in terms of emotional feelings that guide behavior required for self-preservation and the preservation of the species.

Earlier, we compared nerve cells to people with special jobs to do. The limbic system comprises three great subdivisions of nerve cells having different functions. The subdivisions might be imagined as having developed somewhat like the colonial settlements around New York, Boston, and Chicago. On the brain map in figure 5 they are identified by the numerals 1, 2, and 3. Cortex, it will be recalled, is characterized by being arranged in layers. Unlike the new cortex, which is all "high-rise," the early nerve cell settlers of the limbic cortex housed themselves in one and two-story dwellings and only later moved into multistory apartments.

The three subdivisions have an extensive communications system. The amygdala (#1) and septal (#2) divisions receive slowly conducted olfactory messages somewhat in the manner in which old New York and Boston were supplied by slowly moving surface

38. Paul Broca, "Anatomie comparée des circonvolutions cérébrales: Le grand lobe limbique et la scissure limbique dans la série des mammifères," *Revue d'Anthropologie* 7 (1878): 385-498.

39. Paul D. MacLean, "Some Psychiatric Implications of Physiological Studies on Frontotemporal Portion of Limbic System (Visceral Brain)," *Electroencephalography and Clinical Neurophysiology* 4 (1952): 407-18.

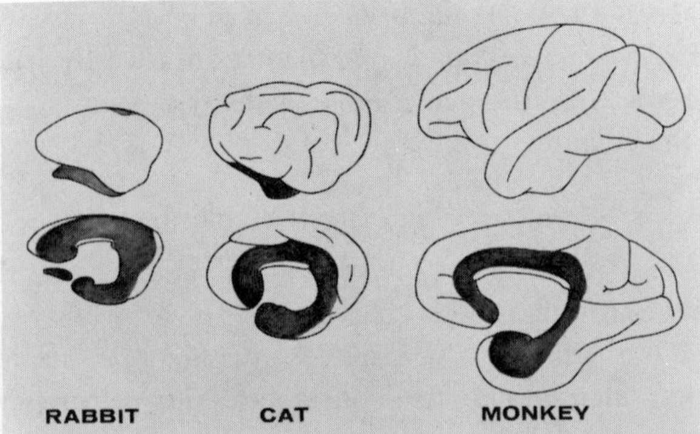

Fig. 4. The limbic lobe of Broca in mammals. The limbic lobe (shaded) is found as a common denominator in the brains of all mammals. It contains the greater part of the cortex corresponding to that of the paleomammalian brain. The cortex of the neomammalian brain (shown in white) mushrooms late in evolution.

Source: Paul D. MacLean, "Studies on Limbic System ("Visceral Brain") and Their Bearing on Psychosomatic Problems," in *Recent Developments in Psychosomatic Medicine*, ed. R. A. Cleghorn and Eric D. Wittkower (London: Sir Isaac Pitman and Sons; Philadelphia: Lippincott and Co., 1954), pp. 101-25.

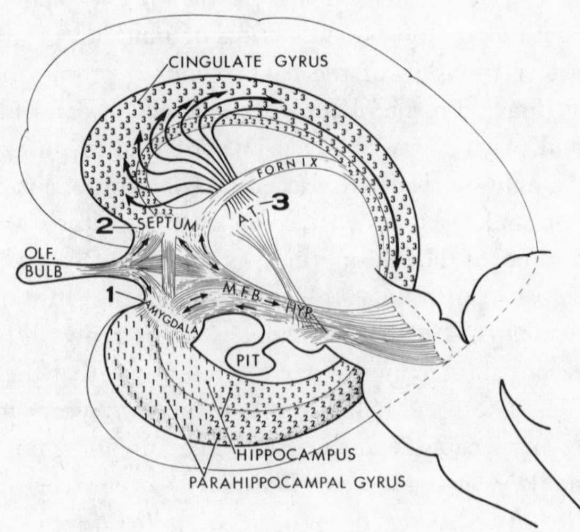

Fig. 5. Three main subdivisions of the limbic system and their major pathways. The systems are identified by the overlying numbers. See text for a summary of their respective functions. Abbreviations: AT, anterior thalamic nuclei; HYP, hypothalamus; MFB, medial forebrain bundle; PIT, pituitary; OLF, olfactory.

Source: Paul D. MacLean, "A Triune Concept of the Brain and Behavior," in *The Hincks Memorial Lectures*, ed. Thomas J. Boag and Dugal Campbell (Toronto: University of Toronto Press, 1973).

ships, whereas the communication of these divisions with the rest of the brain would be comparable to that afforded by barge, highway, and rail systems making connections with Chicago and other parts of the country.

FUNCTIONS OF THE THREE LIMBIC DIVISIONS

Experimental work on animals and observations in the clinic have shown that the nerve cells of the amygdala division (#1) have the job of administering functions of the organism that center around the mouth and are concerned with self-preservation.[40] These functions include feeding, fighting, and self-protection. The cells of the septal division (#2), on the contrary, are occupied with primal functions required for the procreation of the species.[41] In animals, stimulation in the region of the amygdala results in oral responses related to feeding and the expression of anger and defense, while stimulation of the septal region elicits sexual arousal and behavior of an affectionate nature. Because of strong interconnections (fig. 5) excitation in one region may spill over into the other, with a resulting combination of oral and genital effects. The intimate relationship of the two regions is presumably due to their connections with the olfactory sense, which dates far back in evolution and plays a primary role in both feeding and mating, as well as in the fighting that may precede. Male hamsters, for example, cease to mate and fight if deprived of their olfactory apparatus.[42] Under the guise of liberation there is currently at the cinema a considerable preoccupation with "oral sex" and the sadistic behavior that may accompany it. Many people are inwardly disturbed by such inclinations and feelings. They are not aware that these subjective heirlooms date back millions and millions of years before the laws against perversion were written. The fulvus lemur, an early form of monkey, has a greeting display that is relevant to this matter. When two mates have been separated for a time, they

40. MacLean, "A Triune Concept of the Brain and Behavior," pp. 14-15.

41. Ibid., pp. 15-16.

42. Michael R. Murphy and Gerald E. Schneider, "Olfactory Bulb Removal Eliminates Mating Behavior in the Male Golden Hamster," *Science* 167 (1970): 302-4.

greet each other by mutually licking the ano-genital region.[43]

We have seen, on the contrary, that the greeting display of a more advanced form of monkey—the squirrel monkey—depends on visual, rather than olfactory, communication. This distinction should be kept in mind as we consider next the third subdivision. This division becomes progressively larger in primates and reaches its greatest development in human beings. It will be noted that the main lines for communication (which in terms of our analogy would be comparable to Chicago's network of communications with the middle western belt) bypass the olfactory apparatus (see fig. 5). There is some evidence that the great expansion of the third division reflects a shift in emphasis from olfactory to visual and other forms of communication in procreational behavior. The junctional center of this division was named the mammillary bodies by an early anatomist because its shape was suggestive of two breasts. This naming now seems rather provident because there is evidence in rats that it is implicated in nursing,[44] while the great community of cortical cells connected with it is concerned with maternal behavior.[45] These discoveries of parental functions become of still greater interest when it is recalled that there is no counterpart of the third subdivision in the brains of reptiles.

With respect to the ascendancy of vision in prosematic sociosexual communication, it is to be noted that in monkeys (both male[46] and female[47]) electrical stimulation in parts of the third division results in erection of the genital organ, with or without

43. R. J. Andrew, "The Displays of the Primates," in *Evolutionary and Genetic Biology of Primates*, vol. 2, ed. John Buettner-Janusch (New York: Academic Press, 1964), pp. 227-309.

44. Burton M. Slotnick, unpublished observations.

45. John S. Stamm, "The Function of the Median Cerebral Cortex in Maternal Behavior of Rats," *Journal of Comparative and Physiological Psychology* 48 (1955): 347-56; Burton M. Slotnick, "Disturbances of Maternal Behavior in the Rat Following Lesions of the Cingulate Cortex," *Behavior* 24 (1967): 204-36.

46. Paul D. MacLean and Detlev W. Ploog, "Cerebral Representation of Penile Erection," *Journal of Neurophysiology* 25 (1962): 29-55.

47. M. Maurus, J. Mitra, and Detlev W. Ploog, "Cerebral Representation of the Clitoris in Ovariectomized Squirrel Monkeys," *Experimental Neurology* 13 (1965): 283-88.

an ejection of urine. Animals such as the cat and dog with a large olfactory apparatus, mark their territories with urine. The message, so to speak, is "stay away." We have seen on the other hand, how the squirrel monkey uses the visual display of the genital as a gesture of dominance. All three limbic subdivisions are known to be connected with the R-complex, as is also the new cortex. Several examples have been cited elsewhere of the symbolic significance of the genital in mythology and in everyday life.[48] For example, house guards—stone monuments showing an erect phallus—have been used by primitive peoples in all parts of the world as territorial markers. People continue to draw phallic representations in public toilets and to leave their names or initials as a kind of marker. Periodically, adolescents go on the rampage displaying their nakedness in public. Eibl-Eibesfeldt has described a genital display among Bushmen children with features of the display of squirrel monkeys.[49] Vandalism at schools and elsewhere represents another form of visual marking. A refined type of visual marking is typified by the custom of signing a register at a marriage or funeral.

GLOBAL FUNCTIONS OF LIMBIC SYSTEM

Emotion. Clinical findings on patients with psychomotor epilepsy provide the best evidence that the limbic system is basically involved in the experience and expression of emotion.[50] Scarring of the limbic cortex secondary to birth trauma, head injury, or infection has the effect of creating bioelectrical storms that, because of extensive interconnections, may spread to affect populations of nerve cells in *parts* or *all* of the limbic system. At the beginning of a storm, depending on what populations are affected, the patient's

48. Paul D. MacLean, "New Findings on Brain Function and Sociosexual Behavior," in *Contemporary Sexual Behavior: Critical Issues in the 1970s*, ed. Joseph Zubin and John Money (Baltimore, Md.: Johns Hopkins University Press, 1973), pp. 33-74.

49. I. Eibl-Eibesfeldt, "!Ko-Bushleute (Kalahari): Schamweisen und Spotten," *Homo* 22 (1971): 261-66.

50. See MacLean, "The Triune Brain and Scientific Bias," pp. 337-38, regarding the definition of emotional feelings (basic affects, special affects, and general affects).

mind lights up with vivid emotional feelings that range all the way from intense fear to ecstasy.

A storm may also spark eureka-type feelings like those associated with discovery, or free-floating feelings of conviction of what is real, true, and important. When we think of how we evaluate the importance of things, nothing could be more fundamental than the realization that the primitive limbic system has the capacity to generate the strong feelings of conviction that we attach to our beliefs, regardless of whether they are true or false.

The epileptic storms commonly result in a temporary black-out of function of parts or all of the limbic system, while the lights stay on in the rest of the brain. If the brain of the rational mind has not been hit by the storm, sufferers of limbic epilepsy may continue to engage in complicated behavior such as driving a car or doing a job,[51] and yet have no memory of it afterwards. At such times they behave like disembodied spirits.

In between generalized storms there may continue to be small, local storms near the damaged part of the brain. These local storms may generate symptoms of the kind associated with insanity or the use of psychedelic drugs—namely, feelings of depersonalization, distortions of perception, hallucinations, and paranoid feelings. Many of the drugs now used to treat mental illness owe their effects to an action on the limbic system and R-complex. As was initially emphasized, each of these two older formations of the brain has a distinctive chemistry.

Memory and personal identity. In some cases limbic storms may activate a memory of some specific event, or more commonly, only the feeling attached to the memory (déjà vu).[52] On the contrary, limbic blackouts of the kind mentioned above, or extensive damage to parts of the limbic system, interefere with the recording of memories. In this respect, it should be emphasized that memory, just as a feeling of personal identity, depends on the brain's ability to combine internal experience with external experience. The condition that makes us unique as individuals is this private, combined

51. MacLean, "The Triune Brain and Scientific Bias," p. 342.

52. Wilder Penfield and Herbert Jasper, *Epilepsy and the Functional Anatomy of the Human Brain* (Boston: Little, Brown and Co., 1954).

form of experience. Only the information from the external world is publicly available to everyone. Hence it is significant that in the manufacture of experience pertaining to personal identity and to memory, the limbic cortical cells utilize and combine messages pouring in from both the inside and outside world, whereas, as we shall see, the cells of the new cortex are primarily occupied with events in the outside world.

The New Brain and the Rational Mind

There are indications that insistent signals from the inside world make it difficult for the organism to make coldly reasoned decisions required for survival. In the evolution of the neocortex, nature attempts to remedy this situation. Compared with the limbic cortex the neocortex (shown in white in figure 4) is like an expanding numerator. As Herrick has commented, "It's explosive growth in phylogeny is one of the most dramatic transformations known to comparative anatomy."[53] The massive proportions of the neocortex in higher mammals explains the designation of "neomammalian brain" applied to it and structures of the brain stem with which it is primarily connected. The neocortex culminates in the human brain in which there develops a megapolis of nerve cells devoted to the production of symbolic language and the associated functions of reading, writing, and arithmetic. Mother of invention, and father of abstract thought, the new cortex promotes the preservation and procreation of ideas.

Looking at our hand model again—our two fists—we are reminded that all of the exposed surface corresponds to the neocortex. We should also take a moment to reread the initial anatomy lesson regarding the location of the neocortical areas concerned with vision, hearing, and bodily sensations. For solutions of situations that arise in the external world, nature designs the neocortex so that it receives signals primarily from the eyes, ears, and body wall—signals, incidentally, that unlike those for smell and taste going to the limbic cortex, lend themselves to amplification and radiotransmission. With its focus on material things, the neocortex

53. C. Judson Herrick, "The Functions of the Olfactory Parts of the Cerebral Cortex," *Proceedings of the National Academy of Sciences* 19 (1933): 7-14.

develops at first somewhat like a coldly reasoning, heartless computer. Later, and finally, we shall see how nature devised a heart for this computer. In the meantime, a further consideration of neocortical functions will be more meaningful if we keep in mind its working relationship with the R-complex and the limbic system.

A Meeting of Minds

THE BASIC PERSONALITY

In developing an appreciation of what the neocortex contributes to psychological functions, we may first ask what an animal would be like without it. By special treatment near the time of birth one can prevent the neocortex and its related structures from developing in such animals as rats or hamsters. Laqueur and coworkers originally reported that rat preparations of this kind were able to mate, breed, and rear their young[54] and were almost indistinguishable from normal animals in a variety of psychological tests.[55] We have since found that hamsters growing up without the neocortex show all the naturally occurring behaviors typical of hamsters. Such animals, for example, develop play behavior at the appropriate time. Since I have never seen anything resembling play behavior in reptiles, I would presume that the retention of this capacity can be attributed to limbic structures. In regard to "routine" mentioned earlier, it is to be noted that these animals have the daily routines of normal hamsters.

Contrariwise, we may ask what an animal would be like with only its new brain and not the other two. An approximation to such a condition is provided by experiments on monkeys in which major connections of the R-complex and limbic system with the neural chassis are destroyed.[56] With the massive connections to and from the neocortex largely intact, such animals recover the

54. R. K. Haddad, Ausma Rabe, Gert L. Laqueur, et al., "Intellectual Deficit Associated with Transplacentally induced Microcephaly in the Rat," *Science* 163 (1969): 88-90.

55. Ausma Rabe and R. K. Haddad, "Methylazoxymethanol-induced Micrencephaly in Rats: Behavioral Studies," *Federation Proceedings* 31 (1972): 1536-39.

56. MacLean, "On the Evolution of Three Mentalities," p. 320.

ability to move around and feed themselves. The profound alteration in these monkeys is that although they look like monkeys, they no longer behave like monkeys. Almost everything that one associates with typical simian behavior has disappeared. These kinds of experiments, together with certain findings on patients with brain disease, indicate that the R-complex and limbic system provide the neural substrate for the basic personality and the organized expression of prosematic behavior.

To credit the two older evolutionary formations with providing the underpinnings of most forms of naturally occurring behavior is not to downplay the importance of the neocortex. Nothing is more neurologically certain, for example, than that the neocortex is necessary for language and speech, and that we owe to it the infinite variety of ways in which we can express ourselves. It cannot, to be sure, give a sense of humor to the reptilian part of us, but it can respond to the playfulness of the old mammalian brain with an infinite play on words.

EVOLUTION OF HANDEDNESS AND SPEECH

According to some estimates more than 90 percent of us are right-handed.[57] Referring again to our brain model, we are reminded that the exposed part of our middle finger (move it slightly) corresponds to the motor area responsible for our voluntary movements. Since the nerve fibers from that area cross to the other side of the body, the left hemisphere controls the right hand. Why should so many of us be right-handed? Just as mysterious, why should more than 95 percent of us also have our faculties for speech represented in the left (or so-called dominant) hemisphere?

In suggesting some explanations, I shall begin with the primary question of handedness. The oldest human drawings indicate they were made by right-handed individuals. The early bronze tools and weapons were made for right-handed people. Indeed, handedness is recognized to be an inherited and not an acquired trait. Raymond Dart, the discoverer of *Australopithecus africanus*, has presented evidence that this creature with human-like features, as well as

57. Norman Geschwind and Walter Levitsky, "Human Brain: Left-right Asymmetries in Temporal Speech Region," *Science* 161 (1968): 186-87.

subsequent human-like primates and primitive peoples of 15,000 years ago, used bones for utensils, tools, and weapons.[58] When a long bone is hit at midpoint and then twisted, it can be broken into the form of long, sharp daggers. Other bony artifacts have been found that resemble bone utensils still used in New England for coring apples. The American Indians are said to have made similar utensils and weapons.

If as Dart claims, *Australopithecus* used bony weapons for murder,[59] then right-handedness might have developed in the following manner. Suppose that like some monkeys, there had been a chance favoring of the left or right hand. In the case of the right-hander, the left upper extremity would have been left free to flex as a shield to the heart against a sharp, penetrating object. Under these conditions, the right-hander might have had a better chance than the left-hander to survive and reproduce. Later, an actual shield was to take the place of the flexed left arm. It is said that the custom of driving on the left-hand side of the road in England is a carryover from the days when knights rode horseback with the shield carried on the left and the sword on the right.

SPEECH

Before proceeding to the matter of speech, it is necessary to say a word about the representation of vocalization in the brain. It will be recalled that vocalization is of questionable significance in the communication of reptiles, whereas it becomes of vital significance in mammals. Experimentally, most vocal productions in monkeys are elicited by stimulation of limbic-related structures,[60] a finding that reminds one that prosematic vocalization in animals and human beings usually has an emotional overlay. Among human beings,

58. Raymond A. Dart, *Adventures with the Missing Link* (Philadelphia: Institutes Press, Institutes for the Achievement of Human Potential, 1959).

59. Ibid., pp. 106, 113. What I propose here might be considered a variation of the "primitive warfare hypothesis" that has been attributed to Thomas Carlyle (diary entry for June 15, 1871) and to Dr. Phillip Henry Pye-Smith, *Guy's Hospital Reports* 16 (1871): 141.

60. Detlev W. Ploog et al., "Neuroethologic Studies of Vocalization in Squirrel Monkeys with Special Reference to Genetic Differences of Calling in Two Subspecies," in *Growth and Development of the Brain*, ed. Mary A. B. Brazier (New York: Raven Press, 1975), pp. 231-54.

such vocalizations commonly occur in the form of expletives expressive of pain (ouch), surprise (shriek), triumph (whoop), and the like. There are neurological and other reasons for believing that most of our expletives, including our aggressive obscenities, could erupt without the help of the neocortex. Furthermore, like many political utterances they could issue independently "from both sides of the mouth at once" without much loss of meaning. Contrast this situation with what is required when enunciating words with precise meanings. Since the tongue is a midline organ, there must be synchronized action of both sides if there is not to be slurring of speech. Since the cerebral hemispheres are mirror images of one another, and since delay may be involved in relaying information from one side to the other, it would seem next to impossible that both could cerebrate exactly alike and "speak as one mind." Each side of the tongue might receive impulses for the same word at slightly different times, or, worse, get the neural command for two different words. The result would be stammering or stuttering.

One solution for obtaining unified control of a midline organ such as the tongue would be to have it receive instructions from only one hemisphere. But why the left hemisphere? It is often proposed that the greater safety and productivity afforded by hunting in bands were conducive to socialization of our progenitors and the use of vocal sounds as a way of communicating.[61] Whenever it was that expletives were no longer good enough for human communication, it was the latest evolved neocortex, and not the less educable limbic cortex, that was called upon to produce the sounds of language. Since the right hand had already become the final effector organ for directing the use of weapon, tool, or utensil, the representation of speech in the left hemisphere would have provided the quickest and most effective means of coordinating speech and action. And whenever it was that things were first jotted down, the right hand was ready and waiting.

As a result of surgical operations separating the two hemispheres, it has been found that whereas the symbolic functions are

61. Robert Ardrey, *The Hunting Hypothesis* (New York: Atheneum Press, 1976).

represented in the dominant hemisphere, the nondominant hemisphere excels in nonverbal spatial tasks and in musical expression.[62] It is known, however, from cases in which the dominant hemisphere has been removed in childhood, that the nondominant hemisphere (usually the right) is capable of assuming all linguistic functions.

NEOCORTICAL MEMORY

Neurologically, it has been considered a great waste that the nondominant hemisphere sits idly by without ever mastering language. One neurologist compared the right hemisphere to a traveller in a foreign land who always relies on an interpreter. A more positive interpretation is suggested by computer technology. With computers, one of the great hindrances to achieving solutions of complicated problems is an insufficiency of memory, or "core" as they say. Perhaps nature, in placing linguistic functions in one hemisphere, has killed two birds with one stone—putting the midline organ, the tongue, under a single command and freeing the nondominant hemisphere to be used for a greatly expanded memory. Indeed there is clinical evidence that with damage or removal of the nondominant hemisphere, there is a measureable deterioration of memory.

Important as memory is, it must be remembered that the creative process is also dependent on forgetting. Depending too much on rote, we might as well return to the condition of reptiles. It may be one of the functions of sleep that it clears the cortical circuits of yesterday's clutter of experiences.

LEARNING

Although the horizontal connections of the neocortex make for a ready association of auditory, visual, and tactile perceptions, there is a significant gut component to learning. This raises an important question in regard to teaching and learning. It has long been recognized that if a pet is not punished at the moment it does something wrong, it will fail to learn the significance of the punishment. Experimentally, an animal such as the cat cannot learn

62. Eric H. Lenneberg, *Biological Foundation of Language* (New York: John Wiley and Sons, 1967).

the simple task of lifting its leg to avoid a shock when a buzzer is sounded if there is too long a lapse of time between the two stimuli. As testing continues, however, changes in heart rate and respiration occur with each sound of the buzzer, suggesting that the animal learns to respond with its viscera, but not with its leg. A possible explanation for this paradoxical situation is suggested by simultaneous recordings of the brain waves from the neocortex and the limbic cortex during a test. In the neocortex one finds a single response to the sound, whereas in the archicortex there is a prolonged perturbation.[63] Perhaps this prolonged perturbation allows limbic structures that influence the viscera to make an association between the sound and the shock. Gantt observed that conditioned cardiac reflexes in dogs may persist for years after the conditioned leg response has been extinguished.[64] In his words, the organism remembers with its heart, but not with specific movements. Pavlov observed that an animal tested in the manner described above, begins to respond to irrelevant stimuli.[65] One can imagine how such a "generalization" might occur in human affairs. In many households, for example, a mother will postpone punishment of a child until the father returns home to administer the whipping. It is evident how such delayed discipline might be conducive to indiscriminate visceral reactions in childhood, with father becoming identified with any authoritative figure such as a policeman, teacher, principal, and so forth. The experimental observations reinforce the generally recognized principle that punishment should be meted out immediately or not at all.

There is a proverb that says, "Train up a child in the way he should go, and when he is old, he will not depart from it."[66] It has been implicit in what was said earlier, that the R-complex represents a neural repository for programming behavior based

63. Paul D. MacLean et al., "Hippocampal Function: Tentative Correlations of Conditioning, EEG, Drug, and Radioautographic Studies," *Yale Journal of Biology and Medicine* 28 (1955/56): 380-95.

64. W. Horsley Gantt, "Principles of Nervous Breakdown: Schizokinesis and Autokinesis," *Annals of the New York Academy of Sciences* 56 (1953): 143-63.

65. Pavlov, *Lectures on Conditioned Reflexes.*

66. Proverbs 22:6.

on ancestral learning and ancestral memories. Elsewhere, I have suggested that nature economically utilizes the R-complex for the reenactment of currently learned behaviors that have been emotionally conditioned through limbic functions or intellectually executed by the new mammalian brain.[67] Once having mastered a verbal, musical, or other exercise, we can later repeat it, so to speak, almost instinctively.

Some Further Evolutionary Developments

Finally, let us turn again to our brain model and, looking at our two thumbs, imagine the location of our most recently evolved neocortex—the so-called prefrontal cortex. Prefrontal means "at the tip." It has long been known that the intelligence quotient as usually measured is unaffected by the loss of this cortex.[68] Then why the development of the prefrontal cortex? Earlier we suggested that the neocortex has the capacity of operating somewhat like a coldly reasoning, heartless computer. It is the kind of computer that makes it possible for monkeys to scheme their way like gangsters into another troop, murder the dominant male, and perform infanticide in the presence of the distressed mothers.[69] It is unnecessary here to draw some human parallels.

Now for some inexplicable reason, nature appears to have concluded that a genie—a veritable Frankenstein—had been let out of the bottle and if it were left unbridled might lead to the destruction of the species. I use the word "inexplicable" because nature itself seems to have given the blessing to the paradoxical principle of the "need to die in order to live." Have you seen the green heron swallow live fish after live fish? Have you seen the fish squirm and wiggle in the heron's crop as it is swept along to be slowly peeled away by burning juices? Have you heard birds

67. Paul D. MacLean, "Cerebral Evolution and Emotional Processes: New Findings on the Striatal Complex," *Annals of the New York Academy of Sciences* 193 (1972): 137-49.

68. Walter J. Freeman and James W. Watts, *Psychosurgery in the Treatment of Mental Disorders and Intractable Pain* (Springfield, Ill.: Charles C Thomas, 1950).

69. Joseph L. Popp and Irven DeVore, "Aggressive Competition and Social Dominance," in *The Great Apes*, ed. David M. Hamburg and E. R. McCown (Menlo Park, Calif.: W. A. Benjamin and Co., forthcoming).

cough themselves to death from air-sacculitis? Have you risen in the night to give them cough syrup? Have you seen the cat play with a mouse? Have you seen cancer slowly eat away or strangle another human being? This has been nature's way for countless millions of years. The misery piles up like stellar gases tortured by a burning sun. Then why, slowly but progressively, did nature add something to the neocortex that for the first time brings a heart and a sense of compassion into the world? Altruism, empathy—these are almost new words. Altruism—"to this other." Empathy—compassionate identification with another individual.

In the progress from Neanderthal to Cro-Magnon man, one sees the human forehead develop from a low brow to a high brow. Underneath that heightened brow is the prefrontal cortex. There are clinical indications that the prefrontal cortex provides foresight in planning for ourselves and others and that it also helps us to gain insight into the feelings of others.[70] The prefrontal cortex is the only neocortex that looks inward to the inside world. Clinically, there is evidence that the prefrontal cortex by looking inward, so to speak, obtains the gut feeling required for identifying with another individual. It is this new development that makes possible the insight required for the foresight to plan for the needs of others as well as the self—to use our knowledge to alleviate suffering everywhere. In designing for the first time a creature that shows a concern for suffering of other living things, nature seems to have attempted a 180 degree turnabout from what had been a reptile-eat-reptile and dog-eat-dog world.

In figure 6 I have emphasized the close tie-in of the prefrontal circuits with the great third subdivision of the limbic system that was discussed earlier in connection with the evolution of parental care. It is possible that these large evolving parts of the brain are incapable of coming into full operation until the hormonal changes of adolescence occur. If so, it would weigh heavily against the claims of those who contend that the personality is fully developed and rigid by adolescence, if indeed not by the age of five or six. The triune brain concept raises many questions with respect to the emergence of moral judgments and other cultural values of so

70. Freeman and Watts, *Psychosurgery in the Treatment of Mental Disorders and Intractable Pain.*

much interest to educators. There is now abundant anatomical and behavioral evidence that if neural circuits of the brain are not brought into play at certain critical times of development, they may never be capable of functioning. Chimpanzees reared in darkness may be forever blind.[71] Is it possible that if empathy is not learned at a critical age, it may never become fully developed?[72] Kubie, who dealt extensively with the education of the young scientist, emphasized that adolescents not only need to be exposed

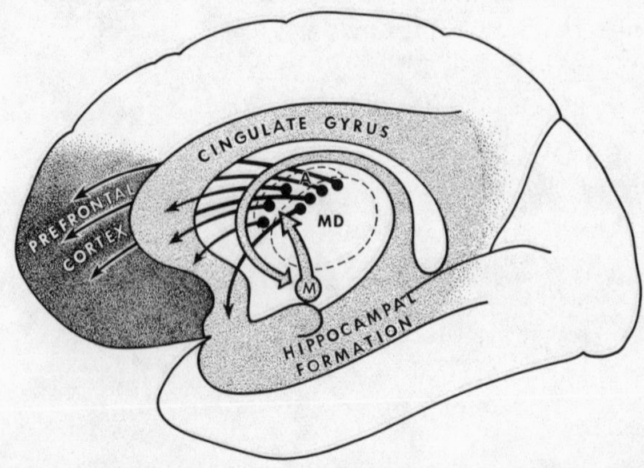

FIG. 6. Anatomical relationship of the limbic system to the prefrontal cortex through the third pathway shown in figure 5. The limbic system is indicated by the light stipple. Abbreviations: M, mammillary bodies of hypothalamus; MD, medial dorsal nucleus; A, anterior thalamic nuclei.

SOURCE: Paul D. MacLean, "The Brain in Relation to Empathy and Medical Education," *Journal of Nervous and Mental Disease* 144 (1967): 374-82.

to human suffering, but also need to be given the responsibility for ministering to it.[73]

In writings that deal with improvement of the external environment, it is repeatedly pointed out how we can "help" nature. There seems to be a contradiction here: since we are part of na-

71. Kao Liang Chow, Austin H. Riesen, and Frank W. Newall, "Degeneration of Retinal Ganglion Cells in Infant Chimpanzees Reared in Darkness," *Journal of Comparative Neurology* 107 (1957): 27-42.

72. Paul D. MacLean, "The Brain in Relation to Empathy and Medical Education," *Journal of Nervous and Mental Disease* 144 (1967): 374-82.

73. Lawrence S. Kubie, "Are We Educating for Maturity?" *National Education Association Journal* 48 (1959): 58-62.

ture, everything that we do must be considered natural. Nevertheless, if we read nature correctly, if we correctly sense its turnabout, its conversion in regard to suffering, then perhaps we can help to speed up the process. As human beings we seem to be acquiring the mental stuff of which we imagine angels are made. Perhaps it is time to take a fresh look at ourselves and try again to act accordingly. Since we know that we may either affect chance or take our chances, no one can argue that we are entirely a product of our genes and that there is not some degree of freedom to change the way things are.

CHAPTER X

Growth Spurts during Brain Development: Implications for Educational Policy and Practice

HERMAN T. EPSTEIN

Introduction

Mental development is manifestly linked to and limited by the development of the child's brain. Because of recently uncovered facts from the neurosciences, we can now suggest a new frame of reference for educational strategies, curriculum planning, and evaluation of educational experiments. To aid the reader in grasping the data and following the arguments supporting the above contentions, I begin by summarizing the main contents of this chapter.

From biology we learn that formation of brain cells ceases early in life; the most recent data indicate its cessation before the end of the second year of life.[1] The cessation contrasts markedly with the increase of about 35 percent in brain weight after that age. This weight increase must appear in the form of (a) more extended and branched axons and dendrites of brain cells, (b) the laying down of the fatty insulation (myelin sheath) of axons, and (c) increased input of energy and materials through an increase in arterial blood supply to the brain. All these sources of increase in brain weight suggest an increase of complexity and speed of intercellular connections, leading to more complex and more reliable neural networks.

If these modifications occur continuously during child development, then each child at any age represents a point on a continuum of development. However, if increases are not continuous, but rather occur at discrete periods during life, then we have to think

1. John Dobbing and Jean Sands, "Quantitative Growth and Development of Human Brain," *Archives of Disease in Childhood* 48 (1973): 757-67.

in terms of *stages* of brain development. Such brain development stages may well manifest themselves in correlated, if not causally related, stages of mental development.

This chapter includes a brief account of my finding that human brain growth indeed occurs primarily during the age intervals of three to ten months and from two to four, six to eight, ten to twelve or thirteen, and fourteen to sixteen or seventeen years, and that these stages correlate well in timing with stages found in mental growth. Further, those experimentally established intervals correlate in time with the classical stages of intellectual development as described by Piaget, except that the fourteen- to sixteen-year brain growth stage has no Piagetian counterpart.[2] We therefore predict a hitherto unknown stage of intellectual development. Very recent work by Arlin yields the beginning of evidence for such a stage, which appears at about the predicted age.[3]

Given the body of facts sketched above, one can think of possible consequences for learning in general and for schooling in particular. One working hypothesis would be that intensive and *novel* intellectual inputs to children may be most effective during the brain growth stages. Anatomical data might be interpreted to lead to the inference that novel challenges to the child's mind that are presented at the wrong time might cause an active and potentially permanent turn-off of the ability to absorb some of those challenges at a later and more appropriate age. The question of what to do during the putative "fallow" periods will be answered definitively only by executing in schools (not in psychology laboratories!) some well-designed experiments aimed directly at that question.

The connection between brain growth stages and the ages of origins of the main Piagetian stages leads to a proposal for a new kind of evaluation scheme for educational experiments. It is known that even in the most affluent of developed countries appreciably fewer than 100 percent of adults manifest concrete operations (the third stage—age seven years), while only 30 percent manifest for-

2. Jean Piaget, *Psychology of Intelligence*, trans. Malcolm Piercy and D. E. Berlyne (Totowa, N.J.: Littlefield, Adams, and Co., 1969).

3. Patricia K. Arlin, "Cognitive Development in Adulthood: A Fifth Stage?" *Developmental Psychology* 11 (1975): 602-6.

mal operations (the fourth stage—age eleven years) that permit solving abstract reasoning problems at the highest level.[4] We may then speculate that even smaller percentages of children from disadvantaged situations will show the onset of the various stages at the normal ages. Thus, we could think of evaluating the effects of an intervention program or any experimental schooling program in terms of what it does to the percentage of children manifesting the *next* Piagetian stage at the expected age.

It is important to emphasize that the brain growth stages are not a theoretical notion but a scientific fact for which the evidence will be sketched in the pages to follow. Mental growth stages have a similar factual character, as does the correlative connection of brain growth stages with the ages of onset of the main Piagetian stages (whose age-linkage will also be demonstrated below).

In contrast, inferences from these facts constitute working hypotheses for adapting schooling strategies and curricula to the facts. We shall begin our study with a brief collection of some twentieth century suggestions that the stagewise mental growth of children has been ignored despite many indications of the existence of such stages.

Stages in Intellectual Development

Why has the idea of intellectual development stages penetrated so little into the thinking about education? It is not because there were no suggestions about such a possibility. Without trying to research the matter completely, I have traced the idea back at least fifty years to Alfred North Whitehead's *The Aims of Education.* In the second chapter, "The Rhythm of Education," the following quotation appears:

> The pupil's progress is often conceived as a uniform steady advance undifferentiated by changes of type or alteration in pace. . . . I hold that this conception of education is based upon a false psychology of the process of mental development which has gravely hindered the effectiveness of our methods. Life is essentially periodic. . . . There are . . . periods of mental growth, with their cyclic recurrences. . . .

4. Pierre R. Dasen, "Cross-cultural Piagetian Research: A Summary," *Journal of Cross-cultural Psychology* 3 (1972): 23-29.

Lack of attention to the rhythm and character of mental growth is a main source of wooden futility in education.[5]

Whitehead goes on to details of these rhythms, but without more than approximate indication of the ages. Between two and four years the child goes from achievement of perception to the acquirement of language. The next cycle ends around age seven years with classification of thought and keener perception. Manifestation of developed powers of observation and manipulation develops between ages eight and twelve. The three years between ages twelve and fifteen, according to Whitehead, should be dominated by a mass attack upon language. Finally, he asserts, the age of precision in language and of romance in science ends about age fifteen and is followed by a period of generalization in language and precision in science. There is a remarkable concordance between this scheme and that derived from forty years of hard work by Piaget and his followers and associates.

Another way to explain the lack of impact of ideas of stagewise development on educational practices is that of Vygotsky, who found it necessary to warn his fellow psychologists to set forth first the factual details of the development of intelligence.[6] As Vygotsky argues so cogently, when one looks at a new phenomenon one should beware of all analogizing until the basic facts of the situation have been set out in terms of the new concept itself. Otherwise one is likely to be misled by the analogies into irrelevant and fruitless paths of investigation. Based on such reasoning, Vygotsky's initial attack on the problem is presented in the same article with the very explicit title of "The Problem of Age-periodization of Child Development."

In this article, Vygotsky discusses what he calls critical periods, defining them as times of rapid change in children, associated with transitions from one level of intellectual functioning to another. Between these critical periods are periods of stable growth. Vygotsky states that critical periods occur during the first year of

5. Alfred North Whitehead, *The Aims of Education* (New York: Mentor Books, 1929).

6. Lev Vygotsky, "The Problem of Age-periodization of Child Development," trans. Mary A. Zender and B. F. Zender, *Human Development* 17 (1974): 24-40.

life, around age three years, and age seven years. Age thirteen years (puberty) is given as a period of stable growth. Vygotsky remarks that there are no critical periods from about age seventeen years through the appearance of final maturity. Again, there is a remarkable concordance with the results of the Piagetian studies.

The Piagetian studies themselves have been the major sources of experimental evidence for four major stages in the development of intelligence: during the first eighteen months, from two to four years, from seven to eleven years, and from eleven to fifteen years. There appears to be a fairly general acceptance of the stages, especially their sequence in normally-raised children; the question remains as to whether the stages are age-linked. Even if age-linkage can be shown, there are two possible prominent interpretations of such a fact. First, the linkage could be cultural in that the usual external factors affecting child development in a society appear at about the same age for most children. Second, the linkage could be the expression of a basis in the biological development of children.

The first interpretation is unlikely because, as set forth by Dasen, the same linkage and sequence have been found in a number of countries that are culturally quite dissimilar.[7] Thus, the observed age-linkage is likely due to biological factors. Recently, Brown and Webb have provided evidence of a very strict linkage to chronological age. Webb studied appearance of the Piagetian stage four (formal operations) in children from ages six to eleven years who had IQs of about 160; their mental ages were therefore between about ten and eighteen years. His results were unequivocal: no child showed any trace of stage four until he reached close to age eleven years chronologically.[8] Brown found a similar result for appearance of stage three (concrete operations) at about age seven years.[9]

Of importance for our later discussion is another aspect of

7. Dasen, "Cross-cultural Piagetian Research."

8. Roger A. Webb, "Concrete and Formal Operations in Very Bright Six- to Eleven-Year Olds," *Human Development* 17 (1974): 292-300.

9. Ann L. Brown, "Conservation of Number and Continuous Quantity in Normal, Bright, and Retarded Children," *Child Development* 44 (1973): 376-79.

Webb's work. He found that the rate of maturation of a new stage depended on IQ. His high-IQ children achieved maturity in the stage in a few months, while normal-IQ children took a year or two. Inferentially, children with subnormal intelligence may never develop the matured aspects of the stage.

In essence, the Piagetian scheme gives us the rises and plateaus in the development of human intelligence—its phenomenological topography. What is lacking is a similar topography of human brain development. The work of White suggests a connection between mental and biophysical growth.[10] First, he showed that the very abundant information is consistent with the inference of a marked shift in level of intellectual functioning of children between ages five and seven years. Second, several of White's studies deal with biophysical parameters that also shift quantitatively and markedly in this interval. The major difficulty with using White's analysis lies in his mixing of body and brain parameters. This is equivalent to the assumption that they change or spurt in parallel, an assumption now known to be incorrect.

Other than White's studies, I have found no published information on the age-linkage of the brain/mind relationship. In the next section we will look at the data for brain and skull growth to see if there are any indications of special events related to any of the intellectual periodization discussed above.

Brain Growth from Birth to Maturity

In a very thought-provoking book, Fodor pointed out that if we accept the existence of stages of development in intelligence, it becomes difficult to understand why and how a child ever goes on to a next stage; this seems to be part of the source of his skepticism about the existence of stages.[11] The argument is that if there is a truly definable stage, it cannot already possess the essential factors needed for going on to the next stage, for there would then be no stable stage in the first place. Some external input is then

10. Sheldon White, "Some General Outlines of the Matrix of Developmental Change between Five and Seven Years," *Bulletin of the Orton Society* 20 (1970): 41-57.

11. Jerry A. Fodor, *The Language of Thought* (New York: Thomas Crowell, 1975).

needed to permit the transition. In our case, this means that to pass from one stage to another requires the prior change in the structure containing the mind: an expansion of the brain.

First, we shall ask if there is any indication of a linkage of any kind between brain and intelligence. It is generally stated that there is no such linkage. In some textbooks we find mention of the fact that Goethe had a 2200-gram brain while Anatole France's brain weighed only 1100 grams. Therefore, runs the implied argument, brain weight is random with respect to intellect. Of course, such comparisons of individuals have no bearing on relations and correlations based on large populations of individuals. Dobzhansky remarked that "it is a fallacy to conclude that, since brain size alone does not unalterably set the level of intelligence, the two variables are not in any way related. Such a conclusion would probably reflect the misconception that a trait is either wholly genetic or wholly environmental."[12] And, indeed, the one set of data I have found seems to show clearly that there is a substantial connection.

Hooton studied the head circumferences of white Bostonians as part of his massive study of criminals.[13] The following table

TABLE 1

MEAN AND STANDARD DEVIATION OF HEAD CIRCUMFERENCE FOR PEOPLE OF VARIED VOCATIONAL STATUSES

Vocational Status	N	Mean (in mm.)	S.D.
Professionals	25	569.9	1.9
Semiprofessional	61	566.5	1.5
Clerical	107	566.2	1.1
Trades	194	565.7	0.8
Public Service	25	564.1	2.5
Skilled Trades	351	562.9	0.6
Personal Services	262	562.7	0.7
Laborers	647	560.7	0.3

SOURCE: Ernest A. Hooton, *The American Criminal*, vol. 1 (Cambridge, Mass.: Harvard University Press, 1939), Table VIII-17.

12. Theodosius Dobzhansky, *Mankind Evolving: The Evolution of the Human Species* (New Haven, Conn.: Yale University Press, 1962), pp. 200-1.

13. Ernest A. Hooton, *The American Criminal*, vol. 1 (Cambridge, Mass.: Harvard University Press, 1939).

shows that the ordering of people according to head size yields an entirely plausible ordering according to vocational status. It is not at all clear how the impression has been spread that there is no such correlation.

The age-relationship of brain growth has been surprisingly rarely studied; I have found only three collections of autopsy data giving average brain weight of humans over the entire period from birth to brain maturity around age eighteen years. The only reason for taking seriously so few studies is that they give the same results. Otherwise the variations I interpret as brain growth spurts would have to be ascribed to statistical fluctuations found in all data.

Analysis of the data into biennial increments shows that brain growth has two components.[14] The first shows the increase in brain weight associated with the increase in body weight. The second component appears in the form of spurts of 5 to 10 percent in brain weight during the periods from two to four, six to eight, ten to twelve, and fourteen to sixteen years, the latter two spurts being slightly earlier for girls and slightly later for boys. The same spurt periods are found by examining the brain/body weight ratios so we know that the spurts are not just expressions of spurts in body growth in general. More recent data from biochemical studies show that there is also a brain growth spurt during the first year of life, roughly between ages three and ten months.[15]

Additional information can be obtained by making use of studies showing that human brain weight is proportional to the cube of the head circumference from birth through brain maturity.[16] Thus, we may use head circumference data to supplement those from brain weight. There are many published studies (including longitudinal ones) of head circumference and they yield the same

14. Herman T. Epstein, "Phrenoblysis: Special Brain and Mind Growth Periods: I. Human Brain and Skull Development," *Developmental Psychobiology* 7 (1974): 207-16.

15. Dobbing and Sands, "Quantitative Growth and Development of Human Brain."

16. Myron Winick and Pedro Rosso, "Head Circumference and Cellular Growth of the Brain in Normal and Marasmic Children," *Journal of Pediatrics* 74 (1969): 774-78; Herman T. Epstein and Erika B. Epstein, *American Journal of Physical Anthropology*, in press.

pattern and ages of growth spurts as found for brain weight.[17] Nellhaus has recently completed preparation of head circumference charts for pediatricians, based on data from a dozen countries.[18] Analysis of his data yields the same pattern of spurts (figure 1) at

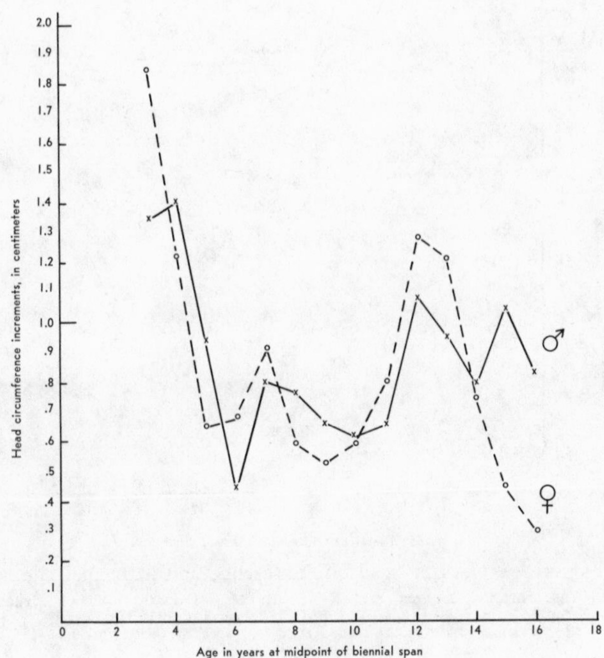

FIG. 1. Head circumference increments
SOURCE: Personal Communication from Gerhard Nellhaus, 1975.

the same ages as found for brain weights. His data include so many thousands of children at each age that the standard errors are smaller than the symbols used to plot the curves in that figure.

The growth of brain weight and head circumference both show a marked difference between the sexes after age ten years. This is clearly evident in the upper graph of figure 2 taken from a longitudinal study of head circumference.[19] Girls' head growth between

17. Epstein, "Phrenoblysis."

18. Gerhard Nellhaus, personal communication.

19. Dorothy Eichorn and Nancy Bayley, "Growth in Head Circumference from Birth through Young Adulthood," *Child Development* 33 (1962): 257-71.

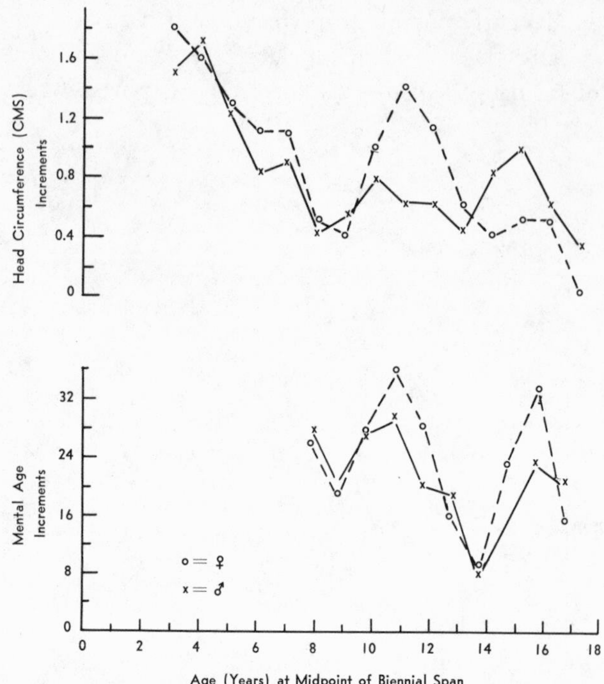

FIG. 2. Increases in head circumference and in mental age

SOURCE: Top, Dorothy Eichorn and Nancy Bayley, "Growth in Head Circumference from Birth through Young Adulthood," *Child Development* 33 (1962): 257-71; bottom, Frank K. Shuttleworth, *The Physical and Mental Growth of Girls and Boys, Age Six to Nineteen, in Relation to Age at Maximum Growth, Monographs of the Society for Research in Child Development* 4, no. 3 (1939): 1-291.

ages ten and twelve years is about twice that of boys, while the situation is reversed for the growth spurt centered around age fifteen years.

The biochemical natures of the various spurts are known only in rather general terms, but one important inference emerges from those data. Cell replication ceases by about age one and a half years.[20] Therefore, increases in brain weight after that age must reflect changes within the cells themselves—in protein, ribonucleic acid (RNA), lipids, and water. The water content was shown to decrease steadily after birth, so that weight increases must be due to the other three substances. These substances would increase as a result of growth of the cells represented in lengthening and/or

20. Dobbing and Sands, "Quantitative Growth and Development of Human Brain."

branching of axons and dendrites or in myelination (insulation) of axons. The latter event would increase the efficiency of signal transmission while the axonal and dendritic changes bespeak increased complexity of neural networks, which should then exhibit increased functional complexity and competence.

The use of brain weight as the defining parameter lets us detect all brain growth substantially exceeding that associated with increase in body weight. But, since it reflects *all* sources of weight increase, we do not know in what region or regions of the brain the growth has taken place nor anything about its anatomical or biochemical nature. And, we surely do not expect that the same localizations and events will be found in all the spurts. Thus, the detailed characterization of each of the spurts awaits the study of the neuroanatomical and neurophysiological correlates of the growth spurts.

Postnatal insults to human brain development mainly take the form of undernutrition and, possibly, environmental deprivation. The former is a well-known cause of decrease in both cell number and network complexity. The latter, which is generally branded in public as a significant source of the poor school performance of many disadvantaged children, is not yet known to affect brain, as distinguished from mind, but there has been no published account of any effort to study the possibility in humans. In rodents, the question is under study in a number of laboratories.

A clue to the role of experience in shaping neural networks (and, eventually, behavior and intelligence) comes from the work on vision in cats and monkeys, initiated mainly by Wiesel and Hubel.[21] In their first experiment, they sutured closed the eyes of newborn kittens. Closing one eye thusly for a month or more results in kittens with essentially no binocular vision, as verified by finding that, unlike the situation in normally raised kittens, no cells could be found in the visual regions of the brain that responded to light impinging on each eye separately. The response was only to light in the eye that had been left open. There are two competing explanations for this result. First, the loss of binocular vision could be due to lack of experience of binocular vision; that experience is

21. Torsten N. Wiesel and David H. Hubel, "Comparison of the Effects of Unilateral and Bilateral Eye Closure on Cortical Unit Responses in Kittens," *Journal of Neurophysiology* (London) 28 (1965): 1029-40.

thus assumed to be the cause of the binocular connections of the eyes to the visual regions of the brain. Second, the binocular connections could have already existed at birth but have been lost due to the lack of experience, which thereby fixes the connections.

The choice between the explanations was gained by the results of the experiment of sewing both eyes closed at birth for periods of up to age one year. In this experiment there could not have been any experience of binocular input. Yet, after removing the sutures, many cells were found to respond to both eyes. Therefore, the network must have existed in the newborn kitten. In the experiments with one eye closed, the connection from that eye to the cells must have been lost due to lack of binocular experience before some critical age.

A similar inference comes from recent studies of nerve-to-muscle connections in rodent fetuses, showing that connections present during fetal life are later lost due to later experience.[22] Thus, there is strong indication that the role of experience is to select from alternative network possibilities that exist before the experience begins.

By analogy, the role of intellectual experience or learning is to select among existing networks created by the genetic apparatus during brain development. If the complete spectrum of needed experience is not available to the organism, it loses forever the possibility of having those functions that are operated by the lost networks. It is possible that during later development another network may take on the lost function, but this is likely to be a secondary strategy of lower effectiveness. In this way, we can understand the role of experience in shaping the minds of men and the drastic consequences of lack of experience or of improper balances of early life events.

Mental Growth from Birth to Maturity

Given the existence of brain growth spurts, their meaning has to be sought in the special functions of the brain. We shall examine first the cognitive or intellectual functions.

A substantial amount of data already exists for what is defined

22. Jeremy Brockes, "Suppression of Foreign Synapses," *Nature* 260 (1976): 281.

as mental age, along with other studies of intelligent performance. All studies we have found that give mental age over a substantial span of ages yield spurts, and these spurts turn out to correlate well in ages with those found for the brain.[23] This may be seen in the results of the mainly longitudinal Harvard Growth Study, from which the biennial increments are given in the bottom half of figure 2.[24] At all ages at which there are data in both halves of that figure, it is seen that there is a good correspondence of spurt ages.

It is surprising that supporters of the Piagetian scheme had not previously examined the data on mental growth to see if there were manifestations of the appearance of the main Piagetian stages. But it is equally surprising that, despite their viewpoints as presented earlier, both Whitehead and Vygotsky did not engage in the testing of the possible implications of their periodization views for the developmental aspects of children's intelligence and school performances.

Probably the strongest test for any theory is the verification of a prediction of an unknown and significant fact. In our case, such a prediction is required by the fact that there is a brain growth spurt between ages fourteen and sixteen, which is after the last known Piagetian stage appears. If there is a hard connection between brain and mind growth spurts, we are forced to predict that a new Piagetian stage will someday be found, and that it will appear first around age fifteen years.

Arlin's recently published paper gives evidence for the existence of a new stage in the development of intelligence that she has found in female college students of ages nineteen to twenty-one years.[25] The new stage is called *problem finding*, to distinguish it from the problem-solving competency that is another way of labelling the

23. Herman T. Epstein, "Phrenoblysis: Special Brain and Mind Growth Periods: II. Human Mental Development," *Developmental Psychobiology* 7 (1974): 217-24.

24. Frank K. Shuttleworth, *The Physical and Mental Growth of Girls and Boys, Age Six to Nineteen, in Relation to Age at Maximum Growth*, *Monographs of the Society for Research in Child Development* 4, no. 3 (1939): 1-291.

25. Arlin, "Cognitive Development in Adulthood."

earlier fourth stage; other descriptive terms could be inductive reasoning, creative thought, or divergent thinking.

Since the publication of that paper, Arlin has completed work on grade school children to verify that the new stage does not appear at any age through thirteen years.[26] At the other end of the age spectrum children in grades ten and eleven (ages sixteen and seventeen) manifest stage five to about the same extent as the college students, and both sexes have been shown to display stage five. Thus, there is presently good reason to assume that this new stage is congruent in age of appearance with the fifth and last postnatal spurt in human brain growth. The prediction may already have been verified.

A major problem with the study of stages in the development of intelligence is that their universality is not yet proven. Dasen has summarized the data on cross-cultural studies of the Piagetian stages, noting that there are many societies in which many or even most adults do not attain even the third stage (age seven years).[27] It may be that the Piagetian scheme is not universal. Or, the failure may be due to various forms and extents of environmental deprivation. All that we know at present is that those who display the various Piagetian stages first show them at the given ages, so that this normal pattern of stages in the development of intelligence parallels very well the pattern of appearance of the brain growth stages.

The finding of a correlation between brain and mind growth spurts as a normally occurring pattern led to the creation of a new word to prevent confusion with the notion of a critical period that is usually discovered by finding some abnormal functioning caused by earlier deficits. We have chosen the name *phrenoblysis* (derived from the Greek meaning a welling-up or spurting of mind and/or skull) to signify these correlated brain and mind growth spurts. Phrenoblysis does not refer to the separate brain and mind spurts.

Perturbations of Brain and Mind Development

Is there any evidence that interference with brain growth is connected in any way with lowered intellectual competence? The

26. Patricia Arlin, personal communication.

27. Dasen, "Cross-cultural Piagetian Research."

first work on this subject with humans called attention to the effects of marasmus (general food deprivation resulting in lowered protein and calorie intake).[28] The report showed about a 25-point lowering of IQ in the roughly four-year-old children along with a smaller head circumference than both their siblings, the control children, and the general local population. The very low socioeconomic status of these children prevented a clean statement that lowered IQ was a consequence of the effect of nutritional deficit on brain growth and resultant IQ. These workers have continued to follow these same children who, since the time of their hospitalization from marasmus, have been on adequate diets. When tested recently at an average age of about seventeen and a half years, the children had come closer (but not yet equal) to the control group in body parameters.[29] The IQ deficit remained about 25 points, as it had been some thirteen years earlier. As the authors noted, however, the biggest surprise was the fact that head size showed not only no catch-up but it did not even keep pace. There was a larger difference between experimental and control children! To be specific, the head circumference difference increased about 20 percent while body weight difference decreased about 30 percent and, as mentioned above, the IQ difference was an unchanged 25 points.

The conclusion is that there is no catch-up in intellectual level and that the building of an adolescent brain on top of an architecturally abnormal brain yields an even greater abnormality than that existing at the time of the end of the marasmic condition. It is hard to escape the conviction that brain abnormality is linked causally to the intellectual deficits, although clean proof is still lacking and, because the subjects are humans, is likely never to be achieved. The direct evidence on this point will come from animal studies, but until such work is done with the higher primates, it will not be possible to show at all convincingly any deficit in intellectual performance that is similar to human kinds of intelligence.

From the point of view of phrenoblysis, it will be important

28. M. B. Stoch and P. M. Smythe, "Does Undernutrition during Infancy Inhibit Brain Growth and Subsequent Intellectual Development?" *Archives of Disease in Childhood* 38 (1963): 546-52.

29. M. B. Stoch and P. M. Smythe, "Fifteen-year Developmental Study on Effects of Severe Undernutrition during Infancy on Subsequent Physical Growth and Intellectual Functioning," *Archives of Disease in Childhood* 51 (1976): 327-36.

to look into two aspects of these human studies. First, head size deficit will have to be studied as a function of the age of the children at which the deprivation first starts. It is not unlikely that such data exist and can be obtained by a survey of populations in any of several countries. Second, it will be important to follow the head circumferences of marasmic children on a yearly, if not a half-yearly, basis to learn about the longitudinal development after an early deprivation.

There is a small amount of evidence supporting the idea that deprivations during later growth spurts can affect brain growth substantially even when the first years of life are without trouble. Baertl et al. have supplemented nourishment of newborn children from families that had already produced marasmic children, the supplement continuing until an average age of nearly eighteen months. At that age statistics for these children showed generally normal development. The children were then released to total care of their families, and within a half-year their measurements had dropped to about the substandard environmental norms through a total cessation of growth in height and in head circumference, plus a loss of nearly 1 kg. in body weight.[30]

Implications of Phrenoblysis

LEARNING CAPACITY

Mental age may be expressed as a compound of the child's inherent learning capacity and the richness of his life experience. By this expression, mental age measurements do not permit us to estimate learning capacity by itself. Of the few studies that purport to get at the learning capacity directly, the following is the best executed.

The work of Cattell and his associates has resulted in a separation of the general intelligence factor, g, into two components: g_c and g_f. The former is called the crystallized intelligence factor and can be roughly related to mental age since it purports to give an estimate of the developed intelligence at the time of measurement. The latter,

30. Juan Baertl, Blanca Adrianzen, and George G. Graham, "Growth of Previously Well-nourished Infants in Poor Homes," *American Journal of Diseases of Children* 130 (1976): 33-36.

the fluid intelligence factor, is an estimate of the child's ability to develop new intellectual competencies—his creative intelligence at the age of measurement; the value varies between 0 and 1.

Estimates of these two components have been given in a recent review.[31] The value of g_f in verbal, numerical, and reasoning capacities has a peak near age eleven years, thus correlating with the brain growth spurt at that age. Age thirteen and a half years, however, is certainly a low point, because the g_f values in all three capacities are very close to zero. Thus, there would appear to be little or no store of creative intelligence around ages twelve to fourteen years, in good agreement with the brain growth plateau found at that period.

INTERVENTION PROGRAMS: THE JENSEN CONTROVERSY

I shall show below that the massive failure of Head Start Programs to achieve their goals in cognitive development of disadvantaged children was not due to genetic factors, as suspected by Jensen,[32] but rather to an age-linked development factor unsuspected by both Jensen and the defenders of Head Start Programs. Black children turn out to be not especially, if at all, different from whites in intellectual capacities. But, it is instructive to give an analytical account of the way the controversy developed.

Virtually all the data on remedial programs come from Head Start programs that occurred and occur in the thousands, probably in the tens of thousands. Virtually all of these programs were set in the age bracket of about three and a half to five and a half years. Jensen pointed out the massive failure of these programs in the cognitive growth aspects of their work, using as data the results of the half dozen official evaluations of such programs. The number of programs said to be definitely successful was variously given as between ten and thirty out of the many thousands that existed.

The typical results of these Head Start programs were a rise in IQ of from ten to fifteen points during the first year or so, fol-

31. Raymond B. Cattell, "The Structure of Intelligence in Relation to the Nature-Nurture Controversy," in *Intelligence*, ed. Robert Cancro (New York: Grune and Stratton, 1971).

32. Arthur R. Jensen, "How Much Can We Boost IQ and Scholastic Achievement?" *Harvard Educational Review* 39 (1969): 1-123.

lowed by a steady decay so that by the second grade there was no difference between the experimental and control children.

The brilliant analysis by Jensen was followed by a collection of so-called refutations which did little credit to the subject or to the profession. In essence, these refutations amounted to saying that Jensen might have had one or another source of error in one or more portions of his analysis; it was not shown that, in fact, the postulated source of error actually existed in the data or in the analysis. Indeed, in later writings, Jensen took up these criticisms and showed, in a way convincing to this writer, that the proferred sources of error did not in fact occur.

As an example, take the question of culture-fair IQ tests. Jensen pointed out that revision of some of the obviously unfair items did *not*, in fact, alter the results *on those very items* for which black children were presumed to be penalized. Thus, this potentially explanatory criticism does not apply to the situation.

It is correct to say that Jensen was wrong, but such a statement does wrong to Jensen because of the context of controversy surrounding his work. His argument was that if no experiential (environmental) changes helped the black children to attain white norms, then we should entertain the interpretation that blacks are genetically different from whites and, in IQ terms, inferior. The only writer I have found who seems to have looked carefully at the real thrust of the argument is Hunt, who had already pointed out in 1961 the possibility of developmental features that could be deterministic in child development.[33]

Jensen's error was in supposing that the only alternative interpretation that remained was that of genetic difference. In fact, as Hunt had already pointed out, there may be a developmental program that was somehow being bypassed. In other words, Jensen did not realize (any more than did his detractors) that there could have been an unlikely accidental choice of exactly the wrong ages for the intervention. From the point of view of phrenoblysis, the four-to-six year age period is one of minimal brain and mind growth, so that Head Start programs at this age should fall short of their cognitive goals for *biological* reasons. Further, phrenoblysis leads

33. J. McVicker Hunt, *Intelligence and Experience* (New York: Ronald Press, 1961); idem, "Reflections on a Decade of Early Education," *Journal of Abnormal Child Psychology* 3 (1975): 275-336.

to the prediction that both earlier and later programs (for children aged two to four and six to eight years) should have much greater likelihood of success. The facts below support this prediction.

The Milwaukee Project worked with black children who were taken in to the project before the age of six months.[34] The children were brought to a day-care setting under the supervision of middle-class black women for about eight hours per day. The twenty-five matched control children exhibited the steadily deteriorating IQs and failing school performances characteristic of most of the sub-population from which the experimental and control children were drawn. The twenty-five experimental children registered IQ gains from the very first test, and their presently estimated average IQs of about 115 are a match to the expected values based on school performance of these children who have completed fourth grade. Hunt gives a detailed analysis.[35]

The Mother-Child Home Program,[36] also analyzed by Hunt,[37] has now spread to at least a half dozen cities. It takes two-year-old children and produces normal IQ children who have remained at that level to the fourth grade. In this project the IQ increase is only about 17 points over the control children compared with the roughly 30-point effect in the Milwaukee Project. But, the Mother-Child Home Program interacts with each family only about one hour per week compared with about eight hours per day, five days per week in the Milwaukee Project.

The Robinsons' project in North Carolina also started with two-year-old children in a day-care setting and produced IQ gains about the same as those obtained in Milwaukee by age four years, which was the termination point of this study.[38]

34. Howard Garber and Rick Heber, "The Milwaukee Project: Early Intervention as a Technique to Prevent Mental Retardation" (Storrs, Conn.: University of Connecticut National Leadership Institute, Teacher Education/Early Education, 1973).

35. Hunt, "Reflections on a Decade of Early Education."

36. Phyllis Levenstein, "The Mother-Child Home Program," in *The Preschool in Action: Exploring Early Childhood Programs*, ed. Ronald K. Parker (Boston: Allyn and Bacon, 1972).

37. Hunt, "Reflections on a Decade of Early Education."

38. Halbert B. Robinson and Nancy M. Robinson, "Longitudinal Development of Very Young Children in a Comprehensive Day Care Program: The First Two Years," *Child Development* 42 (1971): 1673-83.

Thus, all three projects have produced seemingly permanent increased intellectual functioning of children from disadvantaged homes provided the intervention started by age two years and lasted at least through age four years. Hunt reported the existence of several additional programs that cover much of this age period and seem to have been similarly highly effective.[39]

The upshot of all the work discussed in this section is that the Jensen inference was not logically compelling because he did not take into account the possibility of age-linked child development stages of mental growth. In addition, there appears to be at least some support for the predictions of the phrenoblysis approach for the ages of greater and lesser effectiveness of intervention programs.

It should be stressed that phrenoblysis could also predict limited novel intellectual growth at the other brain growth plateau periods: eight to ten and twelve to fourteen years. The data for such periods are scanty, so that no analysis will be attempted. It is worth pointing out, however, that those who believe that junior high school students are not at ages of great intellectual growth can find compelling support in the fact that there is very little brain growth at that period.

GOALS OF SCHOOLING

The most obvious working hypothesis for schooling that can be drawn from the existence of phrenoblysis is that intensive intellectual input should be situated at the spurt ages. To this end we have given samples of the evidence that learning capacity and the success and failure of intervention programs are tied directly to the periods of the brain growth spurts.

The general idea is not a new one. We have quoted Whitehead and Vygotsky as among the early proponents of such an idea. More recently, this idea has been broached by the Piagetians who point out that their stages of intelligence development cry out for applications to schooling. The most direct of these proponents is Hans Furth, who has not only written a book entitled *Piaget For Teachers*,[40] but also, in collaboration with Harry Wachs, has run a Piage-

39. Hunt, "Reflections on a Decade of Early Education."

40. Hans Furth, *Piaget for Teachers* (Englewood Cliffs, N.J.: Prentice Hall, 1970).

tian type of program in a grade school in West Virginia, as described in their book *Thinking Goes to School.*[41] Furth and Wachs have tried to use Piagetian characterization of the development of intelligence in children to deduce what kinds of school activities will spur the child's development of his thinking capacity. The idea is that if he develops his capacities at the indicated normal ages, he will be able to utilize those developed capacities to acquire more readily and more deeply the informational content of school curricula.

An article by Kohlberg and Mayer may be cited as one more example.[42] Kohlberg is also a Piagetian, presumably because his own work showing the appearance of novel moral outlooks can be tied to the Piagetian stages. Kohlberg and Mayer argue that the benchmarks of development are the simultaneous appearance of cognitive and moral stages, whose fostering should be a minimal goal of both home and school activities. (This broadening of the stage idea to include both cognition and morality raises the question of whether still other aspects of child development might appear in correlation with those first two aspects. I am presently assembling the extant data on emotional or psychological development to determine if there are detectable stages and, if so, whether they appear to be correlated age-wise with the others).

From the point of view of phrenoblysis, the picture of development is even more supportive of such hypotheses because the occurrence of periods of little or no brain and mind growth raises the possibility that attempts to inject novel intellectual competencies not only will fail if tried at certain age periods, but that such attempts may be counterproductive. Children exposed to intellectual pressures and inputs for which they have no proper receptive circuitry may learn to reject such inputs; such a rejection might even result in an inability to take in such inputs later when the circuitry has developed.

On a subjective level, many school officials and teachers have talked about their pupils as "turning off" at certain ages, most

41. Hans Furth and Harry Wachs, *Thinking Goes to School: Piaget's Theory in Practice* (New York: Oxford University Press, 1974).

42. Lawrence Kohlberg and Rochelle Mayer, "Development as the Aim of Education," *Harvard Educational Review* 42 (1972): 449-96.

notably on entering high school. Teachers have described the bright youngsters entering junior high school as manifesting little interest in new intellectual challenges for a time and then, when entering senior high school, appearing to have lost interest in any and all learning challenges.

This matching of inputs and receptor circuitry is probably related to the well-known pedagogical concept of *readiness*, which is, parenthetically, an expression of the only accepted indication of the existence of stagewise intellectual growth to have penetrated the school systems.

From an experimental point of view, however, the concept of "turn-off" would be impossible to study, for there is no way to know what any individual would have done if he had been raised and educated in a different way. We will, however, later show a way of evaluating whether *groups* of children may be helped to reach higher stages of development by various intervention devices or by new schooling strategies. It should also be stressed at this point that there are more usual explanations of the turn-off in terms of puberty and its associated psychological correlates. Before invoking the psychological level of explanation it is wiser, in my judgment, to explore first the biological level of explanation, and in this instance the aspect of biology (brain growth) that is more directly related to the function involved—mental function.

The proposal to give new intellectual challenges to children during brain growth spurts leaves unanswered the question of what to do during the plateau periods. I offer the following as my own best guess. The child should be exposed to large amounts of information and to a wide variety of direct experiences with nature, science, people, and work, all from the point of view of enlarging his direct experience base and avoiding much pressure for elaborate inferences about the natures and interrelationships of such experiences. Furthermore, these would be periods for perfecting the long neglected memorization skills involved in the learning of poetry and songs, of the important facts of history, the facts of geography of the nation and of the whole earth, of health science facts, of legal facts, of citizenship facts, and so forth. During such periods we could also help children increase their skills in already initiated competencies. The details of many such activities should not be difficult to discover because the Piagetian studies give the competencies at many substages of the main stages, and the ages for particular activities can then be fairly well estimated.

From the point of view of experimentation, one could argue that the fact of phrenoblysis could logically lead to a very different hypothesis about what to do during slow-growth periods. This alternative viewpoint is that precisely because the children are in a slow-growth period, the input should be intensified. For example, children should be given intensive tutoring so as to maximize their learning at the slow-growth ages. All such inferences from phrenoblysis are in the nature of working hypotheses, so that it would be desirable to run such an intensive tutoring trial in parallel with the direct experience experiment in order to learn which paradigm best accords with nature's designs.

EVALUATION

The ways of characterizing intelligent people are many. Of these, the one that has always intrigued me most is the statement ascribed to a British nobleman to the effect that the mark of an intelligent person is that he knows what to do in the situation where he does not know what to do. This means, of course, that he can see what additional information will help him arrive at the position of being able to make a decision.

This way of thinking is also contained in the essence of a proposal made informally by the late Leo Szilard, who suggested that the intelligence quotient be replaced by the development of a stupidity quotient. Szilard argued that schooling and life experience can produce people who know what to do in certain situations not very different from those about which they have received instruction, but that we really want to know what they will do in novel situations. This can only be done by placing them in novel situations and seeing what they do, especially seeing which children or adults behave stupidly. Such people may be said to have acquired rote learning but no real thinking capacities.

Development of thinking capacities is equivalent to manifestation of the Piagetian stages. The achievement of the normal pattern of stages in the development of intelligence in children and their maturation at an adequate rate would be a goal substantially different from those normally pursued in our schools today. In addition, the extent to which the achievement is reached would constitute the proper means of evaluating any particular schooling paradigm.

To this end, then, I propose an evaluation scheme based on (a) the existence of stages in development of intelligence, and (b) the fact that few apparently normal adults manifest stage 5 intelligence, most do not manifest stage 4, and many do not even manifest stage 3. Presumably, disadvantaged children will grow up to be adults with even lower-than-average achievement of these stages. Only at this time could this evaluation scheme be set forth because its realization depends on the recent expansion of its Piagetian base through the work of Webb, Brown, and Arlin.

The idea is that the results of any educational experiment or strategy concluding at some given age will be measured in terms of the fraction of experimental children displaying the *next* Piagetian stage at its normal age. If this fraction is increased over that of the control children, the experiment will be considered successful. For example, an intervention program with children ages seven to nine years will be evaluated in terms of the fraction of such children who reach the next stage (stage 4, the age eleven-year stage of formal operations) at about age eleven years. As mentioned earlier, in the United States the percentage of adults displaying stage 4 is about 30 percent. The intervention program will be considered successful if the percentage reaches above 30 percent or whatever figure obtains for control children.

This part of the evaluation scheme could have been used even before the recent studies mentioned above. Now we can use Webb's result that maturation of new Piagetian competencies follows a time course inversely related to IQ. For children with normal IQs the maturation rate is typically a year or so at each stage. Thus, we should not only determine the age of onset of the next Piagetian stage but we should also study the children at, say, a year after the onset to see how much maturation of that stage has taken place. One can imagine that an intervention program or some changed curriculum could bring about the onset at the normal age but might not have laid the basis for its normal maturation. This stagewise evaluation can be used for all ages through the end of typical schooling around age eighteen because the work of Arlin has now given us the additional data needed to cover intelligence development up through that age. And, it is worth suggesting that along with the altered schooling should go a program of head circumference measurements designed to check the correlations inherent in the concept of phrenoblysis.

In general, the idea is that education, better called schooling, should be aimed at helping children arrive at biological and mental check points with the proper biological and mental equipment to enter the next stage and to accomplish that stage at a suitable rate. This gives an internal rhythm to schooling strategies. Once a stage has been reached, the new competencies should be extensively utilized to acquire the new and detailed understandings of many processes and subjects that have become accessible to the newly upstaged mind.

Two Further Comments

SEXUAL DIMORPHISM

It was pointed out above that the brain growth spurt of girls at age eleven years is about twice that of boys, while something like the converse is true of the brain growth spurt that occurs around age fifteen years. If we connect brain growth with mental growth, the question arises about the implications of a quantitative difference in brain growth during a spurt period. In this instance of a quantitative difference, it might be possible to discover the implications because it accompanies a sexual dimorphism so that the two classes of individuals are readily distinguished.

A simple hypothesis would be that girls need a very different, and more challenging, curriculum from that of boys at both ages, the input being far more intense and complex for girls around age eleven, and correspondingly less intense and complex around age fifteen. One can imagine that curricula developed mainly for boys could be inadequate or even harmful for girls at age eleven. Indeed, the failure to adapt educational inputs at this age to the far greater capacities of girls might be responsible for the relative lack of females in the more theoretical or abstract professions. Presumably, moreover, the inadequate program for age eleven girls would later make the girls' smaller development at fifteen even less effective.

This line of thought can be related to the famous proposition enunciated by Bruner stating that "the foundations of any subject may be taught to anybody at any age in some form."[43] Our failure to recognize the higher-level form accessible to girls around age eleven may deprive them of the needed background on which to build their subsequent intellectual growth.

A second hypothesis would be that the more substantial later brain and mind growth of boys is responsible for the differential competencies and that there is no way to make up for the relative brain growth deficit of girls at the later (and intellectually more important) age at which Arlin has shown that creative thinking emerges.

Some indications of the ramifications of the brain dimorphism might be gained from determining the fractions of males and females that show Piagetian stages 4 and 5 at their normal onset ages. A significant difference at either of these ages would signal the need for experimentation to try to discover ways of bringing the lower-ranking sex up to the fraction of the other sex showing the stage. Or, if the fractions parallel the brain dimorphism, it would give support to the inference that the sexes should be separately educated after age ten years in order to maximize each child's development of his native intellectual competence. The number of experiments that can readily be imagined is so great that there is no need to try to list them. What is needed is careful planning to do just those experiments whose results will give guidance to the later research on the functional implications of sexually dimorphic brain growth spurts.

SENSORY PROGRAMMING

If there is a stagewise character to development, perturbations are likely to be more damaging if they occur at ages of rapid development. Dobbing has already pointed out this likelihood as the basis of the extremely severe effects on *body growth* if humans or animals are undernourished during times of rapid *brain growth*; the

43. Jerome Bruner, *The Process of Education* (New York: Vintage Books, 1960).

greater effect on brain growth itself is self-evident.[44] We shall use this insight to guide our brief presentation of the appearance of sensory development in humans. Our purpose is to see if there is any reason to associate appearance of new sensory functioning with any ages or stages. The data available are for hearing/talking, language learning, and binocular vision. At birth, children do not talk or understand language; their vision is so rudimentary that it is clear that perception develops postnatally although the child can readily be shown to detect light at birth.

Few children manifest any great amount of language competence before the end of the first year of life. Therefore, if programming of the brain for language is to be shown to correlate with any brain growth spurt, the programming would have to occur during the two to four year period. The data assembled by Lenneberg give the consequences for language production of injuries to or tumors in the left hemisphere of the brain.[45] His data show that if a child suffers one of these two insults before about age twenty months, his eventual production of language is not measurably delayed or abnormal. If the insult occurs between that time and about four years of age, the child loses whatever language he had acquired, reverts to babbling, and learns language all over again. If the insult occurs after age four years, the child does not lose language and recovers whatever is consonant with the extent of the injury. Thus, we may infer that active programming of the left hemisphere for language has its onset at about age twenty months and lasts until age four years. The period is clearly similar to the two to four year period discovered from brain and cognition data.

The data for hearing/speaking refer to the problem of teaching the virtually deaf to use language. The data of interest were obtained by Wedenberg in Sweden.[46] He developed an auditory training method for handling profoundly deaf children. His success may be measured by the fraction of normal speaking vocabulary

44. Dobbing and Sands, "Quantitative Growth and Development of Human Brain."

45. Eric Lenneberg, *Biological Foundations of Language* (New York: John Wiley and Sons, 1967).

46. Erik Wedenberg, "Auditory Training of Severely Hard-of-Hearing Preschool Children," *Acta Oto-Laryngologica*, Suppl. 110 (1954).

possessed by these children at about age nine years, at which age most of the testing was done. If the auditory training was begun at any age up to two years, the children reached maximum success, which is typically 80 percent. If the training began after that age, there was a precipitous drop in success, so that by age three and a quarter years the success was down to 40 to 50 percent and reached a basal level of about 5 percent by about age four years. Thus, auditory training is effective only during the period of spurt in brain growth between ages two and four.

Recently Banks, Aslin, and Letson published the first collection of data on the age-dependence of the effectiveness of surgery in producing binocular vision in children suffering from strabismus.[47] They found that if the strabismus began at any age from birth to about two years, surgery by age two years restored about 75 percent of normal binocular vision. Surgery after age four years was useless for other than cosmetic purposes. On the other hand, if the strabismus began after age five years (there were no data between three and five years), surgery at any later age was 100 percent successful.

All these studies lead to the same conclusion: when the human brain is being programmed for the mental growth spurt correlated with the spurt in brain growth between ages two and four it is simultaneously being programmed for vision, language, and hearing/speaking. Those workers trying to help very young children to overcome physical handicaps impinging on their learning capacities should be aware of the much greater positive prognosis if their efforts are concentrated during the spurt period. It would be very interesting to know the results of similar remedial efforts during later spurt and plateau periods.

47. Martin S. Banks, Richard N. Aslin, and Robert D. Letson, "Sensitive Period for the Development of Human Binocular Vision," *Science* 190 (1975): 675-77.

Part Five

CHAPTER XI

The Implications for Education

JEANNE S. CHALL AND ALLAN F. MIRSKY

In this concluding chapter we shall identify and comment briefly upon those themes that seem to emerge with great force from the information, the empirical findings, the provocative hypotheses and theories, and the implications contained in the preceding chapters. We shall be especially concerned with the themes that have particularly strong implications for education.

One of the strongest themes relates to the central role of environmental stimulation and experience in the growth and development of the brain—animal and human—and in overcoming the effects of inherited deficiencies or acquired injuries. In essence, the neuroscientists writing in this volume are saying to educators that education is central for optimal brain development. Indeed, the more recent the findings, the stronger the evidence for the importance of education appears to be. Recent discoveries, however, also point to the importance of physical aspects of the brain for the functioning of the psychological processes central to learning, such as attention, cognition, motivation, and language. And some progress has been made with pharmaceutical means for effecting behavioral and cognitive changes. Yet, overall, the authors of this volume seem to place a greater stress on education.

From Teyler's introductory chapter noting that stimulation and experience change the brain to Epstein's chapter stressing the importance of education during spurts in brain growth, we are informed about the importance of the environment in the development of the brain. The neuroscientists have presented evidence here that environmental stimulation helps the "healthy" brain develop to its optimal condition.

The emphasis on education may strike many readers as ironic, for brain injury or neurological impairment or dysfunction have been most feared for their effects on learning. Learning difficulties or behavioral problems that may stem from neurological defects, differences, or deficiencies are usually regarded fatalistically, with the expectation that little or nothing can be done about them. Yet over and over again the evidence indicates that practice and stimulation at the right time will foster learning, particularly among those with brain injuries or dysfunctions. The neuropsychologists and neurophysiologists, including clinical neurologists and clinical neuropsychologists, are saying that hope, not fatalism, is appropriate.

Denckla's chapter on "Minimal Brain Dysfunction" provides example after example of the potentially constructive influence of home and school for the education and development of children diagnosed as having learning difficulties, hyperactivity, or behavior disorders—subclassifications of some of the possible minimal brain dysfunctions. Armed with somewhat different evidence from a different body of research, Rudel demonstrates that the young child's brain is highly plastic, and that portions of the brain injured when the child is young may lose some of their full functioning, but that over time, with proper stimulation, the functions may reappear, although often at the cost of sometimes subtle disruptions of other processes. Rudel's chapter, based on laboratory research with animals as well as with children, seems to have a lesson for teachers that has long been known to them, yet somewhat forgotten in recent years. The generalization is that, even if immediate success is not evident, it is helpful for the learner to continue to practice.

For educators who fear that physical brain dysfunctions or defects are permanent and irreversible, the evidence presented in this volume is reassuring. At appropriate times, the research indicates, stimulation will produce a change for the better. Because of this strong relationship between the brain and the stimulation it is given, many of the authors state directly that collaboration of educators and brain scientists in research and in practice is essential.

For almost every brain difficulty reported in this volume, particularly in chapters 7 and 8, the solution proposed is training or retraining—practice under the supervision of a knowledgeable and sensitive teacher who gears instruction to the child's strengths and weaknesses. When drugs are mentioned, they are placed in a broader context of environmental stimulation and learning. Without suitable education through some behavior control at home and school, drugs will not work for long, according to Denckla.

A second theme running through the volume is the importance of timing. MacLean notes that the development of the emotion of empathy, for example, must start early because the regions of the brain responsible for these processes develop early. And to an even greater extent, Epstein's theory of brain growth spurts is concerned with "proper timing." More effective cognitive development can be achieved, he claims, if proper timing is observed.

Generally, the earlier years are emphasized with the implication that as far as stimulation is concerned, "the earlier, the better." However, "later" does not seem to mean that all is lost. Thus, according to Rudel, the injuries suffered early seem to bring on less of a loss of functioning, and with time, there may be a regaining of all but the most subtle processes. There is seldom a permanent loss of language in children as great as the loss that occurs in adults, although there may be some subtle differences in later child language. But even among adults, there can be some recovery of function with proper stimulation and retraining.

A third theme is that certain kinds of training are more effective than others. This raises the problem of the interaction between aptitude and instruction. Will instructional methods that match the aptitudes of the learner be more effective than methods that do not match those aptitudes? Wittrock implies that such matching, based on research from the neurosciences, seems to lie ahead. Thus, it may be possible in the foreseeable future to match some instructional methods most useful to the left-brained and others to the right-brained and still others to differentially organized brain typologies.

A fourth theme running through the volume is the importance of cerebral lateralization for the development of human cognition and for understanding differences in learning style. Almost every chapter touches on this theme. Its implications are currently among the most popular topics in the neurosciences and are also among the most common concerns expressed in this volume. The implications of cerebral lateralization have a central position in the chapter by Kinsbourne and Hiscock. According to Wittrock these implications offer exciting hypotheses for education regarding different cognitive strengths and weaknesses in individuals by sex, by social class, and by cultural background.

The implications for education of recent research on brain lateralization are in all probability quite substantial. Yet the exact applications in educational practice are far from clear. No simple inferences for what and how schools should teach the various curriculum areas can be drawn from the knowledge that the left hemisphere specializes more in analytic and/or sequential processing, such as language, while the right tends to specialize in parallel processing, more characteristic of spatial learning. What does this mean for how and when to teach reading and writing, for example? What does it mean for students who have difficulties in these areas? And what does it mean for those with strengths in the right hemisphere rather than in the left?

It appears that in the general literature on lateralization and learning two kinds of inferences for education are being drawn. First, there are suggestions to strengthen the "weak" left-hemisphere processes by using more the intact right hemisphere for learning of left-hemisphere processes. Thus, Wittrock reports on various experiments to improve reading comprehension with students who have difficulty understanding reading passages. Reading comprehension improves by teaching students to visualize and use imagery, which presumably are right-hemisphere capabilities.

A second recommendation is that students who are weak in academic skills (based heavily on the left hemisphere) be taught music, construction, and other activities involving right-brain processing in order to provide these right-brained children with some activities in which they can excel. It is not enough, these proponents say, to provide these children with remedial training in reading and other subjects that require left-hemisphere processing. Their weakness will expose them to constant frustration and failure. They need "right-brained" activities to give them a sense of success and self-worth.

A more extreme form of this position is taken by those who call for drastic curricular changes so that the academic curriculum would be based less on left-hemisphere processing, which favors the high achiever from high socio-economic backgrounds, and balanced more toward right-brained processing so as to give a greater opportunity to low achievers and to those children from low socio-economic backgrounds. (In this connection, see Bob Samples, "Mind Cycles and Learning," *Phi Delta Kappan 58* [May, 1977]: 688-92).

What would these recommendations mean for schools? They would seem to deserve serious study and controlled tryout. The extreme forms of the solution that stresses teaching to the strengths—the right hemisphere—seem to call for a considerable amount of caution and considered analysis. It may conceivably be that a curriculum more favorable to the right-brained can bring about an even greater gap between the children of the affluent and the children of the poor. Since national surveys indicate that children of the less affluent tend to be the lower achievers, and other research tends to indicate that more of them are right-brained, it is conceivable that if schools concentrated on right-brained activities even lower achievement in literacy-related studies could result among the less affluent. Since reading and writing are needed for all school learning, it would seem essential for the individual and for society that all means be used to improve these skills, particularly the knowledge available from the neurosciences. Since the application of the neurosciences to education is still relatively new, it must therefore be approached with caution as well as with the excitement that comes from viewing old problems in a new light.

It is also important that we do not turn the slogan suggested by Denckla, "Remember the brain" into "Remember *only* the brain." In the enthusiastic applications of psychiatry and clinical psychology to learning problems about thirty years ago it was not uncommon to view most educational difficulties as stemming from psychological problems. We have learned much since then, but the same could happen to the applications of the neurosciences to education. It may even be happening now with the decrease in concern for psychological problems, while there is an increase in concern for neurological factors. Thus, while in the 1940s and 1950s reading and learning disabilities tended to be viewed as psychological problems, today they tend to be viewed as neurological.

The greatest danger of all is that what has been learned about teaching and learning from educational research and practice may be abandoned in the rush to study the effects of various neurological factors, particularly the condition of being left- or right-brained. Some pupils may not learn to read and write well, not because they are right-brained rather than left-brained, but because they may not have been taught well, or were not sufficiently motivated at home and/or school. It is hoped that the findings and insights from the neurosciences will be added to what we already know—not replace it.

Every chapter author acknowledges the great complexity of the brain and the theoretical disagreements that arise from this complexity. If this brings confusion and uncertainty to the different neuroscientists, it brings an even greater sense of insecurity to the nonspecialist. In the search for certainty, there may be a tendency to hold on to one simple theory. It is important for the nonspecialist to know that the various brain theories are being constantly refined and modified.

Because the brain is so complex and the theories are constantly being modified, labeling children and adults whose brains are thought to be different becomes a difficult task. The brain is constantly growing and changing, and teachers need to be apprised of the changes that may affect the ability of the pupil to respond to different kinds of learning. This view of the changing, plastic brain requires not only extra vigilance and care, but also brings with it greater opportunities. Although learning disability and dyslexia require special care, the prognosis is hopeful if proper instruction is provided.

It would appear from the neuroscientists writing in this volume that the next decade should bring a fruitful collaboration between neuroscientists and educators. This collaboration may be as fruitful ultimately as the long collaboration between educators and psychologists. Hopefully, the collaboration between the neurosciences and education will also include collaborators from speech and hearing, linguistics, anthropology, psychology, and other related areas.

To be fully beneficial to both groups, the collaboration must be a mutual one. Neurological hypotheses and theories will need to be tested and applied in classrooms and clinics. And knowledge from the classroom and from educational research will need to be fed back to the neuroscientists for the modification and refinement of their theories.

It is tempting to speculate on a possible future collaborative effort between educators and neuroscientists as we enter the twenty-first century. Conceivably, a new specialty of educational neuroscientist, or educational neuropsychologist could emerge and would combine both kinds of expertise. The discipline of neuropsychology itself is such a blend of interests and skills, and now includes a relatively new subspecialty of clinical neuropsychology. The new professional of whom we speak would be well versed in all of the latest pedagogical information concerning effective methods of teaching and modern developments in curriculum; in addition, this person would be trained in neuropsychological and neurophysiological knowledge and techniques. Each child in the school system needing special assistance would, according to this scheme, be tested by this new professional.

The test battery of the twenty-first century would be the responsibility of a team of specialists including the educational neuroscientist. It would encompass behavioral and photographic analyses designed to identify motor patterns, cerebral dominance and related psycho- and physiomotor capacities; it might also include electrographic and sensory tests that would provide data about the relative maturity and efficiency of processing information in all relevant sensory modalities. Attentional capacities would be assessed by both behavioral and electrophysiological means, and the sources of attentional difficulties (if any) categorized and identified with respect to intra- as opposed to extra-cerebral causes. Brain size, maturity, and relative degree of myelinization in key areas would be assessed by means of noninjurious neuroradiological techniques (the progeny of today's computerized axial tomography scanners). Oxygen utilization in various brain regions at rest and during a variety of mental activities would be assessed by means of dynamic energy utilization techniques. Such methods currently exist and need only to be refined further. Brain neurohumoral balance and maturity would be assessed by means of biochemical assays performed on a few drops of urine and blood. Computer-assisted analyses of these data would enable the educational neuroscientist to perform an accurate assessment of the child's developmental stage, his particular strengths and weaknesses, the instructional materials he would best be able to handle, and the problem areas that would most likely be encountered during his educational career. This information would be made available to the child's teacher or teachers, and would be continuously updated and upgraded at regular intervals.

This program would permit the early identification, forecasting and remediation of educational difficulties; but more than that, it should help in the development of a pedagogical effort and program designed on the basis of how *each* child is growing and maturing, on each child's talents and weaknesses, and not on the basis of an average, normative set of values that fits any single pupil in only a loose way.

As exciting as this utopian aid to education may be in the twenty-first century or a few years earlier, it must be realized that it cannot be applied in the absence of that most effective and essential of all educational forces—able, patient, and caring teachers.

Index

CONSTITUTION AND BY-LAWS OF THE NATIONAL SOCIETY FOR THE STUDY OF EDUCATION

(As adopted May, 1944, and amended June, 1945, February, 1949, September, 1962, February, 1968 and September, 1973)

Article I

NAME

The name of this corporation shall be "The National Society for the Study of Education," an Illinois corporation not for profit.

Article II

PURPOSES

Its purposes are to carry on the investigation of educational problems, to publish the results of same, and to promote their discussion.

The corporation also has such powers as are now, or may hereafter be, granted by the General Not For Profit Corporation Act of the State of Illinois.

Article III

OFFICES

The corporation shall have and continuously maintain in this state a registered office and a registered agent whose office is identical with such registered office, and may have other offices within or without the State of Illinois as the Board of Directors may from time to time determine.

Article IV

MEMBERSHIP

Section 1. *Classes.* There shall be two classes of members—active and honorary. The qualifications and rights of the members of such classes shall be as follows:

(*a*) Any person who is desirous of promoting the purposes of this corporation is eligible to active membership and shall become such on payment of dues as prescribed.

(*b*) Active members shall be entitled to vote, to participate in discussion, and, subject to the conditions set forth in Article V, to hold office.

(*c*) Honorary members shall be entitled to all the privileges of active members, with the exception of voting and holding office, and shall be exempt from the payment of dues. A person may be elected to honorary membership by vote of the active members of the corporation on nomination by the Board of Directors.

(*d*) Any active member of the Society may, at any time after reaching the age of sixty, become a life member on payment of the aggregate amount of the regular annual dues for the period of life expectancy, as determined by standard actuarial tables, such membership to entitle the member to receive all yearbooks and to enjoy all other privileges of active membership in the Society for the lifetime of the member.

Section 2. *Termination of Membership.*

(*a*) The Board of Directors by affirmative vote of two-thirds of the members of the Board may suspend or expel a member for cause after appropriate hearing.

(*b*) Termination of membership for nonpayment of dues shall become effective as provided in Article XIV.

Section 3. *Reinstatement.* The Board of Directors may by the affirmation vote of two-thirds of the members of the Board reinstate a former member whose membership was previously terminated for cause other than nonpayment of dues.

Section 4. *Transfer of Membership.* Membership in this corporation is not transferable or assignable.

Article V

BOARD OF DIRECTORS

Section 1. *General Powers.* The business and affairs of the corporation shall be managed by its Board of Directors. It shall appoint the Chairman and Vice-Chairman of the Board of Directors, the Secretary-Treasurer, and Members of the Council. It may appoint a member to fill any vacancy on the Board until such vacancy shall have been filled by election as provided in Section 3 of this Article.

Section 2. *Number, Tenure, and Qualifications.* The Board of Directors shall consist of seven members, namely, six to be elected by the members of the corporation, and the Secretary-Treasurer to be the seventh member. Only active members who have contributed to the yearbook shall be eligible for election to serve as directors. A member who has been elected for a full term of three years as director and has not attended at least two-thirds of the meetings duly called and held during that term shall not be eligible for election again before the fifth annual election after the expiration of the term for which he was first elected. No member who has been elected for two full terms as director in immediate succession shall be elected a director for a term next succeeding. This provision shall not apply to the Secretary-Treasurer who is appointed by the Board of Directors. Each director shall hold office for the term for which he is elected or appointed and until his successor shall have been selected and qualified. Directors need not be residents of Illinois.

Section 3. *Election.*

(*a*) The directors named in the Articles of Incorporation shall hold office until their successors shall have been duly selected and shall have qualified. Thereafter, two directors shall be elected annually to serve three years, beginning March first after their election. If, at the time of any annual election, a vacancy exists in the Board of Directors, a director shall be elected at such election to fill such vacancy.

(*b*) Elections of directors shall be held by ballots sent by United States mail as follows: A nominating ballot together with a list of members eligible to be directors shall be mailed by the Secretary-Treasurer to all active members of the corporation in October. From such list, the active members shall nominate on such ballot one eligible member for each of the two regular terms and for any vacancy to be filled and return such ballots to the office of the Secretary-Treasurer within twenty-one days after said date of mailing by the Secretary-Treasurer. The Secretary-Treasurer shall prepare an election ballot and place thereon in alphabetical order the names of persons equal to three times the number of offices to be filled, these persons to be those who received the highest number of votes on the nominating ballot, provided, however, that not more than one person connected with a given institution or agency shall be named on such final ballot, the person so named to be the one receiving the highest vote on the nominating ballot. Such election ballot shall be mailed by the Secretary-Treasurer to all active members in November next succeeding. The active members shall vote thereon for one member for each such office. Election ballots must be in the office of the Secretary-Treasurer within twenty-one days after the said date of mailing by the Secretary-Treasurer. The ballots shall be counted by the Secretary-Treasurer, or by an election committee, if any, appointed by the Board. The two members receiving the highest number of votes shall be declared elected for the regular term and the member or members receiving the next highest number of votes shall be declared elected for any vacancy or vacancies to be filled.

Section 4. *Regular Meetings.* A regular annual meeting of the Board of Directors shall be held, without other notice than this by-law, at the same place and as nearly as possible on the same date as the annual meeting of the corporation. The Board of Directors may provide the time and place, either within or without the State of Illinois, for the holding of additional regular meetings of the Board.

Section 5. *Special Meetings.* Special meetings of the Board of Directors may be called by or at the request of the Chairman or a majority of the directors. Such special meetings shall be held at the office of the corporation unless a majority of the directors agree upon a different place for such meetings.

Section 6. *Notice.* Notice of any special meeting of the Board of Directors shall be given at least fifteen days previously thereto by written notice delivered personally or mailed to each director at his business address, or by telegram. If mailed, such notice shall be deemed to be delivered when deposited in the United States mail in a sealed envelope so addressed, with postage thereon prepaid. If notice be given by telegram, such notice shall be deemed to be delivered when the telegram is delivered to the telegraph company. Any director may waive notice of any meeting. The attendance of a director at any meeting shall constitute a waiver of notice of such meeting, except where a director attends a meeting for the express purpose of objecting to the transaction of any business because the meeting is not lawfully called or convened. Neither the business to be transacted at, nor the purpose of, any regular or special meeting of the Board need be specified in the notice or waiver of notice of such meeting.

Section 7. *Quorum.* A majority of the Board of Directors shall constitute a quorum for the transaction of business at any meeting of the Board, provided, that if less than a majority of the directors are present at said meeting, a majority of the directors present may adjourn the meeting from time to time without further notice.

Section 8. *Manner of Acting.* The act of the majority of the directors present at a meeting at which a quorum is present shall be the act of the Board of Directors, except where otherwise provided by law or by these by-laws.

Article VI

THE COUNCIL

Section 1. *Appointment.* The Council shall consist of the Board of Directors, the Chairmen of the corporation's Yearbook and Research Committees, and such other active members of the corporation as the Board of Directors may appoint.

Section 2. *Duties.* The duties of the Council shall be to further the objects of the corporation by assisting the Board of Directors in planning and carrying forward the educational undertakings of the corporation.

Article VII

OFFICERS

Section 1. *Officers.* The officers of the corporation shall be a Chairman of the Board of Directors, a Vice-Chairman of the Board of Directors, and a Secretary-Treasurer. The Board of Directors, by resolution, may create additional offices. Any two or more offices may be held by the same person, except the offices of Chairman and Secretary-Treasurer.

Section 2. *Election and Term of Office.* The officers of the corporation shall be elected annually by the Board of Directors at the annual regular meeting of the Board of Directors, provided, however, that the Secretary-Treasurer may be elected for a term longer than one year. If the election of officers shall not be held at such meeting, such election shall be held as soon thereafter as conveniently may be. Vacancies may be filled or new offices created and filled at any meeting of the Board of Directors. Each officer shall hold office until his successor shall have been duly elected and shall have qualified or until his death or until he shall resign or shall have been removed in the manner hereinafter provided.

Section 3. *Removal.* Any officer or agent elected or appointed by the Board of Directors may be removed by the Board of Directors whenever in its judgment the best interests of the corporation would be served thereby, but such removal shall be without prejudice to the contract rights, if any, of the person so removed.

Section 4. *Chairman of the Board of Directors.* The Chairman of the Board of Directors shall be the principal officer of the corporation. He shall preside at all meetings of the members of the Board of Directors, shall perform all duties incident to the office of chairman of the Board of Directors and such other duties as may be prescribed by the Board of Directors from time to time.

Section 5. *Vice-Chairman of the Board of Directors.* In the absence of the Chairman of the Board of Directors or in the event of his inability or refusal to act, the Vice-Chairman of the Board of Directors shall perform the duties of the Chairman of the Board of Directors, and when so acting, shall have all the powers of and be subject to all the restrictions upon the Chairman of the Board of Directors. Any Vice-Chairman of the Board of Directors shall perform such other duties as from time to time may be assigned to him by the Board of Directors.

Section 6. *Secretary-Treasurer.* The Secretary-Treasurer shall be the managing executive officer of the corporation. He shall: (*a*) keep the minutes of the meetings of the members and of the Board of Directors in one or more books provided for that purpose; (*b*) see that all notices are duly given in accordance with the provisions of these by-laws or as required by law; (*c*) be custodian of the corporate records and of the seal of the corporation and see that the seal of the corporation is affixed to all documents, the execution of which on behalf of the corporation under its seal is duly authorized in accordance with the provisions of these by-laws; (*d*) keep a register of the postoffice address of each member as furnished to the Secretary-Treasurer by such member; (*e*) in general perform all duties incident to the office of secretary and such other duties as from time to time may be assigned to him by the Chairman of the Board of Directors or by the Board of Directors. He shall also: (1) have charge and custody of and be responsible for all funds and securities of the corporation; receive and give receipts for moneys due and payable to the corporation from any source whatsoever, and deposit all such moneys in the name of the corporation in such banks, trust companies or other depositories as shall be selected in accordance with the provisions of Article XI of these by-laws; (2) in general perform all the duties incident to the office of Treasurer and such other duties as from time to time may be assigned to him by the Chairman of the Board of Directors or by the Board of Directors. The Secretary-Treasurer shall give a bond for the faithful discharge of his duties in such sum and with such surety or sureties as the Board of Directors shall determine, said bond to be placed in the custody of the Chairman of the Board of Directors.

Article VIII

COMMITTEES

The Board of Directors, by appropriate resolution duly passed, may create and appoint such committees for such purposes and periods of time as it may deem advisable.

Article IX

PUBLICATIONS

Section 1. The corporation shall publish *The Yearbook of the National Society for the Study of Education*, such supplements thereto, and such other materials as the Board of Directors may provide for.

Section 2. *Names of Members.* The names of the active and honorary members shall be printed in the Yearbook in alternate years or, at the direction of the Board of Directors, may be published in a special list.

Article X

ANNUAL MEETINGS

The corporation shall hold its annual meetings at the time and place of the Annual Meeting of the American Association of School Administrators of the National Education Association. Other meetings may be held when authorized by the corporation or by the Board of Directors.

Article XI

CONTRACTS, CHECKS, DEPOSITS, AND GIFTS

Section 1. *Contracts.* The Board of Directors may authorize any officer or officers, agent or agents of the corporation, in addition to the officers so authorized by these by-laws to enter into any contract or execute and deliver any instrument in the name of and on behalf of the corporation and such authority may be general or confined to specific instances.

Section 2. *Checks, drafts, etc.* All checks, drafts, or other orders for the payment of money, notes, or other evidences of indebtedness issued in the name of the corporation, shall be signed by such officer or officers, agent or agents of the corporation and in such manner as shall from time to time be determined by resolution of the Board of Directors. In the absence of such determination of the Board of Directors, such instruments shall be signed by the Secretary-Treasurer.

Section 3. *Deposits.* All funds of the corporation shall be deposited from time to time to the credit of the corporation in such banks, trust companies, or other depositories as the Board of Directors may select.

Section 4. *Gifts.* The Board of Directors may accept on behalf of the corporation any contribution, gift, bequest, or device for the general purposes or for any special purpose of the corporation.

Section 5. *Dissolution.* In case of dissolution of the National Society for the Study of Education (incorporated under the GENERAL NOT FOR PROFIT CORPORATION ACT of the State of Illinois), the Board of Directors shall, after paying or making provision for the payment of all liabilities of the Corporation, dispose of all assets of the Corporation to such organization or organizations organized and operated exclusively for charitable, educational, or scientific purposes as shall at the time qualify as an exempt organization or organizations under Section 561(C)(3) of the Internal Revenue Code of 1954 (or the corresponding provision of any future United States Internal Revenue Law), as the Board of Directors shall determine.

Article XII

BOOKS AND RECORDS

The corporation shall keep correct and complete books and records of account and shall also keep minutes of the proceedings of its members, Board of Directors, and committees having any of the authority of the Board of Directors, and shall keep at the registered or principal office a record giving the names and addresses of the members entitled to vote. All books and records of the corporation may be inspected by any member or his agent or attorney for any proper purpose at any reasonable time.

Article XIII

FISCAL YEAR

The fiscal year of the corporation shall begin on the first day of July in each year and end on the last day of June of the following year.

Article XIV

DUES

Section 1. *Annual Dues.* The annual dues for active members of the Society shall be determined by vote of the Board of Directors at a regular meeting duly called and held.

Section 2. *Election Fee.* An election fee of $1.00 shall be paid in advance by each applicant for active membership.

Section 3. *Payment of Dues.* Dues for each calendar year shall be payable in advance on or before the first day of January of that year. Notice of dues for the ensuing year shall be mailed to members at the time set for mailing the primary ballots.

Section 4. *Default and Termination of Membership.* Annual membership shall terminate automatically for those members whose dues remain unpaid after the first day of January of each year. Members so in default will be reinstated on payment of the annual dues plus a reinstatement fee of fifty cents.

Article XV

SEAL

The Board of Directors shall provide a corporate seal which shall be in the form of a circle and shall have inscribed thereon the name of the corporation and the words "Corporate Seal, Illinois."

Article XVI

WAIVER OF NOTICE

Whenever any notice whatever is required to be given under the provision of the General Not For Profit Corporation Act of Illinois or under the provisions of the Articles of Incorporation or the by-laws of the corporation, a waiver thereof in writing signed by the person or persons entitled to such notice, whether before or after the time stated therein, shall be deemed equivalent to the giving of such notice.

Article XVII

AMENDMENTS

Section 1. *Amendments by Directors.* The constitution and by-laws may be altered or amended at any meeting of the Board of Directors duly called and held, provided that affirmative vote of at least five directors shall be required for such action.

Section 2. *Amendments by Members.* By petition of twenty-five or more active members duly filed with the Secretary-Treasurer, a proposal to amend the constitution and by-laws shall be submitted to all active members by United States mail together with ballots on which the members shall vote for or against the proposal. Such ballots shall be returned by United States mail to the office of the Secretary-Treasurer within twenty-one days after date of mailing of the proposal and ballots by the Secretary-Treasurer. The Secretary-Treasurer or a committee appointed by the Board of Directors for that purpose shall count the ballots and advise the members of the result. A vote in favor of such proposal by two-thirds of the members voting thereon shall be required for adoption of such amendment.

ANNUAL MEETINGS OF THE SOCIETY

In 1977, meetings of the Society were held in Chicago, Las Vegas, and New York. At each of these meetings one part of the Seventy-sixth Yearbook was presented.

Part I: *The Teaching of English*

Part I *(The Teaching of English)* was formally presented at the opening general session of the Sixty-sixth Annual Convention of the National Council of Teachers of English in Chicago in November, 1976. At that meeting, the secretary of the Society presented a copy of the volume to Charlotte S. Huck, president of the National Council, in recognition of the very substantial contributions of members of the National Council to the preparation of the yearbook. The volume was presented and discussed at a session the next day in which the following persons participated:

Presiding: Kenneth J. Rehage, Secretary-Treasurer of the National Society for the Study of Education.

Presenting the Yearbook: James R. Squire, Ginn and Co., Editor of the Yearbook.

Commenting on the Yearbook: Margaret Early, Syracuse University, Walter T. Petty, State University of New York at Buffalo, and Ralph W. Tyler, Science Research Associates, Chicago.

Part II: *The Politics of Education*

Part II *(The Politics of Education)* was presented at a meeting cosponsored by the American Association of School Administrators in Las Vegas with the following persons participating:

Presiding: Luvern L. Cunningham, The Ohio State University.

Presenting the Yearbook: Jay D. Scribner, Temple University, Editor of the Yearbook.

Commenting on the Yearbook: Alonzo Crim, Atlanta Public Schools, and Dale Mann, Teachers College, Columbia University.

The Politics of Education was also presented and discussed at a meeting cosponsored by the American Educational Research Association in New York, with the following persons participating:

Presiding: David L. Colton, Washington University.

Presenting the Yearbook: Jay D. Scribner, Temple University, Editor of the Yearbook.

Commenting on the Yearbook: James Mecklenburger, National School Boards Association, Anthony Cresswell, Northwestern University, and Robert Salisbury, Washington University.

SYNOPSIS OF THE PROCEEDINGS OF THE BOARD OF DIRECTORS OF THE SOCIETY FOR 1977

I. Meeting of February 4 and 5, 1977

The Board of Directors of the National Society for the Study of Education met at the O'Hare Hilton Hotel (Chicago) on Friday, February 4, 1977 at 7:30 p.m. and again on Saturday, February 5, 1977, with the following members present: Jeanne S. Chall, Jacob W. Getzels, A. Harry Passow (presiding), Harold G. Shane, Ralph W. Tyler, and Kenneth J. Rehage, secretary-treasurer. N. L. Gage was unable to attend because of illness. Herbert Walberg, cochairman of the Society's Committee on the Expanded Publication Program, was present for part of the meeting on Saturday morning.

1. The secretary reported that Arthur Combs and John I. Goodlad were elected to the Board for three-year terms beginning March 1, 1977. (Note: Mr. Combs subsequently notified the secretary that he did not wish to serve on the Board. After consultation with Board members, and in accordance with the Constitution and By-Laws, Article V., Section 3(g), the secretary notified Mr. Tyler, who had received the next highest number of votes in the election, that he had been declared elected to the Board.)

2. The secretary presented reports on membership, income, and expenditures for the first seven months of the current fiscal year. Mr. Getzels and the secretary were asked to make arrangements for an audit of the Society's financial records.

3. The secretary reported on sales of recently published yearbooks as well as a report on some of the older volumes in the yearbook series for which there continues to be a demand.

4. The secretary reported that the volume on *The Teaching of English* was formally presented at the annual meeting of the National Council of Teachers of English in November, 1976, and that arrangements were being made for presentations of that volume at other meetings. The volume on *The Politics of Education* is to be presented at the annual meeting of the Society held in conjunction with the Las Vegas meeting of the American Association of School Administrators in February and again at the New York meeting of the American Educational Research Association in April.

5. The Board heard reports on progress of yearbooks currently in preparation: *The Courts and Education* and *Education and the Brain* (1978); *The Gifted and the Talented* and *Classroom Management* (1979); *The Middle School* (1980).

6. Proposals for yearbooks on the governance of education, on second language learning, on the social studies were discussed but no action

was taken pending the receipt of more information on the proposals. Plans were made for exploring the matter of publishing a yearbook on the philosophy of education.

7. The secretary reported on several communications from members suggesting various topics for yearbooks or expressing interest in writing for the Society's publications.

8. Mr. Walberg presented a report prepared by the Committee on the Expanded Publication Program at the request of the Board. The report included the following items: the number of persons taking out the Comprehensive Membership each year since that membership category was established in 1974; royalties received from the sale of hardcover editions of the volumes in the series on Contemporary Educational Issues; a list of reviews of the publications in that series; and a listing of the names of all editors and contributors to the series and their respective institutional affiliations. In the discussion that followed Mr. Walberg's report the Board authorized the committee to proceed with its plans to provide a broader range of inputs to the commitee's deliberations. At the conclusion of the discussion the Board expressed its appreciation to Mr. Walberg and the Commitee for their work and for their report.

9. Mr. Passow was reelected as chairman of the Board for the coming year.

10. The next meeting of the Board was scheduled for September 30-October 1 in Chicago.

II. Meeting of September 30 and October 1, 1977

The Board of Directors of the National Society for the Study of Education met at the O'Hare Hilton Hotel (Chicago) on Friday, September 30, 1977 and again on Saturday, October 1, 1977, with the following members present: N. L. Gage, Jacob W. Getzels, John I. Goodlad, A. Harry Passow (presiding), Ralph W. Tyler, and Kenneth J. Rehage, secretary-treasurer. Harold G. Shane was unable to attend the Friday evening meeting, but was present for the Saturday session.

1. The secretary reported on membership, on the income and expenditures of the Society for the fiscal year ending June 30, 1977, and on assets of the Society as of that date. Mr. Getzels read a letter from Mr. Sidney Davidson who had been requested to examine the Society's financial records for the 1976-77 fiscal year. Mr. Davidson stated that he had examined the evidence of the cash and securities position of the Society and had found that all items listed in the statement of June 30, 1977 are on hand and in good order. He also made some suggestions in procedures for record keeping that are reflected in the financial report for the 1976-77 fiscal year. Mr. Davidson said that he had not carried out a full-scale audit of the Society's operations for 1976-77 but that

he would recommend that such an audit be carried out from time to time. Mr. Getzels and Mr. Rehage were asked to inquire into the cost of an audit of the Society's books at the close of the 1977-78 fiscal year and report to the Board at the next meeting.

2. The secretary reported that all manuscripts for the three forthcoming publications in the series on Contemporary Educational Issues were ready in advance of the deadline. He also stated that the Committee on the Expanded Publication Program is planning a meeting in October to which several other persons will be invited in line with plans made earlier to enlarge the number of participants in the committee's deliberations.

3. The secretary reported that the volume on the *Courts and Education*, Part I of the Seventy-seventh Yearbook, is proceeding on schedule, but that work on the companion volume (Part II: *Education and the Brain*) is behind schedule. Mr. Passow reported that he expected to be submitting the completed manuscript for the volume on *The Gifted and the Talented* on schedule. The Board authorized an appropriation of $2,000 to meet expenses incurred in connection with the volume on Classroom Management, which is to be edited by Mr. Daniel Duke.

4. During discussion of pending proposals for future yearbook volumes Mr. Passow agreed to have further conversations with Mr. Jonas Soltis regarding a yearbook on the philosophy of education and Mr. Shane consented to arrange for further discussions on the possibility of a volume on the social studies. Further reports on these matters will be heard at the next meeting of the Board. The Board heard reports from Messrs. Shane, Tyler, and Rehage on their meeting with representatives of the American Council on the Teaching of Foreign Languages. After discussion of a detailed proposal for a yearbook on second language learning the Board authorized the preparation of such a volume and appropriated $2,000 to meet expenses incurred in connection with this work. Mr. Frank Grittner will serve as chairman of the committee for this volume and will serve as editor. Mr. Passow reported that Mr. Mauritz Johnson will be requested to serve as editor for the previously authorized volume on the Middle School.

5. Other proposals for yearbooks were discussed by the Board but no action was taken pending further information on those proposals.

6. Following discussion in executive session, the Board authorized an increase in the salary of the Secretary-Treasurer, the exact amount of the increase to be determined following further inquiry by a subcommittee of the Board.

7. The date of the next meeting of the Board, to be held in Chicago, was set for February 3-4, 1978.

REPORT OF THE TREASURER OF THE SOCIETY

1976-77

Receipts and Disbursements

Receipts:	
Membership dues and fees	$ 74,677.50
Sales, royalties, and permissions	56,134.08
Interest	8,747.77
Transfers	178.92
Miscellaneous	364.03
Total	$140,102.30
Disbursements:	
Yearbooks:	
Manufacturing	$ 56,877.03
Reprinting and binding	4,000.00
Preparation	2,987.46
Mailing	4,208.30
Meetings of Board and Society	2,900.41
Secretary's office:	
Salaries (editorial, secretarial)	28,856.09
Supplies, equipment, telephone	5,188.80
Promotion	1,864.45
New publication program	
Preparation of manuscripts and meetings of committee	699.90
Purchase of paperbacks for 1977	21,186.79
Refunds/transfers	201.89
Bank charges	94.30
Miscellaneous	127.09
Total	$129,192.51
Summary of receipts and disbursements:	
Total receipts	$140,102.30
Total disbursements	129,192.51
Excess of receipts over disbursements	$ 10,909.79
Purchase of Certificate of Deposit	10,000.00
Net excess of receipts over disbursements	$ 909.79

Statement of cash on hand:

Cash on hand, July 1, 1976	$ 12,213.25
Cash on hand, June 30, 1977	13,123.04
Increase in cash on hand	909.79

STATEMENT OF CASH AND SECURITIES
as of June 30, 1976

Cash:	
University National Bank, Chicago, checking account	$ 13,123.04
Savings Account:	
University National Bank, Chicago	3,684.37
Savings and Loan Certificates:	
Chicago Federal Savings and Loan Association	10,000.00
Home Federal Savings	10,000.00
Certificate of Deposit:	
Certificate #1116	30,000.00
Bonds:	
American Telephone and Telegraph	14,679.42
ML Corporate Income Fund (25 units)	25,925.25
U.S. Government Bonds (Series H)	15,000.00
Stock:	
First National Bank (Boston), 114 shares common stock (par $6.25)	712.50
Total Cash and Securities on Hand	$123,124.58

Charges against Current Assets

Annual dues paid for 1978	$ 40.00
Paid up Life Memberships	4,358.00
Balance due on purchase of paperbacks for 1977	3,013.21
Balance due on reprinting and binding ordered prior to June 30, 1977	2,095.57
Total charges	$ 9,506.78
Unencumbered assets	$113,617.80

A Note to Members of the Society

An updated list of members of the Society as of January 1, 1978 is now in preparation. A copy of the list will be mailed to members upon receipt of their written request.

KENNETH J. REHAGE
Secretary-Treasurer

INFORMATION CONCERNING THE NATIONAL SOCIETY FOR THE STUDY OF EDUCATION

1. *Purpose.* The purpose of the National Society is to promote the investigation and discussion of educational questions. To this end it holds an annual meeting and publishes a series of yearbooks and a series of paperbacks on Contemporary Educational Issues.

2. *Membership.* Any person interested in the purpose of the Society and in receiving its publications may become a member by sending in name, title, address, and a check covering dues and the entrance fee (see items 4 and 5). Graduate students may become members, upon recommendation of a faculty member, at a reduced rate for the first year of membership. Dues for all subsequent years are the same as for other members.

Membership is not transferable. It is limited to individuals and may not be held by libraries, schools, or other institutions, either directly or indirectly.

3. *Period of Membership.* Membership is for the calendar year and terminates automatically on December 31, unless dues for the ensuing year are paid as indicated in item 6. Applicants for membership may not date their entrance back of the current calendar year.

4. *Categories of Membership.* The following categories of membership have been established:

Regular. Annual dues are $13.00. The member receives a clothbound copy of each part of the current yearbook.

Comprehensive. Annual dues are $27.00. The member receives a clothbound copy of the current yearbook *and* all volumes in the current year's paperback series on Contemporary Educational Issues.

Special Memberships for Retired Members and Graduate Students.

Retired members. Persons who are retired or who are sixty-five years of age *and* who have been members of the Society continuously for at least ten years may retain their Regular Membership upon payment of annual dues of $10.00 or their Comprehensive Membership upon payment of annual dues of $20.00.

Graduate Students. Graduate students may pay annual dues of $10.00 for Regular Membership or $20.00 for Comprehensive Membership for their first year of membership, plus the $1.00 entrance fee in either case.

Life Memberships. Persons sixty years of age or above may become life members on payment of a fee based on the average life expectancy of their age group. Regular life members may take out a Comprehensive Membership for any year upon payment of an additional fee of $10.00. For further information apply to the Secretary-Treasurer.

5. *Privileges of Membership.* Members receive the publications of the Society as described above. All members are entitled to vote, to participate in meetings of the Society, and (under certain conditions) to hold office.

6. *Entrance Fee.* New members are required to pay an entrance fee of one dollar, in addition to the dues, for the first year of membership.

7. *Payment of Dues.* Statements of dues are rendered in October for the following calendar year. Any member so notified whose dues remain unpaid on January 1 thereby loses membership and can be reinstated only by paying the dues plus a reinstatement fee of fifty cents ($.50).

School warrants and vouchers from institutions must be accompanied by definite information concerning the name and address of the person for whom the membership fee is being paid. Statements of dues are rendered on our own form only. The Secretary's office cannot undertake to fill out special invoice forms of any kind or to affix a notary's affidavit to statements or receipts.

Cancelled checks serve as receipts. Members desiring an additional receipt must enclose a stamped and addressed envelope therefor.

8. *Distribution of Yearbooks to Members*. The yearbooks, normally ready prior to the February meeting of the Society, will be mailed from the office of the distributor only to members whose dues for that year have been paid.

9. *Commercial Sales*. The distribution of all yearbooks prior to the current year, and also of those of the current year not regularly mailed to members in exchange for their dues, is in the hands of the distributor, not of the Secretary. Orders may be placed with the University of Chicago Press, Chicago, Illinois 60637, which distributes the yearbooks of the Society. Orders for paperbacks in the series on Contemporary Educational Issues should be placed with the designated publisher of that series. The list of the Society's publications is printed in each yearbook.

10. *Yearbooks*. The yearbooks are issued about one month before the February meeting. Published in two volumes, each of which contains 300 to 400 pages, the yearbooks are planned to be of immediate practical value as well as representative of sound scholarship and scientific investigation.

11. *Series on Contemporary Educational Issues*. This series, in paperback format, is designed to supplement the yearbooks by timely publications on topics of current interest. There will usually be three of these volumes each year.

12. *Meetings*. The annual meeting, at which the yearbooks are presented and critiqued, is held as a rule in February at the same time and place as the meeting of the American Association of School Administrators. Members will be notified of other meetings.

Applications for membership will be handled promptly at any time. New members will receive the yearbook scheduled for publication during the calendar year in which application for Regular Membership is made. New members who elect to take out the Comprehensive membership will receive both the yearbook and the paperbacks scheduled for publication during the year in which application is made.

Kenneth J. Rehage, Secretary-Treasurer

5835 Kimbark Avenue
Chicago, Illinois 60637

PUBLICATIONS OF THE NATIONAL SOCIETY FOR THE STUDY OF EDUCATION

1. The Yearbooks

NOTICE: Many of the early yearbooks of this series are now out of print. In the following list, those titles to which an asterisk is prefixed are not available for purchase.

*First Yearbook, 1902, Part I—*Some Principles in the Teaching of History.* Lucy M. Salmon.

*First Yearbook, 1902, Part II—*The Progress of Geography in the Schools.* W. M. Davis and H. M. Wilson.

*Second Yearbook, 1903, Part I—*The Course of Study in History in the Common School.* Isabel Lawrence, C. A. McMurray, Frank McMurry, E. C. Page, and E. J. Rice.

*Second Yearbook, 1903, Part II—*The Relation of Theory to Pratice in Education.* M. J. Holmes, J. A. Keith, and Levi Seeley.

*Third Yearbook, 1904, Part I—*The Relation of Theory to Practice in the Education of Teachers.* John Dewey, Sarah C. Brooks, F. M. McMurry, *et al.*

*Third Yearbook, 1904, Part II—*Nature Study.* W. S. Jackman.

*Fourth Yearbook, 1905, Part I—*The Education and Training of Secondary Teachers.* E. C. Elliott, E. G. Dexter, M. J. Holmes, *et al.*

*Fourth Yearbook, 1905, Part II—*The Place of Vocational Subjects in the High-School Curriculum.* J. S. Brown, G. B. Morrison, and Ellen Richards.

*Fifth Yearbook, 1906, Part I—*On the Teaching of English in Elementary and High Schools.* G. P. Brown and Emerson Davis.

*Fifth Yearbook, 1906, Part II—*The Certification of Teachers.* E. P. Cubberley.

*Sixth Yearbook, 1907, Part I—*Vocational Studies for College Entrance.* C. A. Herrick, H. W. Holmes, T. deLaguna, V. Prettyman, and W. J. S. Bryan.

*Sixth Yearbook, 1907, Part II—*The Kindergarten and Its Relation to Elementary Education.* Ada Van Stone Harris, E. A. Kirkpatrick, Marie Kraus-Boelté, Patty S. Hill, Harriette M. Mills, and Nina Vandewalker.

*Seventh Yearbook, 1908, Part I—*The Relation of Superintendents and Principals to the Training and Professional Improvement of Their Teachers.* Charles D. Lowry.

*Seventh Yearbook, 1908, Part II—*The Co-ordination of the Kindergarten and the Elementary School.* B. J. Gregory, Jennie B. Merrill, Bertha Payne, and Margaret Giddings.

*Eighth Yearbook, 1909, Part I—*Education with Reference to Sex: Pathological, Economic, and Social Aspects.* C. R. Henderson.

*Eighth Yearbook, 1909, Part II—*Education with Reference to Sex: Agencies and Methods.* C. R. Henderson and Helen C. Putnam.

*Ninth Yearbook, 1910, Part I—*Health and Education.* T. D. Wood.

*Ninth Yearbook, 1910, Part II—*The Nurses in Education.* T. D. Wood, *et al.*

*Tenth Yearbook, 1911, Part I—*The City School as a Community Center.* H. C. Leipziger, Sarah E. Hyre, R. D. Warden, C. Ward Crampton, E. W. Stitt, E. J. Ward, Mrs. T. C. Grice, and C. A. Perry.

*Tenth Yearbook, 1911, Part II—*The Rural School as a Community Center.* B. H. Crocheron, Jessie Field, F. W. Howe, E. C. Bishop, A. B. Graham, O. J. Kern, M. T. Scudder, and B. M. Davis.

*Eleventh Yearbook, 1912, Part I—*Industrial Education: Typical Experiments Described and Interpreted.* J. F. Barker, M. Bloomfield, B. W. Johnson, P. Johnson, L. M. Leavitt, G. A. Mirick, M. W. Murray, C. F. Perry, A. L. Stafford, and H. B. Wilson.

*Eleventh Yearbook, 1912, Part II—*Agricultural Education in Secondary Schools.* A. C. Monahan, R. W. Stimson, D. J. Crosby, W. H. French, H. F. Button, F. R. Crane, W. R. Hart, and G. F. Warren.

*Twelfth Yearbook, 1913, Part I—*The Supervision of City Schools.* Franklin Bobbitt, J. W. Hall, and J. D. Wolcott.

*Twelfth Yearbook, 1913, Part II—*The Supervision of Rural Schools.* A. C. Monahan, L. J. Hanifan, J. E. Warren, Wallace Lund, U. J. Hoffman, A. S. Cook, E. M. Rapp, Jackson Davis, J. D. Wolcott.

*Thirteenth Yearbook, 1914, Part I—*Some Aspects of High-School Instruction and Administration.* H. C. Morrison, E. R. Breslich, W. A. Jessup, and L. D. Coffman.

*Thirteenth Yearbook, 1914, Part II—*Plans for Organizing School Surveys, with a Summary of Typical School Surveys.* Charles H. Judd and Henry L. Smith.

*Fourteenth Yearbook, 1915, Part I—*Minimum Essentials in Elementary School Subjects—Standards and Current Practices.* H. B. Wilson, H. W. Holmes, F. E. Thompson, R. G. Jones, S. A. Courtis, W. S. Gray, F. N. Freeman, H. C. Pryor, J. F. Hosic, W. A. Jessup, and W. C. Bagley.

*Fourteenth Yearbook, 1915, Part II—*Methods for Measuring Teachers' Efficiency.* Arthur C. Boyce.

*Fifteenth Yearbook, 1916, Part I—*Standards and Tests for the Measurement of the Efficiency of Schools and School Systems.* G. D. Strayer, Bird T. Baldwin, B. R. Buckingham, F. W. Ballou, D. C. Bliss, H. G. Childs, S. A. Courtis, E. P. Cubberley, C. H. Judd, George Melcher, E. E. Oberholtzer, J. B. Sears, Daniel Starch, M. R. Trabue, and G. M. Whipple.

*Fifteenth Yearbook, 1916, Part II—*The Relationship between Persistence in School and Home Conditions.* Charles E. Holley.

*Fifteenth Yearbook, 1916, Part III—*The Junior High School.* Aubrey A. Douglas.

*Sixteenth Yearbook, 1917, Part I—*Second Report of the Committee on Minimum Essentials in Elementary-School Subjects.* W. C. Bagley, W. W. Charters, F. N. Freeman, W. S. Gray, Ernest Horn, J. H. Hoskinson, W. S. Monroe, C. F. Munson, H. C. Pryor, L. W. Rapeer, G. M. Wilson, and H. B. Wilson.

*Sixteenth Yearbook, 1917, Part II—*The Efficiency of College Students as Conditioned by Age at Entrance and Size of High School.* B. F. Pittenger.

*Seventeenth Yearbook, 1918, Part I—*Third Report of the Committee on Economy of Time in Education.* W. C. Bagley, B. B. Bassett, M. E. Branom, Alice Camerer, J. E. Dealey, C. A. Ellwood, E. B. Greene, A. B. Hart, J. F. Hosic, E. T. Housh, W. H. Mace, L. R. Marston, H. C. McKown, H. E. Mitchell, W. V. Reavis, D. Snedden, and H. B. Wilson.

*Seventeenth Yearbook, 1918, Part II—*The Measurement of Educational Products.* E. J. Ashbaugh, W. A. Averill, L. P. Ayers, F. W. Ballou, Edna Bryner, B. R. Buckingham, S. A. Courtis, M. E. Haggerty, C. H. Judd, George Melcher, W. S. Monroe, E. A. Nifenecker, and E. L. Thorndike.

*Eighteenth Yearbook, 1919, Part I—*The Professional Preparation of High-School Teachers.* G. N. Cade, S. S. Colvin, Charles Fordyce, H. H. Foster, T. S. Gosling, W. S. Gray, L. V. Koos, A. R. Mead, H. L. Miller, F. C. Whitcomb, and Clifford Woody.

*Eighteenth Yearbook, 1919, Part II—*Fourth Report of Committee on Economy of Time in Education.* F. C. Ayer, F. N. Freeman, W. S. Gray, Ernest Horn, W. S. Monroe, and C. E. Seashore.

*Nineteenth Yearbook, 1920, Part I—*New Materials of Instruction.* Prepared by the Society's Committee on Materials of Instruction.

*Nineteenth Yearbook, 1920, Part II—*Classroom Problems in the Education of Gifted Children.* T. S. Henry.

*Twentieth Yearbook, 1921, Part I—*New Materials of Instruction.* Second Report by Society's Committee.

*Twentieth Yearbook, 1921, Part II—*Report of the Society's Committee on Silent Reading.* M. A. Burgess, S. A. Courtis, C. E. Germane, W. S. Gray, H. A. Greene, Regina R. Heller, J. H. Hoover, J. A. O'Brien, J. L. Packer, Daniel Starch, W. W. Theisen, G. A. Yoakam, and representatives of other school systems.

*Twenty-first Yearbook, 1922, Parts I and II—*Intelligence Tests and Their Use*, Part I—*The Nature, History, and General Principles of Intelligence Testing.* E. L. Thorndike, S. S. Colvin, Harold Rugg, G. M. Whipple, Part II—*The Administrative Use of Intelligence Tests.* H. W. Holmes, W. K. Layton, Helen Davis, Agnes L. Rogers, Rudolf Pintner, M. R. Trabue, W. S. Miller, Bessie L. Gambrill, and others. The two parts are bound together.

*Twenty-second Yearbook, 1923, Part I—*English Composition: Its Aims, Methods and Measurements.* Earl Hudelson.

*Twenty-second Yearbook, 1923, Part II—*The Social Studies in the Elementary and Secondary School.* A. S. Barr, J. J. Coss, Henry Harap, R. W. Hatch, H. C. Hill, Ernest Horn, C. H. Judd, L. C. Marshall, F. M. McMurry, Earle Rugg, H. O. Rugg, Emma Schweppe, Mabel Snedaker, and C. W. Washburne.

*Twenty-third Yearbook, 1924, Part I—*The Education of Gifted Children.* Report of the Society's Committee. Guy M. Whipple, Chairman.

*Twenty-third Yearbook, 1924, Part II—*Vocational Guidance and Vocational Education for Industries.* A. H. Edgerton and others.

*Twenty-fourth Yearbook, 1925, Part I—*Report of the National Committee on Reading.* W. S. Gray, Chairman, F. W. Ballou, Rose L. Hardy, Ernest Horn, Francis Jenkins, S. A. Leonard, Estaline Wilson, and Laura Zirbes.

*Twenty-fourth Yearbook, 1925, Part II—*Adapting the Schools to Individual Differences.* Report of the Society's Committee. Carleton W. Washburne, Chairman.

*Twenty-fifth Yearbook, 1926, Part I—*The Present Status of Safety Education.* Report of the Society's Committee. Guy M. Whipple, Chairman.

*Twenty-fifth Yearbook, 1926, Part II—*Extra-Curricular Activities.* Report of the Society's Committee. Leonard V. Koos, Chairman.

*Twenty-sixth Yearbook, 1927, Part I—*Curriculum-making: Past and Present.* Report of the Society's Committee. Harold O. Rugg, Chairman.

*Twenty-sixth Yearbook, 1927, Part II—*The Foundations of Curriculum-making.* Prepared by individual members of the Society's Committee. Harold O. Rugg, Chairman.

*Twenty-seventh Yearbook, 1928, Part I—*Nature and Nurture: Their Influence upon Intelligence.* Prepared by the Society's Committee. Lewis M. Terman, Chairman.

*Twenty-seventh Yearbook, 1928, Part II—*Nature and Nurture: Their Influence upon Achievement.* Prepared by the Society's Committee. Lewis M. Terman, Chairman.

Twenty-eighth Yearbook, 1929, Parts I and II—*Preschool and Parental Education*, Part I—*Organization and Development.* Part II—*Research and Method.* Prepared by the Society's Committee. Lois H. Meek, Chairman. Bound in one volume. Cloth.

*Twenty-ninth Yearbook, 1930, Parts I and II—*Report of the Society's Committee on Arithmetic.* Part I—*Some Aspects of Modern Thought on Arithmetic.* Part II—*Research in Arithmetic.* Prepared by the Society's Committee. F. B. Knight, Chairman. Bound in one volume.

*Thirtieth Yearbook, 1931, Part I—*The Status of Rural Education.* First Report of the Society's Committee on Rural Education. Orville G. Brim, Chairman.

Thirtieth Yearbook, 1931, Part II—*The Textbook in American Education.* Report of the Society's Committee on the Textbook, J. B. Edmonson, Chairman. Cloth, Paper.

*Thirty-first Yearbook, 1932, Part I—*A Program for Teaching Science.* Prepared by the Society's Committee on the Teaching of Science. S. Ralph Powers, Chairman.
*Thirty-first Yearbook, 1932, Part II—*Changes and Experiments in Liberal-Arts Education.* Prepared by Kathryn McHale, with numerous collaborators.
*Thirty-second Yearbook, 1933—*The Teaching of Geography.* Prepared by the Society's Committee on the Teaching of Geography. A. E. Parkins, Chairman.
*Thirty-third Yearbook, 1934, Part I—*The Planning and Construction of School Buildings.* Prepared by the Society's Committee on School Buildings. N. L. Engelhardt, Chairman.
*Thirty-third Yearbook, 1934, Part II—*The Activity Movement.* Prepared by the Society's Committee on the Activity Movement. Lois Coffey Mossman, Chairman.
Thirty-fourth Yearbook, 1935—*Educational Diagnosis.* Prepared by the Society's Committee on Educational Diagnosis. L. J. Brueckner, Chairman. Paper.
*Thirty-fifth Yearbook, 1936, Part I—*The Grouping of Pupils.* Prepared by the Society's Committee. W. W. Coxe, Chairman.
*Thirty-fifth Yearbook, 1936, Part II—*Music Education.* Prepared by the Society's Committee. W. L. Uhl, Chairman.
*Thirty-sixth Yearbook, 1937, Part I—*The Teaching of Reading.* Prepared by the Society's Committee. W. S. Gray, Chairman.
*Thirty-sixth Yearbook, 1937, Part II—*International Understanding through the Public-School Curriculum.* Prepared by the Society's Committee. I. L. Kandel, Chairman.
*Thirty-seventh Yearbook, 1938, Part I—*Guidance in Educational Institutions.* Prepared by the Society's Committee. G. N. Kefauver, Chairman.
*Thirty-seventh Yearbook, 1938, Part II—*The Scientific Movement in Education.* Prepared by the Society's Committee. F. N. Freeman, Chairman.
*Thirty-eighth Yearbook, 1939, Part I—*Child Development and the Curriculum.* Prepared by the Society's Committee. Carleton Washburne, Chairman.
*Thirty-eighth Yearbook, 1939, Part II—*General Education in the American College.* Prepared by the Society's Committee. Alvin Eurich, Chairman. Cloth.
*Thirty-ninth Yearbook, 1940, Part I—*Intelligence: Its Nature and Nurture. Comparative and Critical Exposition.* Prepared by the Society's Committee. G. D. Stoddard, Chairman.
*Thirty-ninth Yearbook, 1940, Part II—*Intelligence: Its Nature and Nurture. Original Studies and Experiments.* Prepared by the Society's Committee. G. D. Stoddard, Chairman.
*Fortieth Yearbook, 1941—*Art in American Life and Education.* Prepared by the Society's Committee. Thomas Munro, Chairman.
Forty-first Yearbook, 1942, Part I—*Philosophies of Education.* Prepared by the Society's Committee. John S. Brubacher, Chairman. Cloth, Paper.
Forty-first Yearbook, 1942, Part II—*The Psychology of Learning.* Prepared by the Society's Committee. T. R. McConnell, Chairman. Cloth.
*Forty-second Yearbook, 1943, Part I—*Vocational Education.* Prepared by the Society's Committee. F. J. Keller, Chairman.
*Forty-second Yearbook, 1943, Part II—*The Library in General Education.* Prepared by the Society's Committee. L. R. Wilson, Chairman.
Forty-third Yearbook, 1944, Part I—*Adolescence.* Prepared by the Society's Committee. Harold E. Jones, Chairman. Paper.
*Forty-third Yearbook, 1944, Part II—*Teaching Language in the Elementary School.* Prepared by the Society's Committee. M. R. Trabue, Chairman.
*Forty-fourth Yearbook, 1945, Part I—*American Education in the Postwar Period: Curriculum Reconstruction.* Prepared by the Society's Committee. Ralph W. Tyler, Chairman.
Forty-fourth Yearbook, 1945, Part II—*American Education in the Postwar Period: Structural Reorganization.* Prepared by the Society's Committee. Bess Goodykoontz, Chairman. Paper.
*Forty-fifth Yearbook, 1946, Part I—*The Measurement of Understanding.* Prepared by the Society's Committee. William A. Brownell, Chairman.
*Forty-fifth Yearbook, 1946, Part II—*Changing Conceptions in Educational Administration.* Prepared by the Society's Committee. Alonzo G. Grace, Chairman.
*Forty-sixth Yearbook, 1947, Part I—*Science Education in American Schools.* Prepared by the Society's Committee. Victor H. Noll, Chairman.
Forty-sixth Yearbook, 1947, Part II—*Early Childhood Education.* Prepared by the Society's Committee. N. Searle Light, Chairman. Paper.
Forty-seventh Yearbook, 1948, Part I—*Juvenile Delinquency and the Schools.* Prepared by the Society's Committee. Ruth Strang, Chairman. Cloth.
Forty-seventh Yearbook, 1948, Part II—*Reading in the High School and College.* Prepared by the Society's Committee. William S. Gray, Chairman. Cloth, Paper.
Forty-eighth Yearbook, 1949, Part I—*Audio-visual Materials of Instruction.* Prepared by the Society's Committee. Stephen M. Corey, Chairman. Cloth.
*Forty-eighth Yearbook, 1949, Part II—*Reading in the Elementary School.* Prepared by the Society's Committee. Arthur I. Gates, Chairman.
*Forty-ninth Yearbook, 1950, Part I—*Learning and Instruction.* Prepared by the Society's Committee. G. Lester Anderson, Chairman.
Forty-ninth Yearbook, 1950, Part II—*The Education of Exceptional Children.* Prepared by the Society's Committee. Samuel A. Kirk, Chairman. Paper.
Fiftieth Yearbook, 1951, Part I—*Graduate Study in Education.* Prepared by the Society's Board of Directors. Ralph W. Tyler, Chairman. Paper.
Fiftieth Yearbook, 1951, Part II—*The Teaching of Arithmetic.* Prepared by the Society's Committee. G. T. Buswell, Chairman. Cloth, Paper.

Fifty-first Yearbook, 1952, Part I—*General Education.* Prepared by the Society's Committee. T. R. McConnell, Chairman. Cloth, Paper.

Fifty-first Yearbook, 1952, Part II—*Education in Rural Communities.* Prepared by the Society's Committee. Ruth Strang, Chairman. Cloth, Paper.

*Fifty-second Yearbook, 1953, Part I—*Adapting the Secondary-School Program to the Needs of Youth.* Prepared by the Society's Committee: William G. Brink, Chairman.

Fifty-second Yearbook, 1953, Part II—*The Community School.* Prepared by the Society's Committee. Maurice F. Seay, Chairman. Cloth.

Fifty-third Yearbook, 1954, Part I—*Citizen Co-operation for Better Public Schools.* Prepared by the Society's Committee. Edgar L. Morphet, Chairman. Cloth, Paper.

Fifty-third Yearbook, 1954, Part II—*Mass Media and Education.* Prepared by the Society's Committee. Edgar Dale, Chairman. Paper.

*Fifty-fourth Yearbook, 1955, Part I—*Modern Philosophies and Education.* Prepared by the Society's Committee. John S. Brubacher, Chairman.

Fifty-fourth Yearbook, 1955, Part II—*Mental Health in Modern Education.* Prepared by the Society's Committee. Paul A. Witty, Chairman. Paper.

*Fifty-fifth Yearbook, 1956, Part I—*The Public Junior College.* Prepared by the Society's Committee. B. Lamar Johnson, Chairman.

Fifty-fifth Yearbook, 1956, Part II—*Adult Reading.* Prepared by the Society's Committee. David H. Clift, Chairman. Paper.

Fifty-sixth Yearbook, 1957, Part I—*In-service Education of Teachers, Supervisors, and Administrators.* Prepared by the Society's Committee. Stephen M. Corey, Chairman. Cloth, Paper.

Fifty-sixth Yearbook, 1957, Part II—*Social Studies in the Elementary School.* Prepared by the Society's Committee. Ralph C. Preston, Chairman. Cloth, Paper.

Fifty-seventh Yearbook, 1958, Part I—*Basic Concepts in Music Education.* Prepared by the Society's Committee. Thurber H. Madison, Chairman. Cloth.

Fifty-seventh Yearbook, 1958, Part II—*Education for the Gifted.* Prepared by the Society's Committee. Robert J. Havighurst, Chairman. Cloth, Paper.

Fifty-seventh Yearbook, 1958, Part III—*The Integration of Educational Experiences.* Prepared by the Society's Committee. Paul L. Dressel, Chairman. Cloth.

Fifty-eighth Yearbook, 1959, Part I—*Community Education: Principles and Practices from World-wide Experience.* Prepared by the Society's Committee. C. O. Arndt, Chairman. Cloth, Paper.

Fifty-eighth Yearbook, 1959, Part II—*Personnel Services in Education.* Prepared by the Society's Committee. Melvene D. Hardee, Chairman. Paper.

*Fifty-ninth Yearbook, 1960, Part I—*Rethinking Science Education.* Prepared by the Society's Committee. J. Darrell Barnard, Chairman.

Fifty-ninth Yearbook, 1960, Part II—*The Dynamics of Instructional Groups.* Prepared by the Society's Committee. Gale E. Jensen, Chairman. Cloth.

Sixtieth Yearbook, 1961, Part I—*Development in and through Reading.* Prepared by the Society's Committee. Paul A. Witty, Chairman. Cloth, Paper.

Sixtieth Yearbook, 1961, Part II—*Social Forces Influencing American Education.* Prepared by the Society's Committee. Ralph W. Tyler, Chairman. Cloth.

Sixty-first Yearbook, 1962, Part I—*Individualizing Instruction.* Prepared by the Society's Committee. Fred T. Tyler, Chairman. Cloth.

Sixty-first Yearbook, 1962, Part II—*Education for the Professions.* Prepared by the Society's Committee. G. Lester Anderson, Chairman. Cloth.

Sixty-second Yearbook, 1963, Part I—*Child Psychology.* Prepared by the Society's Committee. Harold W. Stevenson, Editor. Cloth.

Sixty-second Yearbook, 1963, Part II—*The Impact and Improvement of School Testing Programs.* Prepared by the Society's Committee. Warren G. Findley, Editor. Cloth.

Sixty-third Yearbook, 1964, Part I—*Theories of Learning and Instruction.* Prepared by the Society's Committee. Ernest R. Hilgard, Editor. Paper.

Sixty-third Yearbook, 1964, Part II—*Behavioral Science and Educational Administration.* Prepared by the Society' Committee. Daniel E. Griffiths, Editor. Paper.

Sixty-fourth Yearbook, 1965, Part I—*Vocational Education.* Prepared by the Society's Committee. Melvin L. Barlow, Editor. Cloth.

Sixty-fourth Yearbook, 1965, Part II—*Art Education.* Prepared by the Society's Committee. W. Reid Hastie, Editor. Cloth.

Sixty-fifth Yearbook, 1966, Part I—*Social Deviancy among Youth.* Prepared by the Society's Committee. William W. Wattenberg, Editor. Cloth.

Sixty-fifth Yearbook, 1966, Part II—*The Changing American School.* Prepared by the Society's Committee. John I. Goodlad, Editor. Cloth.

Sixty-sixth Yearbook, 1967, Part I—*The Educationally Retarded and Disadvantaged.* Prepared by the Society's Committee. Paul A. Witty, Editor. Cloth.

Sixty-sixth Yearbook, 1967, Part II—*Programed Instruction.* Prepared by the Society's Committee. Phil C. Lange, Editor. Cloth.

Sixty-seventh Yearbook, 1968, Part I—*Metropolitanism: Its Challenge to Education.* Prepared by the Society's Committee. Robert J. Havighurst, Editor. Cloth.

Sixty-seventh Yearbook, 1968, Part II—*Innovation and Change in Reading Instruction.* Prepared by the Society's Committee. Helen M. Robinson, Editor. Cloth.

Sixty-eighth Yearbook, 1969, Part I—*The United States and International Education.* Prepared by the Society's Committee. Harold G. Shane, Editor. Cloth.

Sixty-eighth Yearbook, 1969, Part II—*Educational Evaluation: New Roles, New Means.* Prepared by the Society's Committee. Ralph W. Tyler, Editor. Paper.

Sixty-ninth Yearbook, 1970, Part I—*Mathematics Education.* Prepared by the Society's Committee. Edward G. Begle, Editor. Cloth.

Sixty-ninth Yearbook, 1970, Part II—*Linguistics in School Programs.* Prepared by the Society's Committee. Albert H. Marckwardt, Editor. Cloth.

Seventieth Yearbook, 1971, Part I—*The Curriculum: Retrospect and Prospect.* Prepared by the Society's Committee. Robert M. McClure, Editor. Paper.

Seventieth Yearbook, 1971, Part II—*Leaders in American Education.* Prepared by the Society's Committee. Robert J. Havighurst, Editor. Cloth.

Seventy-first Yearbook, 1972, Part I—*Philosophical Redirection of Educational Research.* Prepared by the Society's Committee. Lawrence G. Thomas, Editor. Cloth.

Seventy-first Yearbook, 1972, Part II—*Early Childhood Education.* Prepared by the Society's Committee. Ira J. Gordon, Editor. Cloth, Paper.

Seventy-second Yearbook, 1973, Part I—*Behavior Modification in Education.* Prepared by the Society's Committee. Carl E. Thoresen, Editor. Cloth.

Seventy-second Yearbook, 1973, Part II—*The Elementary School in the United States.* Prepared by the Society's Committee. John I. Goodlad and Harold G. Shane, Editors. Cloth.

Seventy-third Yearbook, 1974, Part I—*Media and Symbols: The Forms of Expression, Communication, and Education.* Prepared by the Society's Committee. David R. Olson, Editor. Cloth.

Seventy-third Yearbook, 1974, Part II—*Uses of the Sociology of Education.* Prepared by the Society's Committee. C. Wayne Gordon, Editor. Cloth.

Seventy-fourth Yearbook, 1975, Part I—*Youth.* Prepared by the Society's Committee. Robert J. Havighurst and Philip H. Dreyer, Editors. Cloth.

Seventy-fourth Yearbook, 1975, Part II—*Teacher Education.* Prepared by the Society's Committee. Kevin Ryan, Editor. Cloth.

Seventy-fifth Yearbook, 1976, Part I—*Psychology of Teaching Methods.* Prepared by the Society's Committee. N. L. Gage, Editor. Cloth.

Seventy-fifth Yearbook, 1976, Part II—*Issues in Secondary Education.* Prepared by the Society's Committee. William Van Til, Editor. Cloth.

Seventy-sixth Yearbook, 1977, Part I—*The Teaching of English.* Prepared by the Society's Committee. James R. Squire, Editor. Cloth.

Seventy-sixth Yearbook, 1977, Part II—*The Politics of Education.* Prepared by the Society's Committee. Jay D. Scribner, Editor. Cloth.

Seventy-seventh Yearbook, 1978, Part I—*The Courts and Education,* Clifford P. Hooker, Editor. Cloth.

Seventy-seventh Yearbook, 1978, Part II—*Education and the Brain,* Jeanne Chall and Allan F. Mirsky, Editors. Cloth.

Yearbooks of the National Society are distributed by

THE UNIVERSITY OF CHICAGO PRESS, CHICAGO, ILLINOIS 60637

Please direct inquiries regarding prices of volumes still available to the University of Chicago Press. Orders for these volumes should be sent to the University of Chicago Press, not to the offices of the National Society.

2. The Series on Contemporary Educational Issues

In addition to its Yearbooks the Society now publishes volumes in a series on Contemporary Educational Issues. These volumes are prepared under the supervision of the Society's Commission on an Expanded Publication Program.

The 1978 Titles

Aspects of Reading Education (Susanna Pflaum-Connor, ed.)

History, Education, and Public Policy: Recovering the American Educational Past (Donald R. Warren, ed.)

From Youth to Constructive Adult Life: The Role of the Public School (Ralph W. Tyler, ed.)

The 1977 Titles

Early Childhood Education: Issues and Insights (Bernard Spodek and Herbert J. Walberg, eds.)

The Future of Big City Schools: Desegregation Policies and Magnet Alternatives (Daniel U. Levine and Robert J. Havighurst, eds.)

Educational Administration: The Developing Decades (Luvern L. Cunningham, Walter G. Hack, and Raphael O. Nystrand, eds.)

The 1976 Titles

Prospects for Research and Development in Education (Ralph W. Tyler, ed.)

Public Testimony on Public Schools (Commission on Educational Governance)

Counseling Children and Adolescents (William M. Walsh, ed.)

The 1975 Titles

Schooling and the Rights of Children (Vernon Haubrich and Michael Apple, eds.)

Systems of Individualized Education (Harriet Talmage, ed.)

Educational Policy and International Assessment: Implications of the IEA Assessment of Achievement (Alan Purves and Daniel U. Levine, eds.)

The 1974 Titles

Crucial Issues in Testing (Ralph W. Tyler and Richard M. Wolf, eds.)

Conflicting Conceptions of Curriculum (Elliott Eisner and Elizabeth Vallance, eds.)

Cultural Pluralism (Edgar G. Epps, ed.)

Rethinking Educational Equality (Andrew T. Kopan and Herbert J. Walberg, eds.)

All of the above volumes may be ordered from

McCutchan Publishing Corporation
2526 Grove Street
Berkeley, California 94704

The 1972 Titles

Black Students in White Schools (Edgar G. Epps, ed.)

Flexibility in School Programs (W. J. Congreve and G. L. Rinehart, eds.)

Performance Contracting—1969–1971 (J. A. Mecklenburger)

The Potential of Educational Futures (Michael Marien and W. L. Ziegler, eds.)

Sex Differences and Discrimination in Education (Scarvia Anderson, ed.)

The 1971 Titles

Accountability in Education (Leon M. Lessinger and Ralph W. Tyler, eds.)

Farewell to Schools??? (D. U. Levine and R. J. Havighurst, eds.)

Models for Integrated Education (D. U. Levine, ed.)

PYGMALION *Reconsidered* (J. D. Elashoff and R. E. Snow)

Reactions to Silberman's CRISIS IN THE CLASSROOM (A. Harry Passow, ed.)

A limited number of copies of the above titles (except PYGMALION *Reconsidered*) are still available from the Office of the Secretary, NSSE, 5835 Kimbark Avenue, Chicago, Ill. 60637.